CONTENDING REPRESENTATIONS II *Entangled Republican Spaces in Early Modern Venice*

Contending Representations II
Entangled Republican Spaces in Early Modern Venice

Edited by Giovanni Florio and Alessandro Metlica

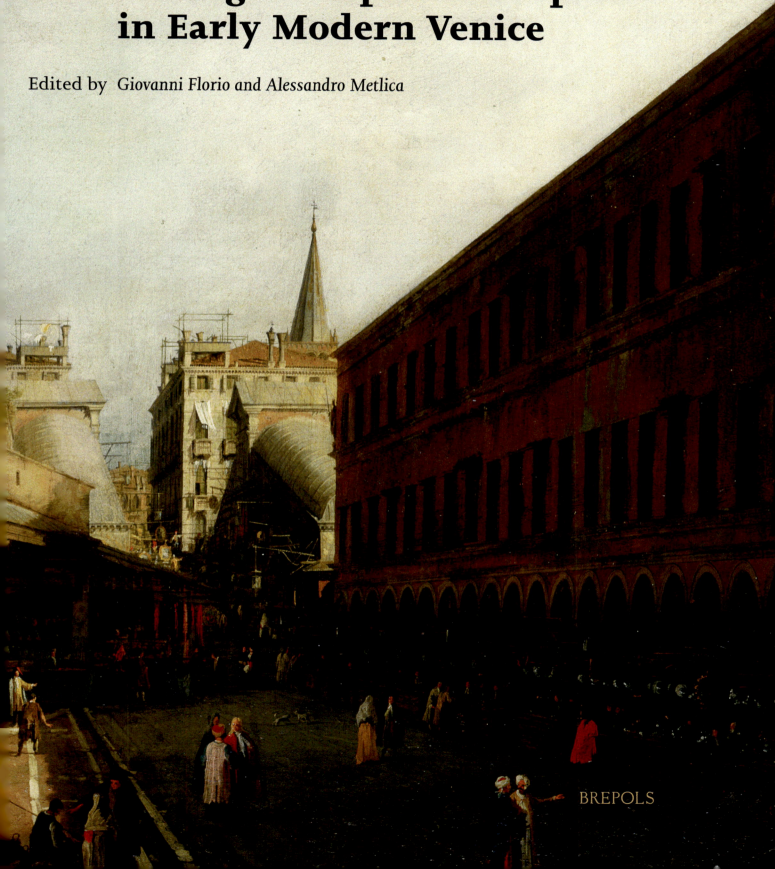

BREPOLS

DUNAMIS   Studies in the empowerment of early-modern representations

Series Editors
Ralph Dekoninck
Agnès Guiderdoni
Alessandro Metlica

This book received funding from the European Research Council (ERC) under the European Union's Horizon 2020 Research and Innovation programme (G.A. 758450 – StG2017 "Republics on the Stage of Kings. Representing Republican State Power in the Europe of Absolute Monarchies, late 16th – early 18th century")

Language correction: Amanda Swain
Editorial assistance: Laura Armillotta

ISBN 978-2-503-60519-7 (HB); 978-2-503-60520-3 (e-book)
D/2024/0095/69
DOI 10.1484/M.DUNAMIS-EB.5.132879

Copyright © 2024 Brepols Publishers, Turnhout, Belgium

This is an open access publication made available under a CC BY-NC 4.0 International License: https://creativecommons.org/licenses/by-nc/4.0/. No part of this publication may be reproduced, stored in a retrieval system, or transmitted, in any form or by any means, for commercial purposes, without the prior permission of the publisher, or as expressly permitted by law, by licence or under terms agreed with the appropriate reprographics rights organization.

Designed by Paul van Calster

Printed in the EU on acid-free paper.

CONTENTS

1
Giovanni Florio & Alessandro Metlica
Civic Ritual and Popular Politics in the Republic of Venice   6

2
Giorgio Tagliaferro
The Meeting of Sebastiano Ziani with Alexander III in the Great Council Hall: Staging, Viewing, and Understanding the Body Politic in Late Sixteenth-Century Venice   44

3
Monique O'Connell
Representative Spaces of Republicanism: Constitutional Thinking, Virtue Politics, and Venice's Great Council Hall in Early Modern Europe   66

4
Massimo Rospocher
'Una parola in piazza fa più male che dieci libri in un gabinetto': The Square as Political Space in Sixteenth Century Venice   78

5
Iseabail Rowe
'From the Clocke to the Shore': Thomas Coryat's 'Streets' of Piazza San Marco   88

6
Evelyn Korsch
A Republic Becomes Divine: The Sacred Role of Topography in Venetian Civic Ritual   98

7
Umberto Cecchinato
Beyond the Ceremonial City: Music, Public Revelries, and Urban Spaces in Everyday Renaissance Venice   118

8
Marco Bellabarba
Power, Friendship, and Protection: Venetian Rectors in Verona Between the Sixteenth and Seventeenth Centuries   128

9
Erika Carminati
Celebrations of Venetian Terraferma's Rettori: From the Good Fama to its Subversion in Bergamo's Public Ritual Sphere   138

10
Alfredo Viggiano
The Good Use of 'People' in Fifteenth-Century Venice: Reflections over a Controversial Term   148

11
Matteo Casini
Venice Beyond Venice: The Foreign Approach to Venetian Rituals, 1400–1600s   160

List of Abbreviations   173
Bibliography   174
Notes on Contributors   192

Giovanni Florio
Alessandro Metlica

CIVIC RITUAL AND POPULAR POLITICS IN THE REPUBLIC OF VENICE

Twenty men dressed in white throng the stage, wearing golden shoes over white stockings and off-white robes embroidered with gold. As a sign of respect, they hold their bejewelled hats, which are adorned with gaudy plumes; the young man on the left, at the back of the squad, has just taken his off. All eyes are on the scene unfolding in front of them: our young man seems amazed by what he sees, but the man beside him, holding behind his back a sumptuous blue hat with a ruby in the middle, looks focused and almost tense. Even the Venetian patricians seated in the upper right grandstand, whose identities are revealed by their lavish crimson robes, gaze absorbedly in the same direction, bowing their heads and venerable beards.

The cover of this volume does not reveal what they are watching with such interest — to break the suspense, just turn the page. In the other half of the painting, Michele Steno, the doge of Venice, who is also dressed richly in white and gold and crowned with a gem-studded horn-like bonnet (the *zoja*, which the doge wore only on ceremonial occasions), receives from the hands of the procession leaders the banner and keys of the city of Verona. We thus discover that our band of men are Veronese ambassadors and that the event portrayed is Verona's submission to Venice on 12 July 1405.

Painted by Jacopo Ligozzi and his workshop around 1619, *The handing over of the keys of Verona to doge Michele Steno* (fig. 1.2) was commissioned by the city council of Verona in 1595 to renovate its meeting room.[1] Accordingly, the iconography of this large canvas (which stands three and a half by six metres) resemantises the subjection of the city by turning a military occupation into a voluntary act of submission: a reframing in line with other celebrative accounts of the event such as the work of Veronese historiographer Girolamo Dalla Corte.[2] The ceremonial structure of the depiction accentuates the two-fold nature of the agreement, which Ligozzi represents as the result of a mutually beneficial negotiation. This is why St Mark and St Zeno, the patron saints of the two cities who flank the Virgin in the upper part of the painting, witness the ritual so benevolently. Even the portrayal of the Venetian patriciate gestures more toward desire for political equilibrium than the truth of history: the red-robed wise men sitting next to the doge are too many in number to be the Signoria (the magistracy that, according to Dalla Corte, actually welcomed the Veronese ambassadors in 1405) and are too few to be the Pien Collegio (which welcomed ambassadors in Ligozzi's time).[3] However, their quantity exactly mirrors that of the arriving delegation, allowing for balance not only in the composition of the canvas but also in the political forces it represents.[4]

There is another detail in this painting that overshadows reality — and proves most significant for our volume. Just above the young ambassador who raises his hat to the doge we see a round arch piercing the backdrop of the scene that, against the blue sky, shows a bell tower and some elegant, mysterious buildings. At first, the beholder is puzzled. What kind of city is this? And where are we looking at it from?

More than one clue seems to suggest that the ritual takes place indoors: the heavy throne of the doge under the canopy, the senatorial tribune set against a wall, and the dark tones of the painting more generally, since the faces and precious robes of the figures are brightened by light which enters only from the left. In this respect, Ligozzi's work looks akin to paintings by Pietro Malombra, which faithfully portray the Pien Collegio gathered in the hall of the same name

1.1 Jacopo Robusti (Tintoretto), *The voluntary submission of the provinces*. Detail of 1.20.

1.2
Jacopo Ligozzi and workshop, *The handing over of the keys of Verona to doge Michele Steno*. Verona, Musei Civici, c. 1619. Photo: Archivio fotografico, Musei Civici di Verona.

REPRESENTING POWER IN THE DUTCH REPUBLIC

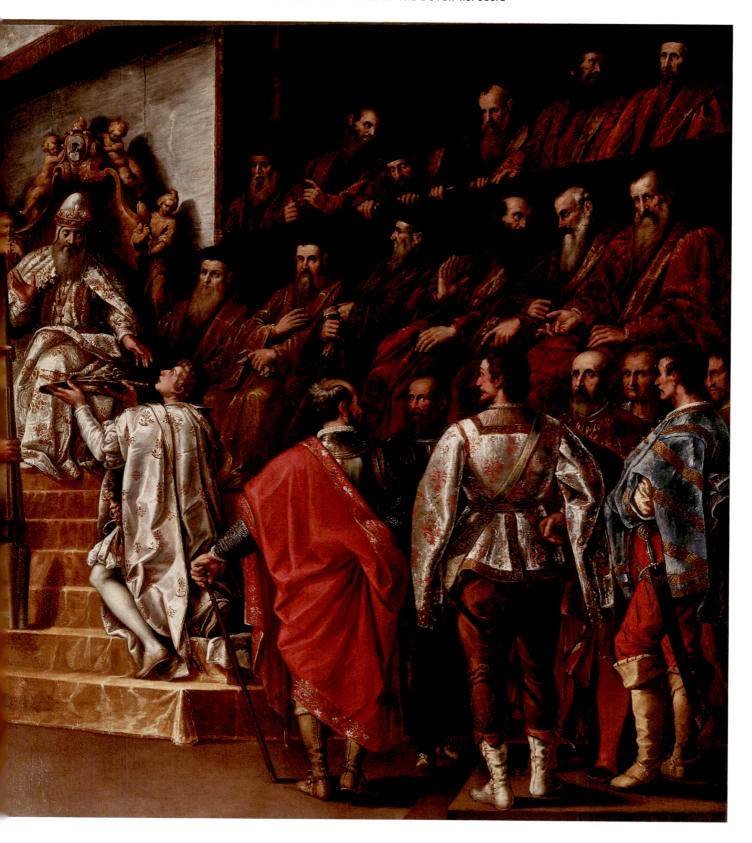

in the Ducal Palace and receiving foreign ambassadors in the early seventeenth century (fig. 1.3). The arch on our volume's cover, however, cannot be a window. Although on one side (that of the city view) it is clearly open to the outdoors, on the other (that of the ambassadors) it is also externally facing – because it is part of a façade, as evidenced by the tympanum windows next to it and, most importantly, the clock above it. We thus must conclude that the diplomatic mission is taking place in the open air. Indeed, as soon as we recover from our disorientation, we easily recognize the building as the Clock Tower in St Mark's Square (fig. 1.4).

The setting of the painted scene is not surprising in itself. Dalla Corte reports that the handover of the keys and banner actually took place in the Piazza, right in front of the Basilica, which would allow for having the Clock Tower as a theatrical backdrop.[5] In the painting, however, art works on the Venetian topography and transforms it. If the building were St Mark's Clock Tower, the view beyond the arch should correspond to the Mercerie: a street that was also relevant in the ceremonial context, since in Ligozzi's time the embassies of subject cities travelled that route to come before the doge.[6] Still, what we see beyond the arch looks nothing like the Mercerie. They are instead imaginary buildings: a sort of capriccio, stylised yet fascinating, recalling an idea of Venice as a monumental city.

This dreamlike environment, deliberately ambiguous, casts a peculiar light on the ritual represented by Ligozzi. The witty composition of the painting makes different ceremonial spaces clash, overlap, and intertwine. The Piazza enters the Palace as the Hall of the Collegio exits into the Piazza, so that outdoor and indoor merge until they blur into one another; past and present also overlap, through a mixing-up of protocols, magistracies, and political codes that were separated by centuries. More importantly, Verona goes to Venice

1.3
Pietro Malombra, *The Hall of the Pien Collegio in Venice*. Madrid, Prado, c. 1610s. Photo: Public Domain.

1.4
Giacomo Guardi after Francesco Guardi, *The Clock Tower of St Mark, from the Front of the Basilica*. New York, Metropolitan Museum of Art, after 1793. Photo: Public Domain.

(the Veronese embassy in St Mark's Square in 1405) only to bring Venice back to Verona (the Venetian capriccio hanging in the hall of the city council in 1619).

Such spatial and conceptual entanglements, of which Ligozzi's painting constitutes a striking example, is the subject matter of this volume. The eleven chapters of this book explore intersections between the Palace and the Piazza, between ceremonial routes and everyday streets, between the dominant city (the *Dominante*) and its dominions. In doing so, the volume aims to connect the rituals of the rulers with the politics of their subjects and to foreground how this juxtaposition sheds new light on each. We argue that investigating these entanglements, which calls for a hybridisation of theoretical models and disciplinary approaches, tells us more about early modern Venice than its much celebrated 'myth' – as its allegedly piercingly lifelike representations are often less transparent than they appear.

Portraying the myth

At the beginning of the seventeenth century, the engraver and publisher Giacomo Franco created a very successful series of engravings that were collected in 1610 in a volume entitled *Habiti d'huomeni et donne venetiane*.[7] As the following subtitle advertises, the series, which consists of a variable number of plates (from 20 to 29, depending on the editions),[8] is devoted not only to Venetian traditional clothing ('*habiti*'), but also to the 'triumphs, festivals and public ceremonies of the most noble city of Venice'. Indeed, in addition to a series of portraits showing the lavish costumes of the Serenissima – including those of the doge, the dogaressa, the naval commander in chief (*capitano generale da mar*), and the procurators of St Mark – the volume offers a rather detailed catalogue of the performative events marking the Venetian civic and religious calendar: the processions in St Mark's Square (fig. 1.5–1.6), bridge wars (fig. 1.7), competitive regattas (fig. 1.8), and the famous marriage of the sea, the Sensa (fig. 1.9).

In early modern Venice, these festivals were much more than a folk curiosity or a tourist attraction. They played a key role in the cross-media narrative promoted by the Serenissima: a system of symbols and tales, or, in the words of James Grubb, 'an accumulation of historical explanation and contingent propaganda',[9] which twentieth-century historiography later defined as the 'myth of Venice'.[10] This interpretative category was coined to frame the multi-layered self-portrait of the ruling elite: the Venetian patriciate. Patricians claimed symbolic prerogatives and exclusive virtues for the city as diverse as devotion (Venice is a city blessed by God and protected by St Mark), liberty (Venice is born and has lived ever since free from any external control), dominion (at least since 1204, Venice rules over a land and sea empire), perfect constitutional balance (as argued by Gasparo Contarini in his widely read and translated *De magistratibus et republica venetorum*), and clockwork laws and regulations that, according to what has been called the 'mechanisation of virtue',[11] purportedly settled all social and political struggles in advance, thus earning Venice the title of Most Serene Republic.

Civic ritual played a substantial role in the 'myth of Venice'.[12] The republic's authority was reenacted on a regular basis through a series of highly codified performances, following a tight agenda that combined secular and liturgical events. Processions held on religious occasions, festivities celebrating key historical dates, receptions welcoming foreign guests, elections, and popular games helped to visualise the state's power. During the solemn parades that crossed St Mark's Square, for example, symbols of Venetian power and independence (the *trionfi dogali*) were exhibited, including the eight banners granted – according to the 'myth' – by pope Alessandro III in 1177 (fig. 1.10). On the Feast of the Ascension (the Sensa), the doge sailed from the Piazza to the open sea and symbolically married the Adriatic by dropping a golden ring into the water (fig. 1.11). He thus claimed the maritime supremacy of Venice and its sovereignty on the Adriatic.

Giacomo Franco's *Habiti* series mirrors how these ceremonies reshaped Venice's urban spaces and imbued the city's topography with sacral and political meanings. This is made clear in the frontispiece (fig. 1.12). Inscribed in a perfect circle unnaturally centred on the religious-political space constituted by the Ducal Palace, St Mark's Basilica, and the Piazza, a bird's eye view of Venice is presented as the scenic backdrop for the engravings that follow. Venice's amphibious topography is thus presented by Franco as programmatically enclosed in a narrow perimeter: an unchanging, self-sufficient space, self-referentially conceived for self-celebration. Festivals and public ceremonies are hence understood

1.5

1.5
Giacomo Franco, *Procession in St Mark's Square during the recruitment of men for the fleet*. Engraving from Id., *Habiti d'huomeni et donne venetiane con la processione della Ser.ma Signoria ed altri particolari*, 1614. Photo: BnF, Gallica. Reproduced with permission.

1.6
Giacomo Franco, *Procession in St Mark's Square during the handover of the baton to the Capitano generale da mar* (ibid.). Photo: BnF, Gallica. Reproduced with permission.

1.7
Giacomo Franco, *The "War of the Fists"* (ibid.). Photo: BnF, Gallica. Reproduced with permission.

1.8
Giacomo Franco, *Women's regatta* (ibid.). Photo: BnF, Gallica. Reproduced with permission.

1.9
Giacomo Franco, *The Feast of the Ascension ("Festa della Sensa")* (ibid.). Photo: BnF, Gallica. Reproduced with permission.

CIVIC RITUAL AND POPULAR POLITICS

Ordine che tiene la Sereniss. Republica Veneta nel dare il bastone all' Ecc.mo General di Mare.
Giacomo Franco Forma Con Privilegio

1.6

Perche sie passato di tanto eccesso di contesa, che con i segni seguono spesso grand.mi inconvenienti la baruffa... Giacomo Franco For. Con Privilegio

1.7

le donne habitanti ne i lidi circostanti a Ven.a concorrono parimente à cosi fatta festa, vogando insieme, et contendendo i premij con universal piacere de riguardanti.
Giacomo Franco fe. Con Privilegio

1.8

Il Doge di Venetia con tutta la Sig.ria il giorno dell' Ascensione à sposare il Mare con questa solenità la quale et per dignità et per concerto e la piu bella pompa che si vegga in Venetia.

1.9

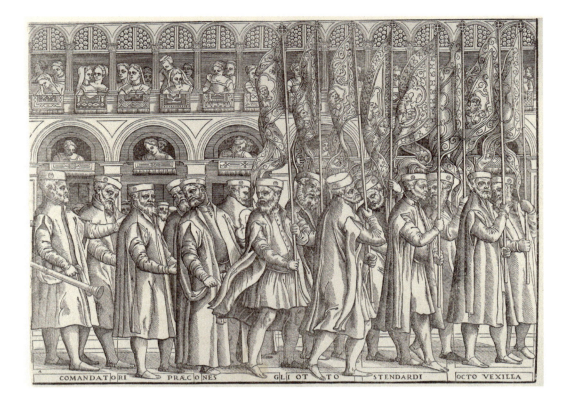

1.10
Matteo Pagano, *Procession of the Doge in Venice*. New York, Metropolitan Museum of Art, 1556-1561. Photo: Public Domain.

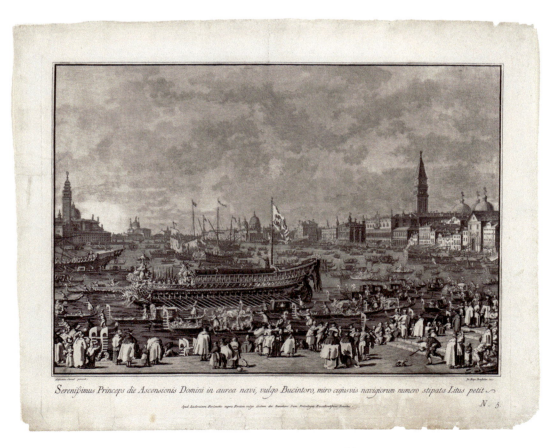

1.11
Giovan Battista Brustolon after Giovan Antonio Canal (Canaletto), *The depart of the doge for the Feast of the Sensa*. Amsterdam, Rijksmuseum, 1766. Photo: Public Domain.

1.12
Frontispiece of Giacomo Franco, *Habiti d'Huomeni e Donne Venetiane Con la Processione della Ser.ma Signoria Et altri particolari cioè Trionfi feste et cerimonie publiche della nobilissima città di Venetia*, 1610. Amsterdam, Rijksmuseum. Photo: Public Domain.

as urban performative devices celebrating the perfection of the Venetian polity and the uniqueness of the geography of Venice, as both the republican government and the marvellous appearance of the city pivot on the site of St Mark's. The Palace and the Piazza thus become not only the conceptual source but also the most iconic representation of civic republicanism.

This 'mythology', or 'accumulation of inherited beliefs and meanings',[13] was not created by Franco, of course. It was well rooted in humanist historiography and grew considerably via sixteenth-century literary production – where the works of polygrapher Francesco Sansovino stand out. Having published a short booklet in 1556 about 'all the beautiful and remarkable things in Venice', and expanded it after 1560 into a more structured 'dialogue',[14] in 1581 Sansovino recast these materials as a text that quickly became a bestseller: *Venetia città nobilissima e singolare*. A sort of touristic guide avant la lettre, the book describes the most distinguished palaces and institutions in Venice in a celebratory tone, but also dwells on the city's ceremonies and public rejoicings, as Sansovino considered Venice's festivals no less unique ('*singolari*') than its republican government or dreamlike topography. Due to the book's huge success, a couple of updated versions of *Venetia* were published in the seventeenth century, adding subsequent events and new information to the original account.[15]

This body of celebratory writings, consistent in motifs and quite widespread thanks to reprints and new editions, exerted a strong influence on Franco's imagery. Proof of this is his interest in the works of a scholar from Belluno, Giovan Niccolò Doglioni, who had in turn 'reformed, rearranged and greatly extended' the 'marvellous things of the glorious city of Venice' first published by Sansovino.[16] In 1614 Franco edited the reissue of a 1594 leaflet by Doglioni: a single sheet publication bearing a woodcut illustration with a map of Venice and captions to decipher it, which depicted 'the origin and government' of the city and included 'a list of all the doges who were there'.[17] Franco reprinted the woodcut separately, reproduced Doglioni's text (which takes up six leaves in his 1614 reissue), and added a series of new plates (from 12 to 16, depending on the edition). Easily confused with the earlier 1610 series, since the two are often bound together, these engravings adopt the same 'mythological' perspective: they depict renowned buildings (the Procuratie), social practises (the courtesans at the hairdresser), military events (the deployment of the fleet at the battle of Lepanto), and civic rituals. In these engravings, the area of St Mark's once again appears as the beating heart of the city's iconography – as demonstrated in the plate representing the procession for the feast of Corpus Christi (fig. 1.13).

In and out of the ceremonial city

It is no surprise that, in the eyes of Franco and Sansovino, the 'myth of Venice' appeared an integrated repertoire despite the striking heterogeneity of its sources and themes. Sixteenth- and seventeenth-century encomiastic production aimed to hold together what might fall away from the centre – and the centre, in the 'myth of Venice,' was the patriciate. As J.R. Mulryne argues, the self-portrait of 'a governing class' constitutes an attempt

> to create or sustain political and social consent, a 'common voice' among the élite of a society – among 'opinion formers', those with hereditary, military or financial power – and by consensual or trickle-down effect to root that consent among the common people.[18]

1.13

Giacomo Franco, *Procession in St Mark's Square: view from the top.* Engraving from Id., *Habiti d'huomeni et donne venetiane con la processione della Ser.ma Signoria ed altri particolari*, 1614. Photo: BnF, Gallica. Reproduced with permission.

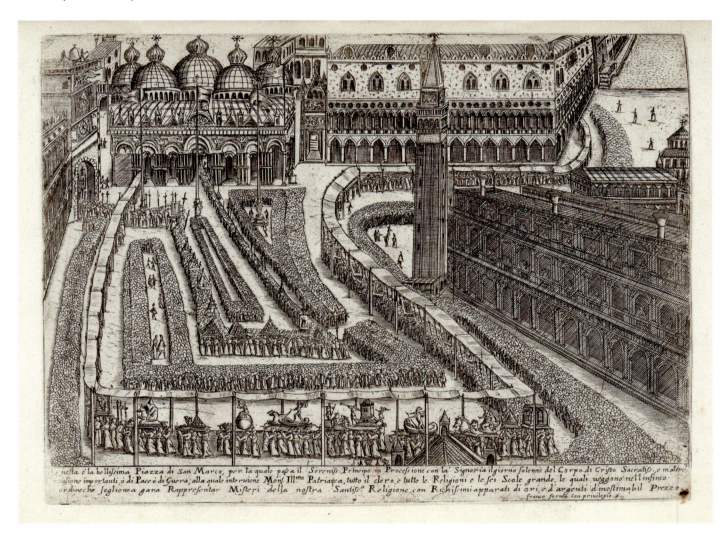

Although Mulryne referred to ceremonial entities in monarchic Europe, Venetian civic ritual reflected similar purposes. Venetian festivals, despite their uniqueness, were also intended to buttress the city's social structure and reaffirm symbolic and political hierarchies. Every celebration reconsecrated the dominance of the city of Venice by leaving the maritime and mainland dominions of the Republic outside the perfect circle engraved by Franco and by refixing the centre of this circle in St Mark's Square, the seat of political and religious power.

Evaluating the 'myth of Venice' today, however, is a whole other matter.[19] Surprisingly, scholars have rarely questioned the framework outlined by Franco's engravings and Sansovino's guide. Venetian festivals have been studied in detail, and their actual costs, ceremonial rules, and sophisticated arrays have been convincingly illustrated. Yet, the notion of 'civic ritual' has never really been called into question. Instead, it has been addressed within the same narrow perimeter outlined by Franco, leading to the definition of Venice as a 'ceremonial city':[20] a limited and well-ordered urban space, where the 'common voice' of the 'governing class' feels loud and clear, but the 'common people', especially those living outside the 'ceremonial city', in the vast and diverse domains of the Republic, are not audible. In order to fill this gap, this volume focuses instead on the 'consensual or trickle-down effect' that allowed the 'governing class' to communicate with 'the common people'. At the same time, we strive for a more ambitious objective: to put 'civic ritual', a notion key to the scholarly paradigm of the 'myth of Venice', in dialogue with a more recent category to gain relevance in the literature, 'popular politics'.

Just like 'civic ritual', 'popular politics' is an umbrella category which brings together a heterogeneous set of methodological tools and critical contributions. On the one hand, it mobilises the Habermasian paradigm of the 'public sphere', and more specifically, applies this model to early modern Venice, a historical context very different to the one for which Habermas first developed the notion.[21] On the other hand, the debate about popular politics pivots on the juridical-anthropological definition of a social group that, despite recent investigations, still proves elusive: Venetian people.[22] However, both approaches to popular politics call into question the idea that the patriciate exerted a factual and symbolic monopoly in early modern Venice. Indeed, such approaches stress the dialectic – i.e. the extensive negotiation among actors – underlying the republican deliberative processes, arguing that the patriciate played a part in the process that was major but not exclusive. Thus far from upholding the functionalist apology codified by the 'myth of Venice', popular politics reads the republican model as the result of interactions among different and even opposing forces. The political vision of those excluded from power – although often latent, sometimes mocking, and even more rarely externalised into violent actions or subversive aspirations – must be included in this framework.

Nevertheless, even this methodological perspective focusing on what Michel Foucault would have defined as the microphysics of Venetian power is not without risks. It could end up confirming a strictly polarised structure: the 'institutionalised power' of the patrician offices, on the one hand, and, on the other, a 'popular politics' framed *ex negativo* by prioritising what is left outside the sphere of the ruling authority. In this sense, the sphere itself would remain unequivocally aristocratic.[23] This volume goes a step further, as it aims to examine the dialectic between rulers and ruled from an unconventional vantage point: the cultural production surrounding the extra-ordinary (but also, as we have noticed, intra-institutional) events of the ceremonial agenda. By connecting the two opposing poles of the historiographical debate, 'civic ritual' and 'popular politics', we aim not only to fill a gap in the literature, but also, and especially, to provide a comprehensive understanding of the way power was represented in early modern Venice.

Our approach also calls into question the topography of this power. Indeed, our goal is to undermine both the strictly urban reading of the civic ritual and the perimeter of Venetian popular politics, which has been traced preferentially (although not exclusively) within the city of Venice. The eleven chapters of this book investigate the socio-political features of early modern cultural production in both Venice and the Venetian dominions according to the so-called spatial turn in the humanities.[24] We do not assume urban spaces are passive, artificial backgrounds for the unfolding of events and practices, but active participants in the ongoing process (re)shaping social, political, cultural, and anthropological identities.[25] This applies primarily to the spaces where civic ritual was performed, starting with the Ducal Palace and the Piazza. The topography of the St Mark's area should thus be considered neither a transposition of republican self-consciousness nor a mere reflection of the rationalising will of aristocratic institutions,[26] but rather as a variable, composite, and polysemic space, constantly redefined by the many people and practices that it daily hosted.[27]

The same approach urges a shift from this space, where 'institutionalised festivals' were performed, towards other 'festive spaces' that may appear peripheric, eccentric, or ephemeral, but which nonetheless prove crucial to rethinking the relationship between civic ritual and popular politics.[28] The novel archival findings and new understanding of visual sources that are presented in this volume[29] foreground a festival system that was more diffuse and less disciplined than has been traditionally recognized: a network of hubs in continual redefinition, through cooperation or conflict, which were enlivened and promoted by actors other than patrician political authorities. This polycentric festival system was not restricted to the city of Venice and importantly included the Venetian dominions. In this sense, the volume replaces the civic-republican framework that authors like Franco and Sansovino helped construct with a territorial state model reflecting wider institutional perimeters. The following chapters examine diverse social and political identities expressed via writings, visual culture, and architectural symbols like piazzas, churches, and governmental buildings. What emerges is a 'concatenation of public spaces' that, while also serving 'as a ceremonial civic stage',[30] do not merely restate the 'myth of Venice', but rather leave space for interactions and negotiations among different institutional powers, social entities, and cultural identities.

The issue at stake is therefore not how these festive spaces were disciplined by the aristocratic ruling class.[31] Indeed, it would be naive to consider them empty spaces available for the expansion of the 'myth of Venice'. Using their own ritual languages, subject communities in the Venetian dominions conveyed political demands and social visions both cooperating and conflicting with those of the *Dominante*. In other words, subject cities, territories, and communities were active stakeholders who interacted with the self-celebratory

1.14

Jacopo de' Barbari, *The City of Venice (Venetie MD)*, 1500. Photo: Public Domain.

1.15

Vincenzo Maria Coronelli, *City of Venice described by the cosmographer Coronelli*. Engraving from Id., *Isolario, descrittione geografico-historica, sacro-profana, antico-moderna, politica, naturale, e poetica*, 1696. Photo: Padua, Biblioteca dell'Orto Botanico. Reproduced with permission.

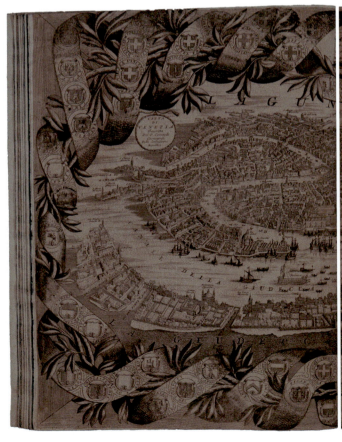

Venetian system by charging it with further, alternative, or even inverted meanings.[32] The same applies to the reception and reworking of Venetian ceremonial practices in other European contexts, as well as among the foreign communities settled (more or less permanently) in Venice.[33]

By investigating the festive spaces and entanglements characterising the Venetian system, this volume intends to reconsider the plurality of cultural practices, social bodies, and political actors involved in these phenomena. In so doing, we build on studies dedicated to both civic ritual and popular politics, in order to challenge the steady vision of the 'myth the Venice' as a symbolic repertoire that has been established once and for all. Our methodological shift from a civic to a state framework could be represented by abandonment of the famous map of Venice by Jacopo de' Barbari (fig. 1.14), and its reinterpretation by Giacomo Franco, in favour of the one Vincenzo Maria Coronelli includes in his Isolario – where the familiar shape of the 'ceremonial city' is surrounded by the coats of arms of its subject lands and cities da Terra and da Mar (fig. 1.15).[34]

More equal than others

The alleged immobility of the Venetian civic ritual applies to both space (the fixed routes around St Mark's) and time (these routes were supposedly established once and for all in the late Middle Ages and Renaissance). In this respect, it is revealing that the scholars who address this issue have focused almost exclusively on the fifteenth and the sixteenth centuries,[35] implicitly assuming that, even if the Republic was fully independent until 1797, during the last two centuries of the Serenissima the performative rhetoric of the 'myth of Venice' was simply adjusted, not altered or modified.[36] In other words, patricians would have preserved festivals because any change to their symbolic capital was unbearable.

Of course, this interpretation is far from unfounded: the redundancy of these cultural productions in terms of words, images, symbols, and gestures – which aimed precisely to reaffirm the continuity of the republican tradition – suggests few apparent differences between the festivals depicted by Giacomo Franco and those engraved by Giovan Battista Brustolon after Canaletto a century and a half later (fig. 1.9–1.11). However, our investigations show that Venetian pageantry and encomiastic production did undergo a change in the seventeenth century.[37] A new representation of power hinging on a new social basis was established, since power relationships within the patriciate and between the patriciate and its subjects radically changed during that time.

As Gaetano Cozzi has argued,[38] the economic and political crisis culminating in the Ottoman-Venetian wars of Candia (Crete, 1645–1669) and Morea (the Peloponnese, 1684–1699, 1714–1718) exacerbated the atavic contrasts between rich and poor patricians.[39] Nominally equal in rights and power, patricians had increasingly different prerogatives depending on the private fortune of their houses (casate). Although the 'myth of Venice' portrayed the patriciate as a socio-political body without internal contrasts, whose decisions were unanimous and highly coherent, starting in the 1630s the most wealthy and powerful patricians openly challenged this vision, as they claimed an unprecedented protagonism in both politics and culture.[40] Several collections of encomiastic texts were printed, and churches arose with façades adorned by the portraits of their worldly patrons in place of angels and saints.[41] Despite sumptuary laws and the republican mistrust towards cult of personality, sculptures portraying Venetian statesmen and naval commanders in chief, quite rare in public and semi-public spaces before the 1620s, now appeared in squares, churches, and public buildings in both in Venice and its dominions.[42] A case in point is the church of Santa Maria Zobenigo: lacking any Christian imagery, its façade is decorated with a statue of the church's chief patron, patrician Antonio Barbaro, who is surrounded by sculpted portraits of his brothers and by marble-relief maps of the sites important to his military service (fig. 1.16).

Beneath its apparent immutability, civic ritual was affected by this process as well. Proof of this can be found in the evolution of a ceremony that was central to early modern Venice: the inaugural entry of the procurators of St Mark. Traditionally elected from among the economically powerful and politically experienced 'greater patriciate', the procuratori were top-ranked magistrates in charge of St Mark's Basilica and its economic assets. They held the most prestigious office in the Republic after the doge and, like the doge (though different to all other Venetian offices), they were appointed for life. Most of the doges themselves were selected from among the procurators. The office of procuratore was created in the eleventh century and had since grown in power: procurators distributed alms, took care of orphans,

1.16
Giovan Antonio Canal
(Canaletto), *Campo Santa Maria
Zobenigo, Venice*. New York,
Metropolitan Museum of Art,
1730s. Photo: Public Domain.

1.17
Gabriel Bella, *The entry of a procurator of St Mark*.
Venice, Fondazione Querini Stampalia, 1780s. Photo:
Public Domain.

executed wills, and administered perpetual trusts made by private testators. This positioned them among the most powerful men in Venice, since these financial duties granted them prestige, a body of clients among the urban plebs, and large influence over Venetian money markets.[43]

The most ritualised moment in the career of a procurator was his election. When the news broke, bells rang for three days in celebration. Drums and trumpets sounded in the streets, as the newly elected handed out wine, bread, and money near the ferry stops (*traghetti*) at his own expense. At night, churches and buildings were decorated with lamps, and there were fireworks in many parts of the city. Then the actual entry was scheduled. On the appointed day, friends and relatives picked up the newly elected procurator in front of his home and took him by boat to the Fondaco dei Tedeschi, near the Rialto, on the Grand Canal. Here the group landed to access the nearby church of San Salvador. A first solemn mass was celebrated, allowing the crowd to gather. Afterwards, the *procuratore* left San Salvador amidst an imposing procession (fig. 1.17), consisting of up to five or six hundred people and including servants, foreigners, musicians, soldiers, captains, and knights from the dominions, as well as the other procurators and most of the senators. Arranged in pairs, the cortege marched past the Mercerie (the streets with the most refined shops in Venice) and paraded from the Rialto to St Mark's Square. Another mass was celebrated in St Mark's Basilica. Then the procurator entered the Ducal Palace for his formal investiture in the presence of the doge. Those who had marched with him from San Salvador to St Mark either received four *pani di zuccari* (Venetian sweets) as a gift or were invited to join the banquet that concluded the celebrations.

Literary sources[44] stress the superb decorations that adorned the ceremonial route, which was transfigured by ephemeral arches and architectures bearing the coat-of-arms of the procurator's family. The *campo* of San Salvador was filled with priceless tapestries, and the surrounding streets and alleys, as well as the Rialto Bridge, were papered with festoons. Persian drapes hung from the windows, and several paintings, including allegorical compositions and portraits of the elected, were exhibited along the path taken by the procession. The shops on the Mercerie played a key role too, as owners put their most polished items on display. Gems, pearls, mirrors, rare feathers, and precious fabrics were arranged to compose the procurator's crest. Sumptuous laceworks, decorated in gold and silver and bearing the procurator's name, were placed next to the engravings with his portrait which many shops displayed in their windows. Like these engraved portraits, printed sheets with sonnets and other encomiastic compositions hung on the walls or were distributed to the crowd.

It would be wrong to describe these entries as centralised performances running like clockwork. Far from being managed or controlled remotely by the Venetian institutions, these rituals were the result of more comprehensive dialogue among the procurator, the patriciate, and the city. First of all, the massive expenditure and lavish displays in the Mercerie were not directly related to the 'myth of Venice', for they did not contribute to the symbolic capital of the government (e.g. to social peace, constitutional balance, or fairness in judgement). Instead, they aimed to project the exceptional status of the few families inside the aristocracy able to attain the highest levels of the ducal offices. In this respect, magnificence – in the sense of both munificence and, more properly, *magnum facere* (to make it big) – proved to be an individual, not a collective virtue: as in many seventeenth-century monarchical contexts, where magnificence exhibited one's wealth and political authority,[45] the entry of a procurator of St Mark was primarily intended to extoll the newly elected patrician and his *casata*.

In Venice, however, magnificence was also exploited to include these displays of personal power, which remained unconventional with respect to republican ideology, in a collective framework. The standard definition by Aristotle of magnificence as an individual quality is hence inadequate to understand the phenomenon. Moreover, this collective framework did not apply, as one might imagine, to the patriciate as a whole, but to other strata of the population. The shopkeepers on the Mercerie, for instance, were personally involved in the celebration, which shows that the new dialectic between private and public virtues did influence the ritual of the entry.

A good example of this dialectic is the commendatory description of the entry of procurator Girolamo Basadonna (1622–1697) written in 1682 by Cristoforo Ivanovich.[46] A canon of St Mark's Basilica, Ivanovich was also a man of letters: he wrote several opera librettos and a treatise, the *Memorie teatrali di Venezia*, which is deemed to be the first historiographical work on Venetian opera.[47] It is not surprising, then, that his account of Basadonna's entry employs the rhetorical resources of the festival book as a genre (i.e. figures of speech such as ineffability and *recusatio*).[48] Ivanovich declares that he will not 'talk of the generosity of his Excellency', 'because such generosity is an inborn talent of the House Basadonna'. Still, he hardly discusses anything else: 'immediately after his election, as proof of his charity', Basadonna 'distributed plenty of money, bread, and wine to the poor and the ferrymen of the city'.[49] Far from a rhetorical commonplace, the motif of the patron's *generosità* runs throughout the text: it defines its encomiastic goals, and implies, as was customary in early modern entrances,[50] a negotiation between the parties involved in the ritual.

Less than a week before Basadonna's entrance, Ivanovich notes, another procurator, Marco Ruzzini, had made his entry. The décor set up for the latter was so splendid that it required four days to be dismantled, leaving the former with just one night to stage his own celebration. Whereas 'those who were less familiar with the generosity innate in this most noble House' were ready to bet that Basadonna would make a modest entry to avoid confrontation, those who knew 'the prodigal nature, which noble minds reveal through the decorum of the public actions' were expecting 'appropriate pomp'.[51] Of course, overnight the Mercerie was completely transformed, and the pageant far exceeded any expectations.

The issue at stake in Ivanovich's account concerns not the performance per se, but rather the definition of prodigality as a positive virtue, though seemingly unrelated (if not in complete contradiction) to the core values of the 'myth of Venice'. Indeed, Ivanovich's praise of Basadonna's 'prodigal nature' as an assurance of the 'decorum of the public actions' points toward the new idea of magnificence that we discussed. Ivanovich also states that the shopkeepers on the Mercerie played a key role in the process, as they glorified not only the procurator but also themselves and, consequently, the whole city. Indeed, by exposing their most lavish merchandise during the parade and contributing actively to the ephemeral event, Venetian merchants 'honoured their own magnificence'.[52]

A sumptuary law approved by the Great Council on 8 May 1683, a few months after (and probably because of) Basadonna's entry, provides greater insight into this passage. From this document, which specifically addressed the entrances of procurators, we learn that the Magistrato alle pompe[53] intended to regulate excessive décor set up between the Rialto and St Mark's, namely by forbidding the 'presents' (*regali*) that the newly elected procurator offered shopkeepers. No wonder the Venetian merchants were magnificent! Since they were financed by the procurator under the counter, the goods they exhibited during the procession were actually part of his display of wealth.

The unofficial agreement between procurators and store owners proves that, even in early modern Venice, civic ritual was far from monolithic. Its political meanings, social implications, and celebratory strands could change according to specific circumstances and party negotiations. In the case of Basadonna's entry, one such agreement sped up the decoration process and left the audience in awe, as the Mercerie were transformed over the course of just one night; yet, it also entailed an entanglement of private wealth and public decorum that did not belong to the pageant traditions of the Serenissima. In the late Middle Ages and Renaissance, when Venetian ceremonial life was outstandingly rich, solemn masses, water parades, and ritual processions did not offer the individual nobleman a chance to stand out. Even in the second half of the seventeenth century, the entanglement of private wealth and public decorum did not fail to alarm the Republican institutions, as the 1683 decree testifies. At that point, however, the process had become unstoppable. Indeed, the government surrendered a few years later, and by 1692 a costly licence sold by the Senate permitted the procurator to celebrate in whatever way he chose to spend his money.[54]

Unchanging routes

The evolution of the entry of the procurators of St Mark in the seventeenth-century is also significant in the context of our investigation for another reason: the transformation that the ritual underwent in post-Renaissance Venice affected not only its meanings and implications, but also its actual topography. To comply with new representation of patrician power, a new use of the urban spaces was established that specifically involved the Mercerie. In this respect, the festival offers a model case study for our general hypothesis, grounded in the spatial turn in the humanities: even in the 'ceremonial city', supposedly frozen in sixteenth-century etiquette, the routes of civic ritual did change, and this evolution mirrored changing power balances within the patriciate and between the patriciate and the rest of the city.

Although it has been assumed that the itinerary for the entry of a procurator had been codified in the Renaissance,[55] the rewritings of Sansovino's *Venetia* tell a very different story. Sansovino's original 1581 text recalls the three-day celebrations following the election of a *procuratore*, but does not mention an entry. Even these celebrations seem marginal, however, with respect to the historical origins and duties of the office: Sansovino addresses the topic quickly while discussing the *Procuratie* (the palace on the Piazza) in book 7 (*Delle fabbriche publiche*, 'On public palaces')[56] but glosses over it in book 10 (*De gli abiti, costumi e usi della città*, 'On city clothes, customs, and habits'), where other Venetian ceremonies are described in more detail. Of course, this does not mean that the ceremony of the entry did not exist at this time. The reissue of *Venetia* edited by Giovanni Stringa (1604) actually fills this gap, adding a description of the procession as it had been performed already at Sansovino's time. However, the event looks quite different from the one reported in later sources.[57] Firstly, the degree of magnitude was different. About three hundred people (not five or six) attended the procession; at the end two (rather than four) *pani di zucchero* were given. Secondly, the ceremonial route was not only shorter, but also, and more importantly, radically dissimilar, since the parade started from the church of San Moisè instead of from San Salvador and did not include the Mercerie.

Most of the literature on the topic, assuming that the procession had always departed from San Salvador, has not made notice of this change of route. Yet, it is clearly reported in the 1663 reissue of *Venetia*, where Giustiniano Martinioni adds a new paragraph explaining that senators and procurators 'do not gather anymore in the church of San Moisè, like Stringa said, but in the church of San Salvador'.[58] We can assign a more accurate date to this substitution: it occurred shortly after the plague of 1630–1631. Indeed, the first document attesting that San Salvador was papered for the entry of a procurator dates back to the election of Francesco Molin in 1634.[59] The new itinerary was quickly codified, and in 1641, when Giovanni Pesaro was elected, it was described in detail in the festival book printed for the occasion. It was the first festival book entirely devoted to the entry of a *procuratore*.[60] A few years later, the exceptional witness Francesco Pannocchieschi d'Elci – nephew of the papal nuncio of the time, Scipione – stated that the entry of the procurators of St Mark was 'the most relevant' of the lavish festivities that struck him while in Venice (1647–1652).[61] Thus, in the span of a few decades, the ritual had expanded in political and cultural relevance to such an extent that it climbed to the top of the ranks of civic ritual: from minor event (Sansovino, 1581) to flagship occasion (Pannocchieschi, c. 1650).

During the sixteenth century, the Mercerie were already the most famous streets in Venice, and many cardinals and ambassadors explicitly asked the Venetian authorities to visit these shops at the heart of the European luxury market.[62] Still, this chain of streets played a secondary role in the framework of civic ritual, at least before 1634. Indeed, although it could be used, the axis San Salvador – St Mark was less travelled than that of San Moisè – St Mark.[63] As the latter route was a straighter path with no luxury shops, it can be assumed that, at the time, neither the profusion of decorations nor the exhibition of luxurious goods were deemed necessary to the ritual.

The immobile prince

On 10 January 1690, when the doge Francesco Morosini returned to Venice after a six-year military campaign in the East Mediterranean, sumptuous ceremonies took place to celebrate his arrival.[64] Twelve patricians appointed by the Senate, leading twelve pleasure barges superbly decorated with wooden statues, gold plating, and crimson clothes, welcomed the doge's galley at the entrance to the lagoon and escorted it to the Lido. Morosini disembarked, attended a solemn mass at the church of San Niccolò, and boarded the Republic's state vessel, the Bucintoro. A fleet of boats then followed him to St Mark's Square amidst salvos of artillery, which gave rise to a triumphant waterborne pageant (fig. 1.18).

Pomp was even greater before the Ducal Palace. In the Piazzetta, the entrance to the city from the sea, an ephemeral arch about twelve metres in height was erected, supported by two loggias and adorned with galleries of arms. Moreover, there were two fountains, each four and a half metres high, representing the figure of Neptune between two dolphins; both fountains spouted wine, to the joy of the crowd attending the event. Morosini passed through the triumphal arch,

1.18
Alessandro Piazza, *The return of Francesco Morosini*, Venice, Museo Correr. 1699. Reproduced with permission.

flanked the fountains, and finally reached the Ducal Palace. Damask fabrics and trophies hung from the façade, while the courtyard was decorated with fifty-two paintings displaying the heroic deeds of the doge, who could contemplate his own victories once more before climbing the Giants' Staircase and entering the Palace.

This ritual entry was totally unusual in early modern Venice. After he was elected, the doge did not have to make an entrance to the city, because he was already there. Exceptions to this general rule mainly took place in the medieval period, in the cases of Renier Zen in 1253,[65] Lorenzo Celsi in 1361,[66] Andrea Contarini in 1368,[67] and Tommaso Mocenigo in 1414.[68] Of the thirty-five doges elected in the sixteenth and seventeenth centuries, only Antonio Priuli in 1618 and Francesco Erizzo in 1631 were far from Venice at the time of their elections,[69] and only the former enjoyed a waterborne entrance, though it was incomparable, in terms of luxury and media resonance, with that of Morosini.[70] Above all, neither Priuli nor Erizzo had risen to the dogado from a position of personal prestige and authority, comparable to that of Morosini, who still led the military fleet as naval commander in chief when he was elected on 3 April 1688, following the death of previous doge Marcatonio Giustinian.

Indeed, between 1684 and 1690 Morosini led one of the most successful campaigns in the history of the Serenissima. As the Turks were defeated in front of the walls of Vienna in

1.19

Filippo Parodi, *Bust of Francesco Morosini*, Venice, Museo Correr. 1687. Reproduced with permission.

1683, the Venetians attacked the Ottoman Empire in what is now modern Greece, emerged victorious, and gained significant territory: Aegean islands, strategic strongholds, and the entire Peloponnese peninsula (or Morea, as the Venetians called it).[71] The hype and commotion surrounding these military successes were just as uncommon as the election of Morosini, who was now known by the title of *Peloponnesiacus* and already (1687) honoured by the Senate with a bronze bust placed in the armoury of the Council of Ten 'when he was still breathing' (*adhuc viventi*), a unique honour in the history of the Republic (fig. 1.19). The shared excitement that swept through Venice during the First Morean War transcended the boundaries between the Piazza and the Palace, prompting the Republic to waive its traditional distrust of excessive cult of personality. Voted for unanimously by the ducal electors and celebrated by the city, Morosini's election was an anomaly in itself and marked a significant departure from the Republic's electoral customs: the new doge was not a procurator of St Mark with a past in Venetian diplomacy or the administration of the dominions[72] but a charismatic leader still engaged on the battlefield.

A doge who led military operations, sailed on his own, and made a ritual entry into Venice was not at all envisaged by the norms of Venetian civic ritual, despite how articulate and detailed they were. On the occasion of Morosini's entry to Venice in 1690, ceremonial adjustments were introduced to temper the exceptional nature of the moment and personality of the elected doge. Once on the threshold of the Ducal Palace, for instance, the actual boundary between the Palace and the Piazza, Morosini sanctioned his change of status with a ritual gesture of performative power. Before ascending the Giants' Staircase and being enthroned in the hall of the Great Council, Morosini resigned his position as naval commander in chief by relinquishing his baton to the secretary of the Senate.[73]

Nevertheless, two years later the Senate itself gave it back to him. In 1692, Morosini was once again required to simultaneously hold the office of doge and command of the fleet, as he had in the period between his ducal election (1688) and triumphal coronation (1690). This unusual decision responded to a twofold need: to revive the languishing military operations on the Greek front and to move the cumbersome presence of the *Peloponnesiacus* away from Venice. It was the beginning of a gradual dampening of the paroxysm of celebration that had culminated in the previous decade (1683–1692). When Morosini died in Nafplio in 1694, the Great Council reformed the Ducal Oath (*Promissio ducis*), regulating the constitutional prerogatives and ceremonial behaviours of the doge. From then on, the doge was prohibited from serving as fleet commander in chief, and the two positions were considered incompatible.[74]

By introducing this norm, the republican 'body politic' was reacting to the personal protagonism and militarism characterising Morosini's dogado. The justifications made to explain this measure, however, show that the Great Council had other concerns as well, related to the representation of republican power. Like other early modern sovereigns, the Venetian Republic needed a physical body to make its power perceivable.[75] Making sovereignty visible was even more urgent in a republic like Venice, a polity within which the *summa potestas* – constitutionally shared among the members of aristocracy and institutionally exercised by a plethora of patrician offices – was hardly identifiable. As the Great Council admitted in 1694, the presence of the doge in Venice was necessary not only for constitutional reasons but also because his 'body natural' added 'gravitas' to the magistracies he presided over and 'majesty' to the 'ceremonies' these magistracies performed. In order to present itself as the 'perfect body of the Republic', the ruling patriciate needed a 'visible head' that came from the doge's 'figure'.[76]

The 1694 amendment of the Ducal Oath reveals the resilience of the constitutional mythology developed in the early Renaissance, as well as its capacity to imbue even the lexicon of the Venetian politics. As the reformers argued, by balancing the republican constitution with a monarchic-like magistrate (the doge), the patrician 'ancestors' successfully addressed the need to stabilise the political system while making its power convincing.[77] The hieratic physiognomy of the republican prince strongly contributed to giving both Venetian civic ritual and the republican political machinery the sense of institutional perfection and immutability that we are problematizing in this volume. The princely persona (in the sense of performative mask)[78] that the doge showed on public occasions was supposed to absorb and neutralise any social or political contrast, manifesting through gestures and etiquette, if not solely through presence, the clockwork functioning of the Republican magistracies, the unity of the patriciate, and the harmony of this political structure with the other parts of Venetian society.

The doge has often been referred to as a 'paradoxical prince',[79] but what is paradoxical, first and foremost, is the constitutional 'myth' he embodies. The idea of Venice as a pacified 'mixed government' incorporating democratic, aristocratic, and monarchic elements within a perfectly balanced constitution[80] implies the existence of an ongoing institutional dialectic. Yet the equilibrium claimed by the 'myth' was nothing but the result of structural tensions that ran through the Venetian polity at all levels. These various lines of tension converged and were absorbed in the doge's princely persona: its constitutional profile was shaped by the unceasing dialectic between the Republic's 'body politic' and its 'visible head'. Starting from the late thirteenth century *serrata*[81], and continuing throughout the early modern period, the Great Council managed to reduce the dogado (a monocratic organ inherited from a deliberately neglected Byzantine past)[82] to a mostly representative office, by limiting its political autonomy and subjecting its pseudo-monarchic prerogatives to ever-stricter restrictions. As we have seen in the case of Morosini, the periodic emendation (*correzione*) of the Ducal Oath was the main legal device implemented to this end: revised at each ducal vacancy by a patrician committee elected by the Great Council (*correttori della Promissione ducale*), the Ducal Oath regulated the constitutional and ceremonial prerogatives of the doge and compelled him to perform his role with princely magnificence, while preventing him from taking any personal initiative.[83]

A significant part of these regulations applied specifically to the doge's freedom of movement and rights of mobility and travel. The prohibition introduced in 1694 openly refers to a series of regulatory precedents dating back to at least the late fourteenth century. Those 'decrees contained in the Ducal Oath'[84] aimed to put the movements of the Republic's 'visible head' under the control of its 'body politic'. After 1501, only via express authorisation by both the Great and Minor Councils could the republican prince leave the city of Venice and cross the border of the lagoon.[85] From a textual point of view, the 1694 reform was closer, however, to that of 1605. On that occasion, the Great Council had already referred to the doge as the 'head of our republic', stressing that it was suitable for reasons of 'public reputation' that 'the person of the Most Serene Prince' never leave the lagoon.[86] The immobilisation of the prince's physical body in Venice, if not in the Ducal Palace, helped not only legitimise but also locate and visualise sovereignty within a political system that was much more entangled than its Renaissance 'myth' suggests.

This need was all the more felt in the fifteenth century, as a consequence of the sudden expansion of the Venetian territorial state,[87] and again in the following century, with the consolidation of the mainland dominions after their temporary loss during the Italian Wars (1509–1516).[88] During the long sixteenth century, which saw the battle of Lepanto (1571) and concluded with the Venetian victory over the Pope's jurisdictional claims during the Interdict crisis of 1606–1607,[89] the Republic of Venice expanded its authority over a *respublica* stretching from the Adda to the Isonzo rivers and from the Istrian peninsula to the eastern Mediterranean. Therefore, the idea took root of Venice as a dominant city-state republic (*Dominante*) ruling as queen over a twofold territorial state that extended over both land (*da Terra*) and sea (*da Mar*). Progressively integrated into Venetian material constitution and political culture,[90] this idea was contextually accepted and developed in art and literature, historiography and rhetoric, architecture and urban planning, public ceremonies and civic ritual.[91] The decoration of the ceiling of the Hall of the Great Council, in the Ducal Palace, was the culmination of this process: Palma the Younger depicted Venice as a warrior queen triumphing militarily over the peoples subjected to her; Paolo Veronese painted Venice as a sovereign guardian providing these peoples with wealth and prosperity; and Jacopo Tintoretto portrayed her as a divine monarch assisting its earthly embodiment, i.e. the doge's 'body natural', and blessing the voluntary submission of the subject provinces (fig. 1.20–1.22).

Considered as a whole, these three large-scale paintings present a terrific synthesis of the 'myth'. A wise and mighty matron, offering social tranquillity and economic well-being

1.20
Jacopo Negretti (Palma the Younger), *Venice crowned by Victory*. Venice, Ducal Palace, Sala del Maggior Consiglio. 1584. Photo: Scala, Firenze.

1.21
Jacopo Robusti (Tintoretto), *The voluntary submission of the provinces*. Venice, Ducal Palace, Sala del Maggior Consiglio. c. 1580-1584. Photo: Scala, Firenze.

to those who worship her (Veronese), queen Venice reigning with benevolence, in full accordance with human and divine law (Tintoretto), but striking out violently at those who do not submit to her magnificent sovereignty (Palma).[92] This could be interpreted as an assertive message intended exclusively for the patriciate, who gathered in that hall to vote. In the same years, however, royal representations of submissions to Venice multiplied, not only in the Ducal Palace[93] but also in the town halls of the subject territories. As Ligozzi's *The handing over of the keys of Verona to doge Michele Steno* suggests, the imagery of the 'myth' was often employed, reshaped, and developed further by subject communities as well.[94]

A case in point is Cesare Vecellio's *The Submission of Cadore to Venice*, which was painted only a few years after the ceiling of the Hall of the Great Council (1582–1584 and 1599 respectively) (fig. 1.23). Static, hieratic, and enthroned, here queen Venice receives homage from the Community of Cadore which, in humbly kneeling, recognizes the sovereignty of

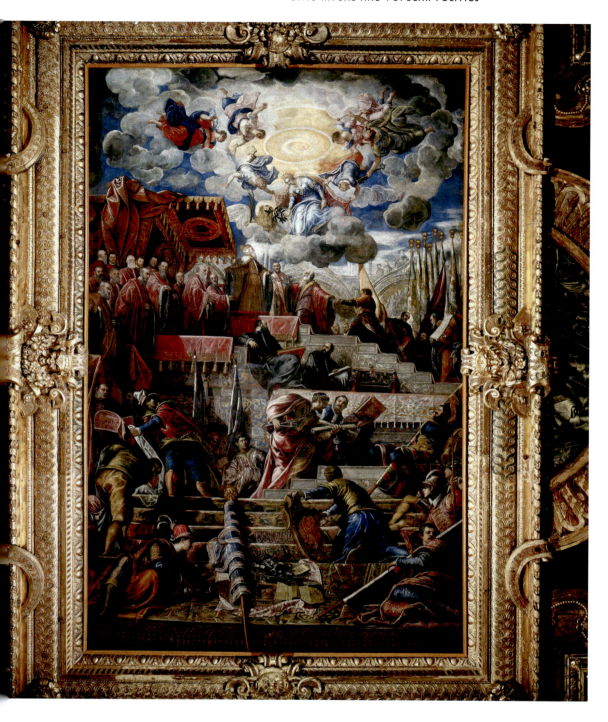

the Republic. This gesture triggers reciprocity:[95] in return for its submission, the Community receives the recognition of privileges, which are represented as a sealed document listing the requests granted it by the Serenissima. Depicted by Vecellio with great attention to its extrinsic and material features, this 'foundational chart'[96] stands out as the only realistic element in the otherwise allegorical composition. The handing over of the *pacta deditionis* between the queen and the subject community thus makes possible a contact, albeit mediated, between political bodies at separate layers of the constitutional edifice of the Venetian state: the former enthroned between St Mark and the Virgin Mary (and transfigured in them), the latter invited by the allegory of Faith to bow at the foot of the throne.[97]

Since it was anchored to the doge's unmoving persona and, as a consequence, to the city of Venice, the celebration of republican power played a significant role in tracing and making visible the constitutional border between the throne

1.22
Paolo Caliari (Veronese), *Apotheosis of Venice*.
Venice, Ducal Palace, Sala del Maggior Consiglio.
1585. Photo: Scala, Firenze.

1.23
Cesare Vecellio, *The Submission of Cadore to Venice*,
Pieve di Cadore, Palazzo della Magnifica Comunità del
Cadore. 1599. © Magnifica Comunità del Cadore, p.g.c.
Reproduction forbidden.

of republican sovereignty and the territories subjected to its rule. The whole ceremonial system which pivoted on the doge has been correctly defined as a 'civic ritual', according to a twofold interpretation that applies both the adjectival and noun form of the definition: on the one hand, it conveys the republican (and humanist) nature of the 'myth'[98] celebrated by the Venetian 'political festival';[99] on the other hand, it gives a sense of the strictly urban scope of this celebration, which was mostly confined to Venice's city boundaries.[100] As Giacomo Franco's engravings recalled, even two centuries after the Venetian conquest of the mainland the 'public ceremonies' performed by the 'doge and the Serenissima Signoria' celebrated Venice as a self-sufficient city-state republic rather than a republican territorial state.

In this regard, civic ritual perfectly reflected the asymmetric constitutional order identifying Venice with the republican government and Venetian dominions with political entities subdued to the Republic but excluded from its government. Following in the wake of the contrasting legacies of Marino Berengo, Gaetano Cozzi, and Angelo Ventura,

notions such as 'non-inclusion'[101] and 'separateness'[102] still underlie much contemporary analysis of Venetian rule over these territories. With respect to its political body, Venice always remained separate from its dominions: while expanding over these territories, the city-state republic neither assimilated nor included the subdued bodies, but merely overlapped with them as a superordinate political power.[103]

Nevertheless, as Vecellio shows, there was always room for negotiation, however narrow it might have been. Formally secured by compliance with the agreements granted to subject communities at the moment of their submission (*pacta deditionis*), the maintenance of local jurisdictional prerogatives and political identities, which counterbalanced their total lack of inclusion in the republican government,[104] offered the chance to put the borders between rulers and the ruled into question. This was made possible through peculiar communicative and ceremonial practices, which Vecellio hints at in his painting's backdrop (fig. 1.24). Behind the allegorical meeting between queen Venice and the Community of Cadore, a more concrete encounter unfolds: as in Tintoretto's painting for the ceiling of the Hall of the Great Council, the doge welcomes the ambassadors of the community submitting to Venice on the Giants' Staircase.

The historical realism of the scene is only apparent and should not mislead. Unlike Ligozzi's painting for the Veronese town hall, Vecellio's work does not memorialise the original event of the submission to Venice, but rather implies its consequences: because of the asymmetrical relationship established through the *pacta deditionis*, the sovereign power located in Venice and embodied by the doge's immobile persona becomes accessible to subjects hailing from the dominions. Framed between the faces of Venice and Cadore and grounded almost physically in the legal documents legitimising it, the view of the Giants' Staircase alludes to the possibility, guaranteed to subjects by the pact of submission, of breaching the constitutional divide between the *Dominante* and its dominions, climbing the steps to the immobile seat of republican sovereignty, and addressing it directly by voicing petitions, complaints, and political visions.

Moving subjects

The very notion of boundary implies its crossability, even if only as something to be prevented. Even the strictest boundary is still a frontier: a threshold that, in defining separate entities and identities, makes communication between them possible.[105] The existence of an actual boundary, both ceremonial and constitutional, between Venice and its dominions shaped the forms of political communication rather than forbidding it. Ritual and politics, in the Venetian context, involved crossing the border that separated the immobile prince from his subjects. A change in perspective, however, is necessary if we are to comprehend how and to what extent such a border was permeable. To do so, the narrow ceremonial map outlined by Giacomo Franco must be situated within the broader context of which it was actually a part.

1.24
Cesare Vecellio, *The Submission of Cadore to Venice.*
Detail of 1.22.

1.25
Jacopo Negretti (Palma The Younger), *Commemorative Painting of Doges Gerolamo and Lorenzo Priuli*, Venice, Ducal Palace, Sala del Senato, 1583–1587. Photo: Scala, Firenze.

Several chapters of this volume[106] are devoted to representations of Venetian rule on its subject territories and polities. The 'rituals of power negotiation' disallowed to the doge due to his immobility (e.g. inaugural entries, ceremonial journeys, and official visits)[107] were regularly performed by the patrician magistrates in charge of administering the subject territories. The immobility of the 'head' of the republic was hence matched by the high degree of mobility of its political body, whose 'limbs' (the patricians) frequently alternated peripheral offices.[108] The Republic relied on these peripheral offshoots of its 'body politic' to project its majesty outside the urban perimeter and make its authority felt in the subject territories (fig. 1.25).

Unlike monarchic officials such as viceroys and royal envoys, Venetian provincial governors (*rettori*) as well as other peripheral and itinerant magistrates (*camerlenghi*, *provveditori*, *sindaci inquisitori*, etc.) were not mere proxies of the sovereign.[109] As members of the Venetian patriciate, they were instead a full-fledged part of the sovereign body itself. They were therefore supposed to act in this capacity during the festivals, ceremonies, and political occasions[110] that were performed as ritual re-establishments (and actual reenactments) of the power hierarchies separating Venice and its dominions. Their peculiar status allowed a direct connection between rulers and ruled, between the collective sovereign body of the republic they represented, on the one hand, and the several subject bodies inhabiting its composite state, on the other. Often portrayed as idyllic encounters restating the 'natural order' of the Venetian society, these ceremonial events were actually far from devoid of tensions. The sumptuary laws were redundant and several treaties were published to discipline the ceremonial conduct of local governors and élites, which suggests the difficulties the Republic encountered in this regard.[111] The key issue at stake was giving the representatives who embodied the Republic a princely aura while preventing them from exceeding personalism (fig. 1.26).[112]

Major tensions also emerged when the ceremonial boundary between the Serenissima and its dominion was crossed in the opposite direction. Republican subjects needed a direct contact with the 'head of the state', just like subjects of any

1.26
Jacopo Negretti (Palma The Younger), *Exaltation of the rectors of Padua Jacopo and Giovanni Soranzo.* Padua, Musei Civici, end of the 16th century. Reproduced with permission.

monarch.[113] The lack of any supra-local or multi-estate representative institutions (i.e. parliaments, estates general, diets, cortes *et similia*), which were almost completely foreign to the Venetian polity,[114] fostered this need. Therefore, to make their voices heard in the *Dominante*, in the mid-sixteenth century several subject cities and territories began to stabilise a diplomatic presence in Venice.[115] A network of 'subject embassies' (*case*) was created, traces of which are still legible in the current toponymy of the city of Venice. Most of these 'embassies' – such as those of Vicenza (fig. 1.27), Verona and Feltre – were located in the area between Santa Maria Zobenigo and San Moisè, whose relevance for the celebration of republican power has already been stressed. Other embassies, such as that of Brescia (fig. 1.28), were located in the area near the Basilica of Santi Giovanni e Paolo and were connected to St Mark's Square and the Ducal Palace via the Mercerie.[116] Thus, although seemingly inviolable, the constitutional perimeter centred on the doge's immobile persona and underscored by Venetian civic ritual, was trespassed daily by subject legations flocking to the seat of republican power for judicial, political, or celebratory reasons.

The presence of this internal diplomacy became particularly evident at celebrations for the election of a doge. Since the fifteenth century, the subject cities and quasi-cities paid homage to the newly elected doge by sending ceremonial delegations appointed to recognize his authority. These declarations of loyalty involved both verbal and non-verbal

those that had been employed, especially in the early fifteenth century, to ratify 'voluntary submissions' of the subject cities to Venice. The similarity is such that Ligozzi, despite having been commissioned to depict an event of ancient 'voluntary submission', was able to use modern descriptions of 'congratulatory embassies' from his own time.[118] Such descriptions were readily available, since the congratulatory ceremonies had a relevant impact on the Venetian information market. Largely entrusted with epistolary writing, handwritten descriptions of the event became widespread; the orations delivered before the doge were quickly printed in law-quality editions (today we would call them instant books) and widely disseminated.[119] Starting with another text by Sansovino (1562), who once again identified the new cultural trend first, these orations were even gathered in printed anthologies with literary and editorial ambitions.[120]

The very existence of these ceremonies and texts challenges the perimeter drawn by the notion of 'civic ritual'. Indeed, a significant part of this 'ritual' complex was not really 'civic' at all: some external actors, coming from outside Giacomo Franco's map, could burst into Venice's urban spaces (like the Veronese ambassadors painted by Ligozzi) and celebrate republican power in their own ways. Subject communities insisted on presenting this practice as part of their own traditions, as if it was not prescribed by any Venetian law or mandate. Venice, indeed, never openly discussed the matter. On the contrary, throughout the early modern era Venetian magistracies cautiously avoided implementing or even promoting laws that would force subject communities to revere the doge by sending ambassadors or orators.[121] For the same reason, no protocol for congratulatory embassies was ever recorded in Venetian ceremonial registers (libri cerimoniali). The Serenissima had considerable interest in allowing its subjects to stage this homage as unforced, since it put on public display their loyalty towards the new prince and the Republic that he embodied. In this regard, congratulatory embassies and orations also played a significant role in the framework of the 'myth of Venice'. 'Spontaneously' performed by subjects, they backed up the apologetic (self)representation of the Venetian sovereignty as a desirable yoke and suggested its dominion was based on consent.

Nevertheless, it would be incorrect to reduce the contribution of these subjects to the 'myth of Venice' to passive endorsement. Congratulatory embassies and orations complicated and

communication. By the mid-sixteenth century, the core of the congratulatory ceremony consisted in a sumptuous pageant performed by the subject ambassadors that took place along the same ceremonial route used for the procurators' entry: arranged in pairs and accompanied by a crowded retinue of former rettori and other patrician patrons, the representatives of the subject community marched from San Moisè (later San Salvador) through St Mark's Square and up to the Ducal Palace. Here the official audience took place in the presence of the Pien Collegio and a congratulatory oration was delivered. Finally, the whole delegation knelt before the doge.[117]

The ceremonial pattern adopted on these occasions and the rhetorical choices made by the orators deliberately echoed

1.27
Sotoportego e corte de la Vicenza, Venice.
Photo: Public Domain.

hybridised the *topoi* of the 'myth' by increasing their polysemy. Subject communities conceived their homage as performative reenactments of the pacts through which they had negotiated the terms of their 'voluntary submission'.[122] As the cases of Ligozzi and Vecellio demonstrate, periodic reenactment of the foundational moment of capitulation – which could occur through performance, oration, or the visual arts – not only implied recognising a status of subjection, but also the existence of local institutions, privileges, and exemptions that had been granted by the *pacta deditionis*. Indeed, in spite of its commendatory nature, the cultural production surrounding the congratulatory embassy was aimed precisely at limiting, in performative terms, the full and undifferentiated deployment of Venetian sovereignty on its dominions.

The orator Mario Frecavalli, for instance, who praised doge Marino Grimani on behalf of the city of Crema in 1595, claimed the right to renegotiate the 'privileges' that his community had obtained by means of its voluntary submission to Venice in 1449:

> In several places, servant cities are used to presenting themselves to those who, by inheritance or by other kinds of fortune, succeed to princedoms or empires […] and to renewing their oath of loyalty, from which they could be relieved due to the advent of the new Prince, in order to impetrate, [once] declared [their] readiness and most loving willingness to serve, the conservation and increase of their privileges, or to recommend themselves [to the new Prince], and [thus] bode themselves […] a favourable rule.[123]

Here, as in other orations from the same period, Frecavalli assumes the power discontinuity caused by in the ducal succession to be a potential reason to revoke the bonds of subjection linking the subject communities to the Serenissima. He hence infers the need for a periodic renewal with both legal and ritual value. Frecavalli's statement is intentionally hyperbolic, as the orator deliberately ignores the durability of the Republic's 'mystical body politic' and focuses exclusively on the 'body natural' of its prince.[124] His purpose, however, is very practical: by leveraging the 'honourable custom' of the congratulatory embassy, the subject community attempts to preserve its own political and juridical identity despite its submission. Meant to be a recognition of Venice's sovereignty over its dominions, these orations thus reveal the limits and unresolved tensions of the Venetian state. In this respect, the congratulatory embassy sent to the republican prince fulfilled a function mirroring that performed, during the same period, by the *joyeuse entrées* of monarchs. Whereas in the monarchic context it was the *dominus* who entered the subject community to recognise its privileges and re-establish his authority,[125] in the Republic of Venice it was the subject community which entered the *Dominante* and, by recognising its authority, claimed its own privileges.

Ceremonial practices were an integral part of this latent process of re-negotiation. The necessity of having an embassy to finally gain contact with the 'immobile prince' encouraged subject cities to represent themselves as autonomous political bodies, subdued to Venice but still endowed with their own political and legal identities. The medium also proved to be the message,[126] because embassies were conceived and performed as a declaration of 'otherness' with respect to the *Dominante*.[127] Justified since the early fifteenth century by the employment of sumptuous ceremonial apparatuses, a comparison was established, in both handwritten and printed accounts, between subject ambassadors and the representatives of sovereign foreign states. Describing the homage paid by Verona to Leonardo Donà in 1606, polygraph Francesco Pola[128] captured the wonder of the crowd thronging St Mark's Square at the sight of the Veronese orators approaching the Ducal Palace with a retinue of about two-hundred men, who were almost equally divided between Veronese citizens and Venetian patricians. The ambassadors represented Verona, a 'subject city' ('*alieno imperio obnoxia*'), but several people mistook them for 'illustrious little kings' ('*inclytos* […] *regulos*') making their entry to Venice.[129] The resident agent of Vicenza (*nunzio*) wrote similarly of the celebrations addressed to Francesco Contarini in 1624: the ambassadors of Vicenza reached Venice 'with great pomp', escorted by 'a retinue that could be suitable for an emperor'.[130]

Representations of Venice as a ruling queen did not prevent the subject communities from cloaking themselves in princely robes. Indeed, these congratulatory embassies might actually

1.28
Corte Bressana, Venice.
Photo: Public Domain.

have conveyed messages that were seemingly incompatible with notions and actual practices of 'republican dominion'. In spite of the apparent immutability of the 'myth of Venice', the forms of such dominion changed radically during the early modern age, becoming no stranger to the lure of absolutism.[131] This is apparent in how Venetian legislation on congratulatory embassies (otherwise rather scarce, as mentioned above) addressed their performances. Starting in the late fifteenth century, the Great Council leveraged the periodic amendment of the Ducal Oath to impose gradually stricter sumptuary restrictions on ducal homage and on the subject communities' self-celebration as a consequence. Formally, the Venetian 'body politic' disciplined the conduct of its 'visible head' and not those of its subjects. Since 1476, the doge was prohibited from receiving congratulatory embassies composed of more than twenty members and listening to orations that were too long.[132] The alleged justification for such measures relied on the doge's role as 'legal guardian' of the subject communities: embodied by the doge, the Republic was responsible for the economic behaviours of these communities, as if they were unable to act autonomously. This attitude drew on a royal understanding of Venetian rule[133] but also on the 'myth of Venice', since the erosion of both local communities' autonomy and 'princely' self-fashioning ambitions was legitimised by the notion of republican 'good governance'. Even in the seventeenth century, when Venetian control of the behaviour of congratulatory embassies became more direct, both the Great Council and the Senate justified their conduct by citing the intention of saving local communities from excessive expense.[134]

In this sense, the amendment of the Ducal Oath addressed the issue of celebrating republican power in two directions: indeed, the need to contain its spatial range, outward costs, and self-celebrative implications applied to both the republican prince and the subject communities. Sumptuary laws reflected a new semantics of power which overlapped with humanist civic-republican discourses about patrician equality and the mixed constitution. At the beginning of the seventeenth century, the issues at stake had already made the urban boundaries of Venetian civic ritual quite anachronistic: in a Europe where absolute monarchy emerged as the leading political benchmark,[135] the 'myth' of Venice had to stretch its perimeter and reframe its shape in both Bodinian and Boterian terms. Some of the key concepts of the 'myth' (such as good government, original liberty, devotion) also evolved and transformed to present the Republic as a fully sovereign prince, subjecting its *potestas* only to God (according to Jean Bodin's thinking) and exerting undisputed dominion over its subject peoples (in the wake of Giovanni Botero's ideas).[136] The paintings on the ceiling of the Hall of the Great Council, as we have seen, point toward this transformation: Venice still grants privileges to subject communities, but also rules firmly as an Amazon warrior, a demigoddess, and an undisputed monarch.

Thus, throughout the early modern period, the republican discourse on sovereignty and dominion was far from smooth and linear: as we have seen, in both the Ducal Palace and the town halls, in both the Piazza and the town squares, queenly representations of Venice still coexisted with those of her subjects' political power. A seemingly minor episode – which was omitted from official historiography and chancellery's records, but reported in detail in the correspondence between the subject communities and their representatives in Venice[137] – highlights the complexity, and even the contradictions, inherent to this discourse. On 11 September 1623, a few days after his election, doge Francesco Contarini informally summoned the *nunzi* of the major mainland communities. At this unofficial meeting, he communicated his wishes regarding the upcoming visits of ceremonial embassies hailing from the dominions. Expecting scrupulous compliance with the sumptuary restrictions, the doge requested that the orators refrain from praising his person:

> [the doge] will gladly hear the praises of his Republic and its [subject] cities, but he will be mortified to hear his own [praises; and this mortification] will increase further [the] latter.[138]

The unofficial reform that Contarini attempted to implement addressed both structural tensions that we discussed: on the one hand, the (self)celebratory ambitions of the subject communities and Venice's long-term efforts to discipline them; on the other hand, the presence of a (pseudo)monarchical figure at the top of a republican system and the consequent need to control celebrations of this 'visible head' in a political context based on the collegial exercise of power. This latter matter was emerging as particularly urgent: just a few years later, the atavic resentments spreading through the lower echelons of the Venetian patriciate would find an outlet in the aristocratic-egalitarian 'movement' led by Renier Zeno against the overbearing power of the Council of Ten and the princely excesses of doge Giovanni Cornaro (1625–1629).[139]

In such a context, tensions from inside and outside the republican 'body politic' converged in the ceremony of ducal homage. On 3 July 1624, the city deputies of Vicenza were informed by their *nunzio* of the imminent death of doge Francesco Contarini. According to the *nunzio*, a 'rumour' was spreading 'among the Venetian nobility': during the upcoming interregnum,

> the Reformers [of the Ducal Oath] will pass a law to the effect that [subject] cities should no longer send congratulatory ambassadors, but do so only every ten years as a token of gratitude to their Prince; on the occasion of the Princes' creations the nuncios will substitute them.[140]

When doge Contarini died, nothing was done in this regard. However, the very circulation of this 'rumour' within and beyond the ruling body denotes, once again, the problematic nature of ducal praise in the 1620s. Not only were the ceremonial features of ducal homage questioned, but also the need of the ritual itself. Established in the early fifteenth century as a periodic reenactment and a symbolic renegotiation of the dominions' submission to the Serenissima, two centuries later the congratulatory embassies were experiencing a profound loss of meaning and performative effectiveness.

Fearing the risks inherent to both the personalism of the doge and the (self)celebratory strategies of the subject communities, broad sections of the Venetian patriciate began questioning the liminal function of the interregnum.

In 1625, for instance, the Collegio's secretary Giulio Priuli rejected the 'points of honour' (*pontigli*) raised by the city of Padua, which was sceptical about sending an ordinary embassy to Venice before the congratulatory one. In other words, the city council of Padua refused to submit petitions before having ritually re-established its subjecthood, which had theoretically been interrupted because of the ducal succession. Priuli, however, dismissed this concern as a mere 'superstition'.[141] Another diplomatic incident occurred upon the arrival of the Paduan ambassadors in Venice. Many patricians encouraged the orator Giovanni Battista Selvatico to pay homage to Giovanni Cornaro in his absence, for the doge was ill and could not reach the Hall of the Collegio. Despite reluctantly accepting, Selvatico replied that 'it seemed not good to congratulate for the elevation to principality of a prince without his presence'.[142] The Collegio's spokesperson (*savio di settimana*), Girolamo Lando, reassured him by explaining that in the current magistracy, as in any others of the Republic, 'the prince was always present', regardless of the physical location of the doge.[143]

Beneath the apparent fixity of Venetian rituals, in the seventeenth century the 'body politic' of the Republic struggled to emancipate itself from the doge's 'body natural' to express its sovereignty over 'subject bodies'. Francesco Morosini's dogado is a rather telling example in this respect as well. During the period in which the warrior doge was engaged on the Greek battlefront (1688–1691 and 1693–1694), the patrician 'body politic' consciously ran the institutional machinery of the Republic without the performative and constitutional assistance of a 'visible head'. In announcing Morosini's election as doge despite his absence from Venice, the Senate made the point clear: from that moment, when addressing the sovereign power both the subject communities and their Venetian *rettori* would have to refer to the 'Serenissimo Dominio Venetiarum' – and not to 'its Most Serene prince'.[144] For the first time in the history of the Republic, the functioning of both the republican institutions and the political communications linking the Palace, the city of Venice, and its dominions were supposed to work without a 'body natural'. In this sense, the dogado of Morosini represented a unique constitutional experiment, during which the patriciate assessed the possibility of maintaining the 'mythical' balance supporting the Venetian constitution in the absence of an actual (pseudo)monarchic element at its top.

The results of this experiment, as we have seen, were paradoxical. The doge's anomalous absence came to amplify the rituals marking his return to the ceremonial and constitutional perimeters of the city of Venice; moreover, Morosini's military fame – and, more specifically, the double office he exceptionally held as doge and naval commander in chief – led to the emergence of cultural phenomena unusual for early modern Venice, in which any form of personality cultural was typically forbidden. Even more paradoxically, the dampening of ducal personalism that followed these phenomena resulted in blunt reconfirmation of the doge's role as 'performative mask' and marker of republican sovereignty and its re-inscription on the map of the Venetian state. With the 1694 amendment to the Ducal Oath, the 'head' of the Republic was definitively fixed to its 'body politic'. Once the 'monstrous' hypothesis of a republican body without a head was dismissed, the 'body politic' recognised the need to rely on its 'visible head' to credibly wear a sovereign crown; by once again restraining the mobility of the prince's 'body natural' within the borders of the 'ceremonial city', the Venetian patriciate reaffirmed its authority on the doge but also the existence of a clear-cut constitutional hierarchy separating the *Dominante* from its dominions. After the institutional dismay of the 1680s, the 'myth' still proved a safe haven – once again showing its flexibility.

However, this rediscovery of ceremonial boundaries hailing from the Renaissance was far from painless or linear: despite the permeability of these boundaries, which this chapter has discussed in detail, some pieces of the puzzle constituting the 'myth'[145] no longer seem to fit in place. Indeed, Girolamo Lando's statement ('the prince is always present') implies an idea of statehood significantly different from the one embodied by the doge's 'body natural', as well as from the one visually rendered in the town halls of the dominion or advocated by the subject orators praising newly elected doges. In 1631, the Senate used the concomitant events of plague and war to suspend the congratulatory embassies for doges Nicolò Contarini (1630–1631) and Francesco Erizzo (1631–1646). This emergency measure was renewed throughout the entire Candia War (1645–1669), until it became *de facto* permanent. In 1675, after the war ended, an attempt to revive the congratulatory embassies was attempted under doge Nicolò Sagredo (1675–1678); however, it was not pursued.[146] Even before Francesco Morosini's rise to power a few years later, the failure of this project proved that the perimeter of Venetian civic ritual and popular politics could no longer be contained within the boundaries articulated during the Renaissance.

The entangled chapters to come

The itinerary this volume maps out is divided into five stages. Each consists of two chapters: in some cases (chapters 6–7, 10–11), this division explicitly corresponds to deal the theoretical perspectives that we discussed above, i.e. civic ritual and popular politics; in other cases, it is intended to enable comparison between different disciplinary approaches to the same object of enquiry (2–3, 4–5). The analysis unfolds in concentric centres that become progressively wider. By gradually moving from inside to outside the Palace (2–3), and then across and beyond the Piazza (4–5), our focus shifts from the urban streets of the 'ceremonial city' (6–7) to the ritual spaces of its peripheral dominions (8–9), and finally turns to a pan-European perspective (10–11). This itinerary aims to overcome the ceremonial geography pre-conceptualised in the iconic frontispiece by Giacomo Franco (fig. 1.10). Accordingly, whereas our first two stages challenge the semantics of the more institutionalised spaces of the Republic, the Palace and the Piazza, the last three question the self-sufficiency of the St Mark's area, as they examine how the Palace and the Piazza interacted with other places and actors. On the one hand, this hermeneutic journey takes us to political spaces outside the St Mark's area (urban streets, 6; the lagoon islands, 7), the city of Venice (Verona, 8; Bergamo, 9; the Mediterranean, 10), and even the Republic itself (Lyon and Florence, 11); on the other hand, it leads to meeting social groups outside the ranks of the Venetian patriciate (the urban population, 2, 4, 6; the subject polities, 8, 9, 10; foreign communities, 3, 11).

The first section of the volume, *Representing the Palace*, brings together a study of the pictorial decoration commissioned for the Hall of the Great Council after the fires of the late sixteenth century with a survey of how this very Hall was represented and reinterpreted, in words and images, between the fifteenth and the eighteenth centuries. Both chapters adopt an interdisciplinary methodology: the first, by Giorgio Tagliaferro (2), crosses the fields of art and intellectual history to assess how cultural production and political thinking influenced each other; the latter, by Monique O'Connell (3), welcomes theoretical suggestions from media history, contextualising them in the framework of early modern political history. Chapter 2 pivots on the close reading of a painting signed by the heirs of Paolo Veronese, *The Meeting of Sebastiano Ziani with Alexander III at the Church of the Carità*. Though organised according to the 'myth of Venice' – with each social group in the work, including the 'people', positioned according to the myth's narrative around the ruling patriciate and its 'visible head' (the doge Ziani) – the composition of the canvas is not without ambiguity. As Tagliaferro argues, the painting must bring the 'people' on stage, even if only to celebrate the patriciate; while wanting to exclude the 'people' from politics, the representation also emphasises their conspicuous presence and puts their legitimising devotion on display. Similarly, chapter 3 addresses the processes of mediatization of the republican 'body politic', by investigating descriptions and engravings in which hundreds of patricians dressed in black and gathered in the Hall of the Great Council vote without saying a word or expressing a needless gesture. These representations are designed to showcase the 'mechanised virtue' extolled by the 'myth of Venice'; yet, as O'Connell shows, the process is not linear, for the cultural production reshapes and re-functionalises the decision-making procedures depicted and the meanings associated with them, through a system of borrowings, cross-references, interactions, and interpolations.

In the second section, entitled *The Piazza Revisited*, Massimo Rospocher (4) examines the Piazza as a 'practised space', regardless of any institutional norms or ceremonial events. Individual and collective subjects took their needs and demands to the streets even when they were contrary to the directives of the government. However, this does not make the Piazza an alternative or opposite to the Palace, but rather a prolongation of it, a widening of its scope and integration of its functions – which allows Rospocher to postulate a connection between 'institutionalised' and 'popular' politics. In chapter 5, Iseabail Cameron Rowe studies the different trajectories that defined the space of St Mark's Square for English traveller Thomas Coryat, whose *Crudities* was published in 1611. Although designed by the republican authorities for ritual and celebratory use, the Piazza remains subject to external and even eccentric interpretations, proving to be a polysemic space which changes according to who experiences it.

In *Sacred Streets and Public Spaces*, the third section of the volume, Evelyn Korsch (6) reconsiders civic ritual and its actual topography in light of the new strategies that were implemented in late sixteenth-century Venice for sacralising republican power. On the entrance into Venice of Henry III of France in 1574, for instance, a *via sacra* was established that exploited both imperial and papal Roman models. The following chapter instead focuses on far less sacred *viae*, as Umberto Cecchinato (7) argues for the need for a bottom-up approach to understanding social and festive street practices. Based on legislative and procedural documentation, chapter 7 shows that categories such as 'public ceremonial' and 'private party', 'institutionalised' and 'spontaneous' festivals frequently overlapped in early modern Venice, because they came to identify the same phenomena, despite the disciplining efforts put in place by authorities wanting to differentiate them.

The fourth section of the book, *The Ceremonial Mainland*, opens with a chapter by Marco Bellabarba (8), which centres on the lost cycle of frescoes in the Pretorio Palace of Verona commissioned by the city governor (*podestà*) Agostino da Mula at the beginning of the seventeenth century. This case study fuels a comprehensive rethinking of the figure of the Venetian governor (*rettore*) with implications for both republican ideology and governmental practice. As Bellabarba argues, the ceremonial works celebrating the governor (e.g. laudatory texts, statues and portraits, performative events) expressed the underlying tension between the office, which represented the collective sovereignty of the patriciate, and its holder, whose personal authority and patronal capacity were at stake. Although delving into a similar topic, Erika Carminati (9) addresses a different case study, shifting attention to the city of Bergamo between the seventeenth and eighteenth centuries. Carminati reads the ceremonies that welcomed and greeted the *rettore* in Bergamo as part of the power negotiations that took place among the local community, the Serenissima, and its representative. By analysing some conflicting episodes, in which ritual forms were challenged if not overthrown, Carminati argues in favour of the existence of a public sphere, however ephemeral. This applies especially to the appropriation and subversion of ceremonial spaces usually reserved for republican authorities.

In the fifth and last section of the volume, *Mythmaking Across Boundaries*, Alfredo Viggiano (10) and Matteo Casini (11) start from very different, yet concurrent assumptions to rethink the 'myth of Venice'. In chapter 10, Viggiano adopts a long-term institutional perspective to show how the notion of 'people', in early modern Venice as well as in Europe, was far too elusive and controversial to be boxed into a passive role, as the 'myth' does. In chapter 11, Casini focuses on the reception and reworking of Venetian festive practices abroad, emphasising the contributions made by the foreign communities living both inside and outside Venice. In light of novel archival findings, Casini shows the civic ritual to be far less monolithic repertoire than has been traditionally assumed, especially because some of its key elements – which the 'myth' crystalized as republican prerogatives – were actually recovered, exploited, and re-semantised in princely and royal contexts. At the end of our itinerary, therefore, the intertwining of republican spaces turns out to be so intricate that it even entangles some monarchic ones.

1. On this painting, see Florio, 'Inchini e carte bollate', pp. 88–92; Varanini, 'L'uso pubblico della storia', pp. 88–90; Peretti, Artoni, Marini, and Napione, eds, *Museo di Castelvecchio*, pp. 219–20. On Ligozzi's figure and artistic production, see Faietti, Nova, and Wolf, eds, *Jacopo Ligozzi 2015*; Cecchi, Conigliello, and Faietti, eds, *Jacopo Ligozzi, 'pittore universalissimo'*; De Luca and Faietti, eds, *Jacopo Ligozzi, 'altro Apelle'*.
2. Dalla Corte, *L'istoria di Verona*, vol. II, pp. 275–94. On the Veronese *deditio*, see Messedaglia, *La dedizione di Verona*.
3. Florio, *Micropolitica della rappresentanza*, pp. 66–77.
4. In Peretti, Artoni, Marini, and Napione, eds, *Museo di Castelvecchio*, pp. 219–20, Ettore Napione argues that the twenty patricians represent the Great Council, but their crimson robes, which belonged to higher magistracies (simple patricians routinely wore black), suggest otherwise.
5. Dalla Corte, *L'istoria di Verona*, vol. II, p. 288.
6. Both the role played by the Mercerie and the conduct of the subject embassies are discussed later in this chapter.
7. Franco, *Habiti d'huomeni et donne venetiane*. About this author, see Pasero, 'Giacomo Franco, editore, incisore e calcografo nei secoli XVI e XVII'; Stefani, 'Franco, Giacomo'.
8. Pasero, 'Giacomo Franco, editore, incisore e calcografo nei secoli XVI e XVII', p. 351.
9. Grubb, 'When Myths Lose Power', p. 43.
10. On this widely debated topic, see Fasoli, 'Nascita di un mito'; Gaeta, 'Alcune considerazioni sul mito di Venezia'; Gaeta, 'L'idea di Venezia'; Gaeta, 'Venezia da "Stato misto" ad aristocrazia "esemplare"'; Crouzet-Pavan, *Venezia trionfante*; Rosand, *Myths of Venice*.
11. See Pocock, *The Machiavellian Moment*, pp. 283–85; Conti, 'The Mechanisation of Virtue'.
12. See Muir, *Civic Ritual in Renaissance Venice*; Ambrosini, 'Cerimonie, feste, lusso'; Casini, *I gesti del principe*; Casini, 'Cerimoniali'; Urban, *Processioni e feste dogali*; Fenlon, *The Ceremonial City*.
13. Fenlon, *The Ceremonial City*, p. 325.
14. Sansovino, *Tutte le cose notabili e belle che sono in Venetia*; Sansovino, *Dialogo di tutte le cose notabili che sono in Venetia*.
15. Sansovino, *Venetia città nobilissima e singolare* (1581).
16. Sansovino, *Le cose meravigliose dell'inclita città di Venetia*.
17. Doglioni, *La città di Venetia con l'origine e governo di quella*.
18. Mulryne, 'Ceremony and the Iconography of Power', p. 1.
19. See Grubb, 'When Myths Lose Power'; Martin and Romano, eds, *Venice Reconsidered*.
20. Fenlon, *The Ceremonial City*.
21. Rospocher, ed., *Beyond the Public Sphere*; Salzberg, *The Ephemeral City*; Rospocher and Salzberg, '"El vulgo zanza"'; Rospocher and Salzberg, *Il mercato dell'informazione*; De Vivo, *Information and Communication*.
22. See Judde de Larivière and Salzberg, 'The People Are the City'; Judde de Larivière, 'De quel peuple parle-t-on?'. See also chapter 10 by Viggiano.
23. Van Gelder and Judde de Larivière, eds, *Popular Politics in an Aristocratic Republic* (from which the expressions 'institutionalised power' and 'popular politics' are taken). Also see Judde de Larivière, *The Revolt of Snowballs*.
24. For a working definition of this concept and the previous debate, see Rau, *History, Space, and Place*.
25. See chapter 4 by Rospocher.
26. Muir, 'Images of Power'; Tafuri, 'Renovatio Urbis'.
27. See Van Gelder, 'Ducal Display'; Van Gelder, 'The People's Prince'.
28. See chapters 7 and 10 by Cecchinato and Viggiano.
29. See chapters 1 and 2 by Tagliaferro and O'Connell.
30. See chapter 9 by Carminati.
31. See Povolo, 'Uno sguardo rivolto alla religiosità popolare'; Povolo, 'Ambigue descrizioni'. Also see Bellabarba, 'Controlling Officials' and chapter 8 by Bellabarba.
32. See Varanini, ed., *Rituali civici e continuità istituzionale*; O'Connell, 'The Multiple Meaning of Ritual'; O'Connell, 'Voluntary Submission'; O'Connell, 'Venetian Empire'; Špoljarić, 'Power and Subversion'; Lavarda, *Vicenza nel Seicento*; Florio, 'Acciocché i popoli'; Florio, 'Venezia e le comunità di Terraferma'; Florio, 'S'incliner devant un prince républicain'; Florio, '"Ai piedi di Sua Serenità"'; Florio, 'Inchini e carte bollate'; Florio, 'Celebrating the Prince from Afar'; Carminati, 'La Repubblica in scena'.
33. See chapters 5, 6 and 11 by Rowe, Korsch and Casini.
34. See Milanesi, *Vincenzo Coronelli, cosmographer*.
35. The only remarkable exception is Casini, 'Cerimoniali'.
36. See Fenlon, *The Ceremonial City*, 331.
37. See Metlica, 'Magnificence and Atticism'; Metlica, 'Reshaping the Republican Ritual'; Florio, 'L'inventio della consuetudine'.
38. Cozzi, 'Dalla riscoperta della pace all'inestinguibile sogno di dominio'. On the same topic, also see Candiani, 'Conflitti d'intenti e di ragioni politiche'.
39. For a long-term view of the phenomenon, see Cozzi, *Repubblica di Venezia e stati italiani*; Cozzi, 'Venezia, una Repubblica di principi?'; Hunecke, 'Il corpo aristocratico'.
40. On the 'antimyth of Venice' in the seventeenth century, see Del Negro, 'Forme e istituzioni del discorso politico veneziano'; Mandelli, ed., *La copella politica*. On the internal contrasts and collective identity of the patriciate, see Raines, *L'invention du mythe aristocratique*; Hunecke, *Il patriziato veneziano*.
41. See Gaier, *Facciate sacre a scopo profano*; Favilla and Rugolo, 'Frammenti dalla Venezia barocca'.
42. For naval commanders in chief, whose role stood out in the Ottoman-Venetian wars, see Casini, 'Immagini dei capitani generali'.
43. See Burke, *Venice and Amsterdam*; Mueller, 'The Procurators of San Marco'; Chambers, 'Merit and Money'; Van Gelder, 'The People's Prince'.
44. A list of these texts appears in Delorenzi, *La galleria di Minerva*, pp. 301–48. Also see Minuzzi, *Il secolo di carta*, pp. 29–33; Metlica, 'Reshaping the Republican Ritual', pp. 171–80.
45. Versteegen, Bussels, and Melion, eds, *Magnificence in the Seventeenth Century*.
46. Ivanovich, *Minerva al tavolino*, II, pp. 118–30.
47. On Ivanovich's librettos, see Bellina, 'Brevità, frequenza e varietà'; Rosand, *Opera in Seventeenth Century Venice*, p. 151.
48. See Bolduc, *La Fête imprimée*; Metlica, *Le seduzioni della pace*.
49. 'Non entro nella generosità di questa Eccellenza, che subito seguita la di lui elezione, in argomento di sua beneficenza, fece dispensare denaro, pane, vino profusamente a' poveri e a' traghetti della città, perché questi è pregio innato della Casa Basadonna'. Ivanovich, *Minerva al tavolino*, II, p. 120.
50. See Russel and Visentin, eds, *French Ceremonial Entries*; Mulryne, Aliverti, and Testaverde, eds, *Ceremonial Entries*; Fosi, 'Court and City in the Ceremony of the Possesso'.

51 'I meno pratici della generosità connaturale di questa nobilissima Casa, teneano concetto, che positiva seguir dovesse la giornata. Alcuni stimavano lo scanso degli addobbi, per non poter gareggiare con quelli del procurator Ruzzini; ma i pratici dell'emulazione e della natura prodiga, che mostrano col decoro dell'azioni publiche i Genii nobili, aspettavano un'improvisa comparsa di qualche pompa convenevole'. Ivanovich, *Minerva al tavolino*, II, 118–30.
52 'Basta concluder, che dove in simili congiunture ogni mercante procura di comparire sontuoso, questa volta ogn'uno ha singolarizato la propria magnificenza'. Ivanovich, *Minerva al tavolino*, II, 122–23.
53 On this Venetian office, see Bistort, *Il Magistrato alle pompe*, which quotes the document in its entirety (267).
54 See Casini, 'Some Thoughts', p. 194.
55 See Ambrosini, 'Cerimonie, feste, lusso', p. 450.
56 Sansovino, *Venetia città nobilissima et singolare* (1581), 108r.
57 Sansovino, *Venetia città nobilissima et singolare* (1604), 211r-213r.
58 Sansovino, *Venetia città nobilissima et singolare* (1663), p. 306.
59 See Delorenzi, *La galleria di Minerva*, 19. Delorenzi quotes ASVE, Correr, reg. 165, 'Sumario delle spese fatte nell'occasione di procurator di San Marco dell'eccellentissimo signor Francesco Molino, creato adì XI genaro 1633 stil veneto'.
60 Vincenti, *Gli apparati veneti*.
61 'Come appunto avviene in questa di fare il procuratore, che per avventura è la più rilevante di tutte'. Pannocchieschi D'Elci, 'Relazione sulle cose di Venezia', p. 315.
62 See De Vivo, 'Walking in Sixteenth-Century Venice'.
63 Sansovino, *Venetia città nobilissima e singolare* (1581), 158rv-159r. On this topic, see Infelise, 'Professione reportista'.
64 On this event and its written sources, see Metlica, 'La "gioiosa entrata" di Francesco Morosini'; Metlica, *Lessico della propaganda barocca*, pp. 48–64. Also see Mancini, Guerriero, and Casini, eds, La *'splendida' Venezia di Francesco Morosini*.
65 Pozza, 'Zeno, Ranieri'.
66 Ginnasi, 'Celsi, Lorenzo'.
67 Cavazzana Romanelli, 'Contarini, Andrea'.
68 Gullino, 'Mocenigo, Tommaso'.
69 Trebbi, 'Priuli, Antonio' and Gullino, 'Erizzo, Francesco'.
70 See Florio, *Micropolitica della rappresentanza*, pp. 59–60.

71 See Cozzi, 'La Repubblica di Venezia in Morea'; Infelise and Stouraiti, eds, *Venezia e la Guerra di Morea*; Ortalli, Gullino, and Ivetic, eds, *L'inestinguibile sogno del dominio*; Stouraiti, *War, Communication, and the Politics of Culture*.
72 On the upper patriciate's *cursus honorum*, see Mandelli, ed., *La copella politica*; Grendler, 'The leaders of the Venetian State'; Hunecke, 'I Savi grandi'.
73 Damerini, *Morosini*, p. 25.
74 *Promissio*, not numbered, 22 February 1693 *more veneto*. On the Ducal Oath, see Musatti, *Storia della promissione ducale*; Cecchetti, *Il doge di Venezia*; Girgensohn, ed., *Francesco Foscari*.
75 Kantorowicz, *The King's two Bodies*.
76 See *Promissio*, not numbered, 22 February 1693 *more veneto*: 'Stabilito da progenitori nostri al corpo perfetto della Republica per capo visibile d'essa la persona del Serenissimo Principe, il quale assistendo al governo della medesima con la presenza e con la mente, aggiunge maestà alle fonzioni e gravità ne conseglii e collegi'.
77 See *Promissio*, not numbered, 22 February 1693 *more veneto*.
78 On the notion of persona as applied to seventeenth-century rulers, see Metlica, *Lessico della propaganda barocca*, pp. 11–26.
79 Muir, *Civic Ritual in Renaissance Venice*, p. 296.
80 See Venturelli, 'La costituzione mista'; Venturelli, 'Mito di Venezia e governo misto'. Also see Gaille-Nikodimov, ed., *Le gouvernement mixte*.
81 See Rösch, 'The Serrata of the Great Council'; Chojnacki, 'Social Identity'; Chojnacki, 'La formazione della nobiltà'; Chojnacki, 'Identity and Ideology'.
82 See Ortalli, *Venezia inventata*; Ravegnani, *Bisanzio e Venezia*; Ravegnani, *Venezia prima di Venezia*.
83 Cozzi, *Repubblica di Venezia e Stati italiani*, p. 96.
84 *Promissio*, not numbered, 22 February 1693 *more veneto*.
85 ASVE, MC, Del., Reg., r. 24, fol. 189r-v.
86 *Promissio*, fol. 111r.
87 See Knapton, 'The Terraferma State'; Arbel, 'Venice's Maritime Empire'; Ortalli, Schmitt, and Orlando, eds, *Il Commonwealth veneziano*.
88 See Del Torre and Viggiano, eds, *1509–2009*; Del Torre, *Venezia e la Terraferma*.
89 Cozzi, *Venezia barocca*; Bouwsma, *Venice and the Defence of Republican Liberty*; De Vivo, *Information and Communication*. On the cultural production of this period see Paul, ed., *Celebrazione e autocritica*; Tagliaferro, 'Il "Mito" ripensato'.
90 See Cozzi, *Repubblica di Venezia e Stati italiani*; Cozzi, *Ambiente veneziano, ambiente veneto*; Gullino, 'L'evoluzione costituzionale'; Christ and Morche, eds, *Cultures of Empire*.

91 See Cozzi, 'Venezia regina'; Tagliaferro, 'Le forme della Vergine'; Rosand, *Myths of Venice*; O'Connell, 'Venetian Empire in Oratory and Print'; Weststeijn, 'Imperial Republics'; Toffolo, *Describing the City*.
92 See Wolters, *Storia e politica*, pp. 260–65; Wolters, 'L'autocelebrazione della Repubblica', pp. 497–500; O'Connell, 'Voluntary submission', pp. 35–36.
93 Colombo, 'Portraits of Sovereignty'.
94 Bergamini and Puppi, eds, *La galleria d'arte antica dei Civici Musei di Udine*, I, p. 164; Varanini, 'L'uso pubblico della storia'; Da Deppo, ed., *Venezia in Cadore*; Florio, 'Inchini e carte bollate'.
95 On the Maussian paradigm, see Zemon Davis, *The Gift*; Kettering, 'Gift-giving and patronage'; Algazi, Groebner, and Jussen, eds, *Negotiating the Gift*; Faggion and Verdon, eds, *Le don et le contre-don*.
96 On the 'constitutional value' of the *pacta deditionis*, see Varanini, 'Gli angusti orizzonti'.
97 Reolon, 'La Dedizione del Cadore'.
98 Muir, *Civic Ritual in Renaissance Venice*.
99 Casini, *I gesti del Principe*.
100 Fenlon, *The Ceremonial City*.
101 Berengo, *La società veneta*; Ventura, *Nobiltà e popolo*.
102 Povolo, 'Centro e periferia'; Povolo, *L'intrigo dell'onore*; Povolo, 'Un sistema giuridico repubblicano'.
103 Panciera, *La Repubblica di Venezia nel Settecento*, pp. 36–39.
104 Rizzi, 'Dominante e dominati'; Zenobi, 'Venice's Terraferma Expansion'.
105 Backouche, Cosandey, Duhamelle, Ducreux, Haddad, Joly, and Marraud, eds, 'Borders, Thresholds, Boundaries'.
106 See chapters 8, 9 and 10 by Carminati, Bellabarba, and Viggiano.
107 An overview of these festivals in the European context appears in Mulryne, Aliverti, and Testaverde, eds, *Ceremonial Entries*, and Checa Cremades and Fernández-González, eds, *Festival Culture*. On the notions of 'rituals of power negotiation', see Mulryne, De Jonge, Morris, and Martens, eds, *Occasions of State*.
108 See Tagliaferri, ed., *Relazioni dei rettori veneti*; Viggiano, 'Il Dominio da terra'; Viggiano, *Governanti e governati*; O'Connell, *Men of Empire*; Melchiorre, *Conoscere per governare*; Setti, *Una Repubblica per ogni porto*.
109 An example is Mauro and Flores, 'Una ceremonia coral'.

110 See chapters 8 and 9 by Bellabarba and Carminati. Also see Carminati, 'La Repubblica in scena'; Bellabarba, 'Rettori veneti e città di Terraferma'; Valseriati, 'Ingressi e uscite dei rettori veneziani a Brescia'.

111 See, for instance, Tazio, L'ottimo reggimento; Tazio, La 'immagine del Rettore.

112 See Viggiano, Governanti e governati; Viggiano, 'La disciplina dei rettori'; Povolo, 'Il protettore amorevole'; Revest, 'Ciceronianismo e ideale repubblicano'.

113 See Della Misericordia, '"Como se tuta questa universitade parlasse"'; Alvarez-Ossorio Alvariño, '"Pervenire alle orecchie della Maestà"'; Alvarez-Ossorio Alvariño, 'Corte, reinos y ciudades'; Alvarez-Ossorio Alvariño, 'Del reino al palacio real'; Angulo Morales, 'Representación y negociación'; Irace, 'Una voce poco fa'; Martínez Aznal, 'El agente navarro en la Corte'; Mauro, 'La rete diplomatica'.

114 Koenigsberger, 'The Italian Parliaments'. On the Patria del Friuli, which is partly an exception, see Casella, ed., Rappresentanze e territori; Casella, Il Parlamento friulano.

115 See Florio, Micropolitica della rappresentanza, pp. 35–90.

116 See Tassini, Curiosità veneziane, pp. 109–12; pp. 259–60; pp. 771–72.

117 See Florio, 'S'incliner devant un prince républicain'.

118 Florio, 'Inchini e carte bollate', 90. On the deditio's ceremonial protocol see Melchiorre, I patti con Padova.

119 Doglio, 'La letteratura ufficiale'; Florio, '"Ai piedi di Sua Serenità"'.

120 Sansovino, Delle orationi recitate. Some of the congratulatory orations gathered in 1562 were later included, as a sort of rhetorical subgenre, in a more comprehensive collection: Sansovino, Delle orationi volgarmente scritte. The last of the work's many reeditions was printed in 1584.

121 The complete legislation is summarised in ASVE, CL, S. II, b. 17, fasc. 26.

122 O'Connell, 'Voluntary submission'. On the notion of reenactment, see Muhle, 'Reenactments du pouvoir'; Bussels and Van Oostveldt, 'Restored behaviour and the performance of the City Maiden'.

123 'A quelli che per heredità o per altra fortuna succedono ne' precipati et imperi […] sogliono in molti luoghi le città serve, quasi per conditionata natura, rappresentarsi e rinovare il giuramento di fedeltà dal quale per variatione de' Prencipi poteano esser disobligate a fine che, dichiarata la medesima prontezza et affettionata volontà de' sudditi a servire, impetrino esse d'altra parte conservatione et aumento de' loro privilegi ovvero raccomandino se stesse e con più ardita speranza si promettano benigno e favorevole imperio'. Frecavalli, 'Oratione', p. 47.

124 On this topic, see Bertelli, The King's Body.

125 For a comparative perspective, see Murphy, Ceremonial Entries, and Breen, 'Addressing La Ville des Dieux'.

126 McLuhan and Fiore, The Medium is the Massage.

127 See Florio, S'incliner; Florio, «Ai piedi di Sua Serenità»; Florio, Inchini e carte bollate.

128 On Francesco Pola, see chapter 9 by Bellabarba.

129 Pola, Elogium.

130 'Hieri sera gionsero gli ambasciatori di congratulatione con gran pompa, e certo hanno una compagnia che potrebbe servir ad un imperatore'. BCBVI, AT, f. 1382, n.n., dated 14 April 1624, nuncio Giovanni Biagio Malchiavello to Vicenza's deputies.

131 See Sarpi, Consulti; Sarpi, Della potestà de' principi; Pin, 'Progetti e abbozzi sarpiani'; Baldin, 'Filosofie della sovranità'; De Franceschi, 'Entre antiromanisme catholique et républicanisme absolutiste'.

132 ASVE, CL, S. II, b. 17, fasc. 26; Promissio, fols. 19v–20r.

133 See Mannori, Il sovrano tutore.

134 ASVE, CL, S. II, b. 17, fasc. 26; Florio, '"Ai piedi di Sua Serenità"'.

135 Metlica, Lessico della propaganda barocca.

136 On the relation between Botero's thought and the Bodinian tradition, see Descendre, Lo stato del mondo.

137 On these kinds of sources, see Florio, Micropolitica della rappresentanza.

138 'Si come sentirà volentieri quelle [lodi] della sua Repubblica e delle sue città, così in sentir le sue resterà con molta mortifficatione la qual s'augumenterà tanto più quanto andassero più in longo'. BCBVI, AT, f. 1383, n.n., dated 11 September 1623, nuncio Giovanni Biagio Malchiavello to Vicenza's deputies.

139 Cozzi, Venezia barocca, pp. 185–228; Gullino, 'Zen, Ranieri'.

140 'Li Riformatori [della Promissione ducale] farano una legge che le città non debbino mandar più ambasciatori di congratulatione ma si ben ogni dieci anni per riconoscenza del suo Prencipe solamente, e che alla creatione de Prencipi i nontii suplischano'. BCBVI, AT, f. 1382, n.n., dated 03 July 1624, nuncio Giovanni Biagio Malchiavello to Vicenza's deputies.

141 ASPD, ACA, Nunzi, b. 64, n.n., dated 14 March 1625, nuncio Bonifacio Papafava to Padua's deputies.

142 'Repplica[ndo]… che il rallegrarsi dell'assontione al principato di un principe senza la sua presenza non […] pareva bene'. ASPD, ACA, Nunzi, b. 64, n.n., dated 22 October 1625, Giovanni Battista Selvatico to Padua's deputies.

143 'Il Principe vi era sempre'. ASPD, ACA, Nunzi, b. 64, n.n., dated 22 October 1625, Giovanni Battista Selvatico to Padua's deputies.

144 'Per la detta lontananza di Sua Serenità doverete in avvenire addiriciarci le vostre lettere con il titolo Serenissimo Dominio Venetiarum'. ASPD, ACA, Ducali, reg. 13, fol. 84v, dated 3 April 1688.

145 See Chapter 10 by Viggiano.

146 Florio, '"Ai piedi di Sua Serenità"'.

Giorgio Tagliaferro

2

THE MEETING OF SEBASTIANO ZIANI AND ALEXANDER III IN THE GREAT COUNCIL HALL

Staging, Viewing, and Understanding the Body Politic in Late Sixteenth-Century Venice

Replacing a cycle destroyed by the infamous fire of 1577, the paintings that decorate the Great Council Hall (*Sala del Maggior Consiglio*) in the Ducal Palace portray events that occurred between 1176 and 1177. The Venetians, led by doge Sebastiano Ziani, were said to have defeated the army of emperor Frederick I Barbarossa in defence of pope Alexander III, though the veracity of these events has never been established.[1] This alleged feat and the peace that followed constituted a mainstay of Venice's claim to sovereignty, for Alexander rewarded the Republic with full jurisdiction over the Adriatic Sea and bestowed upon Ziani a series of *regalia insignia*, known as *trionfi*, which then became permanent emblems of the authority of the doges and, by extension, of the Republic. The ducal cortege revolved around the *trionfi* that took place during the *andate*, namely the processions held on dates of the liturgical calendar to important churches of the city during which the body politic showed itself to the citizens. Through the *trionfi*, collective memory became a self-perpetuating ritual practice that transfigured those events into a legendary past that nurtured the community's identity.[2]

This state of affairs had important repercussions for depictions of the episodes. Considering the function of the Great Council Hall as a state room, where the plenary assembly of noblemen gathered to elect the officials of the public administration and legislature, it can be assumed that the paintings in question would not be perceived by audiences during the period as the mere illustration of remote historical facts. Read through the lenses of codified civic ritual, it can be safely assumed they would have appeared as broader manifestations of the prerogatives of the Republic, in which the singularity of the past combined with the permanency of its ritual reiteration. Although in these paintings the insignia are removed from the ritual context and projected backwards into history, they still function as primary 'visual foci' which, as Patricia Fortini Brown has pointed out, have the power to turn each scene into a 'lasting civic icon'.[3] From the perspective of the Venetian ruling class that commissioned these paintings, the events depicted were important in that they attested to a temporal continuity between the past and present, the same continuity that was established through the perpetuity of ritual. Historical accuracy was secondary by comparison.

Fortini Brown has underlined how Renaissance Venetian painters modelled their historical narratives on the actual forms of rituals such as entries, progressions, processions, receptions, and donations.[4] The use of this 'ceremonial paradigm', as Fortini Brown calls it, is evident in works by fifteenth-century artists such as Gentile Bellini and Vittore Carpaccio, where attention is focused on organised ritual performances that are set apart from surrounding everyday activities. For instance, in the *Miracle of the Relic of the Cross* painted by Carpaccio for the Scuola Grande di San Giovanni Evangelista (fig. 2.2), the healing of a madman is staged on the left of the composition in the form of a private event which very few can see: an exclusive group of brethren of the Scuola wait downstairs and a hooded procession crosses the bridge, while life in the city goes on. According to Fortini Brown, the presence of bystanders and other trivial or accidental details in

2.1
Francesco Dal Ponte (Bassano), *Pope Alexander III Bestows the Sword on Doge Sebastiano Ziani*. Detail of 2.3.

2.2
Vittore Carpaccio, *Miracle of the Relic of the True Cross at the Rialto Bridge*. Venice, Gallerie dell'Accademia, 1494–1496, cm 371 x 392, cat 566. Photo: Venice, G.A.VE, Photographic archive, with permission from the Italian Ministry of Culture.

pictures like this one provide 'a sense of the fortuitous' that is meant to 'confer upon a particular version of an event a look of documentary authority'.[5] To describe this approach to visual storytelling, which she compares to the vernacular mode of contemporaneous chronicles, Fortini Brown has famously coined the expression 'eyewitness style'.[6]

In the post-1577 Great Council cycle this interconnection between historical narrative and ritual is taken to a new level, especially by changing the relationship between the audience and the principal action depicted. In these scenes spectators are more closely and actively involved as observers, thanks in part to a different organisation of the city space, which is expanded and facilitates an interaction between protagonists and bystanders. In Francesco Bassano's *Alexander III Bestows the Sword on Doge Sebastiano Ziani* (fig. 2.3), the event is no longer hidden within an urban reality but rather

2.3
Francesco Dal Ponte (Bassano), *Pope Alexander III Bestows the Sword on Doge Sebastiano Ziani*. Venice, Ducal Palace, Sala del Maggior Consiglio, 1585–1590. Photo: Scala, Firenze.

becomes the centre of action: the happening is the main fulcrum of the city space and the catalyst of the attention of the figures depicted.[7] Rather than attended by select groups of high-ranking citizens and members of a confraternity, here the event of the symbolic donation of the sword is witnessed by crowds of people which fill nearly every inch of available space. This primary event is centralised; there is no room for secondary activities unrelated to it, and any distracting action is subordinated to the happenings at the centre. Bassano thus stages a different kind of ceremony than his predecessors, one in which the emphasis is not just on the object of viewing but also on the subject viewers.

This shift away from the framing used by the previous generation of late fifteenth-century painters likely reflects the natural evolution of aesthetic taste and artistic practice from the late fifteenth to the late sixteenth century. However, a closer, more systematic inspection may complicate our understanding of these images, allowing us to see them as products of more substantial changes in the political agenda of the ruling class. The new cycle was realised at a time when the Republic had received significant blows to its position in international affairs and to its territorial integrity. It is sufficient to recall the loss of Cyprus to the Ottomans in 1573, the tensions with Rome over ecclesiastical jurisdiction within the Venetian dominion which culminated in the 1606–1607 Interdict crisis, the increasing political and territorial pressure put on the Republic by the Holy Roman Empire and Spain, and the internal political stagnation as well as factionalism and electoral antagonism that climaxed in the reform of the Council of Ten in 1582–1583, just as the decorative programme in the Great Council was underway. Against this backdrop, the pictorial cycles that refashioned the Ducal Palace in the last quarter of the century, considered altogether and in connection with the public festivals and encomiastic literature of the period, can be interpreted as part of a strategy pursued by the patriciate both to revamp the public image of the Venetian state and to reassert its identity and hegemony as a social group.

Fuelled by the aftermath of the victory at Lepanto against the Ottomans in 1571 and imbued with its rhetoric of self-sacrifice and heroism, which lasted for decades after the famous battle, this self-celebratory endeavour may appear a feeble attempt to revive old ideological structures in order to compensate for the waning prestige of the Republic. After all, traditional myths are typical antidotes against crises.[8] In doing so, however, the Venetians developed novel forms of visual expression that reveal an awareness of the changing needs, expectations, and challenges faced by late sixteenth-century European rulers vis-à-vis representation of sovereignty. The new pictorial cycles in the state rooms of the Ducal Palace sought to provide a historical and moral justification for the prerogatives of the Republic and its ruling class by placing emphasis on the virtuous actions performed by the patricians for the benefit of the people, as well as on the happiness of the citizens, the interlinked concepts of liberty and nobility, and underscoring the unity of the dominion. Even more importantly, Venetian subjects were for the first time a tangible presence within the pictures and played a key role in consolidating Venice's sovereignty.[9]

Most of these themes emerge forcefully in the Great Council Hall cycle, whose grandiosity (attested to by its grand scale) was unparalleled not only within the Ducal Palace but also among contemporary state rooms in Europe. In the two previous cycles of 1419 and 1474–1564, the narrative had been confined to the Great Council room and limited to the Alexandrine legend; in the decorative cycle added post-1577, it was expanded into a more elaborate programme that extends into the adjacent Scrutiny Hall and depicts the heroic deeds of the Venetians from a span of eight centuries — from the time the Ducal Palace was founded in the early ninth century up to the most recent military campaign against the Turks in 1572. The Alexandrine story therefore became only a segment of this larger narrative displayed on the north wall of the Great Council Hall, facing the internal courtyard of the palace. Two noblemen, Jacopo Contarini and Jacopo Marcello, and the Florentine historiographer Girolamo Bardi, were entrusted by the Senate with devising the programme, which is known in manuscript copies dating from 1584.[10] The publication of Bardi's *Dichiaratione di tutte le istorie* (1587), a printed booklet containing the résumés of the historical and allegorical subjects depicted in the two rooms, indicates that there was also an intention to spread the contents of the programme beyond the walls of the palace. More generally, the effort put into carefully explaining the contents of the programme attests to the importance that the Venetian authorities attached to the cycle and its communicative power. In fact, as Bardi points out, the programme's main aim was to spur present and future doges and patricians to imitate the actions of their ancestors.[11] All this attention to public reception is also reflected in the cycle itself: apart from the battle scenes, the principal episodes are staged as public spectacles before masses of crowds, like in the Bassano painting described above.

This aspect of the cycle has been mostly overlooked by scholars and deserves further discussion. It would be tempting to explain it in relation to the role that was often attached to painting as a means of validating historical facts through their visual reenactment, which entails the presence of eyewitnesses within (bystanders) as well as without (the viewer). The Great Council has often been seen by scholars as a significant example of this, especially because Bardi himself used painting as historical evidence to support the Venetian version of the 1176–1177 events.[12] A further connection can be made with Francesco Patrizi's emphasis on images as structural elements of memory that the historian must bring back to life and keep alive. In his ten books *Della historia* (1560), which assert the need for historians of knowing the facts they describe, the Dalmatian philosopher claims that 'history is that narration which one tells about things he has seen with his own eyes', namely the act of 'a watching with one's own eyes'.[13] The main example he employs to make this point is the pre-1577 fire Great Council cycle, which he compares to the histories illustrated in ancient Roman columns and arches.[14] Indeed, the presence of witnesses within the pictures — including the innumerable bystander portraits listed by Francesco Sansovino in the previous lost pictures and those visible in the extant ones — can be understood according to this logic.[15] While this is certainly a crucial aspect underlying the historiographical attitude and purposes of the programme that has not yet been sufficiently explored, the present essay takes a different stance, instead discussing the socio-political resonance of the visual strategy described above. It focuses on the first picture of the Alexandrine sequence as a case study in the increasing role taken on by Venetian subjects as spectators and co-protagonists within the celebration of the ducal authority at the turn of the sixteenth century. Finally, it reflects on how painters co-opted ceremonial models that imbued the representation of historical events with a ritual dimension and what this tells us about how the Venetian ruling class conceptualised the image of the Republic as a body politic and civic community during this period.

Vesting the doge with authority

Signed by the heirs of Paolo Veronese ('Aeredes Pauli Caliari Ver. Faciebant') — namely his brother Benedetto and son Carletto, who inherited the workshop — the *Meeting of Sebastiano Ziani and Alexander III at the Church of the Carità* (fig. 2.4) was evidently completed after Veronese's death in 1588.[16] It is hard to determine to what extent Paolo was responsible for the composition. At least one sheet of his sketches has been considered preparatory to this and another painting of the series, although there is no clear indication in the drawing that this was indeed the case; in any case, the arrangement of the picture could have been finalised by his descendants.[17] Regardless of who planned and executed it, the design of the painting is well-thought-out and deserves careful analysis if we are to appreciate its ingenuity. To this end, it

is first necessary to consider the story depicted, a synopsis of which can be found in Bardi's *Dichiaratione*.[18] Bardi provided an even more detailed account in his *Vittoria navale* (1584), a pamphlet which compiled historical evidence to demonstrate the veracity of the controversial victory of the Venetians over the imperial fleet at Punta Salvore and therefore disprove the dismissive accounts by historiographers such as Carlo Sigonio, who had called into question the truthfulness of the event.[19] Published during the period in which the decorative campaign was still ongoing, the *Vittoria navale* is an extremely useful source, as it gathers the results of the historiographical research by Bardi that fuelled the new pictorial programme and reflects the intentions of its creator.[20]

According to Bardi, in 1176 Pope Alexander III set out for Zara, from which he later moved to Constantinople to meet the Byzantine emperor Manuel I Komnenos and beg for his help against Frederick Barbarossa.[21] However, being 'suspicious of the unfaithfulness of the Greeks', the pope changed his mind and, 'clothed as a simple priest', fled to Venice and disguised himself among the Canons Regular of Santa Maria della Carità.[22] There he was eventually detected by a French citizen named Commodus, who was passing through Venice during his pilgrimage to the Holy Land. Commodus, who had previously seen the pope in Rome and France, recognized Alexander while 'he was reciting the office, dressed in unassuming clothes'.[23] Having determined the pope's identity 'after long observation', the Frenchman rushed to the Ducal Palace to report his discovery to the doge and Signoria.[24] Doge Ziani, knowing that the pope had vanished a year earlier and astonished by the discovery, wanted to put Commodus's reliability to the test; yet, 'after examining him several times and talking to him, [the doge] found him consistent with his first statement and judicious (*prudente*) in everything else he said'.[25] Ziani then ordered that Commodus be hidden in the Palace, to prevent the news from spreading, and prepared himself to meet the pope. He put on garments 'seemly for the papal majesty', summoned the bishop of Castello along with the clergy, and made his way to the church of the Carità 'with all the most notable officials of the Republic'.[26] Here the cortege found the pope 'in the attire described by Commodus', kneeling and praying to 'God to free His Church from so many vexations'. Without hesitation, Ziani 'prostrated himself at his feet and, extolling him as the legitimately created Vicar of Christ, reassured him on

public's behalf that he should not fear Frederick [Barbarossa]'.[27] The doge then pledged to stand up for Alexander and fight the emperor to restore the pope's authority and reputation, thus inducing the pontiff to reveal his identity, recount his recent experiences, praise 'the doge's and Signoria's piety with many affectionate words', and 'willingly put himself in the hands of that Republic'.[28] Finally, 'having donned his pontifical vestments, and boarded the ducal boat, he went with all the clergy to the church of St Mark, where [he] blessed the doge and the whole city'.[29]

As this brief summary shows, Bardi presented the meeting between Ziani and Alexander as a public act of recognition concerning the identity and authority of the pope. However, because it was Ziani who acknowledged and restored the pope's legitimacy, the episode also enhanced the prestige of the doge. The change of condition of the two protagonists is heralded by their disrobing and dressing throughout the story, with their vestments functioning as emblems of dignity. The pope is first divested of his robes as a consequence of being stripped of power by Barbarossa; when his public persona is eventually reinstated through the mediation of the doge, Alexander simultaneously regains his papal trappings (which, interestingly, in Bardi's other version of the story are said to be prepared by the doge himself).[30] Likewise, to meet

2.4
Benedetto and Carlo Caliari, *Meeting of Doge Sebastiano Ziani and Pope Alexander III at the Church of the Carità*. Venice, Ducal Palace, Sala del Maggior Consiglio, 1588–1590. Photo: Scala, Firenze.

2.5–6
Benedetto and Carlo Caliari, *Meeting of Doge Sebastiano Ziani and Pope Alexander III at the Church of the Carità*. Details of 2.4.

with the pontiff, the doge puts on robes 'seemly for the papal majesty', thereby indicating the extent to which in this context clothes literally make the man.

This emphasis on dress, with its implications in terms of display of power and status, comes through in the pictorial scene: Ziani, donning an ermine mantle over a brocaded cloak, genuflects before Alexander, who is clad in a white cassock 'as a simple priest' (fig. 2.5); meanwhile, near the left margin of the picture, the papal tiara is borne on a tray along with a golden cope (fig. 2.6), alluding to the 'pontifical vestments' Alexander will then wear during the procession to St Mark's. The pope, bareheaded, stands still while receiving Ziani's homage. The doge is without his horn-like bonnet (*corno*), the pseudo-crown signifying his dignity, and sports only the *camauro*, the white linen skullcap worn underneath the ducal cap. This by no means lessens his status. His genuflection does not indicate submission, unlike in two of the following scenes in the cycle, where prince Otto and his father Barbarossa prostrate before the pope and doge after being vanquished. On the contrary, Ziani's bended knee is a gesture of humility and respect communicating his recognition of the pope's identity and authority. The *camauro* itself enhances the doge's eminence by adding a sense of solemnity and sacrality. As Francesco Sansovino reminds us, the skullcap had served since antiquity as 'almost the insignia of a sacred person, representing some sort of memory of the anointment of the Christian Kings, as if this Prince was of the same body as them', and gracing his head when the *corno* was taken off.[31] The fact that the *camauro* implicitly equated the doge to an anointed prince gains further significance when we consider that Ziani is depicted in front of the pope, who has the power to consecrate emperors. Given that the remainder of the pictorial sequence celebrates the act of conferring the insignia of sovereignty to the doge as a reward for his taking on the role of champion of Christendom in lieu of the disloyal emperor, this first scene can be considered a prelude to and justification of the doge's subsequent status elevation. Accordingly, in both this and other paintings of the series in which Ziani bows to the pontiff while being vested with the insignia, the doge wears only the *camauro*, which is also a sign of his yielding before the pope's authority.

It can be concluded that, even though in this picture Alexander is the guest to whom the city pays tribute, it is Ziani who is tacitly acclaimed as leader. In fact, this can be considered the first act of a triumphal procession the doge performs throughout Venice, before moving to Ancona and Rome in the final episodes of the story. Although the ceremony does not culminate in the donation of an insignia, as in the following scenes, the privileged relationship established between the two protagonists, encapsulated by Ziani's genuflection, paves the way for the doge's ensuing investiture. Finally, the recognition of the pope is witnessed by Venice's citizens, meaning the pope's endorsement of the doge's leadership is validated and amplified before the population. The presence of such a wide and varied audience is a key factor that deserves further attention.

From private meeting to public event

In Bardi's description, the action moves back and forth twice between the Carità and the Ducal Palace, so that the recognition of the pope, with its twofold meaning of revelation and rehabilitation, comes about throughout the city as though in a ceremonial procession. As the procession unfurls, the event turns into a festive reception, resulting in a self-celebratory representation in which Venice's socio-political formation mirrors itself.

Accordingly, the painting is organised in such a way that a private summit is transformed into a public event attended by hundreds of people. The setting itself is strategic: the meeting takes place outdoors in front of the church, rather than inside as indicated in the textual sources. Because this is a story of revelation, comparable to anagnorisis in classical theatre, the possibility of gazing is inherently fundamental. A key function in this act of recognition is performed by Commodus, the French pilgrim who testifies to the pope's identity and thereby acts as a mediator of truth, as subsequently certified by the doge. In Bardi's account, the trustworthiness of the witness, a pilgrim travelling to the Holy Land, is tested against his piety, which stands in opposition to the unfaithfulness of both the Greek and Roman emperors. For this reason, the presence of Commodus in the painting is justified, though in contradiction with Bardi's account in the *Vittoria navale*, which states that the Frenchman was taken into custody in the Ducal Palace. However, Bardi did change this part of the story in the *Dichiaratione*, where Commodus's attendance at the encounter instead becomes crucial. In this version, Alexander first denies his own identity for fear of being handed over to Barbarossa, and eventually caves in after the doge adduces Commodus's testimony.[32] This is reflected in the painting, where the black-clad kneeling figure of the pilgrim Commodus is distinct from the standing pope and his attendant, who are both wearing white tunic. The layman turns his head towards the doge, as if to confirm his testimony. Indeed, this might well be the moment when the pope eventually gives in and admits his identity.

It must be noted that Commodus uncovers the pope only 'after long observation' and, once the pontiff is recognized, his rehabilitation goes hand in hand with his public visibility. The urban space is therefore an ideal location for Alexander's exposure to the public gaze, which warrants his reinstatement. This is ratified through the following procession to St Mark's Square, Venice's religious and political heart, so that the recognition is spread throughout the city. The ritualisation of the event continues with the blessing of Ziani in the ducal chapel, a rite of consecration that ratifies the doge as the head of a mystic body formed by both the body politic and the civic community. Of course, neither the parade nor the consecration could have been depicted without disrupting the unity of action; however, the consecration is prefigured by Ziani's solemn bow in front of the Carità, and the whole scene is presented as a stately ceremony. The doge is accompanied by his train-bearer (*caudatario*) and retinue of officeholders dressed in official togas of various colours, while the papal paraphernalia are carried along, followed by standards and canopies. In this way, the unforeseen encounter between Ziani and Alexander is formalised into a public reception to honour the pope; at the same time, this is also an opportunity to display the authority of the Venetian state, which is embodied by the doge and his cortege.

With its carefully planned arrangement and characterisation of both the figures and the setting, the painting indicates a deliberate intention to stage what looks like a communal performance similar to the ducal *andate*. Comparison of the picture's design and the layout of the *andata* to San Giorgio Maggiore on Christmas day illustrated in an engraving by Giacomo Franco (fig. 2.7) suggests that Veronese and his collaborators could have been inspired by the format of the ducal processions.[33] The meeting between the doge and the abbot of San Giorgio — each followed by their entourages — on the canal bank before the church, with throngs of people crammed on either side and gondolas approaching from the waterway, bears strong resemblance to the ceremony

2.7
Giacomo Franco, *Visit of the doge to the church of S. Giorgio Maggiore for Christmas Vespers*. Engraving from Id., *Habiti d'huomeni et donne venetiane con la processione della Ser.ma Signoria ed altri particolari*, 1614. Photo: BnF, Gallica. Reproduced with permission.

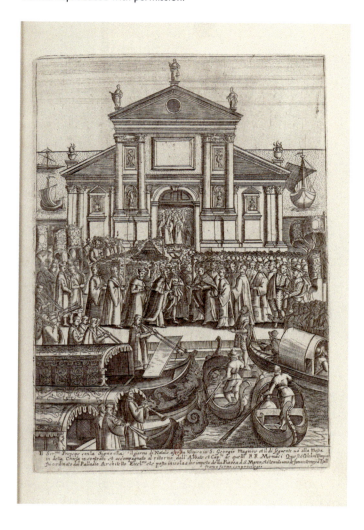

portrayed in the canvas. In fact, the similarities are so striking that one may assume that Franco, who published the print later, around 1610, drew directly on the painting for inspiration; if so, it would be legitimate to infer that the latter was perceived by contemporaries as a convincing depiction of a ducal ceremony and to further argue that this is precisely what the picture was meant to call to the viewer's mind.

Be that as it may, what we see in the painting cannot be understood as the representation of an *andata* in the strict sense: this is not supported by the narrative fiction, nor does the picture present an accurate description of the ceremonial protocol. Rather, the scene combines the features of a ducal procession, to which the whole story of the Alexandrine donations alludes, with those of a welcome ceremony for a prestigious guest. Like any other state ritual, it has the power to focus attention on the charisma of the leader and, through the contact with the authority of the pope, to make perceptible and recognisable what Geertz would call 'the inherent sacredness of central authority'.[34] The historical event is filtered and re-signified through the symbolic forms of the ceremonial, whereby 'the world as lived and the world as imagined' are fused together.[35] One key aspect is that the ceremony does not reflect the cyclical character of civic ritual. In accordance with the story, what we see is a spontaneous gathering of people, with the emphasis placed not on a codified, fixed performance but on the reactions of the various people involved. Even more importantly, there is no distinction between actors and spectators; instead, both the protagonists of the main action and the bystanders are simultaneously actors and acted upon. This seems to give substance to Alberto Tenenti's observation that the scenic character of Venice's urban form lent itself to the staging of spectacular festivals reflecting the structure of the community, in which citizens were not only spectators but also participants.[36] Because of both its uniqueness and the massive participation of the citizenry, the spectacle staged in the painting can to some extent be likened to the festivals held in Venice in the late sixteenth century to celebrate epochal events such as the victory of Lepanto (1571) or the peace of Vervins (1598) or to welcome princes like Henry III of France, 1574 (fig. 2.8).[37] In any case, this mode of representation has repercussions for the perception of the historical narrative, since the picture is pervaded by the same sense of spectatorship that characterised public festivals. Closer analysis of the composition reveals the distinctiveness of such a representation.

Like in the other paintings of the series, there are no ephemeral structures or pomp in this image. The open space of the city, with its architectural and urban configuration, is the only element that renders the scene, amplifying the visibility of the action, which — as we have seen — was a key factor in successfully restoring the pope's authority. Yet the crowd has a more marked structural function than in other paintings of the same sequence: masses of figures, smaller in scale, swarm everywhere, leaving no empty space, while the city's architecture is used as a planar backdrop to accommodate them. The design is organised around juxtaposed horizontal layers that follow the lines of the quays and buildings,

2.8

Andrea Vicentino, *The Arrival of Henry III of France at the Lido*. Venice, Ducal Palace, Sala delle Quattro porte, 1593. Photo: Scala, Firenze.

echoed by striped clouds in the sky. The space is arranged in a succession of narrow planes, in which isocephalic groups of people are lined up, squeezed into a claustrophobic perspective with multiple vanishing points. The consequent impression of flatness and lateral expansion stands in contrast with the pronounced depth effect in Bassano's *Alexander III Bestows the Sword on Sebastiano Ziani*. There, the primary narrative moment is located at the very centre of a telescoped view that catches the eye of the beholder; here, it is instead situated in the mid-ground, slightly off centre, subtly disguised within the choral structure of the scene. The pope and doge mingle with a group of downscaled figures; the viewer needs to look beyond the larger characters in the foreground to pinpoint the protagonists. Moreover, the likeness of Alexander is barely discernible, while Ziani's face is *en profil perdu* and in shade. Their encounter has a humble, unobtrusive tone. Still, its protagonists are spotlighted in different ways: an aperture in the foreground leaves the steps of the quay on which they stand visible to us, thus creating a sort of raised podium; light and colour highlight the two retinues, which are clearly distinguishable amongst the crowd; lastly, the calm composure of Alexander and his train, in contrast with the unseemly gesticulating figures in the foreground, calls attention to the gravitas of the moment.

As a result of this composite, counterbalanced arrangement, the protagonists appear amidst the bystanders rather than isolated from them. As external beholders, we are invited to allocate the same amount of attention to the core event and to the response it elicits among the population. The whole spectacle is presented as a collective act of viewing propagating all around, whose epicentre are the pope and the doge. The protagonists watch, and at the same time are watched, so that the main action fuses with its reception; performance and spectatorship become one and the same. Arranged in this way, this communal act of viewing brings about a manifestation of embodied authority engendering consensus: as the authority of the pope is revealed to and recognized by the doge, the authority of the doge is exposed to and acknowledged by the citizenry. In this respect, the picture mobilises that 'reciprocal spectatorship' which, as Henri Zerner observes, was commonly performed by the ruler and populace in early modern European public ceremonies and festivals, where the participation of large numbers of citizens was crucial to consolidating the public image of the sovereign.[38] This is the first important point about this image, which amplifies the narrative function of beholding as a metaphor of public disclosure: the representation of power is staged in the Piazza and outside the conventions of the Venetian civic ritual, so that the

2.9
Benedetto and Carlo Caliari, *Meeting of Doge Sebastiano Ziani and Pope Alexander III at the Church of the Carità*. Detail of 2.4.

2.10
Cesare Vecellio, *The Great Captain*. Engraving from *De gli habiti antichi, et moderni di diuerse parti del mondo libri due*, 1590. Photo: BnF, Gallica. Reproduced with permission.

people, as spontaneous witnesses to this inaugural act of the doge's authority, generate that *consensus omnium* in which any authority is grounded. The ritual is then designed to renew this authority through the act of reiteration.[39] This viewing performance aggregates the people and incites participation, resulting in civic engagement.

The second crucial aspect of this image is how the depicted act of beholding enables a display of the political and societal order, indexed by different degrees of spectatorship, in which the congregation of citizens becomes an embodied image of social hierarchy and harmony. Through the improvised ceremony, an ephemeral historical event is thus transfigured into a perpetual image of the Venetian community. The attendees are arranged in groups, each with a different range of vision, level of attention, and rate of movement denoting their degree of participation in the ceremony and, by extension, in the public sphere: the closer to the main action, the more attentive, composed, and involved they are. An overview of the groups depicted shows how these correspond to the various layers of the Venetian society, which is presented as a diversified yet harmonious ensemble.

Social harmony and political hierarchy

The focus of the action is the group formed by the pope and canons who, swathed in white tunics, stand still in quietness at the centre of the scene. The doge has the exclusive privilege of looking into Alexander's eyes, whereas the senior officers behind him face the pontiff and join the ceremony from a short distance. The ducal cortege, with its coloured fabrics contrasting with the clerics' robes, is a living image of the body politic. In appearing before the populace, the doge, Signoria, and government establish themselves as the fulcrum of the political and social order. People jostle around them on all sides in attempt to gain a good viewpoint, like the youths who have climbed a podium along the church wall, or to get nearer to the action, like the multitude of bystanders assembled to the right, opposite the ducal retinue. It is not easy to identify the social composition of the

2.11
Benedetto and Carlo Caliari, *Meeting of Doge Sebastiano Ziani and Pope Alexander III at the Church of the Carità*. Detail of 2.4.

2.12
Benedetto and Carlo Caliari, *Meeting of Doge Sebastiano Ziani and Pope Alexander III at the Church of the Carità*. Detail of 2.4.

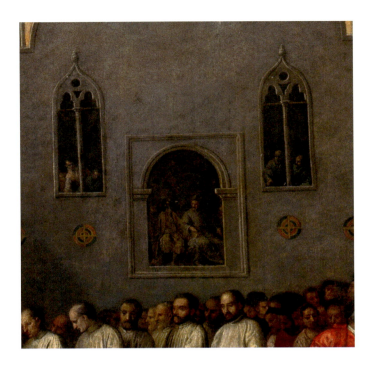

crowd on this side of the picture, especially because the distinction between the clothing of the patricians and of the *cittadini* during this period was admittedly blurred.[40] Some of the men in the first row along the embankment wear black clothes and white collars, an attire that had become very popular in late sixteenth-century Italy and denoted a respectable social standing; however, because it was not only a sign of wealth but also of moral sobriety, it was worn by nobles as well as non-nobles, which makes it difficult to establish the social identity of these figures.[41] Indeed, in his *De gli habiti antichi, et moderni* (1590), Cesare Vecellio reports that the ordinary black dress of Venetian aristocrats was also commonly used by doctors, lawyers, and merchants.[42] The fact that these characters in the picture do not sport the open sleeves typical of the patriciate may indicate that they are *cittadini*, but this must be taken with caution. In any case, it seems plausible that they are upstanding citizens. The ladies enjoying a higher viewpoint in the back tiers are dressed in a way that vaguely resembles the domestic outfits of the Venetian noblewomen illustrated in Vecellio's costume book, but it is hard to accurately identify their status.[43] They differ, in any case, from the few women who appear in the first rows to the right of the monks, whose clothes signal a lower social status. The crowd in this area is mostly indistinct, with only the faces and hats visible. All in all, this seems to be a mixed population, including both well-off citizens and commoners perhaps intended to be parishioners; indeed, the local lay community is represented by the large standard raised in the right rear of the church, its emblem too fuzzy to be discerned.

Regardless of the specific social statuses of these spectators, they all share physical removal from the focal point of the scene. Yet interestingly, this does not apply to the two men seen from the rear, who stand on the steps of the bank to the right, facing the aforementioned group of black-clad men. The logic of the picture suggests that these two characters have just arrived by gondola, which means they circulated freely. Both bow and stare in the direction of the main event. The one on the left dons a light-blue gown with open sleeves that seems to designate him as a public officer, which is probably what gives him right to access the ceremony from a somewhat privileged viewpoint.[44]

The separation between the ceremony and the crowd is further emphasised by the presence of a red-clad official portrayed to the right of the pope's retinue, who clutches the forearm of a man in the first rows to hold him back (fig. 2.9). The latter man, wearing a light-blue garment, holds on to his neighbour, who is clothed in a dark suit. It is difficult to determine whether these two figures are in the company of the previously described men in black, who stand just behind them. It is clear, however, that by denying access to any intruders, the figure in red creates a perimeter that draws a clear demarcation between those performing the ceremony and those attending it from some distance. This is underscored by the emergence of the scarlet robe and its contrast against the colour scheme of the picture. The identification of this character is complicated by the fact that various Venetian state officers used to wear a red gown.[45] Among them was the grand chancellor (*cancellier grande*), who played a role in the ducal procession, where he was the last official to precede the doge.[46] Given that the grand chancellor was the highest charge of the non-patrician officeholders and was popularly known as the *doge del popolo* (the people's doge), it would be somewhat appropriate that in the picture he mediates between the ducal retinue and the citizenry.[47] However, this figure is removed from the cortege and apparently has the task of preventing anyone from trespassing, which was not among the grand chancellor's functions. On

the contrary, this role would be more suitable for the *capitan grande*, the chief of the *zaffi* or *sbirri* (policemen), who was in charge of preserving public peace and order, and whose uniform generally tallied with that of the man depicted here.[48] In Vecellio's costume book (fig. 2.10), the *capitan grande* is portrayed in a velvet or satin crimson robe tied at the waist with a silver-buckled velvet belt and worn above a white-collar shirt, along with a red hose and black biretta.[49] He also wore a surcoat mantle that was usually purple (*pavonazzo*) but 'on certain solemn days' was of the same scarlet (*scarlatto*) as the undergarment. It is true that, unlike in Vecellio's account, the cloak of the man in the painting is not fastened at the sides with laces tied in bows, nor is he equipped with a sword hung at his belt; however, the detail of the red surcoat over a robe of the same colour matches the costume description so closely that it is unlikely accidental, especially since the scene depicted is one of those 'solemn days' on which the *capitan grande* would have sported such an outfit. In addition, Vecellio specifies that the other *capitan minori* who assisted the head captain, each with his own group of *zaffi*, 'preceded the doge every time he left the Ducal Palace in solemnity'.[50] The *capitan grande* would therefore be appropriate in this particular scene. Although on the one hand his inclusion in the scene may be nothing more than pictorial artifice meant to enliven the action, on the other it suggests a deliberate intention to give prominence to a character who is unnecessary within the economy of the narrative but offers a certain twist to the picture. The figure creates a filter or barrier between those on the left who participate in the state affairs and those on the right who do not; moreover, if taken as the officer designated to maintain public order, the character appears to officially enforce this separation between groups, and his presence implies that the social harmony and peaceful unfolding of the ceremony are safeguarded against any potential disruption. This chimes with the *capitan grande*'s role as an 'interface between the ruling class and the population', as the 'representative of that republican justice which the 'myth of Venice' claimed to be equitable, strict, and benevolent', whose responsibilities grew in the last two decades of the sixteenth century.[51]

As these details demonstrate, the authors of the painting did their best to create some sort of hierarchical subdivision but also to avoid a hard break among the different social groups. In this respect, the picture echoed the idea of civic ritual as an instrument of social cohesion functional to show how social hierarchies and differentiations are absorbed into the political organisation of the Republic. It is worth remembering that the doge was seen as the charismatic centre of the social layers excluded from the ruling class and that public rites were meant to reinforce this leading role. The relationship between the government and the *cittadini*, for instance, was cemented through the participation of the latter in the interregnum rites performed in the periods of vacancy after the doge's death, implying a symbolic, temporary elevation of the lower social group.[52] Moreover, the ducal cortege, which was originally composed exclusively of patrician, was modified in the sixteenth century to incorporate a group of ducal secretaries, who came from the ranks of the *cittadini*.[53] This alteration reflected substantial changes that had occurred in the administrative organisation of the Republic. At the same time, the ducal procession maintained long-standing characteristics bearing symbolic significance, though they no longer reflected the political reality, thus facilitating a Geertzian fusion between imagination and experience.[54] In some respects, the picture under examination appropriated this function, in that it abstracts the idea of the Venetian social peace through the form of ritual; nevertheless, the scene transcends the boundaries and prescriptions of ritual to stage a spectacle centred on the visual participation of the city as a whole, denoting various degrees of political discernment.

Among the most privileged onlookers are the two figures accommodated in the loggia on the façade of the Scuola della Carità that towers against the sky in the background (fig. 2.11). One of them, recognisable as a prelate by his long gown and biretta, is likely the bishop of Castello, who, according to Bardi, joined Ziani on his way to the Carità. However, such an ambiguous positioning, which enables this character to enjoy a first-row view of the square while remaining completely removed from the action, is suitable for acknowledging him as head of the Venetian Church without granting him too much prominence: on the one hand he is depicted at the centre of the picture, framed by the open gallery that sets him apart from the crowd; on the other hand, his presence is marginal in relation both to the narrative and to our view. Whether deliberate or not, this marginalisation reflects the fact that the encounter with the pope is presented as a state affair concerning the secular leader, not a celebration of the Church per se. The image, in any case, does not exclude the bystanders from the scene or confine them to the role of mere space-fillers. In one way or another, their presence is made meaningful to us. Even the most distant background figures, some barely distinguishable, are intent on gazing at the main scene, and therefore appear to actively participate as viewers. These include the characters leaning from the two mullioned windows flanking the loggia on the Scuola façade, which include two tonsured clerics on the right and three secular men on the left, plausibly the monks and lay *confratelli* of the Carità respectively.

This situation, however, is somewhat reversed in the foreground (fig. 2.12), where the space is dominated by monumental figures that appear completely disengaged from the primary event. These comprise oarsmen carrying upper-class citizens on gondolas along the canal overlooking the square, as well as other sorts of commoners who populate the bank closer to us, paying little to no attention to what is going on in the background. In fact, their presence distracts and wreaks agitation, somehow perturbing the serene atmosphere of the ceremony. In contrast with the placid composure of the crowd at the opposite end of the canal, the wobbly postures of the gondoliers give a sense of instability, culminating in the ungainly fall of a rower who loses his balance and is thrown off his boat while the passengers aboard hold on to the gondola. Further disruption is caused by two sturdy men carrying baskets full of fish who step onto the nearest embankment and advance towards us; they are completely disconnected from, and unaware of, the primary event taking place behind them. No greater attentiveness is displayed by the two loafers in the right corner, who seem to be playing cards in the company of a stray dog.

Despite their detachment from the narrative, these figures cannot go unnoticed. Their large, wriggling bodies clutter the foreground space from side to side and, as an effect of the low perspective, emerge prominently between the beholder and the main action, so that they inevitably catch our gaze and give us the uncomfortable feeling of blocking our view and obliging us to circumvent them in order to target the focal event. As in Bassano's *Alexander III Bestows the Sword on Sebastiano Ziani*, these characters add a colourful and humorous note to the picture; yet, they have a different impact on the composition. Whereas in Bassano's painting they typically function as *repoussoir* figures, which bracket the main scene and direct the eye to the heart of the composition, in this painting their presence is encumbering and disturbing, as their lack of alertness clashes with the high level of concentration permeating the rest of the image. By no means is the everyday life going on at the margins quiet; on the contrary, these figures intrude on the pictorial space and force themselves into this tableau of Venetian reality, acting as contrasting elements.[55]

The general attitude of these figures can hardly be decoupled from their strong social connotations, for their lower social status is immediately signalled by their clothing, bare feet, and occupations. As a result, the tension between the order of the ducal procession and the disarray provoked by these characters may potentially be read as an index of social conflict. Nonetheless, this tension does not threaten social cohesion; rather, it results in a diversification of the levels of political engagement and comprehension. What these disparities communicate is the different way each figure sets eyes on what is happening. In fact, it is true that these marginal figures carry on their business without enjoying the act of recognition that the rest of the community shares to various degrees. Still, they are not excluded from this choral self-representation of Venetian society, but rather participate as latently discordant elements that are ultimately integrated into the overall image. As our gaze bypasses them, and zeroes in on the main scene, tensions and conflicts are neutralised by the unifying power of the ceremony. In fact, this contrived arrangement is not the most logical and straightforward way of staging a story that apparently lacks narrative complexities or difficulties and could be more easily rendered by focusing attention on the central episode. The composition thus suggests a deliberate intention not only to complicate the subject matter but also to engage the viewer, who must attempt to discern the logic of the picture. It is this aim that encourages further reflection on the possible implications of these internal and external acts of viewing.

Vision and discernment

The artists who designed the painting exploited the actual architecture of the square constituted by the church, Scuola, marginal buildings, and embankment to articulate physical and visual distance from the centre of the action. Considering the significance of the event as a manifestation to the people of the authority of both the pope and doge, distance from the main action implicitly indicates involvement in or separation from governmental action. The fact that this distancing corresponds to an immediately perceivable social hierarchy reinforces this impression. Accordingly, some sort of hierarchy of vision emerges as we are invited to observe the diverse viewing situations, which match the expected differences in political understanding and comprehension of the various social groups. This becomes even more relevant when the importance attached by Bardi to viewing is taken into account.

We need not assume that the authors of the painting had awareness of political theory to argue that the arrangement of the social order in the image absorbs and reflects meanings embedded in the mentality of the Venetian patriciate and their political culture; as demonstrated in a number of Veronese's works, artists do not need to engage with theoretical speculations to interpret, and meet the expectations of the ruling class.[56] Likewise, it is not necessary to imagine that a specific clique of patricians prevailed over another to wield strict control over the development of the pictorial programme and its realisation. In fact, there is evidence to argue that Jacopo Contarini, a learned patron of the arts and sciences often associated with the papalist and conservative patrician wing, played a key role in the Great Council decorative campaign and that, in its initial phases, the programme was reviewed by members of his coterie.[57] However, the cycle of paintings more generally reflects the ideology of the ruling class, in a way similar to how it is expressed in the same years in the work of Paolo Paruta, i.e. in a manner that extends beyond factionalism.[58]

The staging of Venetian society in the painting under examination reflects a typically aristocratic view of republican rule, where the multitudes are excluded from the government and only the few people considered to be real citizens guarantee the happiness of all the inhabitants. In his *De magistratibus et republica Venetorum* (1543), Gasparo Contarini famously illustrated this concept through recourse to the traditional organic metaphor of the state as a human body, with the summit of the government representing the head and eyes and the other parts decreasing in importance as they gain distance from the head.[59] Contarini praises the Venetian ancestors who wisely excluded commoners from the Great Council and gave it only to those who were 'noble by birth, or ennobled by virtue, or well deserving of the Republic'.[60] Indeed, in his treatise nobility is depicted as a mixture of merit, lineage, privilege, propensity towards the *res publica*, and right to rule. By contrast, he did not consider artisans and mercenaries, albeit necessary in a city, worthy of being considered *cittadini*, but instead sorts of 'public servants'.[61] Similar opinions on the exclusion of artisans from the government of a republic were later expressed by Giovanni Maria Memmo and Paruta.[62] Paruta resorts to the metaphor of the body to articulate the various degrees and functions of the members of a city, but adds a new metaphor — likening the latter to the universe with its empyrean concentric circles, where rulers are the unmoved movers who act for the benefit of the populace.[63] In a similar fashion, in his *Breve institutione dell'ottima republica* (1578) Giason De Nores states that 'the citizens of the perfect republic are those who do not move and can participate in its government, not the artificers, mechanics, servants, and strangers, who come and go at their whim and are employed as if they were instruments'.[64] Only true citizens can 'perform virtuous actions' and partake in the public happiness, from which the mechanics are excluded.[65] Finally, the image of heavenly rings was reprised by Agostino Michiel in his speech for the election of doge Pasquale Cicogna (1585), which describes artisans, merchants, citizens, noblemen, and princes as each representing one order of the universe, with the prince at the centre like an angel, standing still and setting in motion all the other circles.[66]

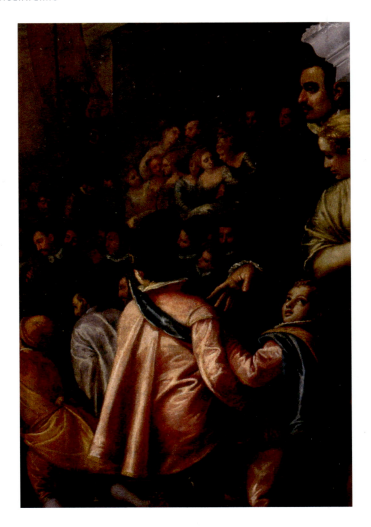

2.13
Benedetto and Carlo Caliari, *Meeting of Doge Sebastiano Ziani and Pope Alexander III at the Church of the Carità*. Detail of 2.4.

In the painting, the inclusion of *artefici* and *mechanici* who writhe, squirm, and move away from the centre of attention reflects their exclusion from the government of the city. This, by contrast, enhances the role of those who stand still and look. These are the citizens who participate actively in the *res publica* and act virtuously for the benefit of the populace. The painting is thus a paean to and legitimation of the ruling class. To this end, it exploits a corollary postulate of the Aristotelian analogy of the body politic, that is, the concept of sight as a metaphor for political understanding and civic participation, whereby only those who administer the government have the right to see.

Tellingly, Gasparo Contarini concludes his treatise by asserting that

> the supreme rule of things in the Republic of Venice is committed to the Gentlemen, as to the eyes of the city, and the lowest offices to the people, therefore the Venetians live in the happiest way as a well united body; for the eyes of the Republic see not only for themselves but also for all other members, and the other parts of the city not so much regard themselves as they willingly obey these eyes as being the principal members of the Republic. And if in whatsoever Republic the citizens shall let themselves be carried away into such folly — as it has happened to many — that the people wished to exercise the function of seeing and usurp the use of the eyes, then it necessarily follows that the whole Republic ruins.[67]

In his dialogue *Della perfettione della vita politica* (1579), Paolo Paruta similarly echoes that

> Servitude does not prevent the servant from acquiring perfection more than blindness does with the mole, for blindness, being natural to the mole, does not make her more imperfect or more miserable in her own right; this would only happen if those animals that are born to see were deprived of sight and if those men who are born to command were deprived of liberty.[68]

Along the same lines, in the painting the act of seeing thematized in the story is also developed into socio-political discourse. The various stances of the spectators outline a spectrum of viewing conditions positioned somewhere between two opposite extremes, which are represented by two different groups of figures standing next to each other in the foreground. In the right margin of the picture, a family of well-dressed citizens consisting of a husband, wife, and two children enjoys a high and stable vantage point provided by a raised podium at the edge of the embankment, from which they look towards the main scene across the canal (fig. 2.13). Their contrast in attitude, composure, appearance, and status with respect to the aforementioned fishmongers, who are placed further down to the left but on the same spatial plane, could not be more forceful. While the latter turn their backs on and completely ignore the main event, the former are fully absorbed in watching it.

This jarring antithesis, accentuated by the high/low positioning of the two groups, fits well into the hierarchical arrangement of the picture. The household unit epitomises the role played by the family as the backbone of civic life.[69] Its function as the 'fundamental political cell, forming the skeleton of the privileged order', as Angelo Ventura described it, is a staple of aristocratic ideology and *topos* of Renaissance political thought, which in Venice takes on a particular significance in light of the polity's peculiar socio-economic organisation.[70] Family, city, and nation, the spheres socially defining the early modern self, are linked by the cognate concepts of love, abnegation, and commitment to the other, which make the individual a member of the community. This relationship is effectively summarised in Paruta's dialogue, which makes a recurring association between *amor familiae* and *amor patriae*, between the behaviour of a good family man and the practice of a good citizen.[71]

As with many figures in the picture, it is hard to determine whether this family is meant to be of noble standing or not. Judging from their clothing, however, there seems to be no doubt about their high status. The husband, for instance, is dressed in a black suit with a white collar, like the previously examined gentleman within the crowd who is painted next to him. The family's high status is further emphasised by their contrast with the fishmongers at the centre. This juxtaposition gains further significance when we consider that, in the late sixteenth century, the age-old accusation that Venetians descended from fishermen and low-class people was still perceived as an insult threatening the aristocratic claims of the Venetian ruling class and was fiercely opposed by writers such as Francesco Sansovino and Leonardo Fioravanti, who asserted that the Venetian ancestors were free, respectable, and illustrious people.[72] It should also be noted that in the Ducal Palace the theme of the nobility of Venice interlinked with that of its original liberty and was given prominence in the ceiling decoration of the Hall of the Four Doors (*Sala delle Quattro Porte*), frescoed by Jacopo Tintoretto in the restoration campaign that followed another fire in 1574.[73]

While the family group occupies a liminal, discreet position in the picture, it also gains prominence due to its size, nearness, and attitude. Standing at the boundary between the image and the real world, these figures drive the beholder's gaze towards the primary narrative moment through well-studied visual axes determined by their postures. With his face turned backwards towards us, the smaller boy catches our eye and invites us to follow his gaze towards his parents, who, in turn, stare at the main event — a connection reinforced by how the father's hand stretches down towards the children. At the same time, the boy's arm is interlocked with that of his taller brother, who is seen from rear while bending forward to gain a better look at the ceremony beyond the canal, prompting us to do the same. This group of figures play a twofold role as spectators within the narrative fiction and mediators between the picture and the viewer. Due to their ambivalent condition within and at the margins of the depiction, and the fact that they are set apart from all other characters, they are liable to take on an emblematic function. In this context, they appear to personify the fundamental unit of the larger body of Venetian society and condense the love for family and country required from a good citizen.

We assume that this group of figures spoke to the noblemen gathered in the Great Council in a more compelling and significant way than they do to the modern viewer. They fulfil an exhortatory purpose in the economy of the image by presenting the patricians with a model of social behaviour; on the other hand, their presence gratifies the *esprit de classe* of the aristocracy by projecting a reassuring image of nobility, self-possession, and discernment. More importantly, they look, see, and understand in the same way the patricians viewing the picture were expected to. The noblemen in the Great Council would be prompted to engage in this act of viewing like the characters in the painting; and, as external beholders, they would activate the function of these characters as metaphors of the political discernment that they themselves embodied as members of the ruling class. In fact, this painting is not just storytelling or a portrayal of 'eyewitnessing'. It is a representation of political authority and the social order that requires the viewer to feed into it. It elicits a reflexive response from its designated audience, urging patrician viewers to exercise their political virtues through visual engagement. Finally, by prodding the patricians into action through their participation as viewers, it informs the dialectic between the individual and the collective on which the ethos of the Venetian elite was founded. All this was in line with the aims and expectations of the Great Hall decorative programme's designers.

Conclusions

The whole Great Council and Scrutiny cycle rests on this duality: while it aimed to exhort the patricians to imitate their ancestors and act virtuously, it also reassured them about their social pre-eminence. Partly didactic and partly celebratory, the programme harnesses the circularity on which the legitimacy of the Venetian ruling class, as well as the fabricated image of Venice as a perfect Republic, was built. It is subtended by and simultaneously reinforces the concept that the patricians possessed inborn virtues deriving from their ancestral nobility, while nonetheless deserving their noble status thanks to their virtuous actions. In the same way, the notion of Venice's good government and sovereignty was underpinned by her original liberty and stability over the centuries, just as much as these liberty and stability were guaranteed by her judicious and unconditional rule.

To some extent, however, the post-1577 cycle attempts to short-circuit this long-established, self-perpetuating mechanism by co-opting Venice's subjects as testimonies to the good effects of the actions of their rulers. As the initial episode of the Alexandrine sequence, the discovery of the pope's presence in Venice is presented as a sign of the city's predestination. The pontiff is the guarantor of divine will who bestows divine approval on the doge's authority, Venetian institutions, and Republic's social order. The pope thus validates an unchanged, fixed configuration that is ratified through a public ceremony. The depiction appealed directly to the sense of civic-political duty and moral responsibility of the noblemen gathered in the council. It also addressed the doge who, seated on the tribune set against the adjacent wall, would see this painting first from his right. On his left, on the opposite wall, he would observe the portrayal of the allocution delivered by doge Enrico Dandolo to the crusaders in St Mark's in 1201. In both paintings the doge's authority is measured against the presence of an engaged audience. In the *Meeting of Sebastiano Ziani and Alexander III*, his public investiture legitimises his leadership before the people, as well as the role of the leading group and the mutual relationship that exists between the state and its citizens.

With its original and carefully thought-out design, the painting reveals the growing need to emphasize the relationship between rulers and subjects that emerged in the forms of self-representation of the Venetian state in the last quarter of the sixteenth century, especially, but not only, in the pictorial cycles of the Ducal Palace. It is as if the prerogatives grounded in the traditional concept of Venice's imperial mission as a *res publica christiana* needed to be validated by attention to the actual benefits that subjects gained from Venetian rule. However, emphasis is not on conquest or supremacy but on time-honoured sovereignty, the continuity of leadership, and consensus. Even if the theme of the *imperium* became increasingly central in these pictorial decorations, the self-eulogising rhetoric developed by the Republic in the decades of its progressive loss of geopolitical influence does not hinge on power and hegemony but on prestige and authority — notions which both rest on public acknowledgment.

This message is clearly communicated by the three allegories in the central row of the Great Council ceiling (fig. 1.20–1.22), which, according to the original plan described by Bardi, were meant to show the political effects of the heroic deeds depicted in the two rooms. Here, Venice's triumph over the provinces, represented in the first allegory by Palma Giovane, is sanctioned by the formal act of their spontaneous submission depicted by Jacopo Tintoretto in the second allegory. Finally, the mutual pact legitimising the authority of the Republic leads to the happiness of the people under the Venetian government, which is celebrated in the third allegory by Veronese, whose theme is expressly inspired by the ancient Roman iconography of the *felicitas publica*.[74] Just as the jubilant people in the final allegory bears witness to the good government of the Republic, thus testifying that the historical deeds depicted in the two rooms were performed by the Venetians rulers for the sake of the citizens, so the audience present in the *Meeting of Sebastiano Ziani and Alexander III* attests to the legitimacy of the authority on which that rule is premised, turning the event into an investiture. This is something more than civic ritual; it is a public staging that vindicates the republican leadership and guarantees the goodness of rulers whose actions benefit the people.

This novel direction taken by the Republic in its strategy of self-representation reflects an ideological stance that is fully expressed by Paolo Paruta in both *Della perfettione* and *Discorsi politici* (1599), which both emphasise ethics as the foundation of the ruling class and civic happiness as the main aim of the state.[75] The increased importance attached to the participation of the subjects as a public testimony to Venetian good government suggests that the Venetian ruling class was no less aware of the urgency of these matters than other sovereigns striving to unify their monarchies. At a time when the cycle was still being prepared and Caliari's painting had not yet been delivered, Elizabeth I was pointing out to the English Parliament, then urging Mary Stuart's execution, that 'We princes […] are set on stages, in the sight and view of all the world duly observed. […] It behooveth us therefore to be careful that our proceedings be just and honourable'.[76] To vouch for the integrity of the Venetian patricians and represent their deeds as virtuous actions, the devisers of the Great Council decorative programme took advantage of the power of images to reify history, to make it believable and relevant to the present, creating immediate associations with allegories that layered the events depicted with a specific moral meaning. Through their power of evocation, these pictures conjure a public stage that, at least at the level of narrative, brings the *Palazzo* out into the *Piazza*; even more evocatively, however, they also bring the representation of the *Piazza* into the *Palazzo*, reminding the members of the Council that they were expected to observe, as much as to be observed.

1. I would like to thank Giovanni Florio and Alessandro Metlica for involving me in this project and for their generous and constructive feedback. I am also grateful to Matteo Casini for his constant exchange of ideas on these topics over the years and, more specifically, for his suggestions in relation to this essay. I moreover owe a huge thanks to Celeste McNamara for kindly proofreading the text. On the controversial nature of the events: Köster, '24 luglio 1177'.

2. The most detailed account of the *andate* and the ducal cortege in the period under examination is provided by Sansovino, *Venetia città nobilissima et singolare* (1581), 193v–206v. On the topic see Mazzarotto, *Le feste veneziane*, 155–79; Muir, *Civic Ritual in Renaissance Venice*, pp. 135–56, 189–211; Foscari Malacrea, 'Il doge nelle cerimonie pubbliche', pp. 105–91; Urban, 'Feste veneziane cinquecentesche', pp. 95–104; Urban, 'L'"andata" dogale a San Vio'; Casini, *I gesti del principe*, pp. 149–68; Urban, *Processioni e feste dogali*, pp. 86–88, 97–149; Fenlon, *The Ceremonial City*, pp. 120–27; Ravegnani, *Il doge di Venezia*, pp. 117–39; Kurtzman, 'Civic Identity and Civic Glue'.

3. Fortini Brown, 'Painting and History in Renaissance Venice', p. 267.

4. Fortini Brown, *Venetian Narrative Painting*, pp. 165–91.

5. Fortini Brown, *Venetian Narrative Painting*, p. 125.

6. Fortini Brown, *Venetian Narrative Painting*, pp. 4–5, 125–32.

7. On the painting, see Arslan, *I Bassano*, I, pp. 199–200; Franzoi, *Storia e leggenda del Palazzo Ducale di Venezia*, p. 252, no. 383; Wolters, *Storia e politica nei dipinti di Palazzo Ducale*, p. 173; Wolters, *Il Palazzo Ducale di Venezia*, pp. 147–48.

8. Grubb, 'When Myths Lose Power', pp. 43–49.

9. Florio, 'Inchini e carte bollate'. See also O'Connell's contribution to this volume, chapter 2.

10. MCV, Ms. Cicogna 105 and Ms. Cicogna 3007/26, the former is transcribed in Wolters, 'Der programmentwurf zur Dekoration', pp. 303–18; BMV, Ms. It. IV, 22 (=5361); ASVE, PS, Misc., b. 49, transcribed in Wolters, *Storia e politica*, pp. 297–310.

11. Bardi, *Dichiaratione*, 63v–64r.

12. Bardi, *Vittoria navale*, pp. 65, 154. On the topic see Wolters, *Storia e politica*, pp. 162–78; Fortini Brown, 'Painting and History', pp. 270–71; Fortini Brown, *Venetian Narrative Painting*, p. 83; Haskell, *History and Its Images: Art and the Interpretation of the Past*, pp. 83–84; De Vivo, 'Historical Justifications of Venetian Power in the Adriatic', pp. 168–69; Van Kessel, 'Artists and Knowledge in Sixteenth-Century Venice', pp. 231–38.

13. Patrizi, *Della historia*, 8r, 13v: 'l'historia è quel narramento, ch'altri fa delle cose, che egli ha con gli occhi proprii vedute'; 'un rimiramento che altri fa con gli occhi propri'.

14. Patrizi, *Della historia*, 14r.

15. Sansovino, *Venetia città nobilissima et singolare* (1581), 124v, 130v–132v; see Van Kessel, 'Venetian Thinking on the Lives of Paintings in the Early Modern Doge's Palace', pp. 99–108.

16. Franzoi, *Storia e leggenda*, p. 250, no. 379; Wolters, *Storia e politica*, p. 171; Wolters, *Il Palazzo ducale di Venezia*, pp. 145–46.

17. ABW, Inv. 24476r, pen and ink and wash, 29.8 × 21.7 cm; see also SGSM, Inv. 1951:63, pen and ink and wash, 30.1 × 20.9 cm. For both drawings see Cocke, *Veronese's Drawings: A Catalogue Raisonne*, pp. 216–19, nos. 92–93.

18. Bardi, *Dichiaratione*, 33r–34v.

19. Bardi, *Vittoria navale*. See Sigonio, *Historiarum de regno Italiae Libri Quindecim*. On the historiographical quarrel over the battle of Punta Salvore, see Cozzi, 'La venuta di Alessandro III a Venezia nel dibattito religioso e politico tra il '500 e il '600'; De Vivo, 'Historical Justifications'. On how visual representations of the events were used as historical evidence in the controversy, see Wolters, *Storia e politica*, pp. 163–64; Fortini Brown, 'Painting and History', pp. 266–72; Fortini Brown, *Venetian Narrative Painting*, pp. 81–86; Cooper, 'Prolegomenon to a Quarrel of Images'.

20. Bardi, *Vittoria navale*, pp. 20–22.

21. The travel to Zara is not mentioned in Bardi, *Dichiaratione*, 33r, where the date of his escape to Venice is said to be 1175.

22. Bardi, *Vittoria navale*, p. 20: 'Ma soprapreso prima, che se ne passasse in Grecia, da varii sospetti, dubitando della poca fede de Greci, deliberò di trasferirsi a Venetia. Et per tanto dato commiato a tutti i suoi, rimandandogli in Italia, et vestitosi in habito di Prete privato, se ne passò del mese di Luglio del presente anno in quella Città'.

23. Bardi, *Vittoria navale*, p. 20: 'Nel qual luogo veduto, a caso, il Pontefice Alessandro, che in habito molto negletto se ne stava dicendo l'Officio, lo raffigurò, avendone certa notitia per haverlo et in Francia et a Roma più volte veduto'.

24. Bardi, *Vittoria navale*, pp. 20–21: 'Tuttavia non si assicurando di se stesso, per meglio avertirsi, postosi con molta attentione a rimirarlo, finalmente doppo un lungo guardare, fra se stesso persuaso, ch'ei fosse il sommo Pontefice Alessandro, si partì frettolosamente della detta Chiesa, et andatosene al Palazzo Ducale, da Sebastiano Ziani in quel tempo Doge, et capo della Republica'.

25. Bardi, *Vittoria navale*, p. 21: 'dubitando, che Commodo non vacillasse, fattolo più d'una volta diligentemente essaminare, et entrato con esso in varii ragionamenti, lo ritrovò non men stabile nel primo detto, che prudente nel resto'.

26. Bardi, *Vittoria navale*, p. 21: 'provedendo con somma prestezza d'habiti, et di vestimenti convenienti alla Maestà Pontificia, havendo fra tanto adunato il Vescovo con la maggior parte del Clero, se n'andò il Doge, et la Signoria con tutti i più riguardevoli della Republica, alla detta Chiesa'.

27. Bardi, *Vittoria navale*, p. 21: 'Dove ritrovato nell'abito assegnato da Commodo, il Pontefice, che prostrato in terra faceva oratione a Dio, che horamai liberasse da tanti fastidii la sua Chiesa, se gli gettò a piedi, et adoratolo come Vicario di Christo legittimamente creato, l'assicurò a nome publico, che non temesse di Federigo'.

28. Bardi, *Vittoria navale*, p. 21: 'lodò con molte affettuose parole la pietà del Doge, et della Signoria, rimettendo liberamente se stesso nelle mani di quella Republica'.

29. Bardi, *Vittoria navale*, p. 22: 'Doppo le quali parole vestitosi de gli habiti Pontificali, e salito nella Barca Ducale, se n'andò con tutto il Clero alla Chiesa di San Marco, dove benedetto il Doge, con tutta la Città, si ritirò nel Palazzo del Vescovo, alla Chiesa di S. Silvestro'.

30 Bardi, *Dichiaratione*, 34r: 'vestitosi de gli habiti Pontificali preparatigli dal Doge'. I want to thank Celeste McNamara for drawing my attention to this detail.

31 Sansovino, *Venetia città nobilissima et singolare* (1581), 177r: 'Sotto alla predetta Corona o Berretta, si vede una scuffia bianca di sottilissimo renso, o cambrà, la quale i Dogi hebbero ab antiquo, quasi come insegna di persona sacra, rappresentandosi con quella, una certa memoria del santo olio col quale s'ungono alcuni Re Christiani, non altramente che se questo Principe fosse uno del corpo loro. La qual scuffia, oltre che habbia sembianza di quella fascia ch'era già antica corona de i Re, aggiugne anco molta gratia alla testa sotto al Corno, il quale prende per quella, molto più fermezza nel suo riposo. Oltre a ciò il Doge trahendosi il Corno per qual si voglia cagione, resta col capo velato, et non del tutto nudo et sfornito'.

32 Bardi, *Dichiaratione*, 33v–34v. Whether Commodus was present or not at the moment of the meeting is not specified in the manuscript; see Wolters, *Storia e politica*, p. 304.

33 On the *andata* to San Giorgio Maggiore, see Urban, *Processioni e feste dogali*, pp. 105–10.

34 Geertz, 'Centers, Kings, and Charisma', p. 171; republished in Geertz, *Local Knowledge*, p. 146.

35 Clifford Geertz, 'Religion as a Cultural System', p. 28.

36 Tenenti, 'L'uso scenografico degli spazi pubblici: 1490–1580', p. 24.

37 On this matter, see the contribution to this volume by Evelyn Korsch, chapter 7.

38 Zerner, 'Looking for the Unknowable', p. 97, note 27; see also pp. 83–84.

39 Bourdieu, 'Les rites comme actes d'institution', p. 63.

40 Newton, *The Dress of the Venetians, 1495–1525*, p. 9.

41 Butazzi, 'Intorno al "Cavaliere in nero"'; Quondam, *Tutti i colori del nero*.

42 Vecellio, *De gli habiti antichi*, 106r ('habito ordinario et commune a tutta la nobiltà Veneziana'): 'Et questo è l'Habito usato non solamente dalla nobiltà, ma da' Cittadini, et da chiunque si compiace di portarlo, come fanno quasi tutti i Medici, gli Avvocati, et Mercanti, i quali tutti se ne vestono volentieri, poiché essendo Habito proprio della nobiltà, porta seco ne gli altri anchora gran riputatione'. See Butazzi, 'Intorno al "Cavaliere in nero"', p. 50; Davanzo Poli, *Abiti antichi e moderni*, p. 75.

43 Similar attire was associated with the 'donne per casa' and the 'gentildonne venetiane, et altre, per casa, et fuori di casa la vernata', Vecellio, *De gli habiti*, 138v–39v, 143v–44r.

44 *Pavonazzo* (purple) or *turchino* (light blue) were used for *cavalieri, procuratori, savi, consiglieri, comandatori* or *banditori*, admirals, and doge's secretaries. See Davanzo Poli, *Abiti antichi e moderni*, p. 68.

45 Crimson was used for senators, *magistrati, avogadori, cavalieri del doge*, and *cancellier grande*. See Davanzo Poli, *Abiti antichi e moderni*, p. 68.

46 The grand chancellor was separated from the doge only by the ballot boy (*ballotino*). See Muir, *Civic Ritual in Renaissance Venice*, pp. 193, 196. On the significance of his office, see Casini, 'Realtà e simboli del Cancellier Grande veneziano in età moderna (sec. XVI–XVII)', p. 242. On the Chancellor's role in the ducal procession, also see Casini, *I gesti del principe*, p. 167.

47 Casini, 'Realtà e simboli', pp. 240–48.

48 I owe this suggestion to Matteo Casini. On the figure of the *capitan grande* in the late sixteenth century, see Pezzolo, 'Fra potere politico e controllo dell'ordine'.

49 Vecellio, *De gli habiti*, 111r–v; see Rosenthal, 'Clothing, Fashion, Dress, and Costume', pp. 908–09. Also see Grevembroch, *Gli abiti*, III, no. 7. The *capitani minori* had an outfit similar in colour and type; Grevembroch, *Gli abiti*, III, no. 12.

50 Vecellio, *De gli habiti*, 112v. Also see Grevembroch, *Gli abiti*, III, no. 7: 'Il di lui geloso carico fu ed è di comandare agli altri Capitani, e di ordinare tutto ciò, che con prudenza, ed impegno devono eseguire serviggio della Giustizia, acciò in pacifico sistema tenghino la Plebe della Dominante, onde continuamente prevedendo, e provedendo stassene Lui vigilante, per riparare i dissordini. […] Nelle funzioni precede il Doge'.

51 Pezzolo, 'Fra potere politico e controllo dell'ordine', pp. 92, 95, 98.

52 Casini, *I gesti del principe*, pp. 54, 167. On the interregnum rites, also see Muir, 'The Doge as Primus inter pares'.

53 Casini, *I gesti del principe*, pp. 163–68.

54 See, in this context, Casini, *I gesti del principe*, pp. 167–68.

55 A completely different interpretation is provided by Wolters, *Storia e politica*, pp. 171, 173.

56 Examples from Veronese's oeuvre and the relevant bibliography are too many to be thoroughly accounted for here. It is enough to mention that this was the main thesis pursued in Holden Evers, 'The Art of Paolo Veronese'. A brilliant and compelling discussion of Veronese's unique ability to interpret the ideology of the Venetian patriciate is provided in Terribile, *Del piacere della virtù*. For a similar analysis, but more specifically addressing the political sphere, see Tagliaferro, 'Le forme della Vergine'.

57 For a list of the *provveditori alla restauration del Maggior Consiglio* who supervised the works see Lorenzi, *Monumenti per servire alla storia del Palazzo Ducale di Venezia*. Although Jacopo Contarini belonged to the *case vecchie* and was close to Romanist families, his papalist connections may have been overemphasised by scholars such as Manfredo Tafuri. Contarini's political ideas are mostly unknown, and his public engagement was fundamentally related to his activity as a patron. Considering the breadth of his interests and the variety of individuals of different extraction with whom he networked, it would be limiting to regard his contribution to the Great Council decorative campaign as an expression of the political orientation of a specific party. On this polyhedric figure, see Savini Branca, *Il collezionismo veneziano nel '600*, pp. 31–32, 201–03; Rose, 'Two Venetian Patrons of the Renaissance of Mathematics'; Rose, 'Jacomo Contarini (1536–1595)'; Rose, 'A Venetian Patron and Mathematician of the Sixteenth Century'; Logan, *Culture and Society in Venice 1470–1790*; Foscari and Tafuri, *L'armonia e i conflitti*, pp. 168–69, note 42; Tafuri, *Venezia e il Rinascimento*, pp. 197–212; Hochmann, 'La collection de Giacomo Contarini'; Hochmann, *Peintres et commanditaires à Venise, 1540–1628*; Tagliaferro, 'Quattro Jacopo per Montemezzano'; Hochmann, 'Giuseppe Porta e la decorazione di palazzo Contarini dale Figure'; Hochmann, 'Giacomo Contarini'.

58 On Paruta see, in particular, Cozzi, 'La società veneziana', re-published in Cozzi, *Ambiente veneziano, ambiente veneto*; Baiocchi, 'Paolo Paruta'; Gaeta, 'Venezia da "stato misto" ad "aristocrazia esemplare"', pp. 454–59. More recently, Giani, 'Paolo Paruta'; Venturelli, 'Mito di Venezia e governo misto'.

59 On Contarini's political thought, see the classic studies by Gilbert, 'Religion and Politics'; Gaeta, 'L'idea di Venezia', pp. 633–41; Gleason, 'Reading Between the Lines'.

60 Contarini, *La Republica*, xv: 'Tutti quegli adunque, che furono o nobili di sangue, o chiari per virtù, o benemeriti della Republica, ricevettero da principio quella authorità de governare la città'. A similar position is espressed by Memmo, *Dialogo*.

61 Contarini, *La Republica*, xr: 'Percioché ciascuna città ha bisogno de gli artigiani, et di molti mercenari, et ancho di servi privati i quali prestano l'opera loro; ma nessuno di questi veramente si può dire Cittadino. Perché il Cittadino è huomo libero; et tutti questi servono o servitù publica, o privata. Percioché tutti i mercenarii, et artigiani sono da essere stimati come servi publici'.

62 Memmo, *Dialogo*, p. 92; quoted in Ventura, *Nobiltà e popolo*, p. 302, note 41 (see also pp. 306–08). Paruta, *Opere politiche*, II, p. 19 (*Discorsi politici*, I, 1); quoted in Baiocchi, 'Paolo Paruta', pp. 194–95.

63 Paruta *Della perfettione*, pp. 85, 289–90.

64 De Nores, *Breve institutione dell'ottima republica*, 32r: 'La moltitudine de' cittadini dell'ottima republica s'intende essere di quegli à punto, che stanno fermi, et possono essere partecipi del governo di essa, et non de gli artefici, de' mechanici, de' servi, de' forestieri, i quali vanno et vengono a loro arbitrio, et sono adoperati come instrumenti'.

65 De Nores, *Breve institutione*, 33v: 'de gli huomini della città, che in essa dimorano, altri sono partecipi di felicità, havendo occasione di operar attioni virtuose specialmente secondo la giustitia, i quali sono assolutamente parti della città. Altri non sono partecipi di felicità, che non hanno occasion di operar attioni virtuose, et giuste, ma esercitano arti vili, et mechaniche, i quali non sono assolutamente parti sostantiali della città, ma necessarie, come instrumenti'.

66 Michiel, *Delle orationi di Agostino Michele*, 22v-22bis (*Oration quarta nella creatione del Serenissimo Prencipe di Vinegia Pasqual Cicogna*).

67 Contarini, *La Republica*, LXXI: 'il sommo governo delle cose nella Republica Vinitiana è imposto a Gentilhuomini, come a certi occhi della città, gli uffici più ignobili a gli altri del popolo, et così come ben congiunto corpo, i Vinitiani vivono felicissimamente, sendo che gli occhi della Republica non a se soli ma a tutte le membra risguardano et l'altre parti delle [sic!] Città non solamente a se habbino riguardo, ma etiandio ubbidiscano di bonissima voglia a questi occhi, come a principali membra della Republica. Et se in alcuna Republica a tanta pazzia si lasciarà trasportare qualche cittadino, il che in parecchi è avenuto, che il popolo volesse usare l'ufficio di vedere, et s'usurpasse l'esercitio de gli occhi, tosto è forza che tutta la Republica vada in rovina'.

68 Paruta, *Della perfettione*, pp. 291–92: 'la servitù niente più è d'impedimento al servo, per acquistare la sua perfettione, che sia alla talpa la sua cecità, la quale, perché a lei è natural cosa, non la fa nell'esser suo, né più imperfetta, né più misera: il che averrebbe, privando quegli animali di vista, che son nati al vedere, et quegli huomini di libertà, che nati sono al comandare'.

69 For a general overview, see Bellavitis, 'Family and Society'.

70 Ventura, *Nobiltà e popolo*, p. 297: 'cellula politica fondamentale, che forma l'ossatura dell'ordine privilegiato'.

71 See for instance the assertion of one of the participants in the dialogue, Niccolò da Ponte, in the third book: 'ricco stimo colui, il cui havere è tanto, che possa fare ufficio di buon padre di famiglia, et di buon cittadino'; Paruta, *Della perfettione*, p. 266.

72 Sansovino, *Dialogo di tutte le cose notabili che sono in Venetia*, pp. not numbered ('Origine di Venetia'): 'quelli, che dicono Venetia nostra haver havuto principio da pescatori, et vil gente, mostrano in tutto di essere ignoranti della vera historia'. Fioravanti, *Dello specchio di scientia universale*, 83r-v; quoted in Gaier, *Architettura "Venetiana"*, p. 298 (see also pp. 295–97).

73 Sansovino, *Venetia città nobilissima et singolare* (1581), 122r-v. See Franzoi, *Storia e leggenda*, p. 66, nos. 77–78; Wolters, *Storia e politica*, pp. 61–64; Wolters, *Il Palazzo Ducale di Venezia*, pp. 81–83; Zamperini, *Palazzo Ducale*, pp. 168, 172.

74 Bardi, *Dichiaratione*, 63r-v; Wolters, *Storia e politica*, p. 310.

75 Baiocchi, 'Paolo Paruta', pp. 176–78.

76 Marcus, Mueller, and Rose, eds, *Elizabeth I*, p. 194. The speech was delivered on 12 November 1586.

Monique O'Connell

3

REPRESENTATIVE SPACES OF REPUBLICANISM

Constitutional Thinking, Virtue Politics, and Venice's Great Council Hall in Early Modern Europe

In the long history of constitutional thinking, Venice stands out as a classic example of institutional stability and governmental complexity.[1] Two texts that have substantially shaped understandings of the Venetian constitution are Gasparo Contarini's *De Magistratibus et republica Venetorum* and Donato Giannotti's *Libro della republica de vinitiani*.[2] Both were written in the early sixteenth century, during a moment when Venice escaped the conquests and factional violence that transformed the governments of many other states during the Italian Wars. Both have also been the subject of extensive scholarly analysis, together and separately.[3] While it is beyond doubt that Contarini's and Gianotti's texts occupied a large role in Europe's political understanding of republics, it is also the case that by the late sixteenth and early seventeenth century the representation of Venice was both visual and textual.[4] The city was an obligatory stop for Grand Tourists and diplomatic travellers, and those who had not been in person could experience Venice's unique geography through maps, paintings, and engravings.[5] For visitors, the insider view of Venetian politics offered by Contarini and Giannotti often contrasted with the external visions of the city available to travellers.

In 1631, the Elsevier edition of Giannotti's work combined the textual tradition of describing the institutions of Venetian government with a visualisation of those mechanics in action.[6] The volume itself included not only a Latin edition of Giannotti's *Dialogi de Republica Venetorum*, but two sets of commentary on Contarini's and Giannotti's works. The first accompanying commentary, Niccolò Crasso's *Notae in Donatum Iannotium et Casparem Contarenum Cardinalem*, is illustrated with a series of images showing a meeting of the Great Council, electoral procedures, and the form of the ballot boxes.[7] A fold-out plate shows the doge and Collegio seated on a platform at the head of the Great Council chamber, with rows of seated patricians filling the hall and *ballottini* ('ballot boys') collecting ballots.[8] Subsequent images show detailed depictions of the balloting urns, patricians in the act of dropping their votes into the urns, and *ballottini* emptying their vote-counting boxes into the larger urns at the front of the hall. Another image shows Venetian patricians in motion on the ceremonial platform at the front of the hall: several patricians at the edges of the platform are in conversation, while two are approaching voting urns at the centre of the hall (fig. 3.2).

The 1631 illustrated volume was part of Bonaventura's and Abraham Elsevier's series of thirty-five Latin volumes on republics: each volume provided information on the history, topography, laws, and government in places across Asia, Africa, Europe, and the Middle East.[9] The majority of the volumes were produced in cheap pocket editions that appealed to diplomats, merchants, and other travellers. A Latin edition of Contarini appeared in the series in 1626, and a second edition in 1628 included several other descriptions and treatises on Venice and its government, including works by Leandro Alberti, Johannes van Cootwijk, and Giulio Belli.[10] These works were explicitly framed for a European audience that was increasingly interested in Venetian governmental principles for structuring their own political affairs.[11] For example, in the 1628 edition Contarini's treatise is complimented by van Cootwijk's *Synopsis Reipublicae Venetae*, an abridgement of Contarini's description of Venetian institutions

3.1
Joseph Heintz the Younger, *The interior of the Sala del Maggior Consiglio, Ducal Palace, Venice*. Detail of 3.7.

3.2
Cornelis Claesz Duysend (?), *Great Council Hall*. Engraving from Donato Giannotti, *Dialogi de Republica Venetorum*, Leiden, Elzevier, 1631, 404–05. Photo: Milano, Biblioteca Nazionale Braidense — Pinacoteca di Brera, with permission from the Italian Ministry of Culture.

of government that was first published in 1619 and later appeared as a separate work in 1626.[12] The edition represents the republic from a variety of perspectives, placing Contarini's work in dialogue with other European visions of the city.

The 1631 Elsevier edition combined visual and textual representations of Venetian government, packaged for an elite European audience interested in a comparative view of political structures. It points to the complex web of textual content, visual representation, and print markets that shaped European access to Contarini's and Giannotti's works. Many intellectual historians have traced linear chains of influence, placing Contarini and Giannotti in a straight line of development with other theoretical texts that built on one another and developed ideas of republican government across time and space.[13] Contarini's text has also been mined for its role in creating the much-discussed 'myth of Venice'; the work has been seen as the end-point of a centuries long-process of myth-building or as a new articulation of that 'myth' shaped by the conflict of the war of Cambrai.[14] This chapter instead relies on the paradigm of entanglement to offer a different perspective on how Contarini's and Gianotti's texts act as iconic representations of the Venetian Republic on the European stage. Rather than considering objects of historical study in parallel and comparing discrete instances, the methodologies of entangled history point toward moments of interconnection, reciprocal influence and emphasize the mutability and malleability of concepts and historical paradigms.[15] Contarini's and Giannotti's works began in the diplomatic spaces of Italian politics during the Italian wars; they existed in dialogue with previous treatments of Venetian government as well as critiques of Venetian character from hostile powers. The print versions removed the immediate political context but introduced a dialogue with audiences who absorbed Contarini's and Giannotti's works at a distance that put them in conversation with other works on republics and on Venice itself. This chapter focuses on textual and visual depictions of the Great Council, the foundational governmental organ in the Venetian constitution, in order to excavate the tangled representations of virtuous noble identity and idealised electoral procedures that informed European visions of the Venetian republic.

The Great Council has a central place in both Contarini's and Giannotti's treatises. For Contarini, it is the key governmental body ensuring 'the practice and exercise of virtue', the main aim of the Republic's wise founders. He describes it as 'this whole assembly of patricians — this Great Council where the ultimate sovereignty of the Republic resides, and on which the Senate and the authority of the magistrates depends — fulfils the role of a popular authority in this Republic'.[16] He explains that the founders had chosen to limit the governing class by patrilineal descent so that 'all those who were noble by birth, renowned for virtue, or meritorious towards the Republic, obtained from the beginning the right to participate in governing the city'.[17] The Great Council's main duty was to enact laws and elect magistrates; Contarini's description of the electoral procedures situates all of the actors in the space of the Council Hall, with patricians seated on ten parallel benches and the officials charged with restraining electoral corruption occupying assigned seats around the Hall, so that 'they may seem to have been appointed guardians of the whole assembly so that not one patrician can act with impunity against the laws and decrees of the assembly'.[18] While Giannotti's treatment of the Great Council follows a roughly similar outline, he begins by situating the creation of the Council historically, describing the so-called Serrata of 1297 before moving to the procedures by which young nobles prove their ancestry and enter the council.[19] Giannotti also emphasises that electoral magistrates are arranged in particular seats around the room, explaining that this is not only to control corruption but also to give the impression that all seats are equally honourable and to ensure that young and old patricians are seated together, to encourage serious and restrained behaviour.[20] In both works, the Great Council is presented as a marker of patrician identity and the home of electoral processes that regularly created and re-created the system of interlocking councils and magistracies that made the Venetian government work.

In this pair of texts, Contarini is the consummate insider and Giannotti is the curious outsider. The Contarini family was one of the largest and best established families of the patriciate; Contarini's treatise is informed by his service in the Venetian councils and his experience in the diplomatic circles of the Italian Wars, first at the court of Charles V and then in Rome, where questions of republican liberty in the emerging peace of Italy were frequently debated.[21] Giannotti was a Florentine political writer and diplomat who visited Venice in 1526–27, when he wrote his *Della republica de vinizinani*; the text is structured as a dialogue between a Venetian noble and a Florentine visitor eager to learn the details of Venice's political arrangements.[22] In May of 1527, the Medici regime fell in Florence and Giannotti returned home to serve as secretary in the chancellery of the re-established Florentine Republic. When the Medici returned to power in 1530, Giannotti spent the rest of his life in exile between Rome and Venice.

After their authors' deaths, the multiple editions and translations of the two works, together and separately, continued to have international appeal to armchair travellers interested in Venetian politics. Even before Contarini's work reached its classic form represented by the edition of his collected works (*Opera*, Paris 1571), the text was translated, mistranslated, amplified, and altered.[23] The effect of many of these adaptations was to make the text more accessible or appealing to distant readers. The 1544 French translation added an epigram calling readers to 'view' Venice through Contarini's detailed description of the republic's constitutional arrangements, saying 'Car si tu lis (comme je t'en advise)/Ce beau livret, sans aultre peine avoir,/De ta maison tu pourras veoir Venise ['If you read this marvellous book (as I advise you to do) you may easily see Venice from the comfort of your home']'.[24] In this translation, Contarini's Latin treatise was transformed into a vehicle for 'seeing' a representation of how the republic worked, and by extension evoked a representation of all of Venice — enabling armchair travel with a political focus.[25] Before the Elsevier Latin edition of 1631, Giannotti's work was published in Rome in 1540 and again in 1542 and translated into German in several

3.3
Paolo Forlani, *Venice's Great Council*, Venice, Bolognino Zaltieri, 1566. © The Trustees of the British Museum.

editions.[26] The two works were printed together in an Italian edition by the Aldine Press in Venice in 1591, supplemented by two other commentaries on republican government by Sebastiano Erizzo and Bartolomeo Cavalcanti.[27] These editions gave a variety of European audiences access to Contarini's and Giannotti's texts, and their publication intersected with a growing interest in travel narratives.

In the sixteenth and seventeenth centuries, Northern European elites visited Venice in increasing numbers as part of the Grand Tour, searching for climates to enjoy, splendours to marvel over, antiquities to collect, and political systems to study.[28] Venice's form of government was renowned among British and French travellers interested in the practicalities of republican politics, but Venetian laws forbidding patricians from speaking to foreigners meant that it was difficult (though not impossible) to get an insider's view of politics simply by being in the city.[29] Print culture therefore had a large role in shaping representations of Venetian political space in the mental universe of learned European citizens, whether they visited the city or not. The content of Contarini's and Giannotti's treatises was referenced in guidebooks, translated, abridged, and annotated by other authors, and visualised in engravings and paintings.

Contarini's and Giannotti's treatises affected visitors' mental representations of Venice before they even arrived in the city, if indeed they visited at all. The Italian author (and son of the famous architect Jacopo) Francesco Sansovino wrote a series of guidebooks to Venice in the second part of the sixteenth century to introduce the city's splendours to the growing number of tourists arriving there: these include his 1561 guidebook to Venice, *Delle cose notabili che sono in Venetia* ('On the notable things which are in Venice'), and the 1581 encyclopaedia, *Venetia città nobilissima et singolare. Descritta in xiiii libri* ('Venice, most noble and singular city, described in xiv books'). [30] Each work contains significant sections describing the functions of different governmental councils, perhaps reflecting Sansovino's training as a lawyer and his other publications devoted specifically to government and administration.

The 1561 guidebook is a dialogue between a Venetian guide and a foreigner; at the outset of book one, the foreigner declares that Venice was an impossibility, 'and this impossibility is furthermore placed within the impossible in that she is built on the sea and as such completely unlike any other city'.[31] Yet after the Venetian asks what he has seen to delight him, the foreigner responds that he has seen many marvellous things, 'but I probably enjoy the things that enchant my ears just as much', going on to explain that he locates Venice's uniqueness not in its physical form but in the mechanisms of its state: 'the actions of princes, the words and deeds of the senators, the origin of the magistrates and other similar matters that are not particularly common elsewhere'.[32] In response to the Venetian's question on what further information he'd like to know, the foreigner declares that 'I have learnt everything from Cardinal Contarini's slim volume which talks about magistrates, and from the book by Messer Donato Gianotti'.[33] This exchange points to the role these two texts had in shaping travellers' preconceptions about Venice; the dialogue in the guidebook between the Venetian and the foreigner also mirrors the insider/outsider perspectives represented by Contarini's and Giannotti's respective treatises.

The guidebook's section on the Great Council Hall evokes the nobility of the patriciate, describing the room as a place where you could 'view' Venetian patrician virtue in action. 'Indeed, where else could you see more solemnity and more modesty that customarily observed by the nobility in the Gran Consiglio?'[34] The Venetian in the guidebook goes on to situate Venetian government officials in space — the doge, in ceremonial dress, seated above the assembly in his *tribunale*, a platform at the head of the hall; three councillors seated to his right; a head of the Council of Ten at the foot of the room; and the *auditori* in the room's corners. Through this description of the physical arrangement of the magistrates in the council chamber, Sansovino evokes a sense of government as performative display. The text of the guidebook may have been augmented for some travellers by a visit to the Great Council itself, but curious political tourists could also experience the idealised spatial arrangement of the Great Council Hall through Paolo Forlani's 1566 engraving *Il Gran Consiglio di Venetia* (The Great Council of Venice), published by Bolognino Zaltieri.[35] Forlani was a prolific engraver and mapmaker, best known for his contributions to mapping the geography of the Americas, but he also produced a detailed engraving of the Great Council Hall; as one of the only depictions of the space before the destructive 1577 fire, it has become iconic and is often reproduced in contemporary guides and books on Venice (fig. 3.3).[36]

Forlani's image allows the viewer to 'see' a Venetian election in action. As in the guidebook and in the spatial

3.4

Georg Hoefnagel, *The Ducal Palace on Fire*. Engraving from Georg Braun, *Civitates Orbis Terrarum*, vol. 5. *Urbium praecipuarum mundi theatrum quintum*, c. 1600. Photo: Roma, Biblioteca Angelica. Reproduced with permission.

descriptions of the Great Council in Contarini's and Giannotti's texts, all the actors are located precisely in the Hall. The doge and his councillors are seated on the *tribunale*, under Guariento's now damaged *Coronation of the Virgin* that once decorated the room. A cartouche at the upper right gives the room's dimensions, explaining that it was designed to hold between 1000 and 1500 nobles. The image is dominated by the parallel rows of Venetian nobles seated back-to-back on nine benches in the centre of the room, all with distinct individual faces and some chatting over their shoulders or dropping their ballots into urns. Despite how crowded the room is, the overall impression is one of order and decorum. The parallel Latin/Italian inscription at the bottom of the image makes clear that an election is in progress: there are *ballottini* passing between the rows, announcing the names of the candidates and collecting the black and white balls signifying yes and no votes. The figures at the head of the room are labelled below: the doge and his party, the secretary in charge of counting the yes and no votes, the grand chancellor who shouts the name of the electors and the elected as they are counted, and the secretary who records the votes. Other labels located the various magistrates and judiciary officials in the space of the hall, again contributing to the overall impression of Venetian elections as taking place in a perfectly organised and dignified manner.

Forlani's engraving worked in tandem with textual descriptions of Venetian electoral processes. As Contarini himself admitted, in the middle of his description of Venetian elections, 'I am aware that it is extremely difficult to explain these details in writing'.[37] Giannotti conjured the physical space of the Great Council through verbal description in his own treatment of Venetian elections. In Giannotti's text, the Venetian interlocutor Trifone Gabriele begins his description of the elections of magistrates by saying, 'io vi descriva la forma della sala, dove il Gran consiglio si raguna. Potrei, se voi l'avete veduta, e notata puntualmente ogni sua particolarità, lassare indietro tale descrizione' ('I will describe to you the form of the room where the Great Council meets. I can, if you have seen it, and carefully noted all of its details, leave you with this description').[38] The Florentine in the text, Borgherini, responds 'Io ho veduta questa sala che voi dite: nondimeno, assai mi sarà grato che la sua figura alla memoria mi torniate' ('I have seen this room that you describe; nonetheless, I would be very grateful if its image would return to my memory'). For a visitor to Venice interested in the mechanics of the city's elections, the text of the treatises was interwoven with other available representations of political space in guidebooks, commentaries, and engravings, creating a detailed representation of the inner workings of the Venetian republic.

Contarini's and Giannotti's works lived on beyond their authors' deaths in representations of Venetian politics aimed at sixteenth century political travellers; they also existed in a complex relationship with descriptions of the Venetian government written before the mid-sixteenth century. Earlier generations of Venetian authors had also seen the Great Council as the central political organ of the Republic; in the generation before Contarini and Giannotti, Paolo Morosini and Girolamo Donà both argued that the Council's stringent controls to ensure true patrician ancestry guaranteed the virtue of the Venetian political body. Morosini's *De Rebus ac Forma reipublicae venetiae* ('On the substance and form of the Venetian republic') connected the Barbarella lottery for council membership to an unbroken tradition of legitimate descent going back to the founding of the city, and Donà's *Apologia* ('Apology') also linked the careful control of noble identity in the Great Council to the natural virtue and nobility of the Venetian patriciate, which allowed Venice to expand its 'just and legitimate' republican empire.[39] Both Morosini and Donà were writing in response to princely detractors who repeatedly defamed Venetian virtue, casting the republicans as low-born merchants with a boundless appetite for territorial expansion.[40] In response, Morosini and Donà both highlighted the Great Council as the continuous embodiment of Venetian virtue and its electoral mechanisms as protecting against corruption.

Contarini and Giannotti inherited a long textual tradition that asserted the virtue of the Venetian system — a virtue that fifteenth-century humanist authors saw as beginning with the wise founders of the city and preserved by the mechanics of its governing councils.[41] In their presentation of institutional arrangements as a sort of mechanised virtue, these fifteenth-century Venetian writers were out of step with what James Hankins has recently identified as a main current of thought in Italian humanist circles: virtue politics.[42] Hankins contends that most of Italy's leading political thinkers in the fifteenth century turned away from a focus on institutions and pointed to humanist education as the path to creating a virtuous ruling class. In Hankins's formulation, it was not

until the Machiavellian political revolution of the early sixteenth century that the power of institutions was again recognized as a potential path to reform. 'Refounding laws, customs, and institutions — not improving individual human character — was Machiavelli's principal avenue to the reform of Italian government in his time'.[43] While Hankins's analysis does not focus on Venice, his work offers a new interpretative key for understanding the widespread popularity of Contarini's and Giannotti's works on the Venetian constitution. If the Venetians had been out of step with the main currents of Italian humanist thinking in the fifteenth century, representing an alternative to virtue politics, their longstanding emphasis on institutions perfectly positioned them to capture Italian and international interest in the sixteenth.

Indeed, by the mid-sixteenth century, Venice's version of virtuous politics – as represented in the idealised space of the Great Council – was something Europeans wanted to see as well as read about. From the 1540s on, elites had access to Giannotti's and Contarini's works in Latin, Italian, and French editions; after the 1560s, visitors to the city could read Sansovino's guidebook and see the Great Council Hall through Forlani's engraving. European attention to Venice's Great Council was intensified by the dramatic events of 1577, when a fire in the Ducal Palace gutted the Hall, destroying the room's decorative programme and the chancery's notarial archives. The Flemish artist, botanical illustrator, and mapmaker Georg Hoefnagel produced an engraving to illustrate the conflagration which appeared in the popular *Civitates orbis terrarum*, a multi volume compendium with maps and views of over five hundred cities around the world.[44] Sansovino was part of the debate on how to rebuild the space; he argued that the building should be rebuilt as it was, the perspective that ultimately prevailed (fig. 3.4).

Once restored, the Great Council Hall remained a point of interest for tourists and armchair travellers alike. The Florentine monk Girolamo Bardi, who collaborated on the visual programme of new paintings in the Great Council

3.5

Giacomo Franco, *Ducal Palace*. Engraving from Id., *Habiti d'huomeni et donne venetiane con la processione della Ser.ma Signoria ed altri particolari*, 1614. Photo: BnF, Gallica. Reproduced with permission.

Hall, also composed a guide to the decorative programme; Bardi's descriptions of the paintings were printed together with the later version of Sansovino's revised guidebook, suggesting visitors were the intended audience for the work.[45] Like Sansovino's guidebook, the book's detailed explanations of the paintings' subjects and themes evoke the space of the Great Council Hall in the mind's eye, creating a vivid visual picture of embodied republican action that could be experienced through text or image at a distance (fig. 3.5).

Venice's flourishing print industry suggests that by the turn of the seventeenth century, images of the Great Council Hall as an emblem of Venice's unusual political life were part and parcel of what the city's visitors and viewers expected to see.[46] Giacomo Franco was one of the most prominent printmakers and print publishers of his generation; he sold prints out of his shop on the busy Frezzerie, positioned to attract the attention of passing tourists.[47] His most popular work, *Habiti d'huomeni et donne venetiane*, includes a wide variety of images from Venetian life: Venetians and visitors can be seen racing gondolas, battling on bridges, marching in ceremonial processions, and hunting ducks in the lagoon.[48] The book included both an interior and an exterior view of the Great Council Hall; in the exterior image, patricians are engaged in discussion in front of the distinctive façade. The caption identifies the building as the place where Venetian magistrates debated and decided the matters of state. The interior image is broadly similar to Forlani's 1566 depiction: rows of patricians appear as orderly as an ornamental garden, with the doge and his councillors on a platform at the head of the room, and ballotini passing through the rows collecting votes. The caption specifies that the room is decorated with beautiful paintings, although the only ones visible in the engraving are the ducal portraits near the ceiling and Tintoretto's *Paradise* over the ducal seat. This pair of images reproduces the

3.6

Giacomo Franco, *The Great Council*. Engraving from Id., *Habiti d'huomeni et donne venetiane con la processione della Ser.ma Signoria ed altri particolari*, 1614. Photo: BnF, Gallica. Reproduced with permission.

insider/outsider perspective seen in both Sansovino's guidebook and in Contarini's and Gianotti's treatises (fig. 3.6).

If we return to the 1631 Elzevier engraving, it is clear that the image draws on earlier visual depictions of Venetian elections as well as on Contarini's and Giannotti's textual descriptions. In a final twist, the Elsevier images first associated with the commentary on Giannotti's text were detached from their original context and re-used in the De la Court brothers' *Politike Weegschaal* (Political Balance) in 1662.[49] De La Court's defence of republican systems of government took Venice as a model; he connected the equality of the Venetian patriciate to the incorruptibility of its electoral procedures, saying that once fair and anonymous voting procedures were in place, 'without much ado, all other good measures and laws leading to a good police, finance, militia, defence etc. can be proposed and worked out'.[50] While the scope of this chapter does not allow for in-depth investigation of painted depictions of Venetian politics, it is worth noting that Joseph Heintz the Younger's painting of an election in the Great Council Hall closely resembles the earlier printed images discussed above, with the addition of detailed reproductions of the paintings on the walls and ceiling.[51] These seventeenth-century illustrations added to textual descriptions of the Venetian government, entangling Venetian electoral practices, representative spaces of republicanism, and broader considerations of constitutional theory (fig. 3.7).

This chapter has argued that the entanglement of text and image in the sixteenth century contributed to the creation of a fixed representation of Venetian politics in elite European minds. The degree to which these impressions had become standardised by the seventeenth century is demonstrated by the moment of mockery in James Harrington's *The Commonwealth of Oceana* (1656). The book is an explication of an ideal republican constitution; at one point, the lord Epimonus de

3.7
Joseph Heintz the Younger, *The interior of the Sala del Maggior Consiglio, Ducal Palace, Venice, with patricians voting on a bulletin for the election of new magistrates.*
Photo: Public Domain.

Garrula, one of the characters of the book, announces that he has been to Venice and seen an election in the Great Council. He was surprised by the silence of the proceedings, and goes on 'but there is such a pudder with their marching and counter-marching as, though never a one of them draw a sword, you would think they were training; which til I found that they did it only to entertain strangers, I came from among them as wise as I went hither'.[52] Harrington's satire turns the Venetian reputation for decorum and order on its head; what is most relevant in this context is that the passage's humour depends on a widespread familiarity with the way Venetians typically conducted elections. Both the direct experience of travel and the indirect experiences of reading treatises contributed to this awareness: travel and reading were entwined with visualisations of republican space to create an enduring representation of Venetian politics.

1. Gordon, *Controlling the State*, pp. 129–62.
2. Contarini, *The Republic of Venice*; Giannotti, *Opere Politiche*, I, pp. 29–151.
3. Fragnito, 'Contarini, Gasparo', p. 28; Marconi, 'Giannotti, Donato', p. 54. For individual treatments and further bibliography, see Gleason, *Gasparo Contarini*; Bowd, '"The Tune Is Marred"'; Soldini, 'Les républiques de Donato Giannotti'. For works considering the two texts together, see Cozzi, 'Cultura politica e religione'; Gilbert, 'The date of the composition of Contarini's and Giannotti's books on Venice'; Bouwsma, *Venice and the Defense of Republican Liberty*, pp. 145–60; Pocock, *The Machiavellian Moment*, pp. 272–327; see the important critique in Pecchioli, *Dal 'mito' di Venezia all''ideologia americana'*; Silvano, *La 'Republica de' Viniziani'*, pp. 39–120;
4. For fifteenth century ideas of Venice as an ideal government, see Toffolo, *Describing the City*, pp. 148–69; for later periods, see Fink, *The Classical Republicans*, pp. 28–41; Bouwsma, 'Venice and the Political Education of Europe'; Haitsma Mulier, *The Myth of Venice*; Rosand, *Myths of Venice*.
5. Nuti, 'Alle origini del Grand Tour', pp. 3–54.
6. Giannotti, *Dialogi de Repub. Venetorum*, pp. 404–16; Conti, 'The Mechanization of Virtue', pp. 73–83.
7. Povolo, 'Crasso, Nicolò', p. 30.
8. All digitised editions of the 1631 *Dialogi* do not include the illustrations.
9. Traister, *The Elsevier Republics*, p. 2; Conti, *Consociatio civitatum*.
10. Contarini, *Casparis Contareni patricii Veneti, de Republica Venetorum*; Traister, *The Elsevier Republics*, pp. 18–19.
11. Conti, 'Mechanization of Virtue', p. 82.
12. Van Cootwijck, *Itinerarium Hierosolymitanum et Syriacum*; Haitsma Mulier, *The Myth of Venice*, p. 60.
13. Bouwsma, 'Venice and the Political Education of Europe', pp. 445–66; Pocock, *The Machiavellian Moment*, pp. 272–327; see the important critique in Pecchioli, *Dal 'mito' di Venezia all''ideologia americana'*; Silvano, *La 'Republica de' Viniziani'*, pp. 39–120.
14. For overviews of Contarini's role in the extensive literature on the 'myth of Venice', see Sabetti, 'Introduction', pp. XXXVIV–XLII; Toffolo, *Describing the City*, pp. 148–49.
15. Entangled history emerged in the 1990s as a response to the problems of comparative history. For an overview and further references, see Kocka, 'Comparison and Beyond'; Burson, 'Entangled History', pp. 3–4.
16. Contarini, *The Republic of Venice*, p. 18.
17. Contarini, *The Republic of Venice*, p. 18.
18. Contarini, *The Republic of Venice*, pp. 22–23.
19. Gilmore, 'Myth and Reality in Venetian Political Theory', p. 435; Bouwsma, *Venice and the Defense of Republican Liberty*, pp. 157–58.
20. Giannotti, *Opere Politiche*, I, p. 75.
21. Gleason, *Gasparo Contarini*, pp. 1–74; Bowd, 'The Republic of Ideas'.
22. Soldini, 'Les républiques de Donato Giannotti', pp. 13–113; Gilbert, 'The Venetian Constitution in Florentine Political Thought', p. 497.
23. Contarini, *Gasparis Contareni cardinalis opera*.
24. Cited and translated in Bowd, '"The Tune Is Marred"', p. 83.
25. Florio, '"So Flourishing a Commonwealth"'.
26. Soldini, 'Les républiques de Donato Giannotti', pp. 9, 123–70.
27. Contarini and others, *Della republica et magistrati di Venetia*.
28. Redford, *Venice & the Grand Tour*. Sabetti, 'Introduction', p. XVII; Pezzini, 'Notes on the translation', p. XLIX.
29. Davis and Marvin, *Venice, the Tourist Maze*, p. 32; De Vivo, *Information and Communication in Venice*, pp. 40–45.
30. Sansovino, *Sansovino's Venice*.
31. Sansovino, *Sansovino's Venice*, p. 77.
32. Sansovino, *Sansovino's Venice*, pp. 77–78.
33. Sansovino, *Sansovino's Venice*, p. 78.
34. Sansovino, *Sansovino's Venice*, p. 93.
35. Forlani, *Il Gran Consiglio di Venetia*; Franzoi and Leonardi, *Il Palazzo Ducale di Venezia*, pp. 66–67; for context, see Bury, *The Print in Italy*, pp. 170–80.
36. Woodward, 'Paolo Forlani'.
37. Contarini, *The Republic of Venice*, p. 26.
38. Giannotti, *Opere Politiche*, I, p. 71.
39. Morosini, 'De rebus ac forma reipublicae venetae', p. 247; Dona's *Apologia* is published in Malipiero and Dolfin, 'Annali veneti dall'anno 1457 al 1500', p. 458; also seen in manuscript in the BMV, Ms. It. VII 913 (8591), fols. 276–89 and in the BAV, Ottob. lat. 1889.
40. The insults Morosini was responding to were likely those of Pius II, who was incensed over the Venetian seizure of Cervia; Donà was responding to a publicly circulated letter from the King of France Charles VIII. For discussion of texts and contexts, see King, *Venetian Humanism*, pp. 46 and 132–40; on hostile views of Venice, see Rubenstein, 'Italian reactions to terraferma expansion'.
41. Robey and Law, 'The Venetian myth and the *De Republica Venetia* of Pier Paolo Vergerio'; Gaeta, 'Storiografia, coscienza nazionale e politica culturale'.
42. Hankins, *Virtue Politics*.
43. Hankins, *Virtue Politics*, p. 466.
44. Nuti, 'Alle origini del Grand Tour', p. 28; the engraving depends on an earlier painting of the event.
45. Sansovino, *Delle cose notabili della città di Venetia*.
46. Van der Sman, 'Print Publishing in Venice in the Second Half of the Sixteenth Century'.
47. Stefani, 'Franco, Giacomo'.
48. Franco, *Habiti d'huomeni et donne venetiane*; Franzoi, *Il Palazzo Ducale di Venezia*, pp. 68–71.
49. Conti, 'Mechanization of Virtue', p. 82; Haitsma Mulier, *The Myth of Venice*, pp. 151–52.
50. Cited and translated in Haitsma Mulier, *The Myth of Venice*, pp. 152–53; Weststeijn, *Commercial Republicanism in the Dutch Golden Age*.
51. Joseph Heintz the Younger, *The interior of the sala Maggior Consiglio, The Doge's Palace, Venice, with patricians voting on a bulletin for the election of new magistrates*; for seventeenth and eighteenth century printed images of the space, see Franzoi, *Il Palazzo Ducale di Venezia*, pp. 83, 87, 92, 103–04.
52. Harrington, *The Commonwealth of Oceana*, p. 114; for analysis on Venice in seventeenth century British political thought, see Eglin, *Venice Transfigured*.

4

Massimo Rospocher

'UNA PAROLA IN PIAZZA FA PIÙ MALE CHE DIECI LIBRI IN UN GABINETTO'

The Square as Political Space in Sixteenth-Century Venice

In the early modern period, Venice was a crucial node in a global communication network and major crossroad linking Europe, Asia, and Africa. Venice was one of the most densely populated metropolises in the world; it was a city of water and land, of goods and people, of books and papers but also of sounds, voices, and words. Also because of its peculiar urban geography, with a dense architectural texture that favoured gatherings and exchanges of opinions, Venice has proved to be a privileged site of investigation for the ephemeral, informal, and daily dimension of politics.[1]

This chapter seeks to analyse the political functions of the main Venetian urban public space, the square. By offering a place where heterogeneous groups of people could assemble, the square shaped the political identity of the city. The aim of the chapter is to investigate the role of the piazza as an everyday political space in the Republic of Venice during the long sixteenth century. As a locus of both the celebration and the contestation of republican power, as a multifunctional urban place and a space of political interaction between the government and the people, this chapter argues that the piazza epitomises the physical and metaphorical representation of early modern popular politics.

Space and (popular) politics

In the last two decades, historical research has taken yet another historiographical turn: the so-called 'spatial turn'. This label evokes the attitude to consider the spatial dimension that is shared by humanities and social sciences, as a result of the reception of seminal works by urban geographers and sociologists such as Henri Lefebvre and Edward Soja.[2] The study of space has also had an undeniable impact on the new political history, contributing to renewing the debate on the emergence of the public sphere and leading to a greater interest in its physical dimension.[3]

For early modern historians, the notion of political space has received increasing attention in studies interested in actors, structures, and practices of political processes.[4] This approach has generated an increased focus on the materiality of the pre-modern political spaces where exchanges took place and opinions flowed. A new political topography has emerged which includes both informal and institutional spaces, squares and palaces, vernacular and official places.[5] Alongside the 'official' political dimension of palaces and courts, this historiography has highlighted the existence of political practices in theatres of everyday life such as squares, barbershops, alehouses, markets, printshops, and coffeehouses. By considering space not just as a passive backdrop but as an active component of socio-political identities, recent research has reconstructed a new historical morphology of the early modern European public sphere. In this broad historiographical framework, the city and Republic of Venice have been the focus of various analyses highlighting the political function of public spaces such as pharmacies, inns, and squares, where men (and occasionally women) could gather and exchange rumours, news, and information or discuss politics.[6]

In addition to new political spaces, the spatial approach has brought to light new political actors, revealing a wide and heterogeneous public interested in early modern politics. Focusing on informal rather than official political spaces, research on urban and popular politics has shown that the social actors on the political scene in early modern Europe came not only from the ruling elites but also from the classes excluded from the direct management of power.[7] Many of these studies have also focused on the ephemeral dimension of orality. The voices of shopkeepers, merchants, notaries, or artisans have been analysed for their contributions to public political debate in different European contexts: from Flanders to Castile, from England to the Italian republics and city-states, from Papal Rome to the Kingdom of Naples.[8] With respect to the Venetian Republic, this has resulted in particular attention to the social category of the *popolani* and recognition of their function as political actors.[9] In the context of the spatial turn, this chapter explores the analytical potential of space as a tool for investigating popular politics in the Republic of Venice.

An ambivalent space: the piazza as a stage of power

The square was the centre around which the political, religious, and social life of the urban community revolved. Yet while the disordered medieval square emerged 'from below', the geometrical Renaissance piazza was modelled 'from above', as an architectural symbol of political authority. The creation of a central public space in the urban topography was itself a political act performed by authorities who carved out their own public stage within the city. Fifteenth-century architectural treatises established the canons of the physical and symbolic centrality of the square in the urban ecosystem.[10]

The Renaissance square combined an urban space and its ideal representation, a material place and its archetype. Alessandro Fontana wrote that the sixteenth-century piazza was 'no longer a real space, a space for civic, religious and commercial activities, but a logical structure, a mental form'.[11] More than a physical site, the main public space became a representative *topos*, 'a theatre for ideal spectators', a 'portrait', 'a true image', 'an idea': this is how Tomaso Garzoni presented to his contemporaries his *Piazza Universale* (1585), on whose stage 'all the professions of the world' are paraded.[12]

Many studies on Renaissance rituals have focused on the representative function of public spaces.[13] Seen from this perspective, the piazza was the ceremonial stage of authority, the outdoor extension of the court, the site where power was acclaimed. The classical triumphs celebrated in the Renaissance by princes and pontiffs, republics and monarchies culminated in the main square. In these rituals, it has been argued, 'the citizen was no longer the actor of the medieval ceremonies, an active and responsible participant in the processions, but the passive spectator of the manifestations of the display of power'.[14] At the height of the urban rationalisation process imposed by authorities, the sixteenth-century piazza 'no longer belongs to the city, but is merely the exterior, the extension and pendant of the court's inner courtyard; expropriated from the citizens, it is no longer more than a 'symbolic' space, the abstract place of princely power'.[15] Taken to its extreme, this definition of the square as a 'neutral' space in which the citizenry was merely the passive receiver of demonstrations of power, would reify Habermas's idea of an early modern purely 'representative public sphere'.

Within Venice's spatial hierarchy, St Mark's area represented the political and religious core of the ceremonial city: it was the central urban and symbolic space, positioned to convey the 'myth' of the Republic.[16] The city's highly choreographed governmental rituals and religious processions culminated in the square and constituted the most striking manifestation of its ceremonial dimension. The public which gathered in this main urban space shared the perception of being part of an 'imagined community', based on a common identity (linguistic, political, or ideological).[17] The piazza was thus a place of 'communal imagination' and 'invention': 'whether it were a public holiday or a weekday, the texts and iconography show it repeatedly, the Venetians are there, coming and going, walking and talking, as if attracted by the socio-symbolic power of an identity space whose meaning consisted in being the space of all the spaces in their city'.[18]

While recognizing the ceremonial dimension of the city's main public space, the role of the urban crowds cannot be reduced to that of passive spectators of politics. Indeed, it is precisely the study of civic rituals in Renaissance Italy that has shown how the people participated as active political protagonists, sometimes reappropriating ceremonies and spaces of power in the most unforeseen ways.[19] Within the spatial dialectic between rulers and ruled, the square appears to be the space 'of the unexpected'.[20] That was the case, for example, when in April 1512 the triumphal procession held in Venice to celebrate the victory of the troops of the Holy League against the French was interrupted by the arrival of a fishing boat at St Mark's *molo*, the quay facing the lagoon at the edge of the Piazzetta. The fisherman brought breaking news about the outcome of the Battle of Ravenna, announcing the victory of the French and turning the official jubilation into collective despair.[21] Sometimes, public rituals were disrupted by violence. This was the case in 1521, when the distribution of coins (*sparsio*) to the population gathered in the square by the newly elected doge Antonio Grimani was abruptly interrupted. This was because a foreigner had chopped off the head of an Arsenal worker who, employed as a guardian of public order, was leading the way to the *pozzetto* ('sedan chair') where the doge sat during the ceremony.[22] Another disruption of a public ritual on 7 April 1595 is perhaps less gruesome but, in terms of political significance, even more dramatic: young boys and common people interrupted the funeral procession for the eighty-sixth doge of the Republic, Pasquale Cicogna, by shouting the name of one of his prospective successors ('viva, viva, Marino Grimani!'), and throwing the solemn ritual into disarray.[23] The population did not limit itself to words but also destroyed the material elements making up the square, such as 'some of the market stalls and covered stands erected on the piazza [...], while also demolishing the benches of various palace tribunals'.[24]

The model of a representative public sphere, in which the population merely attends the spectacle of the magnificence of power, does not explain the multiplicity of interactions between a broad political public and the authorities. Above all, it is the hybridity and multifunctional character of the square that makes it difficult to circumscribe it as a mere scenographic arena for staging the magnificence of power. In the early modern period, sources describe the prosopopoeia of the square, which becomes a political subject with its own, often dissident, voice. As a 'place of invention' and 'space of the unexpected', the square is thus an ambivalent space: it is not only the stage for a *repräsentative Öffentlichkeit*, but also the political space for the constant process of negotiation that took place between the authorities and their subjects.

A theatre of everyday life: the piazza as a space of interaction

The square was therefore not the ideal, empty, geometrically perfect space described in the treatises of Renaissance urban planners; it was instead a space of political and social interaction,[25] constantly transformed by the swarming presence of the people who lived it daily. As Stephen Milner has shown for Piazza della Signoria in Florence, the stone benches scattered around the piazza, outdoor and under the Loggia dei Lanzi, were everyday spaces of sociability and political discussion used by people of all ranks: patricians and artists, clerics and artisans, governments officials and vagrants.[26] Despite the tendency of authorities to rationalise the main civic space, the Renaissance square remained a 'practised place', according to Michel De Certeau's definition, the theatre of a dynamic and socially differentiated public sphere.[27]

Rather than a static entity imposed from above, the square was the dynamic product of the interactions among architecture, material objects, and social actors, designed as much by the authorities as by the everyday actions of those passing through it. In Venice, the built environment of St Mark's was identified with the body public: the square was the people. Marvelling at the diverse crowds crammed into the square ('neither sex, nor age, nor station, was missing'), the poet Francesco Petrarca was fascinated by how the piazza 'dissolved into the unseen substructure of a revealing body politic that spilled across its architectural surfaces'.[28] Petrarca described the unity of the built space and the people during public rituals: 'It would be impossible to say how full the square was of people' ('Come fosse piena la piazza di popolo sarebbe impossibile il dirlo'), such that 'a grain of millet could not have fallen to earth; the huge square, the church itself, the towers, roofs, porches, windows were not only filled but packed. An incalculable and incredible crowd of people covered the face of the earth'.[29] In December 1509, after attending a public execution, Marin Sanudo used a similar expression to conceive the Piazza as a space that personified the city's *popolo*: 'The square was full of *popolo*, so that I can say this: I have never seen so many *popolo*'.[30]

In addition to hosting the large crowds that assembled to participate in civic rituals, the square was also the site of smaller and more spontaneous gatherings. These could be small groups of people (the so called *bozzoli*)[31] who gathered for different reasons, such as entertainment or business. Those occasions would also be characterised by lively discussions about new taxes or the latest political and military events. Sometimes these exchanges could escalate into violence. This was the case in July 1512, when a young boy selling printed political ballads in St Mark's Square was attacked by 'a partisan of the French'. According to the latter, the boy's verses had fuelled a rumour throughout the city that Louis XII's army had been defeated by the English. The 'French partisan' attacked the boy, stole his pamphlets, and disappeared.[32] Sometimes larger crowds would spontaneously assemble to hear news from the Holy Land, to celebrate military triumphs or collectively commiserate over a defeat, or to listen to the performances of street singers or the announcements of a town crier. Thus, in the months following the military disaster suffered by the Serenissima at Agnadello (1509), interest in the evolution of current political events favoured the manifestation of a conjunctural and 'evanescent public sphere' which encompassed not only the official spaces of political debate but also informal ones, such as squares, streets, churches, inns, and markets.[33] 'Now all the world is talking about war, /and singing, writing, and speaking about Venice, /debating only this in the churches and the piazzas'[34], commented an anonymous street singer. Popular ballads on the war were recited and sold for 'a penny' in the crucial passageways of social and economic life: 'in the squares and over the Rialto Bridge', where the people gathered to exchange information.[35]

Despite periodic attempts by the procurators to regulate it and by architects to rationalise it, in sixteenth-century Venice St Mark's Square was a space that was anything but silent, controlled, or exclusive to the celebration of power.[36] The scenic majesty of St Mark's Square should therefore not deceive us about the site's real nature as a 'practised space', whose hybrid function was determined by the many activities that took place there and by the voices or sounds characterising its daily life. All these activities interacted with its architectural context and define the identity of that space, marking it as a political, social, or ritual site. Though the heart of the ceremonial city, St Mark's Square was also the social space par excellence, animated by the presence of meat and fruit shops, taverns, and bakeries as well as by the activities of charlatans, street performers, and news writers. Given its multifunctionality, the St Mark's area was described throughout the sixteenth century as 'more akin to an Arab souk than to the forecourt of Versailles'.[37] Foreign travellers described with admiration the sequence of four or five stages that were set up daily in front of the Basilica for performances by charlatans and ballad singers, while other entertainers 'of the poorer sort' were relegated to the Piazzetta.[38] Hundreds of people gathered around these stages. It was also possible to attend other kinds of performances in the same urban space, including the grammar and philosophy lessons given by humanists that could be attended 'near the bell tower', where 'there are two men paid by St Mark's, very learned in humanities, who read publicly to those who want to hear them without paying any fee, and they are men of great renown'.[39] The different uses of the piazza and other public spaces, where education, entertainment, and information seeking collided, were evoked by Tomaso Garzoni in the late sixteenth century. He painted a moralising portrait of the 'idle people' (*gente ociosa*) who made a completely different use of the square than the one envisaged by the authorities and who could be seen 'strolling through the square, and going from the taverns to the fishmongers, and from the palace to the loggia, doing nothing else all day long but wandering here and there, now listening to street singers, [...] now sitting in some barbershop counting tales and jokes, now reading the news'.[40]

Representations of the square as a place for the spontaneous gatherings of heterogeneous publics continued throughout the sixteenth century. The recurring image of the piazza as a dynamic social sphere is complemented by the *topos* of Venice as a microcosm of the world. Aldo Manuzio defines the square as *Orbis magis quam Urbs* in his preface to the works of Angelo Poliziano that was addressed to Marin Sanudo;[41] Luigi Groto struggles to distinguish 'whether Venice is in the world, or the world is in Venice'.[42] Equally topical is the representation of St Mark's Square as the centre of the world. In the words of an early seventeenth-century English traveller, which echoes those of Manuzio, the flow of people in St Mark's Square was so impressive that it would have been better to call it 'Orbis rather than Urbis forum'.[43]

Protest and control:
the piazza as a space of dissent

According to the Florentine humanist Giovanni Cavalcanti, 'Whoever holds sway over the piazza always controls the city':[44] control of the square was a necessary precondition for maintaining power and preventing conflicts. The square was a powerful catalyst for dissent,[45] not only because it aggregated various social strata within one architectural space but also because of its acoustic qualities, which doubled the power of the sounds and words spoken there. This was a communicative power of which the seventeenth-century writer and satirist Gregorio Leti was fully aware: in one of his piercing dialogues, Leti wrote that 'a word in the piazza does more harm than ten books in a cabinet'.[46]

While seditions and popular revolts were rare events in Venice, since the city's morphology made it difficult for the people to gather rapidly, the latent fear of their occurrence was constant throughout the sixteenth century. Precisely

4.1
Giovan Antonio Canal (Canaletto), *The church of San Giacomo di Rialto, Venice*, 2nd third of the 18th century. © Gemäldegalerie Alte Meister, Staatliche Kunstsammlungen Dresden. Photo: Hans-Peter Klut.

because of its communicative and symbolic value, St Mark's Square was strictly guarded, and crimes committed there carried aggravated penalties.[47] In times of civic tension, the authorities took extraordinary security measures to prevent any disorder in the city's public spaces. The early summer of 1509 was one such moment: fears were growing that the doge might become an object of contention at public ceremonies, and there were doubts as to whether the ritual of Corpus Domini, traditionally celebrated in the St Mark's area, should be held. In the end, those who believed the ancient ritual should be continued prevailed, but a proclamation was published stating that bearing arms would be considered a capital offence, and teams of armed guards were placed at all the crossroads of the *calli* surrounding St Mark's Square to protect the supreme Venetian magistracy.[48] Historical sources suggest an anthropomorphic representation of the piazza. For an anonymous fourteenth-century Florentine chronicler, the narrow access to the main piazza were 'mouths' (*bocche*): they acted as a filter and could be closed to prevent undesirable people from entering. The homology between the physical closure of these narrow urban corridors and the silencing of dissenting voices here is evident.[49]

Because it symbolises the city community as a collective political subject, the piazza acquires its own voice, which often expresses dissent. Statements that the piazza 'murmurs, whispers, shouts, cries' were recurrent in the writings of Venetian diarists. Yet the voice of the square could also manifest itself through 'written voices', such as manuscript flyers or printed placards scattered in the streets, posted on palaces, loggias, and columns or through polemical writings carved with charcoal on the walls of public and private buildings. These episodes recur in literary sources and criminal registers and are evidence of the criticisms citizens and *popolani* harboured against the patriciate. Indeed, a constant flow of insulting writings with political content appeared in the public spaces of the lagoon city. In 1492 defamatory libels against magistrates of the Republic were plastered on the columns of St Mark's Square; in 1497 defamatory posters were affixed to the Ducal Palace and the Basilica; in 1498 other insults against patrician magistrates appeared on the walls of the Ducal Palace, in the piazza, and at the Rialto market.[50] In 1499, after the Ottomans' defeat of the Venetians in the naval battle of Zonchio, graffiti appearing on walls and writings posted on shop doors attacked the *capitano generale da mar* Antonio Grimani: 'Antonio Grimani, / rebel against the Venetians!'. Popular discontent was so widespread that children echoed this dissent, running through the streets singing these acerbic verses: 'Antonio Grimani, / ruin of the Christians / rebel against the Venetians / may you be eaten by dogs'.[51] In April 1500, a poster in the Piazza openly accused the entire republican government of not doing enough in the fight against the Turks.[52] In November 1505, insulting placards against doge Leonardo Loredan were attached to the walls and columns of the church of San Giacomo di Rialto (fig. 4.1) and the Ducal Palace.[53] In March 1514, several handwritten bills were found along the Mercerie inciting people to revolt against the Venetian patriciate in *Terraferma* and wishing 'Death to these thieving Venetian tyrants'.[54] This phenomenon was particularly intense during the dramatic period of the Italian wars, but it continued throughout the sixteenth century. In March 1574, for example, a manifesto was put up on the door of St Mark's Basilica. The author was a goldsmith who intended to stir the 'Venetian people' to revolt against the tyranny of 'nobles and merchants' with the aim of obtaining the 'mutation' of the republican form of government.[55] Disregarding these oral and written voices meant exposing oneself to the risk of revolt. The Venetian authorities were vigilant and reacted by trying to control the practices of dissent that were manifested in the main public space also by intervening from a legislative point of view.[56]

The square is a space of potential contestation and dissent, but also the theatre of consensus and the place where the repressive side of power also materialises. In Venice, though the merchant Girolamo Priuli did not consider the measures adopted by the Council of Ten to be as effective as in the past – when 'everyone used to hold his tongue behind his teeth for fear'[57] – the authorities made every effort to punish the crimes of *lesae maiestatis* that occurred in the main public spaces. In January 1511, an investigation was opened by the Venetian magistracies to uncover the instigators of the protest that occurred on the island of Murano when the outgoing *podestà* was subjected to insulting verses, as well as the target of snowballs, in the public square.[58] In November 1511, the barber Bernardino Malizia was hoisted onto a platform between the two columns in the Piazzetta, between the Ducal Palace and the Basilica, and his tongue was cut out for having spoken defamatory words against the state.[59] In October 1547, in Brescia, the local Venetian authorities reacted harshly to a lame poultry seller who protested against the paving of the Piazza della Loggia, which implied the expropriation of his wooden stall. In that same public space, he had shouted slogans in favour of the emperor and against the rectors, inciting the people to anti-Venetian rebellion: '"Empire! Empire! And kill the Venetian rectors!"'.[60] The itinerant poultry seller was hanged by order of the Venetian *podestà*.

During the sixteenth century, in Venice, as in other Italian cities, there were attempts to institutionalise forms of control over the political discourse circulating in the main public spaces. In Bologna and Florence, for example, wooden boxes (*tamburi*) were set up to receive secret complaints, often concerning acts, writings and words derogatory to the state.[61] A similar system operated in Venice: before the instalment of the more permanent, well-crafted stone-carvings shaped as lions' mouths (*bocche di leone*), by the mid-sixteenth century the Venetian authorities installed wooden post-boxes (*casselle*) for anonymous or eponymous denunciations. These were located in prominent public sites around the city and the wider Veneto area, usually on the walls of entrances to state buildings or outside churches.[62]

The square was a source of concern not only for civic authorities but also for the religious powers. The piazza was

the nexus of a struggle for control not just of physical but also of cultural, political, and religious space. In the same physical space, learned and popular, sacred and profane, secular and clerical, orthodox and heterodox culture were dangerously mixed. During the sixteenth century, for instance, street singers and preachers competed for control of the main public space in Italian cities.[63] In the booksellers' stalls in St Mark's Square, it was possible to find all kinds of printed items, as testified in 1549 by a scribe questioned by the Holy Office, who admitted to having purchased forbidden books under the Clock Tower and arcades of the Piazza.[64] In the second half of the sixteenth century, the theatres of urban public debate were also monitored more strictly by the religious authorities. In 1553, the bishop of Verona, Alvise Lippomano, expressed concern that religious issues were being discussed in public spaces among the popular crowds (persone basse), 'in the squares, in the shops, in the taverns and even in the women's outdoor wash-houses'.[65] The functions of consensus and dissent, interaction and repression, aggregation and surveillance thus constantly overlapped in the square.

Between the palace and the piazza

Francesco Guicciardini states that 'between the palace and the piazza there is often such a thick fog, or such a high wall, that the human eye is unable to discern anything. When that is the case, the people will know as much about the actions of those in government and the reasons behind their decisions as they do about what is happening in India; and for this reason, the world is easily filled with erroneous and idle opinions'.[66] Guicciardini's aphorism entails a division between institutional (palazzi) and informal political spaces (piazze), between the secret and the public, between the government and the people. But was the separation between piazza and palazzo really so strong as to make them incommunicable?

Renaissance republican political imaginary tends to highlight, and often to idealise, the porous nature of these two arenas. The definition of 'parliament' (parlamento) given by Guicciardini in his Storia d'Italia as 'a congregation of all the citizens assembled in the piazza in front of the Communal Palace, at which time, they deliberate in open discussion

4.2
Detail of 4.1, featuring paper leaves put up on the columns.

on proposals put forward by the chief magistracy'[67] emphasises the interaction between the political space of the piazza and that of the civic palace. In republican contexts, this interaction also led to the formation of political institutions: the creation of the *Consiglio Maggiore* in Florence (1494), for example, was nothing other than a shift from the *piazza* to the *palazzo* of the manifestation of the people's opinion, also with the aim of controlling popular actions. However instrumental it might have been, political commentators of the period did not fail to note the weight given to the piazza in the decisions of rulers. Indeed, the very attitude of the Florentine magistrates had given rise to the popular saying that these institutional figures had 'one soul in the square, and one in the palace' ('uno animo in piazza, ed uno in palazzo').[68] This association also became tangible in the architectural elements characterising the squares of many Italian cities. This is reflected, for example, by the loggias of public palaces or the *ringhiera*, a raised platform of civic palaces facing the main square, which both marked passage of political decisions from the secrecy of government rooms to the public dimension of the square. These material constructs represented a 'filter through which the relation of governors to governed was negotiated'.[69]

Historiography has shown that the voices and discussions coming from the squares did not merely contribute to legitimising decisions elaborated within the palaces of power. In Venice too, the political interaction between *piazza* and *palazzo* could take place in different forms and was more or less institutionalised. The murmuring ('mormoratione') of the piazza – widespread criticism or polemical rumour — appears as one of the protagonists of political chronicles of the Republic. In a letter to the Council of Ten (1531), Marin Sanudo recalled that in order to be able to write the 'truth' in his chronicle he had 'routinely been to the piazzas to investigate every fact, even if it was only minor details'.[70] This idea was echoed by Girolamo Priuli, who declared that in his diaries he had described 'what was said in the squares'.[71] The nobility was encouraged to frequent not only semi-official political spaces such as the 'broglio', the Piazzetta in front of the Ducal Palace, but also places of contact between institutional politics and the everyday life of those excluded from institutions.[72] In his manual on the *Perfetto gentil'huomo* (1584), Aldo Manuzio il Giovane explicitly invited young Venetian patricians to 'follow closely the public squares of St Mark and Rialto'. This practice was part of the political education of the aristocracy: 'because, acting otherwise, he would give the impression of being a man who does not consider public affairs seriously'.[73]

Capturing the mood of the square was an essential skill for a politician, especially in moments of alteration of the political and social body. This was the case in the autumn of 1509 during the post-Agnadello crisis, when a heated public debate regarding the progress of the war took place between some nobles and a group of *popolani*. The latter were required to meet 'in campo', by order of the Senate, to clarify the nature of their dissent against the state, as murmurs flowing through the streets suggested their readiness to revolt.[74] A large number of commoners were then summoned to an 'official' political space, the Great Council hall, and publicly reported for their grievances regarding the nature and limitations of the government.[75] These episodes illustrate the extent to which the Venetian ruling class lived not confined within the secrecy of its own political spaces but rather in contact with the city; it also demonstrates the extent to which the voices and moods of the people were closely monitored. The voice of the square was spontaneous, volatile, unreliable, and often used instrumentally by the rulers; and the evolution of this chatter (*ciance*) needed to be politically considered.

Yet if the 'murmurs' of the square had to be listened to, they were not to be pandered to. Merchant Girolamo Priuli commented on the concerns surrounding uncontrolled circulation of gossip and rumours in the city's most crowded public spaces. In a heartfelt monologue, he polemicized against this constant chatter and the circulation of fake news and false opinions 'in the piazzas, in the loggias, at the Rialto Bridge, in the churches and in barbershops' ('per le piazze, le logge et per Rialto et ecclesie et botege de barbieri'). In his view, this reflected a lack of order, since now 'anyone, of whatever status and condition, was permitted to say whatever he liked and whatever came to his lips, in the piazza and loggias and in every place' ('Hera licito a cada uno, de ogni grado et condictione se fusse, dire quanto li piaceva et che li fusse venuto in bocha et in piazza et in le logiette et per ogni locho').[76] From this perspective, the outward dissemination of information generated in the secret rooms of the Palace to more informal public political spaces ('opinione deli nobelli et populli, dicte in lichi sopradicti') would ultimately lead to chaos and the state's collapse.[77]

Thus even in the 'most serene' Republic, there was fear that the high wall separating the square and the palace would be torn down by popular revolt. This was literally the case in March 1569, when hundreds of angered Arsenal workers invaded the government palace and occupied the Collegio Hall.[78] The thick fog separating the 'people' (*piazza*) from the 'rulers' (*palazzo*) was thereby crossed by voices and political opinions coming from the city's main public spaces and reaching the Ducal Palace. Yet by the end of the seventeenth century, this communication operated in two directions — so much so that Guicciardini's aphorism appeared almost inverted in the words of Gregorio Leti, who noted that in the past 'the people (*popolo*) never knew what the prince was doing, but the prince always knew everything the people did. Things are all reversed at present, because the people know everything the prince does, and the prince nothing of what the people do'.[79]

[1] De Vivo, *Information and Communication in Venice*; Horodowich, *Language and Statecraft in Early Modern Venice*; Rospocher and Salzberg, '"El vulgo zanza"'; Judde de Larivière, *The Revolt of Snowballs*; Van Gelder and Judde de Larivière, eds, *Popular Politics in an Aristocratic Republic*; Van Gelder and De Vivo, 'Papering over Protest'.

[2] Rau, *History, Space, and Place*; Kingston, 'Mind Over Matter?'; Warf and Arias, eds, *The Spatial Turn*; Zeller, 'The Spatial Turn in History', pp. 123–24.

[3] With all its limitations, the concept of the public sphere still maintains a strong heuristic value. See Rospocher, 'Beyond the Public Sphere', pp. 9–28.

[4] Kümin, ed., *Political Space in Pre-industrial Europe*; Williamson, ed., *Locating Agency*.

[5] Scott, 'Preface', p. 2.

[6] Welch, 'Space and Spectacle in the Renaissance Pharmacy'; Judde de Larivière, 'Du Broglio à Rialto'; De Vivo, 'Pharmacies as Centres of Communication'; Salzberg, 'Spaces of unrest?'.

[7] Cohn, *Popular Protest and Ideals of Democracy*.

[8] Dumolyn, Haemers, Oliva Herrer, and Challet, eds, *The Voices of the People in Late Medieval Europe*; Horodowich, 'Speech and Oral Culture'; Dumolyn and Haemers, '"A Bad Chicken was Brooding"'.

[9] Judde de Larivière and Salzberg, 'The People Are the City'.

[10] Kruft, 'L'idea della Piazza rinascimentale'; Calabi, *La città del primo Rinascimento*, pp. 46–76.

[11] Fontana, 'La piazza del Cinquecento come 'topos' rappresentativo', p. 171.

[12] 'Un teatro per spettatori ideali', 'un ritratto e una vera immagine, anzi una espressa idea'; Garzoni, *La Piazza Universale*, I, p. 62.

[13] See for instance Mulryne, De Jonge, Morris, and Martens, eds, *Occasions of State*.

[14] Fontana and Fournel, 'Piazza, Corte, Salotto, Caffè', p. 648.

[15] Fontana, 'La piazza del Cinquecento', p. 166.

[16] Fenlon, *The Ceremonial City*; Morresi, *Piazza San Marco*. On the political uses of public spaces, see Crouzet-Pavan, '"Sopra le Acque Salse"', II, in particular pp. 836–55 and 901–38.

[17] Anderson, *Imagined communities*. See also Milner, 'The Florentine Piazza', p. 84: 'The piazza was such a place of communal imagination through which successive forms of spatial, institutional, social and linguistic order were articulated and contested'.

18. Crouzet-Pavan, *Venezia trionfante*, p. 273.
19. Muir, *Civic Ritual in Renaissance Venice*; Bertelli, *The King's Body*; Casini, *I gesti del principe*.
20. Calabi, *La città del primo Rinascimento*, p. 46.
21. Sanudo, *I diarii*.
22. Casini, 'Rituali e violenza pubblica a Venezia', p. 31.
23. Van Gelder, 'The People's Prince'.
24. Van Gelder, 'The People's Prince', p. 278.
25. The metaphor of the square as a space of political interaction was explored in Bakhtin's work; see Hirschkop, *Mikhail Bakhtin*, pp. 249–71.
26. Elet, 'Seats of Power'.
27. Milner, 'The Florentine Piazza'; De Certeau, *The Practice of Everyday Life*.
28. Atkinson, 'The Italian Piazza', p. 569.
29. Petrarca, *Letters of Old Age*, IV, p. 135.
30. Sanudo, *I diarii*, IX, col. 358.
31. De Vivo, *Information and Communication*, pp. 92–93.
32. Sanudo, *I diarii*, col. 75.
33. Briggs and Burke, *A Social History of the Media*, pp. 61–90; Rospocher and Salzberg, *An Evanescent Public Sphere*, pp. 93–114.
34. 'Hor tuto 'l mondo di guerra ragiona /& di Venetia canta scriue & parla /per chiese & piaze sol questo tenzona'. *Laus Venetorum* (BMV, Misc. 2157.01), fol. 28v.
35. 'Per le piaze e sopra il Ponte d'il Rialto' (Priuli, *I Diarii*, MCV, MS. Prov. Div. 252-c, vol. 5, fol. 55r-v).
36. In 1529, Sansovino was granted the commission for the renovation of the Piazza; Howard, *Jacopo Sansovino*, pp. 8–61.
37. Fenlon, *Sung Histories*, p. 76.
38. Coryat, *Coryat's Crudities*, I, p. 51.
39. 'A San Marco appresso il campaniel sono doi pagati per San Marco, in humanità dottissimi, che leggono publice a chi voleno udirli senza pagar alcun premio, e homeni di gran fama'. Sanudo, *Cronachetta*, p. 51.
40. 'Passeggiar per piazza, et andar dall'hostaria in pescaria, et dal palazzo alla loggia, non facendo altro tutto il giorno, che girar di qua, e di là, hora sentendo canta in banchi, … hora posando in qualche barberia a contar frottole, e fanfalucche, hora leggendo le nove di banco'. Garzoni, *La Piazza Universale*, II, p. 987.
41. Poliziano, *Opera*, a1v.
42. 'Se Vinegia è nel mondo, ò il mondo in Vinegia'. Groto, *Le orationi volgari*, 9r.
43. Coryat, *Coryat's Crudities*, I, p. 314.
44. 'Colui che tiene la piazza, sempre è vincente della città'. Cavalcanti, *Istorie Fiorentine*, p. 306.
45. On St Mark's Square as a space of protest, see Van Gelder, 'Protest in the Piazza'.
46. 'Una parola in piazza fa più male che dieci libri in un gabinetto'. Leti, *Dialogo quarto*, p. 265. On this dialogue see Infelise, *Gazzetta*, pp. 85–93.
47. Crouzet-Pavan, 'Potere politico e spazio sociale'.
48. Assonica, *Fragmentum chronicæ*, p. 316.
49. Molho and Sznura, eds, *Alle bocche della piazza*, pp. XXXV–XLVIII; see also Milner, 'The Florentine Piazza'.
50. ASVE, CD, Del., Miste, Reg., reg. 25 fol. 82r; reg. 27, fol. 184r; Fil., f. 11, fol. 38r.
51. 'Antonio Grimani, / ruina de' cristiani / rebello de' venetiani, / puòstu esser manzà da' canni'. Sanudo, *I diarii*, III, col. 5. On Grimani, see chapter 10 by Viggiano.
52. 'Quasi dicat non è tempo di perder, el turcho vien addosso e vuj non provedé!'. Sanudo, *I diarii*, III, col. 269.
53. Finlay, *Politics in Renaissance Venice*, pp. 109, 120–21.
54. 'Su su a la morte, a sacho de questi ladri tyranni venetiani'. Sanudo, *I diarii*, XVIII, coll. 44–45.
55. ASVE, CD, Del., Crim., Fil., f. 17, dated 28 March 1574: 'non dubitiamo che presto faremo mutacion de principe e sarà testa sola'.
56. Crouzet-Pavan, 'Les mots de Venise'.
57. 'Cadauno retiniva la lengua dentro li denti per paura'. Priuli, *I Diarii*, p. 108.
58. Judde, *The revolt of the snowballs*.
59. Sanudo, *I diarii*, XIII, col. 260.
60. 'Imperio! Imperio! Et amazar li rettori'. ASBS, Bib., OL, Op-Q, n° 18, Ludovico Caravaggi, Chronica de Bressa (Caravaggi, Chronica), fol. 77v. 'INRI 1547'. On this episode, see Rospocher and Valseriati, 'Politics in the street'.
61. Terry-Fritsch, 'Networks of Urban Secrecy'.
62. Preto, *Persona per hora secreta*.
63. Rospocher, 'Battle for the Piazza'.
64. ASVE, SE, b. 7, fasc. 18, fols. 1v–2v (22 May 1549).
65. 'Per le piazze, per le botteghe, per le taverne et insino per li lavatoi delle donne'. Prosperi, *Tra evangelismo e Controriforma*, p. 241.
66. 'Spesso tra il palazzo e la piazza è una nebbia sì folta, o uno muro sì grosso, che non vi penetrando l'occhio degli uomini, tanto sa el popolo di quello che fa chi governa, o della ragione per che lo fa, quanto delle cose che fanno in India; e però si empie facilmente il mondo di opinione erronee e vane'. Guicciardini, *Ricordi*, p. 153.
67. Guicciardini, *The History of Italy*, p. 76.
68. Machiavelli, *Discorsi sopra la prima deca di Tito Livio*, I, cap. XLVII.
69. Milner, 'Citing the Ringhiera', p. 54. On the materiality of political public spaces, see Rospocher and Valseriati, 'Politics in the street'.
70. 'Continue stato alle piaze a investigar ogni ocorentia per minima che la fusse'. Sanudo, *I diarii*, XXX.
71. 'Quanto se diceva sopra le piaze'. Priuli, *I Diarii*, II, p. 112.
72. De Vivo, 'I luoghi della cultura a Venezia', p. 708.
73. 'Sollecitare le Piazze publiche di S. Marco et di Rialto', 'perché, altrimenti facendo, dà a credere di esser'uomo, che si prenda le cose publiche per ischerzo'. Manuzio, *Il perfetto gentil'huomo*, pp. 48–49.
74. Da Porto, *Lettere storiche*, pp. 128–29.
75. Da Porto, *Lettere storiche*, pp. 128–29.
76. 'Hera licito a chadauno, de ogni grado et condictione, se fusse, dire quanto li piaceva et che li fusse venuto in bocha et in piaza et in le logiette et per ogni locho'. Priuli, *I Diarii*, IV, pp. 108–09.
77. Priuli, *I Diarii*, IV, p. 246.
78. Van Gelder and de Vivo, 'Papering over Protest'.
79. Leti, *Dialogo quarto*, p. 256.

5

Iseabail Rowe

'FROM THE CLOCKE TO THE SHORE'

Thomas Coryat's 'Streets' of Piazza San Marco

At the end of the sixteenth century, an English courtier, traveller, and writer named Thomas Coryat journeyed from England across continental Europe, passing through France, Italy, and the Low Countries. In 1611 this trip resulted in a book commonly known as *Coryat's Crudities*.[1] The publication, written upon Coryat's return to England, detailed his quick first 'taste' of new lands: it was indeed intended for a readership of fellow travellers and travel enthusiasts, and in particular for fellow courtiers (who contributed poetry and other short extracts to the preface of the travelogue). The book has been analysed from a literary perspective for its metaphors related to food and digestion, its unique use of language (despite the employment of typical travel-writing tropes), and its unusual format and publication process.[2] When taken up as a historical source, it is primarily referenced for its consideration of social interactions or cultural exchanges.[3] This is because Coryat focused much of his descriptions on the dress, behaviours, and customs of those he met. However, in addition to these detailed accounts of people, Coryat also attentively observed the spaces through which he moved. This was achieved through a significant focus on the categorisation and measurement of the urban environments that he explored.

This chapter will focus on one specific site in which Coryat performed these measurements: St Mark's Square in Venice. As such, it will analyse Coryat's reaction to this overwhelming and arguably irregular space and how he made sense of it through measurement and categorisation. Specifically, this chapter will consider his methods of measurement and classification choices, as well as what the features of the Piazza he chose to describe reveal about the Venetian architectural environment. By questioning the connections he drew between architectural features within the urban space, and considering why these connections were formed, it will discuss what Coryat's account tells us about the construction and function of the Piazza. The extent to which temporary structures, or special events in the Piazza, informed Coryat's perceptions of the space will also be investigated. Finally, the chapter will analyse how Coryat's reaction to the piazza as an external visitor reflected the intentions of the adaptations and interventions made to the space during the century preceding his visit.

Walking the Piazza

Coryat begins his description of St Mark's Square with enthusiastic praise, calling it 'The fairest place of all the citie (which is indeed of that admirable and incomparable beauty, that I thinke no place whatsoever, eyther in Christendome or Paganisme may compare with it)'. However, the Piazza did not align with traditional conceptions of architectural beauty in English public squares at the turn of the seventeenth century, which instead situated classical tropes and symmetry at the heart of spatial appreciation. In contrast, St Mark's Square perhaps seemed untraditionally sprawling, having grown almost organically around the restrictions posed by island landforms and developed piece by piece over the centuries as additional land was reclaimed from the lagoon.[4] Although today the term 'Piazza' is often referred to include the entire inverted L-shape at the 'entrance' of the city, it is in fact made up of two distinct spaces. These two spaces were defined separately as St Mark's Square, which was limited to the elongated rectangular area in front of St Mark's Basilica, and the *Piazzetta*, which was simultaneously a ceremonial landing site and the *Piazza* of the Ducal Palace.[5]

Though the Piazza thus represented a vast, complex, and varied space to Coryat, he attempted to make sense of it for himself and readers by breaking it down into four distinct sections. Interestingly, Coryat called these 'streets' and, in so doing, avoided offering a static presentation of the Piazza, instead conveying a sense of purposeful movement or travel through the space, albeit within a series of discrete areas. This sense of movement is enhanced by his measurement of the streets in paces. Moreover, Coryat delimited these streets in relation to the significant architectural features of the Piazza, and as such made various visual or functional connections within the built environment, while also indicating his own direction of travel or that which he observed of others.

Coryat defined the four streets of the Piazza as follows (fig. 5.1): the first was the space between the façade of St Mark's Basilica and the façade of the church of San Geminiano, which was destroyed in the early nineteenth century.[6] The second travelled between the *Torre dell'Orologio* (Clock Tower) — which, as he noted, was the Piazza's entrance from the Merceria — and the twin columns of St Mark and St Theodore ('The second from that notable clocke at the coming into St Markes from the Merceria [...] to the two lofty pillars neare to the shore of the Adriatique gulfe').[7] The third street identified by Coryat ran between the bridge by which one entered the Piazza from the east, arriving in front of the Ducal Palace, and the Venetian Mint known as the *Zecca*, which provided the boundary of the Piazzetta on the opposite side ('The third reacheth from the bridge neare to the prison, along by the South side of the Dukes Palace, and so by the Sea shore, to the end of that stately building a little beyond the foresaid pillars').[8] The final street ran from what Coryat called the 'Canon's house' to the northern side of the Basilica ('The fourth and the last part reacheth from the North side of the S. Markes Church to the Canons houses').[9] Here the 'Canon's house' can be assumed to refer to the Palazzo Patriarcale, given the measurements Coryat used to define the space ('being in length sixty nine paces, in bredth thirty eight') and the fact that it would have filled the fourth remaining space in the Piazza.[10] Each street was measured in length and breadth using the unit of measure, paces, typically reserved for distances that could be walked, whereas the scale of the architectural features in the surroundings were instead described in feet. The delineation of the four streets relatively closely follows Sansovino's description of St Mark's Square in *Venetia città nobilissima et singolare*, where these four zones are instead described as four piazzas.[11]

Coryat not only designated and measured these streets, but ranked them as well, arguing that Streets One and Two competed for greatness, although Street One won outright, that Street Three was inferior to Two, because it repeated the same architectural elements (albeit from a different angle) of the second street but lacked the grandeur of passing between two rows of buildings, and that Street Four seemed unworthy of comment beyond its dimensions.[12] The ranking of these streets coincided with their dimensions, as the highest rated was also the longest (although Streets One and Two were of almost equal length). Though Coryat does not explicitly identify length as a criterion for superiority, his fixation with measurement throughout the text demonstrates that he thought bigger is better.

Of the four sections, Street Three is the only area that could reasonably be called a street according to our contemporary

5.1
Plan of Piazza San Marco with Coryat's Streets. Designed by the author.

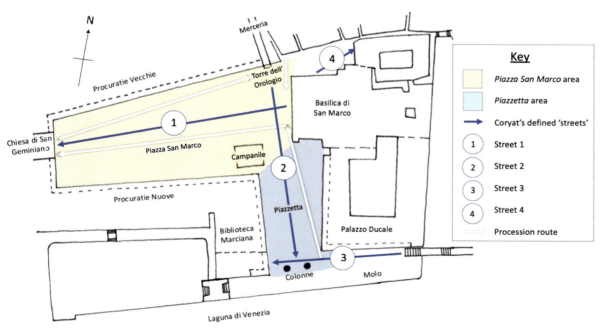

understanding of the word. However, far from being limited to the confines of the Piazza, as Coryat defines it, Street Three was in fact connected with a much longer stretch of walkway running along the southern side of the island-city. As mentioned above, Coryat stated that this street repeated the architectural elements of Street Two, because it also passed by the two large columns and the Ducal Palace.[13] However, this description ignores the Pier (*Molo*) beside the water's edge, a very busy area for the arrival of boats and the embarkment and disembarkment of goods and people both during ceremonial events and everyday life. This is the first indication that Coryat's emphasis was on formal architectural structures as points of interest and on land-based travel via 'streets', rather than on Venice's waterborne activities.

The second of Coryat's streets, which ran from the Clock Tower to the twin columns in front of the *Molo*, further reveals his preference for order and symmetry. Street Two runs between what are arguably two monumental 'gateways': the first embodied by the archway beneath the clock, which is in turn framed (when looking from the water) by the second, and the twin columns of St Mark and St Theodore. Prior to the construction of the clock, this 'gateway to the city' was marked by the columns alone. The Clock Tower was conceived just before the turn of the sixteenth century as a second gateway between the open space of the Piazza and the narrower streets of the city beyond.[14] The understanding of the Clock Tower as a second gateway was certainly recognized by Coryat, who called it 'a very faire gate at one end of this street', and was described similarly by contemporaneous chronicles and travellers.[15] For example, its effectiveness as a device for directing both the eyes and feet of those in the Piazza upon their arrival in Venice was recognized by the writer Francesco Sansovino (author of his own sixteenth-century guidebook to Venice), who in 1581 wrote of the Clock Tower: 'underneath there is a great door through which one can enter the Merceria from the Piazza, that on first sight seems almost to represent the door through which one goes into the city'.[16]

Entering the Piazza: from the water or the Clock?

As Deborah Howard first identified, the Clock Tower's construction recognized the emerging importance of the open Piazza space, especially for ceremonial purposes.[17] It also resulted in a re-orientation of the Piazza, creating a new central axis along the street that Coryat described as Street Two. By contrast, city-views of Venice produced prior to the Clock Tower's construction depict the city from the east, as if the viewer were moving up the Grand Canal from its mouth

5.2

Erhard Reuwich, *Civitas Veneciarum* (detail), woodcut print on paper, 1486. Photo: Venice, Biblioteca Nazionale Marciana, Armadio VI.21. By concession of the Italian Ministry of Culture — Biblioteca Nazionale Marciana, Venice. Any reproduction is forbidden.

in front of the Piazza, as one did when arriving at St Mark's Square by water. An example of this is Erhard Reuwich's rendering of the city in *Civitas Venetiarum*, which was produced in 1486 (fig. 5.2). Although this view still centres the composition on the Piazza, only a portion of the Piazzetta is visible, and it frames the Ducal Palace alongside the first 'gateway' to the city — the twin pillars of St Mark and St Theodore — as the primary focus. This view was later confirmed in the *Nuremberg Chronicle* (also known as the *Liber Chronicarum*) produced c. 1491, which presents a cropped version of Reuwich's view (fig. 5.3). The new cropped parameters positioned the already limited view of the Piazza as the centrefold of the book, definitively recognizing the dominance of the Ducal Palace over the Piazza space beyond, as the identifying and central feature of Venice.

The first depiction of the cityscape after the Clock Tower's completion appears in Jacopo de Barbari's celebratory map of 1500 (fig. 5.4).[18] In this rendering, the direction of depiction has shifted and is now squarely to the north, as if the viewer were approaching the Piazza head on from near the island of San Giorgio Maggiore. Surrounded by the 'outer gateway' of the twin columns, in this framing the Clock Tower takes central focus and is clearly depicted as a second entrance to the city; placed head-on, the archway draws the eye to the centre back of the square, while the rest of the city unfolds behind it. This clearly represents a shift in focus, by around forty-five degrees to the west, which allowed for a more central display of the open space of the Piazza, rather than the Ducal Palace. In her discussion of the map, Deborah Howard even goes so far as to suggest that this shift in perspective may have occurred over the course of the three years during which the map was made, resulting in a 'disjunction evident in the lines on the paving' and 'inspired by the scenographic success of the insertion of the Clock Tower into the space'.[19] Indeed, the construction of the clock and the new viewpoint (and consequential reorientation) it encouraged, certainly resulted in a drawing together of the Piazza and the Piazzetta spaces together along the axis Coryat identified as Street Two. Coryat's designation of Street Two, and his preference for it over Street Three (which mirrored the orientational focus that had dominated prior to the Clock Tower's construction) similarly responded to the intervention produced by the tower and the resulting reorientation of the city.

However, this new view of the Piazza (which by the end of the sixteenth century was the accepted view of the city) drew the viewer northwards from the water, towards the land. This was similarly supported by writings, like that of Sansovino quoted previously, which viewed the Clock Tower as a doorway from the Piazza into the city beyond.[20] Instead, Coryat's description and subsequent notes about the Clock Tower 'at the entrance of St Marks from the Merceria' indicate that he travelled from the Mercerie, underneath the Clock Tower, and into the Piazza.[21] This mirrors the ceremonial entrance of the procurators of St Mark into the Piazza, who walked from Rialto to St Mark's Square via the Mercerie.[22] Coryat's similar perspective reveals that his own travel into the Piazza was also by foot, on land rather than from the water, and this mirrored in his description of the city, which begins with a description and history of Rialto, then the Rialto Bridge, before reaching the Piazza. In fact, Coryat, as an 'outsider' and relatively low-ranking courtier, was almost entirely cut-off from the more elite water travel, which occurred by private gondola (although he highlighted one special trip he was invited to take with Sir Henry Wotton, the English ambassador to Venice who 'admitted me to passe with him in his Gondola').[23] Other than the ambassador's invitation, Coryat warns against the use of private gondolas, hinting at the possibility of bad experiences, such as being taken hostage and carried by gondoliers to unfamiliar places then charged a ransom to be taken back again.[24] Coryat thus had a poor view of Venetian water travel and called the 'boatmen' 'the most vicious and licentious varlets about all the city,' strongly warning his readers against water travel.[25]

This is a remarkable perspective given the ceremonial importance of arrival to the city by water, which was used to impress and welcome foreign diplomats and princes and therefore features heavily in travel accounts praising the city and its beauty.[26] Sir Henry Wotton for example, as an ambassador, was provided with a ceremonial entry into the city by water, albeit this ceremony was somewhat artificial given that he had already been a resident in the city for some weeks.[27] As Fortini Brown notes, a water entry (which was possible only through a few deep, hidden channels) implied an indirect arrival route that showed off the city from a carefully orchestrated perspective.[28] This inevitably led to accounts praising the waterways of the city. French Ambassador Philippe de Commynes, for example, was carried down the Grand Canal for his entry into the city and remarked that it was 'the most beautiful street in the whole world'.[29] Coryat, on the other hand, had a quite

5.3

View of Venice. Woodcut from Hartmann Schedel, *Liber chronicarum*, Nuremberg, Anton Koberger for Sebald Schreyer and Sebastian Kammermeister, 1493, fols. 43v-44r. Photo: Milan, Biblioteca Nazionale Braidense, NBEC0.03.0037. By concession of the Italian Ministry of Culture — Pinacoteca di Brera — Biblioteca Braidense, Milan.

unceremonious entry to Venice, arriving from Pauda along the river Brenta and taking a gondola from Fusina into the city which was apparently so unremarkable that it warranted no further description other than to say 'of these gondolas I will write hereafter in my description of Venice' — which as we have seen was far from a favourable account.[30]

Luckily for Coryat, as Filippo de Vivo points out, 'by 1500 "walkability" dominated the choices of the authorities in charge of public works. Their records show a remarkable concern with enlarging streets and keeping them unencumbered, especially in commercial areas, to facilitate movement back and forth'.[31] New *fondamenta* (walkways running parallel to canals) were constructed, and in St Mark's Square itself the food market was removed and relocated to Rialto, which played a significant role in opening up the space.[32] Coryat clearly benefited from this, and actually specifically mentioned the width of the Mercerie as 'convenient enough in some places for five or six persons to walke together side by side'.[33] Both Coryat's decision to ignore the activity of the Molo in his account of Streets Two and Three in the Piazza and his direction of travel into the Piazza reveal the benefit that this 'walkability' had for early modern travellers.

From the Clock Tower, Coryat's Street Two cut across St Mark's Square and the Piazzetta to the two marble columns 'of equall height and thicknesse very neare to the shore of the Adriatique gulfe, the fairest certainly for height and greatnesse that ever I saw till then' — again indicating the importance of scale in determining value.[34] Coryat's consistent approach to measuring columns revealed it was not only by walking that he used his body to measure, and thereby define and describe, the Piazza space. In fact, throughout his travels Coryat used his body in various ways as a reference point for measurement. He described the circumference of the columns, for example, as 'so great, that I was not able to claspe them with both mine armes at thrice'.[35] This similarly provided readers with an immediate reference point for the scale he was endeavouring to describe.

Interestingly, Coryat considered the two columns the limit of Street Two, rather than seeing it continue through them to the water's edge. This again suggests an avoidance of the Molo, but may also reflect the presence of the temporary architectural structure of gallows that were regularly raised between the two columns. Coryat saw and described this process:

Betwixt the pillars condemned men and malefactors are put to death. For whensoever there is to be any execution, upon a sudden they erect a scaffold there, and after they have beheaded the offendors (for that is most commonly their death) they take it away againe.[36]

When the gallows were not present, the space where they stood was demarcated by a difference in the Piazzetta's paving, as shown by Jacopo de' Barbari's map. There the gallows area is identified as a zone of the Piazza where the relatively static activity of dice throwing was allowed to be played.[37] This, rather than the columns, may in turn have created an abstract limit, thanks to the presence of people standing to play, that shaped movement in the street.

Streets and ceremonial routes

Coryat's description of Street Two focuses heavily on the symmetry and line created between the Ducal Palace to the east and the Marciana Library to the west (built 1537–1553, with the addition of five bays in 1588). Coryat called these constructions 'two very goodly and sumptuous rows of buildings', using the word 'rows' to describe the logge that ran along the respective façades of both buildings. Coryat's description of these two structures as 'rows of buildings' reflects the way a loggia broke up the façade when viewed from the Piazza below, giving the illusion of a series of connected buildings rather than one large imposing edifice. Indeed, he praised the walkways beneath the arches on both sides, measuring their size and depth, their number of columns, the distance between said columns, and their circumference with his arms. An arcade space allowing movement among and around the buildings could arguably have broken up directional movement implied by Coryat's use of the word 'street'. However, like the gallows, other temporary structures along this second part of the route can be seen in prints by Giacomo Franco made around the exact time of Coryat's visit. These structures included stages, market stalls, and benches for a variety of performative and ceremonial reasons (fig. 5.5). Such temporary structures narrowed this part of the Piazza into more of a defined causeway, or specifically constructed it as a processional walkway on special occasions. Although Coryat does not mention either the activities or the structures, they may have influenced his perception of the space and delimitation of the streets.

5.4
Jacopo de' Barbari, *The City of Venice (Venetie MD)*, 1500. Detail of 1.13 featuring St Mark square.

His perception of Street One, which Coryat called the 'fairest of all', may be explained in several ways.[38] The first thing to note is that it travelled between two churches: the St Mark Basilica and the church of San Geminiano (the latter now defunct), and thus reflected part of a standard processional route around the Piazza (fig. 5.6) followed during ceremonial processions involving the doge and the Signoria, most notably that of Corpus Domini.[39] Coryat's description of the hoisting of flags on the flag poles at the Basilica at the end of this street (as occurred on ceremonial occasions) makes it clear that Coryat must have had knowledge of such a procession and likely witnessed one first-hand.[40] Although he again does not recount the proceedings of any ceremony, such events nevertheless seem to have influenced his perception of the space. The visual evidence of such processions once again suggest that Coryat's routes were defined not by the permanent built environment but rather, as with Street Two, by a mixture of temporary structures and people lining the procession route, as can be seen in Giacomo Franco's print of the Corpus Christi procession (fig. 1.13).

Coryat's description of Street One focuses on the narrower, western end of the street that fell between the Procuratie Vecchie (1517–1538) and the Procuratie Nuove (1583–1640), the latter of which was still under construction during his visit. This emphasis again demonstrates his fixation with regularity and symmetry above all else — to the extent that

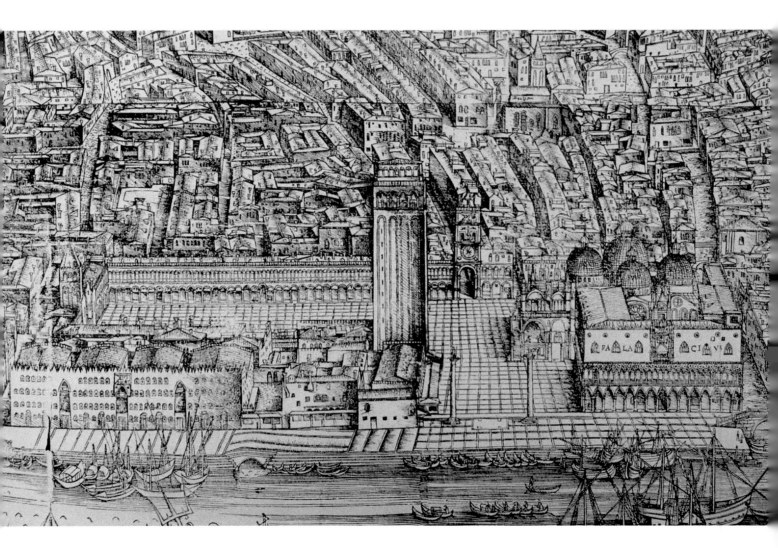

5.5
Giacomo Franco, *Li Ciarlatani*. Engraving from Id., *Habiti d'huomeni et donne venetiane con la processione della Ser.ma Signoria ed altri particolari*, 1610. Amsterdam, Rijksmuseum. Photo: Public Domain.

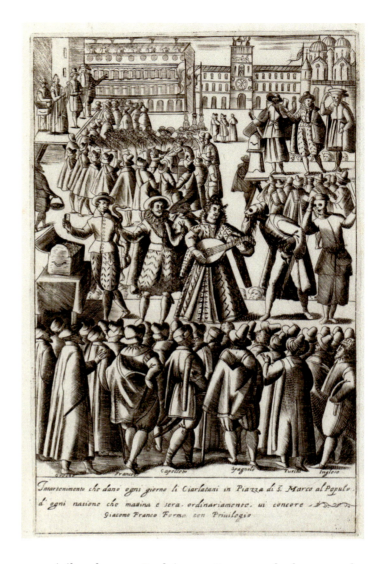

he even overlooked the fact that construction of the Procuratie Nuove in this part of the street was not yet finished. Like the Marciana Library, which was intended to create symmetry with the Ducal Palace, the two Procuratie buildings were developed during the sixteenth century for the same purpose, and they certainly succeeded in drawing Coryat's attention. As in Street Two, he praised the regularity of the vaulted archways with their walkways beneath, and even went so far as to count the number of windows on each floor and measure (in order to compare the southern and northern galleries) the depth of the walkways and distance between columns, ultimately finding them satisfactorily equal.[41] Where Coryat found fault, however, was with the Piazza's brick paving, which he protested ought to have been done in a manner akin to the flooring in the great noble houses of England. This interesting comparison of public and private space perhaps indexes what, for Coryat at least, would have been the Republic's unusually accessible monumental architecture, which interacted with everyday activities; in England, by comparison, it was reserved for the private homes of the nobility.

Conclusions

The idea of physical accessibility is pervasive in Coryat's description of the Piazza, and readers are thus confronted with his bodily presence in every part of his written account. Of course, as was common in travel writing of the sixteenth and seventeenth centuries, Coryat took pains to emphasise his presence in the places and spaces he travelled — as proof of his actually having been there. As this chapter has demonstrated, he achieved this by measuring scale in relation to his body and bodily activity, such as measuring distances with 'paces' (even using this system to measure the Grand Canal, which would have been impossible to pace out) and measuring circumferences, such as those of columns, with his arms.[42] Beyond the humorous impression of a rather embarrassing English tourist stretching his arms to wrap them around columns amidst the beauty and bustle of St Mark's Square, such details once again highlight the accessibility of these sites. Though precluded from the elite form of water travel, and by extension from the interiors of many luxurious private buildings, Coryat was nevertheless able to move among these buildings via the walkways of their loggie — and to compare, measure and touch their columns — without needing any privileged access. In doing so, Coryat made the most of an incredibly important part of the sixteenth-century Venetian programme of Piazza renovations, which aimed to make these grand buildings not only 'accessible' and visible to the public but integral to the activities and movements of everyday life in Venice and regularly celebrated by public ceremony. For Coryat the accessibility of Venetian grandeur under a republican government must have represented a stark contrast with the separation and preservation of palaces for the English nobility. This attitude certainly aligned with other, relatively contemporaneous publications which praised Venetian republican governance and drew comparisons with England, such as Lewis Lewkenor's 1599 translation of Gaspar Contarini's *De Magistratibus et Republica Venetorum* as *The Commonwealth and Government of Venice*.[43]

Coryat's description of St Mark's Square chopped it up into manageable bite-sized chunks. He described his sections as streets in order to make sense of the space with a measured

5.6

Gentile Bellini, *Procession in St Mark square*, 1496. Venice, Gallerie dell'Accademia. Reproduced with permission.

and critical account. His points of focus and inclination toward classical order and symmetry certainly reflect a typical English gaze at the end of the sixteenth century. More importantly, however, the way he perceived the space notably mirrored the intentions of the updates to the architectural framework of the Piazza begun in the preceding century. This shows that these aims to increase the walkability of the city may have built on order and symmetry to enhance the ceremonial potential of the Piazza space. In this respect, Coryat's rare account offers an outsider's perspective that was developed on foot and differs significantly from the accounts of official visits by nobles and ambassadors, who relied heavily on water travel that displayed the city at its finest. Though he does not describe any ceremonial activities in the square in detail, his choice of streets would seem to indicate they had a role in shaping his perceptions, as did the temporary architectural structures such public events employed. Finally, Coryat's commentary responded to the accessible nature of the space and to the state-orchestrated public displays of wealth and grandeur that were so integral to perceptions of the republican governance of the city. Likely without fully understanding such intentions, Coryat's descriptions and response demonstrate the success of the aims underpinning the Piazza's improvements and certainly, its ability to impress.

---

1. Coryat, *Coryat's Crudities*.
2. Palmer, '"The Progress of Thy Glorious Book"'; Ord, 'Textual Experience in Thomas Coryat's Crudities'; Craik, 'Reading "Coryats Crudities"'; Craik, 'Eating His Words'.
3. Frontain, 'Thomas Coryate and the Epistemology of Travel'; Parr, 'Thomas Coryat and the Discovery of Europe'; Jones, 'Italians and Others'.
4. Ammerman, 'Venice before the Grand Canal', p. 142.
5. Here 'the piazza' refers to the space as a whole, as Coryat defined it.
6. 'The first is that which reacheth from the front of St Markes Church to the opposite front of St Geminians Church' (Coryat, *Coryat's Crudities*, I, p. 315).
7. Coryat, *Coryat's Crudities*, I, p. 315.
8. Coryat, *Coryat's Crudities*, I, p. 315.
9. Coryat, *Coryat's Crudities*, I, pp. 315–16.
10. Coryat, *Coryat's Crudities*, I, p. 325.
11. Sansovino, *Venetia città nobilissima et singolare* (1581), 105r.
12. The ranking of the streets was also reflected in the order in which Coryat introduced them and, in turn, in how they have been labelled and listed in his work and in this chapter. The first ranked street is Street One, and so on.
13. Coryat, *Coryat's Crudities*, I, pp. 324–25.
14. Goy, *Building Renaissance Venice*, pp. 193–259.
15. Coryat, *Coryat's Crudities*, I, p. 328.
16. 'Di sotto è un portone per lo quale s'entra di piazza in merceria, onde alla prima veduta rappresenta quasi come una porta per la quale si vada nella città'. Sansovino, *Venetia città nobilissima et singolare* (1581), 117r.
17. Howard, 'Venice as a Dolphin'.
18. Howard, 'Venice as a Dolphin'. Schulz, 'Jacopo de' Barbari's View of Venice'.
19. Howard, 'Venice as a Dolphin', p. 104.
20. Sansovino, *Venetia città nobilissima et singolare* (1581), 117r.
21. Coryat, *Coryat's Crudities*, I, p. 318.
22. Metlica, 'Reshaping the Republican Ritual', pp. 173–75.
23. Coryat, *Coryat's Crudities*, I, p. 332.
24. Coryat, *Coryat's Crudities*, I, pp. 311–12.
25. Coryat, *Coryat's Crudities*, I, pp. 311–12.

26. Fortini Brown, 'Measured Friendship, Calculated Pomp', pp. 140–46.
27. Smith, *The Life and letters of Henry Wotton*, p. 147. Muir, *Civic Ritual*, p. 233.
28. Fortini Brown, 'Measured Friendship, Calculated Pomp', p. 140.
29. Fortini Brown, 'Measured Friendship, Calculated Pomp', p. 140.
30. Coryat, *Coryat's Crudities*, I, pp. 194–95.
31. De Vivo, 'Walking in Sixteenth-Century Venice', p. 125.
32. Svalduz, '"Atorno questa nostra città"; De Vivo, 'Walking in Sixteenth-Century Venice', p. 136. Tafuri, *Renovatio Urbis*.
33. Coryat, *Coryat's Crudities*, I, p. 328.
34. Coryat, *Coryat's Crudities*, I, p. 323.
35. Coryat, *Coryat's Crudities*, I, p. 323.
36. Coryat, *Coryat's Crudities*, I, p. 324.
37. Scarabello and Morachiello, *Guida alla civiltà di Venezia*, p. 117.
38. Coryat, *Coryat's Crudities*, I, p. 316.
39. Sansovino, *Venetia città nobilissima et singolare* (1581), 196r. Matteo Casini, 'Ceremoniali'. Hopkins, 'The Influence of Ducal Ceremony on Church Design', pp. 30, 35.
40. Coryat, *Coryat's Crudities*, I, pp. 329–30.
41. Coryat, *Coryat's Crudities*, I, pp. 316–17.
42. Coryat, *Coryat's Crudities*, I, p. 306.
43. Contarini and others, *The Commonwealth and Gouernment of Venice*. For analysis see Hadfield, *Literature, Travel and Colonial Writing*, pp. 40–51.

Evelyn Korsch

6

A REPUBLIC BECOMES DIVINE

The Sacred Role of Topography in Venetian Civic Ritual

The Serenissima was ambitious. Though a republic, Venice strived for a power position equivalent to the rank of empires and kingdoms, or even higher. Such a goal could be achieved only through a quasi-divine status. This chapter explores the means by which the Republic of Venice succeeded in presenting itself as divine, in particular through examples of how the concept of sacralisation was implemented through aspects linked to festival culture, public rituals, and urban topography.

The Republic of Venice was famous for its festival culture, which it successfully used as a strategy of representation until its demise in 1797. The instrumentalisation of festivals contributed significantly to the elaboration and consolidation of the so-called 'myth of Venice'.[1] The 'myth' fulfilled two functions: at the domestic level, it served to stabilise rule; at the level of foreign policy, it formed the legitimating basis for the Venetian government as a protagonist of equal or higher rank to other European powers. Venetian festival culture reached a high point in the second half of the sixteenth century. Despite, or better because of, recurring military conflicts, famines, and waves of epidemics, the Serenissima performed its own self-glorification whenever an occasion presented itself. In addition to the already extensive regular calendar of religious feasts, celebrations of the visits of foreign princes and cardinals, the inaugurations of ambassadors or Venetian dignitaries, and military victories were organised.[2]

Among the several festivals explored in this chapter, two state occasions stand out for their particular political symbolism and extraordinary high costs: the 1574 visit of Henry III, king of France and Poland, and the coronation festivities for dogaressa Morosina Morosini, wife of doge Marino Grimani, in 1597.[3] On both these occasions, the Venetian government displayed a maximum level of splendour and magnificence in attempt to overcome a crisis situation. Though the two crises were different, the strategies of representation applied were similar. In 1574 the Serenissima was struggling to regain its image as a defender of Christianity. Enthusiasm over the victory of Lepanto in 1571 had quickly faded on the political level, but its mythic value became strong. After the conquest of Cyprus by the Ottomans, Venice decided to make a separate peace with the Sublime Porte in 1573, in order to trade again without restrictions in the Mediterranean. This treaty did not remain secret for long, and the Serenissima soon incurred the wrath and distrust of the European powers.

Whereas the situation in 1574 represented a foreign policy problem, in 1597 things were different. After the plague of 1575–1577, natural disasters, military conflicts, and famines, Venetian domestic politics sought means to improve the mood of a rather demoralised population as well as to restore public order by presenting an image of strength and prosperity. Laws on the carrying of weapons were tightened and even small public gatherings of crowds were banned.[4] Towards the end of the century, the number of decrees related to dancing and playing music outside increased.[5] But according to official historiography, the Serenissima seemed to be free of public disorder and dissent.[6] Since doge Marino Grimani and his wife were not only extremely wealthy, but also very popular with the people because of their generosity, they could benefit from public performances for self-promotion.[7] During the festivities in 1595 and 1597, Grimani used munificence and civic ritual to engage directly with ordinary Venetians as a form of thanks for having supported his election.[8] Nevertheless, the ducal couple's celebrations primarily served to glorify the state they represented.

Initially addressed to different audiences, and therefore integrating different areas of the urban topography, the strategies of state self-representation used in 1574 and 1597 merged into one guiding concept at the end of the sixteenth century. Since in 1574 foreign spectators needed to be convinced of the uniqueness and supremacy of Venice, the entire state territory, including the *Terraferma*, was involved in the festivities.

Henry III thus completed one long *via triumphalis* that started at the border in Pontebba and ended at the border in Rovigo. The entries and festivities offered to the king along the route increased in splendour and effort, climaxing in Venice and then decreasing in pageantry. The outstanding significance of Venice was thus emphasised also in topographical terms, with focus set on the city itself, namely on the lagoon and the area around St Mark's Square.

Although the so-called coronation of Morosina Morosini in 1597 was an event with international participation, the focus of the celebrations shifted to the offices of the Ducal Palace that were partially open to the public. In fact, the dogaresse were not crowned but made triumphal entries to the Palace, their new residence, which confirmed their new statuses. Contemporaneous writers described this ceremony as either an 'entry' or a 'coronation', underscoring the high political symbolism of this kind of civic ritual. After a procession across the Piazza and the singing of a *Te Deum* in the Basilica, the festive company entered the Palace and walked through the offices lavishly decorated by guilds, which offered delicacies and musical performances. The dogaressa's triumphal entry ended in the Hall of the Great Council, where she took her seat on the so-called doge's throne. The highlight of the civic ritual thus moved from outside to inside the palace.

New strategies of political iconography developed in the 1570s and afterward granted the increased importance of the Palace: in this seat of government, a new iconographic programme based on a phenomenon called 'Neobyzantinism' presented the doge as the Redeemer, with his councillors (the *consiglieri ducali*, composing the Signoria) as angels and Venice itself as paradise on Earth. In this sense, the Hall of the Great Council was transformed into a divine Olympus, where a new form of musical performances, called *rappresentationi* or *cantate*, underlined its significance as a channel of God's voice. Celio Magno introduced this new type of musical performance, which presented the doge and the Signoria as Jupiter and his deities, for the coronation of doge Alvise Mocenigo in 1570. Praising the doge also as *vicarius Dei*, *alter ego Christi* and *miles christianus*, the performance created a dual layer of sacralisation, which was based on both Christian and mythological iconography. Such performance enhanced the *maiestas* of the members of government, and thus the sacredness attributed to them.[9] In 1571, on St Stephan's day, Magno delivered another *rappresentatione* to celebrate the victory of Lepanto.[10]

During the state visit of Henry III in 1574, Claudio Cornelio Frangipane similarly relied on the concept of a Venetian Olympus. His *Tragedia*, which depicted the foundations of the Republic, was staged in the Hall of the Great Council.[11] The four allegories represented in the niches of the Sansovinian Loggetta — Athena, Mercury, Apollo and Pax — became part of the performance. Athena, taking the leading role among the gods, was presented as the *alter ego* of *Venetia*, the allegorical personification of Venice. This rendered her not only superior to the French king, to whom she provided political advice, but also to Mars. According to Rome's founding legend, Mars was the father of the twins Romulus and Remus, and therefore the ancestor of the 'Eternal city'. Since Athena-*Venetia* acted as the leader of the deities, she claimed a rank superior to the Roman Empire. Venice's former *imitatio* as *altera Roma* was replaced by a new ideological definition as *Romam superans*. The lyrics of the *Tragedia* created a quasi-divine atmosphere in the Hall of the Great Council by applying continuously terms of light and sound.

Under the dogado of Marino Grimani, the *cantate* became an important part of the official festive calendar. Grimani established the tradition that these musical performances were staged on 25 April (St Mark), on the feast of Christ's Ascension (*Sensa*), on 15 June (St Vitus), and on 26 December (St Stephan).[12] Considering that musical harmony had been understood as a sign of divine emanation since Neoplatonism, it was not by chance that Grimani decreed regular musical performances to stabilise his rule in a time of crisis. Indeed, the harmony of divine order was presented as analogous to the harmony of the *regimen temperatum* of the Republic.[13] This state controlled effect was emphasised by the fact that the St Mark's Chapel performed the *rappresentationi*. Since this institution was responsible for state music, it is clear that these events constituted state acts of crucial importance: they were staged in the presence of foreign ambassadors and other state guests and symbolically assigned the doge a quasi-divine rank that raised him above other rulers. The complex of visual, acoustic, and topographical strategies applied to strengthen the sacred character of the doge as representative of the Venetian state formed the aforementioned 'Neobyzantinism'.[14] However, there is evidence for a contrasting development: the staged sacredness of the Republic proportionally increased as Venice's actual political and economic importance decreased.

Theology of the state

The sixteenth-century authors who commented on the history and politics of Venice already described the ideological basis of the Republic as a 'theology of the state'.[15] Like monarchs, the doge had two bodies: his physical one, as well as the metaphysical political body related not to his person but to his office.[16] It was this latter body that was to be honoured by the civic and diplomatic ritual focusing on the doge's *persona*.[17] As being immortal, the mystical body was considered sacred to such an extent that a royal entry could be perceived as a procession of Corpus Christi.[18] This sacralization was exactly the effect desired by Venetian state ideologists when they implemented the doge as the *alter ego* of Christ in political iconography and 'myth'.

The process of *Christomimesis* echoed even in the orations delivered by the subject ambassadors congratulating the newly elected doge. Focusing on this matter, Giovanni Florio identifies two bodies in the ceremonial envoys from subject communities as well. Due to the restrictions limiting the doge's movements, the dominions sent congratulatory ambassadors to the Ducal Palace. Florio stresses their need to 'embody' the whole subject city that they represented. Thus, the meeting in the Hall of the Collegio took place between the doge, who embodied the Republic, and the orators, who embodied subject communities.[19] These orations represent the most considerable part of a wider epideictic production. In Venice, special events and state occasions — such as the visits of foreign princes, victories, and peace treaties — were traditionally adorned with celebratory speeches, whose public performance was managed by the Signoria. All types of these orations were later usually published to give permanence to the performance. Among the authors were writers like Giangiorgio Trissino, Cornelio Frangipane, and Luigi Groto, but also state historiographers and theorists such as Bernardo Giustinian, Gasparo Contarini, and Paolo Paruta.

Most panegyrists focused on representing Venice as an image of heaven and paradise. In their praises, *Venetia* was always characterised by virginity and virtue, akin to the Virgin Mary.[20] *Venetia* was moreover presented as Astraea, hoping the Golden Age will return.[21] In these accounts, the doge and the Signoria figured as images of God, the sun, or the stars.[22] Trissino defined the doge as 'a fair prince, and saint, and similar to God; that the good prince is really the image of God on earth', and Bartolomeo Malmignatti described the Signoria as 'this famous council which represents the angels' chorus of Paradise'.[23] Members of the government as well as the state itself were always related to the heavenly sphere to emphasize their uniqueness. Since Venice was supposed to have been founded on the day of the Virgin's Annunciation in 421, its constitution could be presented as divine, perfect and eternal. In 1554, Giovanni Maria Masenetti proclaimed:

> Thus, it was necessary that this saint Republic of Venice, born on celestial advice, was granted empress, free and Christian [...]. When the city of Venice emerged from the salty waves adorned with thousand crowns, emerged together with her Faith, Justice and the other virtues.[24]

Masenetti's words perfectly summarise the principal components of the 'myth of Venice', but a myth also could be revealed as such. Internal criticism was present though it usually did not appear in public since secrecy itself was part of the 'myth'.[25] To keep alive Venice's image of political stability and social harmony, the Signoria employed sophisticated strategies. As in 1514, when a devasting fire destroyed the Rialto area and thus allowed a new concept for reconstruction, the Serenissima could benefit from both the fires in the Ducal Palace that occurred in 1574 and 1577. By the end of the sixteenth century, a precisely elaborated political iconography had been developed that exploited the 'myth' to maximum. The most prestigious artists were engaged in this programme, and at the turn of the century, new paintings were mounted in the government seat.

Nevertheless, the 'myth' would be continually challenged over the course of the seventeenth century. Already since the beginning of the sixteenth century, and in particular during the Italian Wars, quarrels about ceremonial protocol and diplomatic precedence occurred. Though the Republic's perception as immortal had an impact on international policies and generated respect for its constitutional structure, foreign ambassadors complained that 'simple merchants' and 'seamen' claimed primacy.[26] Moreover, Venice was accused of being a republic without legitimised titles of nobility and without any imperial or papal authentication. Such accusations increased during the Interdict crisis of 1606–1607 and resulted in a 'war of writings' focusing on the sovereignty issue between the Serenissima and the Papacy. Though the War of Gradisca (1615–1617) provoked a new wave of anti-myth literature, the Signoria refrained from an official reply to the polemic. Instead, authors like Frangipane and Paolo Sarpi defended Venice's claim to dominion over the sea by different lines of argument.[27] However, in 1633, a public debate about the Serenissima's status began. The defenders of the Republic pointed out that it owned two royal titles, i.e. Cyprus and Candia, and that these would be valid in the event of physical loss of the related reigns — which had occurred in 1573 and would again in 1669. Moreover, they emphasised Venice's *maiestas* based on its supremacy in the Adriatic. The critics, however, were not impressed and even mocked the lion of St Mark.[28] In such a hostile atmosphere, the Serenissima replied to the attacks with an improvement of the 'myth' by precisely reconfirming its divine origin and its privileges. Gino Benzoni defines this period as an era of irreversible decline and even attributes a 'crown syndrome' to the Serenissima, as an uncrowned queen desperately seeking a crown. This desire for self-legitimation explains the enthusiasm in Venice when Francesco Morosini conquered Morea in 1687. Indeed, the newly incorporated reign served as a surrogate coronation.[29]

One of the aforementioned efforts to elaborate and increase the myth complex was undertaken by the ceremonial master of St Mark's Basilica, Giovanni Battista Pace. In 1678, he introduced the work *Ceremoniale magnum*, which included the foundation 'myth' of Venice. The text may be considered a late reply to criticism originally triggered by the 'war of writings' and further developed during the entire seventeenth century. Pace refers to all criticism including the lion of St Mark.

> The ever-glorious Republic of Venice took its most fortunate origins from the sea, in the year of our salvation 421, on the day of the Feast of the Annunciation to the Virgin Mary, destined to be a fortunate one for all of Christendom. The Eternal Father himself, considering rightly from eternity to find a bride for his only son, decided that Christ and Venice should be conceived in the Virgin's womb on the same day. This most precious conception of groom and bride took place on 25 March. Since she had to be a place of refuge for Catholic faith, Venice was born amongst the waters, made immovable among the turbulences of the waves and the tempestuous vicissitudes of humans. [...] She is very strong, surrounded by movable walls and guarded by the eye and claws of a lion, the notable impresa of the Most Serene Dominion, as well as the glorious and most propitious emblem of Saint Mark the Evangelist. Immersed in the water like the sun, she shines more vividly, more prestigious and brighter, and has become a spectacle without comparison, admired by all the world.[30]

According to the 'myth', Venice's uniqueness is reflected in the Venetian constitution. The perfection ascribed to the Republic was a pivot of the Venetian theology of state. The Serenissima was supposed to be a hybrid system with monarchic, aristocratic, and democratic elements. Written sources emphasised the role of law and political practice in creating an equilibrium out of the constant tension produced by the 'democratic' base constituted by the members of the noble families seated in the Great Council Hall, the 'aristocracy' represented by the great governing magistracies (Senate, Collegio, Council of Ten), and the doge's 'almost-monarchical' persona.[31] The Venetian political system attracted many admirers, including famous authors such as Francesco Petrarca and Philippe de Commynes, who considered Venice a miracle and the most beautiful spectacle on earth. However, they pointed out that the outstanding benefits of the Venetian state were not only based on republican virtues displayed by a so-called 'good government'. They also derived from a Christian sacredness performed on the religious-political stage of St Mark's area.[32]

Accordingly, in several political writings Venice is described as a ship and the doge as an exemplary shepherd. In 1560, Alessandro Altano praised doge Girolamo Priuli: 'Oh wise and saint shepherd of the most beautiful herd of all which graze in God's sheep shelter. Oh faithful and innocent guardian of the famous virginity of this woman, of which has never been before a similar one nor another one'.[33]

According to the Venetian epideictic tradition, the duty of each state was to obtain eternal beatitude for its subjects in the sight of God. Venice could achieve this goal easier than other states, because it had been created by God himself. Whenever a new doge was elected, this sacred dimension was confirmed by the celebration of a Holy Trinity Mass. Just as Christ is enthroned over the host of angels, so the doge ruled the members of the state.

This function of the doge as a reference to Christ was emphasised visually by monumental paintings with Christ in the centre placed above the platforms, the so-called *tribunali*, of the most important offices hosted in the Ducal Palace. The eye of the beholder is directed by the wooden decoration from the doge's seat to the image of Christ above. This iconographic

6.1
Jacopo Robusti (Tintoretto), *The Paradise*. Venice, Ducal Palace, 1588–92. Photo: Scala, Firenze.

strategy was applied to all four main rooms in the seat of government: the Halls of the Collegio, Senate, Scrutiny, and the Great Council.[34] Jean Habert sums up the message of Jacopo Tintoretto's *Paradiso* situated in the Hall of the Great Council (fig. 6.1): 'Christ is a celestial doge, the only true doge of Venice, and the terrestrial doge is his representative on earth'.[35]

This ideological approach, which has been described as 'Neobyzantinism', can be defined as 'a cultural phenomenon that appears to have been the consequence of a reaffirmation of identity'.[36] It emerged as a reaction to a time of crisis requiring the redefinition of the state, and thus also of its head. The doge was given a new position, in both political and religious terms. David Bryant explains:

> The doge, *princeps in republica*, *princeps in ecclesia*, becomes a kind of modern emperor who is able to unify the church and the state and to render both positions beneficial by a balance which meanwhile had been lost in Byzantium itself.[37]

Hence, the dictum '*Christus vincit*', which was originally reserved for Byzantine emperors, served now as a reference to the doge and was implemented in the iconographic, architectural, literary, and musical works created in Venice in the last quarter of the sixteenth century.[38]

Topographical strategies in the context of the 'crown syndrome'

In his study of the entries of the procurators of St Mark, Alessandro Metlica states that, starting with the entry of Francesco Molin in 1634, the ceremonial itinerary changed: the starting point for the procession became the church of San Salvador instead of San Moisè.[39] After having celebrated mass, the route ran through the Mercerie to the Basilica, where a stop was made for another mass and the newly elected procurator swore the oath of office with both hands on the altar. Then the procurator and his party headed to the

Hall of the Collegio in the Ducal Palace, where he expressed thanks for the honour of being commissioned to serve the Republic.[40] Over the course of the seventeenth century, and particularly from the 1670s onwards, these festivities became more and more ostentatious. As Metlica points out, because of an increasing rivalry among the noble families the display of luxurious decorations and personal allusions drew focus to certain protagonists and their houses (*casate*). Splendour and magnificence meant to glorify the Serenissima were now exploited for auto-celebration. This development undermined the traditional principles of Venice's republicanism, thereby reshaping civic ritual as well as the 'myth' itself.[41]

However, the decision to modify the itinerary of the procurator's entries was not made by chance. In addition to reflecting a certain pragmatism, given the dilapidation of the church of San Moisè, this change occurred in a period when the 'myth of Venice' was harshly questioned.[42] The tarnished credibility of the 'myth' was restored also through visible strategies, by combining civic ritual with topographical implications. Since the Basilica of St Mark was the uncontested religious centre for civic ritual and the location where the oath of office took place, the axis between the church of San Salvador and the Basilica can be understood as a *via sacra*. San Salvador had substantial symbolic significance because of its multi-layered sacred-political connotations: it is one of the eldest churches in Venice, holding the urn with the ashes of St Theodore, the first Byzantine patron saint of Venice (before St Mark assumed this role).[43] According to the 'myth', in 1177 Pope Alexander III consecrated the church after doge Sebastiano Ziani had arranged a peace treaty between himself and emperor Frederick Barbarossa. As a sign of gratitude, the pope allegedly granted the doge the so-called *trionfi*, which also served as the basis for the mystical marriage between Venice and the Sea yearly performed at the feast of the Sensa that assigned to the Republic the role as Queen of the Adriatic.[44]

The sacralising role of San Salvador was also visually stressed: the reconstruction of the church in the sixteenth century formally alluded to the Basilica of St Mark in its design, with cupolas and polychrome floor mosaics. Therefore, San Salvador gained a higher level of sacredness by referring to the Basilica as the religious centre for state occasions. Besides, in 1584 the bones of Caterina Cornaro were transferred to a newly built tomb monument in San Salvador facing the Cornaro's family grave.[45] In 1489, the Republic had forced Caterina to abdicate in order to assume her title as Queen of Cyprus, Jerusalem, and Armenia. The church therefore conveyed the claim of dominion over Cyprus. In addition, the allusion in the title to Jerusalem, site of the Holy Grave, and to Armenia, the first Christian kingdom, strengthened Venice's claims to sacredness. In San Salvador, above the main altar is a painting by Titian depicting the transfiguration. According to the 'myth of Venice', the transfiguration of Christ alludes to a 'transfiguration' of the doge from head of the Republic to a redeemer, and from a political to a mystical body. Starting the entries of the procurators of St Mark at San Salvador therefore infused the event with higher symbolic significance. The office of procurator already created a connection to St Mark. Celebrating mass first in San Salvador, then moving to the Basilica for a second mass, created a *via sacra* reinforced by the sacrality of its start and endpoint. Passing through this route, the procurator served as a bearer of sacredness that was offered to the doge and the Signoria when he paid his respects to them in the Hall of the Collegio. The ceremonial route running from San Salvador to St Mark and from there to the Ducal Palace can be read as complementary to the *via triumphalis* running from San Nicolò del Lido to St Mark.

Occurred in December 1423, the first Venetian visit of the Byzantine (co-)emperor John VIII Palaiologos offered a good occasion to use both 'triumphal' routes.[46] As was usual at that time, John VIII spent the first night in the monastery of San Nicolò, and the next day he made his entry on the Bucintoro (ceremonial state galley) from San Nicolò to St Mark; then he was escorted to his accommodation at the monastery of San Giorgio Maggiore. A rich entertainment programme followed, including the designated highlights for state guests, such as visits to the treasury of St Mark, the Mint, the Arsenal, and the Hall of the Great Council.[47] On 13 January 1424, the doge and Signoria invited the emperor for a walk through the city centre. After enjoying the view from the Campanile, and thereby 'understanding the city and its port', the walk began at St Mark, proceeded along the Mercerie, crossed the Rialto Bridge, turned into Ruga Vecchia San Giovanni (Old St John Street) and ended at the landing stage of San Tomà, from which the group moved by boat along the Grand Canal. After passing St Mark, they reached San Giorgio Maggiore.[48] Horses were deliberately omitted during this walk to impress the emperor by a direct contact with the locations and stores that were passed by. The chronicler Antonio Morosini describes in detail how the itinerary had been prepared. As usual, the shops on the Mercerie were obliged to increase the quality and quantity of their goods and to be decorated splendidly. Crossing the Rialto seemed like bathing in riches.

> Mountains of pure mint gold and pearls and jewels in great multitude, with gold threads and pearls and jewels in great variety, and passed by the stores and sales stalls for cloth, golden cloth of all kinds, and silk.[49]

Along the route, buildings and boats were magnificently adorned, while noble people dressed luxuriously moved on the streets. Although Morosini does not mention it explicitly, acoustic performances, music, and fragrances were also integrated into such state occasions. Thus, the whole city appeared a synesthetic multimedia-spectacle whose unique beauty, addressed to the senses, seemed divine. Since the declared aim of these occasions was to present Venice as a city of miracles that was almost transcendent, the visit of John VIII should serve as a medium for communicating Venice's magnificence, pomp, and pageantry to the rest of the world.

> So that he [the emperor], seeing, admiring and pondering the splendour and great wealth of the city of Venice, and its magnificence, would bring it back to his nobles and to all the Greeks: In all the world there is nothing comparable to this city, if one has seen what he has seen, and such things he could never before neither think nor believe that they exist.[50]

The Byzantine emperor himself unified in his transcendent body both state and church. By assigning him a role in transmitting Venice's uniqueness, the Serenissima appropriated his sacrality to surpass him in rank. Moreover, the doge who walked side by side with John VIII strived to benefit from the *kratos* of the *basileus* through a symbolic transition of his divine origin. Allusion to the Byzantine Empire, which in the past represented the climax of power and pomp, was ideologically motivated. Venice had long appealed at different levels to Byzantine ceremonial and iconographic power, assimilating and transforming its rituals. Symbolic objects such as the organ and the Bucintoro, as well as rituals and festivals that used music and light as emanations of the divine, belonged to this transition.[51] In addition, beginning in 1423 members of the Signoria were required to dress in crimson in public as a means of increasing the prestige of the state. Purple red, the colour originally reserved for Byzantine emperors and later used by the popes as symbol of the martyrial mission of the Church, became a clear manifestation of both the sacredness and power position claimed by Venice. By dressing in purple, the Venetian Senators evoked the

6.2
Detail of. fig. 2.7 featuring the arrival of Henry III of Valois at the Lido.

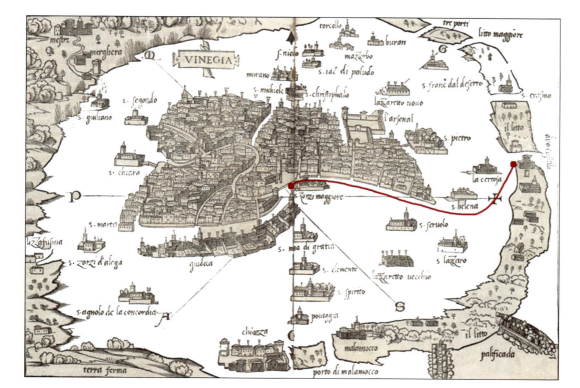

6.3
Itinerary of the Sensa ceremony through the Venetian lagoon. Designed by the author on a view of Venice in *Libro di Benedetto Bordone*, Venice, Nicolò Zoppino, 1528. Photo: Venice, Museo Correr. Reproduced with permission.

College of Cardinals (the Pope's 'Senate') but also the Christ-likeness of the Byzantine emperors, who 'presented in purple as king of the kings'.

On the other hand, the imperial walk itinerary ennobled the area passed through: where the emperor's purple shod feet touched the ground, there remained symbolically a trace of sacredness. In this regard, the Mercerie served not only as connection between the two sacral locations of St Mark and San Salvador, but also reinforced their character as a *via sacra*. As mentioned above, the 'walk of miracles' started with a view over the city from the top of the Campanile. Only by this means the Signoria could point out the city's particular *situ*, surrounded by water, and stress the 'myth' of being waterborne according to God's will. With the term 'to make understand the city' Morosini aimed to emphasise Venice's claim to power.

The fact that the starting point of the procurator's ceremonial route was a church consecrated to the Holy Saviour (that is the literal meaning of San Salvador) indicates its importance to the myth complex built upon the concept of Neobyzantinism. The itinerary to the Ducal Palace made by the procurators of St Mark during their inaugural entries even enhanced its sacralising function by connecting two points of Venice's topography devoted to the celebration of the Holy Saviour. The entry of the procurators ended in front of the doge and the Signoria in the Hall of the Collegio, where each procurator renewed the oath already sworn in St Mark's Basilica. The wooden decoration of the tribunal directed the gaze of the beholder from the doge to Paolo Veronese's painting dedicated to the *Allegory of the battle of Lepanto*. This votive painting depicts Christ as *Salvator Mundi*, St Justina, St Mark, Faith, *Venetia*, Agostino Barbarigo, and doge Sebastiano Venier. Since the latter, in his previous position as naval commander in chief (*capitano generale da mar*), had been responsible on behalf of the Venetians for the victory of Lepanto, he appears as *miles christianus*. The counterpart of Venier is the Faith, which corresponds to the ceiling inscription: 'Rei publicae fundamentum'. As Giorgio Tagliaferro points out, in the image St Justina is dressed like a queen, while *Venetia* is adorned with an aureole. Though usually *Venetia* is presented as a queen, here she becomes a saint.[52] She seems to have swapped roles with St Justina. Her aureole's design moreover evokes the star wreath of the Virgin Mary. This allusion to Virgin Mary, presenting *Venetia* as her *alter ego*, suggests *Venetia*'s immaculate conception and reaffirms her claim to power. A further reference to the founding myth is implied by *Venetia*'s gaze, which is directed toward her bridegroom, Christ, and not toward the central scene of the painting.

The performance of sacredness through topography and festival architecture

When the reception for Henry III at San Nicolò del Lido was completed on 18 July 1574, the doge, king, papal legate, senators, and ambassadors boarded the Bucintoro to make the king's entry into Venice (fig. 6.2). This festive company travelled towards St Mark's Square, but, without stopping there, the ship turned into the Grand Canal and instead took Henry III to his accommodation at Ca' Foscari.[53] The Bucintoro's route from San Nicolò to the centre thus corresponded with that traditionally prescribed for the return of the vessel during the ceremony of the Sensa (fig. 6.3). The ceremonial highlight of this rite occurred at the port entrance between the fortresses Sant'Andrea and San Nicolò, when the doge threw a consecrated golden ring into the water. Then, after a mass in the church of San Nicolò, the festive cohort took the Bucintoro to the Piazzetta and participated in a banquet in the Ducal Palace.[54] The Sensa legitimised Venice's supremacy on the Adriatic. Since, according to the divine founding myth, *Venetia* was born as Queen of the Sea, she was the bride not only of Christ but also of the doge. Any conceptual conflict in this dual marriage was resolved by identifying the doge as Christ's *alter ego*.[55] In this way, *Venetia*'s virginity was respected, while the sacredness of the doge's office was also enhanced On occasion of Henry's entry, the identical itinerary of his *via triumphalis* confirmed the Serenissima's claims to power, which were addressed to both the guest of honour and the invited foreign ambassadors.

The development of this waterborne *via triumphalis* relied also on practical needs. Being surrounded by water, the city's position limited opportunities for triumphal entries or processions on solid ground. During the procession for the founding of the Holy League in 1571, St Mark's Square resembled a labyrinth, as the authorities attempted to control the movement of the crowd by ordering the audience using geometrical patterns. The winding processional route led from the *Porta del Frumento* (Wheat's Gate) of the Ducal Palace across the expanse of the Piazza to the main portal of the Basilica, thus making a symbolic connection between the political and religious centres. On the occasion of the procession celebrating the victory of Lepanto in October the same year, the itinerary had been identical.[56] Although decorations such as garlands, tapestries, and light installations had always been widespread, ephemeral constructions were rarely used on festival occasions because of Venice's traditional perception of itself as already presenting a perfect appearance which made additional architectural decorations unnecessary.[57] From the 1640s onwards, however, festival architecture became more common, as the entries of procurator Giovanni Pesaro and of doge Francesco Morosini show.[58]

The Serenissima overcame its apparent spatial limitations by including the lagoon in its *via triumphalis*. San Nicolò, with its port entrance between the two forts (*castelli*), proved an excellent starting point for waterborne entries and processions, because it offered both a natural access point and was a safe area, being protected by a military fortification. Moreover, the waterborne route to St Mark's was long enough to stage a triumphal entry that was framed by the city as a perfect 'theatre scenery'. However, the symbolic function of San Nicolò was a crucial factor. Only a place with sacred-political connotations could initiate a *via triumphalis*, which also needed to end in another place with sacred-political connotations, such as the St Mark's area. By making use of the *Porta della Carta* (Paper's Gate), another *via triumphalis* could be created between the Basilica and the Palace, by leading up the *Scala dei Giganti* (Giants' Staircase) and the *Scala d'Oro* (Golden Staircase) to the chambers of government. In this way, the Republic generated a complete *via triumphalis* that directly connected the sacred location of San Nicolò to the political centre and thus enhanced the divine character attributed to the government.

Though it was not common to construct festival architecture in the centre of Venice, there had been two attempts to evoke the fascination of a triumphal arch already in the sixteenth century. In 1557, the *Arte dei beccai* (Butchers' guild) had built a triumphal arch on the Piazzetta for the entry of the dogaressa Zilia Dandolo Priuli.[59] Maximilian Tondro notes that the first ephemeral triumphal arch in Venice, commissioned by the butchers for the dogaressa's entry on 18 September, aimed to intervene in a public discussion. In fact, it was not an ordinary arch but a wooden construction consisting of two portals connected by a stage with a table that faced the Ducal Palace. In the Venetian ceremonial books (*Cerimoniali*), it was referred to as a 'theatre', a general term for festival architecture, whereas the chronicler Francesco Sansovino described it as a 'beautiful arch with a big opening on each side'.[60] It was built at the entrance to the Piazzetta, at the corner between the Library and the Mint, exactly in front of the butchers' stalls. During the entry ceremony, the arch complex could be passed through even twice. First, when the Signoria went to the Bucintoro to pick up the dogaressa at her home palace, and a second time after the arrival of the dogaressa and her festive company, as they moved from the Piazzetta to the Basilica.[61]

The whole construction was covered with white fabrics painted with decorations. Fictive rusticated pilasters reflected the real ones of the Library and Mint. The decorations were rather simple, bearing the coats of arms of both the doge and the dogaressa, the four Cardinal Virtues, four giants, an inscription dedicated to St Mark, the saint himself, trophies, and garlands. Butchers cleavers flanking the ducal arms alluded to the commissioners. The 'theatre' moreover made some formal references to the triumphal arch that had been erected in 1556 for Bona Sforza's entry into Padua.[62] The latter was the first temporary triumphal arch commissioned by the Signoria and realised on the *Terraferma*. When one month later the Polish queen made her entry into Venice, no arch welcomed her there.[63] It was not until 1557 that the *Arte dei beccai* introduced this festival architecture to the city centre.

The 'theatre' was meant as a statement to the ongoing project of *renovatio urbis* transforming the area of St Mark from a common marketplace into an exalted space for civic ritual.[64] The butchers' stalls were the last remaining structure of the old market but had already been scheduled for removal.[65] The stalls posed a problem not only for architectural unity, but were also considered by the procurators of St Mark an important aesthetic issue regarding the magnificence of the St Mark's area: 'a monstrosity amidst so many jewels, such as the Mint, the Library, the Ducal Palace, and situated in the most beautiful site of the city'.[66] Critics were aware that the image of the Serenissima, and the persuasive power of the 'myth of Venice', were based on the visual perception of the city.

By the attempt to integrate it into civic ritual, the butchers' arch complex overcame the reproach of being indecorous for this unique 'sacred' location. According to Tondro, the dogaressa's entry served only as a pretext for the *Arte dei beccai* to advance their own prestige and economic interests. However, nobody would have been able to build any construction in a public space, and especially not in the area of St Mark, without the explicit permission of the Signoria. Although the Signoria itself did not commission the butchers' 'theatre', according to the *Cerimoniali* it considered the structure a decoration that honoured the dogaressa and contributed to the glory of the Republic. If it had not, the Signoria would never have granted the *Arte dei beccai* permission to build another triumphal arch for Morosina Morosini's coronation. Indeed, in 1597 the dogaressa and her festive company walked through an arch that was painted on both sides with scenes glorifying Venice and praising the Morosini and Grimani families. This arch was erected on the opposite side of the Piazzetta from the first, in front of the Palace. Since the butchers' stalls had already been removed in 1580, the shift in location of the second arch to the government seat represented a clear signal that festival architecture had to be state controlled. As such, it became increasingly sophisticated — as illustrated by Vincenzo Scamozzi's invention of the so-called 'macchina', a floating island that served as a stage for banquets, music, and dance.[67]

Another moment for building ephemeral architecture might have been the celebrations for the victory of Lepanto in 1571. However, contrary to what the literature on the topic has argued, there were no triumphal arches in the proper sense flanking the Rialto Bridge on this occasion, though there were splendid decorations on both sides.[68] The festivities for these celebrations were initiated immediately after the communication of the victory to the Collegio on 19 October. The doge and the Signoria went promptly for mass at St Mark's Basilica, where they were joined by the ambassadors of foreign rulers. The *Te Deum* was sung by doge Alvise Mocenigo himself, together with the Spanish ambassador and archbishop of Toledo Diego Guzmán de Silva.[69] In the following days, as representative of Venice's most important ally within the Holy League, Guzmán de Silva was honoured by the celebration of solemn high masses; once he also administered communion to the doge and the Senate. On 21 October, Guzmán de Silva celebrated a Mass of the Holy Spirit at St Mark's Basilica that was attended by the doge, the Signoria, and many nobles dressed in crimson. Afterwards, there was a procession across the Piazza in which the Host was carried before the doge under the archbishop's baldachin.[70] Venice and Spain thus demonstrated their alliance as defenders of the Christian faith. In addition, and even more significantly, this procession of Corpus Christi increased the sacredness of the festivities: it took place in front of the Basilica of St Mark — a religious centre and church under the *ius patronatus* of the doge — was conducted by the doge — as *alter ego* of Christ — together with Guzmán de Silva, as archbishop and representative of His Catholic Majesty.[71]

In his festival account, the notary of the ducal chancellery (*cancelleria ducale*) Rocco Benedetti emphasised a suggestive scene that took place at the end of mass when the doge himself carried a crucifix.[72] Though Alvise Mocenigo was personally very pious, this performance can be considered a visualisation of state propaganda, as the reactions of the audience prove. Indeed, this gesture of the doge, who was dressed in crimson, presented him Christlike. As Vicar of Christ and embodying Venice, he was prepared to make any sacrifice necessary for defence of the faith, and could thereby guarantee God's grace for the Serenissima. People were fully aware of this meaning. Benedetti, for instance, states, 'there was also His Serenity carrying the Crucifix before him, which greatly moved everyone to consider how great, and immense was the Lord's clemency and power, who had delivered us from so many distresses, miseries, tribulations, ventures and dangers'.[73] In this special moment in the Basilica of St Mark the doge's function as 'Redeemer' was visually implemented in political iconography and served henceforth as basis for the new iconographic programme in the Ducal Palace. Due to this impact, the victory of Lepanto gained so much symbolic potential. The doge's crimson-coloured clothes evoked not only Christ's blood but also the purple of the Byzantine emperors that characterised the *basileus* as 'king of the kings'. In the figure of the doge both meanings were unified. His authority referred to both state and church.

The significance of the victory of Lepanto, which actually was followed by a loss of territories as Cyprus was conquered by the Ottomans, was strengthened to an extreme to compensate for decades of defeats and centuries of war. Lepanto was thus imprinted in public consciousness as a miracle and clear sign of divine alliance. 'The' victory — as it was henceforth called — was visible evidence that the Republic was in God's grace, no matter what critics accused it of. Such political tactics employed psychological strategies. Accounts of the celebrations describe a population acting in an unreal manner due to excessive joy.[74] Of course, festival reports are based on *topoi*, and their contents have to be contextualised.

Nevertheless, it is clear that these festivities functioned as a social outlet in an era of crisis. State-controlled mythmaking developed accordingly: parallels were drawn between the Peace of Venice in 1177 and the victory of Lepanto. Luigi Groto, congratulatory ambassador of Adria, underscored these as the two most extraordinary events in the Republic's history, and ascribed the merit, in both cases, to a person named 'Sebastiano' (Ziani in the former case, Venier in the latter).[75] By linking Venice's foundation myth with the victory in 1571, he reconfirmed the sacredness of the Serenissima. Groto moreover positions Lepanto in relation to Cyprus. He declares Venier to be a 'relative' of Venus ('Venere') — who in turn is an *alter ego* of *Venetia* — and as divinely chosen to avenge Cyprus.[76] This allusion suggests that the forthcoming loss of Cyprus was already present in people's minds. The 'crown syndrome' thus was born.

After the end of the officially organised celebrations, performances by citizens and foreign merchants were approved but required the inclusion of religious ceremonies. The preparations began in the area surrounding the Rialto Bridge. Special attention was dedicated to the commercial centre, since the victory over the Ottomans generated hope for an economic recovery as it promised revived trade with the Levante.[77] A competition developed among merchants with regard to decorations and performances. The German traders residing in the *Fondaco dei Tedeschi* (Germans' warehouse) decorated their building with tapestries, creating the impression of a starlit sky through sophisticated illumination. Acoustic performances and concerts took place for three nights.[78]

However, the climax of the pageantry was displayed on the other side of the Rialto Bridge: in the area flanked by the Palazzo dei Dieci Savi, the Palazzo dei Camerlenghi, the church of San Giacomo di Rialto, and the adjacent *portici*, a demonstration of luxury and splendour was staged which surpassed in magnificence even the one organised for John VIII Palaiologos in 1424. This area corresponded to the mythic 'insula', where the first masonry building had been constructed — an area that Sansovino considered 'the most important commercial and financial centre of Europe'.[79] The so-called 'Piazza' was a hub for the global economy and supplied European and Asian courts with luxury objects, including crowns and sceptres. It must have been a great satisfaction for Venetians that kings and other rulers reigned with insignia made at the Rialto.[80]

The Rialto area also had a strong symbolic value as being the place where, according to the 'myth', Venice had originated: an inscription in the major chapel of San Giacomo di Rialto mentions that this church was founded on 25 March 421 and consecrated one year later by the bishops of Padua, Altino, Treviso, and Oderzo.[81] Sansovino considers San Giacomo di Rialto as a model for St Mark's Basilica and thus attributes to it architectural and ideological references to St Mark as the most sacred place.[82] San Giacomo also played a significant role within the Venetian civic ritual, as it was the seat of annual ducal procession commemorating the privileges granted to Venice by Pope Alexander III. A formal recognition occurred at the beginning of the sixteenth century: under the dogado of Andrea Gritti, who initiated the city's *renovatio urbis* project, the church came under the doge's *ius patronatus*.[83]

The prestige acknowledged to the Rialto area explained the competition among merchants to offer the best display on state occasions. The *Arte dei drappieri* (Drapers' Guild) arranged an outstanding spectacle. Under the *portici* along the Palazzo dei Dieci Savi, the shops of the drapers, situated one next to the other, constituted one single imposing passage that Benedetti estimated to be longer than one hundred steps.[84] The drapers transformed the ceiling of this passage into a turquoise heaven with stars, other ornaments, and gilded lanterns. They covered the shops, walls, sales desks, and columns with precious fabrics and hung garlands at the vaults. In this way, the drapers created their own little *via triumphalis*.

Benedetti states that the crowds moving back and forth in the antique decorated Ruga degli Orefici (Goldsmiths'

Street) along the *Drapperia* evoked the triumphal procession made by Publius Cornelius Scipio Africanus in Rome.[85] In 202 BC, the Roman general defeated Hannibal Barca in the Battle of Zama, and upon his return to Rome was awarded a triumph. When Scipio invited the people to celebrate the anniversary of the victory of Zama with another triumph to the Capitol, the Roman Senate saw a threat to the Republic and reacted with restrictions.[86]

This *exemplum* drawn from Roman history implied a reminder as it recalled both the Republican principle of equality and the reluctance towards the cult of personality on which the Venetian constitution was founded and which defined the doge as *primus inter pares*. Benedetti's reference to a conqueror who largely expanded the Roman Empire also invoked the Venetian dream of Astraea and of the return of the Golden Age. Indeed, the festivities for the victory of Lepanto celebrated the vision of the rise of a new Venetian empire in the Mediterranean. Imperial connotations were therefore linked to sacred ones as the Signoria integrated an annual ducal procession from St Mark's Basilica to the church of Santa Giustina in memory of the victory of Lepanto into the Venetian festival calendar.[87]

During the celebrations for the victory of Lepanto, the buildings opposite the *Drapperia* were decorated with crimson cloth on which pictures of mythological figures were mounted. The shops were adorned with coats of arms, 'spoglie', trophies from the battle, and works of art by famous masters like Giovanni Bellini, Giorgione, and Titian.[88] This canon of paintings may have served as a marketing strategy indicating that, in daily life, this location housed an art market selling works of high-ranking artists.[89] Canaletto's *veduta* of the square at San Giacomo di Rialto (fig. 4.1) confirms that this business took place there. The stores on the 'Parangone' — a street parallel to the drapers' *portici*, the shops on the Rialto Bridge and the others around the square were decorated similarly. On the square itself were flagpoles with banners featuring St Mark, and all balconies were also adorned with flags. At the foot of the Rialto Bridge a big portal was erected, and another one appeared on the opposite side, close to the goldsmiths' shops.[90]

Benedetti's description does not give a more precise localisation. However, considering the possibilities offered by the 1571 topography, there are only two options. It seems that the two portals created an axis spanning the whole distance between the bridge and the end of the *Ruga degli Orefici* and thus running parallel to the drapers' *portici*. As first option the two portals might have been positioned freestanding at both ends of the *Ruga degli Orefici*. There is, however, no indication that people passed through these portals.

Therefore the other option seems much more convincing: a portal was set at each end of the drapers' *portici*. Attached to the gates, it would not have been necessary to decorate both sides of the portals. The crucial point, however, is that the portals would thus have served as endpoints highlighting the internal *via triumphalis* running under the painted heaven, to which Benedetti ascribed a divine character thanks to its use of light and music as emanation.[91] This solution would have guaranteed the greatest honour for the drapers. Moreover, this *via triumphalis* would have connected two sacred locations with special significance for civic ritual since San Giovanni Elemosinario adjoins the drapers' *portici*. Like San Giacomo di Rialto it was under the doge's *ius patronatus* and part of the festival calendar through a ducal procession during the Holy Week. Thus, the two portals positioned close to these two churches also marked endpoints of a little *via sacra*. Benedetti's aesthetic impression of a divine character would have been formally confirmed. His account avoids the term 'arch'. It can be assumed that he would have used the term if it applied, since ephemeral constructions such as triumphal arches would have increased Venice's prestige. Most likely, these portals were instead a very simple type of festival architecture. Both portals were decorated with the coats of arms of the allies of the Holy League: in the centre stood the papal one, to the right the Spanish and to the left the Venetian emblems. There is no mention of further ornaments, and it seems that the portals were painted on only one side. They thus bore no formal relationship to traditional triumphal arches, and their construction would have been much less challenging than the 1557 butchers' 'theatre'.

Apparently, these simple portals did not make much of an impression on the festival reporters, since both Benedetti and Sansovino describe them with only one sentence.[92] By contrast, the writers have been fascinated by the displays of social harmony that seemed to derive from the celestial sphere. Despite the long-lasting festivities involving masses of people, public order was maintained, and no crime or violence occurred. Since the drapers had, as promised, also organised religious performances such as masses and a procession with a crucifix that had been much appreciated, the Signoria decreed

6.4
Domenico Zenoni, *Triumphal Arch and Loggia at the Lido*. New York, Metropolitan Museum of Art, 1574. Photo: Public Domain.

that other guilds too were allowed to arrange festivities, if they renounced the profane.[93] As a result, jewellers, Tuscan merchants, and 'marzeri' prepared pompous celebrations similar to the drapers', though slightly less magnificent. Their decorations also consisted of precious silk cloth and paintings. A new addition was the pyramid covering the fountain at the centre of the square, which rotated and displayed light installations.[94] Of course, the most spectacular effect of all the festive decorations occurred at night but also during daytime hours the ostentation of conspicuous consumption was overwhelming. Sansovino elevated the performances at the Rialto to a magical, transcendental level, calling them 'an appearance that cannot be described at all'.[95] The representational strategies applied by the Signoria in the area of St Mark were thus imitated by the guilds at Rialto — at a lower level but claiming the same glory to the Republic, and thus also to themselves.

However, the Rialto area was not only Venice's commercial centre but also a crucial site for government affairs. The Palazzo dei Dieci Savi and Palazzo dei Camerlenghi were important seats for state finance. The latter included a prison for debtors and thereby also assumed a juridical function. Analogous to the St Mark's area, official decrees were made public on the square in front of San Giacomo di Rialto. Moreover, what in 1528 became the location of the Palazzo dei Camerlenghi was before an architraved loggia, as the map of Jacopo

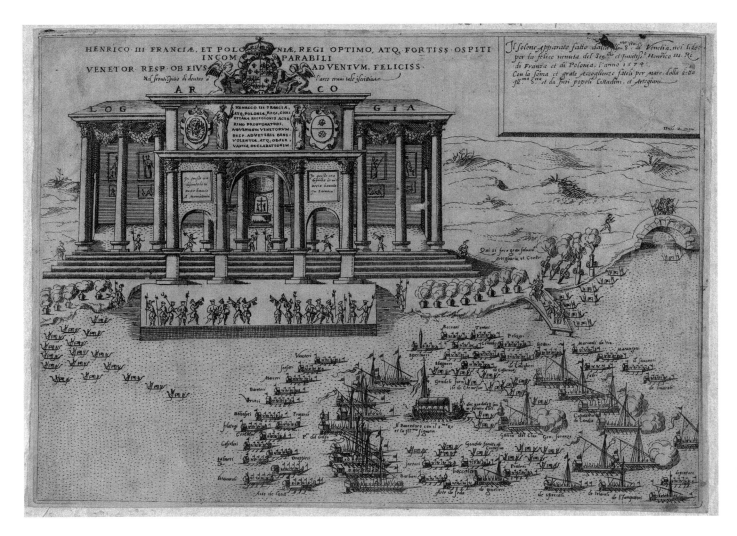

6.5
Rome, Via sacra, Forum Romanum. Plant realised by the author, based on the graphic project by Samuel Ball Platner, *The Topography and Monuments of Ancient Rome*, Boston, 1904, 172.

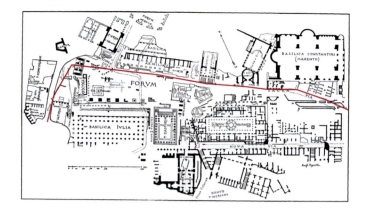

de' Barbari shows. This loggia served as a meeting place for noblemen. In 1424, it had become a prestige object of the Signoria which decreed to build it newly in stone.[96] After its removal to create the Palazzo dei Camerlenghi, the loggia's social function was transferred to the *portici* of the new administration building. The loggia at the Rialto had a counterpart on St Mark's Square at the foot of the Campanile. Since the latter had been severely damaged by a lightning strike in 1489, the Signoria approved a new project for an aristocratic meeting point.[97] This new Loggetta was designed by Jacopo Sansovino and constituted an opportunity to insert references to triumphal architecture into the square in the context of the ongoing programme of *renovatio urbis*.[98] Thus from the turn of the sixteenth century onwards, the Rialto and St Mark's areas both became construction sites — with Sansovino involved in both projects.[99] In addition, an ideological connection was created on several levels that linked both the urban spaces and reinforced the symbolic potential of the Mercerie for civic ritual. Thus, in ceremonial terms, both the *via triumphalis* and the *via sacra* extended from St Mark's Square to San Giacomo di Rialto.

This topographical significance changed again in 1574, when for the first time it was the Signoria and not a guild that commissioned the festival architecture within the city. This time neither the Piazzetta nor Rialto were chosen as the location but the Lido: far away from the commercial areas of the city, the Lido allowed for focus on ceremonial concerns.

Ephemeral architecture for Henry III's entry and the Roman via sacra

On the occasion of Henry III's entry, a triumphal arch was erected at San Nicolò al Lido (fig. 6.4). The awarding of the contract for the festival architecture to Andrea Palladio was the well-considered decision of an elite circle of art experts with important political offices.[100] Giacomo Contarini, a highly cultured art connoisseur and collector, was one of the two people in charge of the project and worked out the concept of the iconographic programme for the state visit. He had become not only a patron of the architect but also a close friend.[101] Marcantonio Barbaro, who also took part in the preparations and acted as one of the six procurators carrying the canopy at the reception ceremony, was also a patron of Palladio and had introduced him to the Venetian aristocracy.[102] Palladio had already designed triumphal arches in Vicenza for the festivities of Cardinal Nicolò Ridolfi in 1543 and Bishop Matteo Priuli in 1565, and thus had gained some experience with this type of construction.[103]

The ephemeral architecture built for the state visit of Henry III introduced three novelties. For the first time a detailed iconographic conception was carried out, a freestanding construction was erected and a location with high symbolic relevance was chosen, i.e. San Nicolò, the endpoint of the Venetian *via sacra* for the Sensa ritual and the starting point of the *via triumphalis* used for solemn entries. The triumphal arch at the Lido had three gates and was designed in imitation of the arch of Septimius Severus in the Forum in Rome, which had been built in honour of the emperor and his sons Caracalla and Geta in 203 AD. The arch of Septimius Severus represented the Roman victory over the Parthians in several campaigns.[104] While the decorations of the ancient arch referred to martial contexts, on the ephemeral arch at the Lido only two reliefs (on the front side) depicted war motifs: the battles of Jarnac (1569) and Moncontour (1569), from which Henry had emerged victorious.

Since the arch had to be passed through twice, it was possible to view an iconographic programme on both sides. The back side, however, did not depict a military theme but instead showed Henry's entry and his coronation in Krakow.[105] Hence, compared to the Roman arch, the iconography of the Venetian model can be considered more pacific and forward-looking. Though the ephemeral arch emphasised the struggle against the heretics, it also evoked the subsequent pacification of the kingdom. Both themes represented the objectives of papal policies, and their realisation was expected from the new king of France.[106]

At a meta-level, the ancient bore further symbolic content. Chronicler Lucius Cassius Dio not only referred to Septimius Severus as a 'new Alexander' but also described in detail his conquest of Byzantium, a widely admired city that was considered impregnable.[107] While Septimius Severus himself fought in Mesopotamia, Byzantium was conquered and destroyed by his troops in 196 AD. The emperor was proud to have defeated this magnificent city. In the Venetian context, reference to the triumphal arch of Septimius Severus can also be understood as a declaration that Venice not only considered itself an *alterum Byzantium*, but also that it believed itself to have surpassed Byzantium in rank.

The ephemeral triumphal arch at the Lido associated Venice not only with the Roman Empire and its tradition of triumphal processions but also with the *via sacra*, which was integrated into Rome's public performances as a route with high symbolic value (fig. 6.5). Like the former processional route that had crossed the ancient Roman Forum, the *via sacra* became part of a modern *via triumphalis* for the first time in 1536, for the triumphal entry of Charles V, when a new *axis urbis* was even created.[108] The *via sacra* started at the arch of Titus, passed through the arch of Septimius Severus, moved to the Temple of Saturn, and from there led to the Capitol. The Capitol, with its Temple of Jupiter Capitoline, represented the religious centre of Rome, where all triumphal processions ended. Symbolic-topographic parallels between Rome and Venice are evident. The Roman Forum performed the same functions as the St Mark's area: both were the political and religious centres of the dominions, as well as of trading activities. The portico of Rome's Curia Iulia, which no longer exists, served as a meeting place of senators in the same way as the Loggetta at the base of the Campanile, while the Temple of Jupiter Capitoline corresponded to the Basilica, since both were spiritual centres and the endpoint of processions. State ideologists and architects in Renaissance Venice were aware of this symbolic value and enhanced such imperial connotations when they undertook the so-called *renovatio urbis* in the first half of the sixteenth century.[109]

The Roman analogy implied in the *via triumphalis* appealed not only to the motifs embedded in imperial iconography, but also to sacred aspects related to Christian practice, since the itinerary corresponded in part to that of the ceremony of *possesso* undertaken by a new pope.[110] In the case of the *possesso*, the route followed the *via papalis* from St Peter to St John Lateran, crossing the Roman Forum by way of the *via sacra*. The highlight and conclusion of the ceremony took place at the Lateran Basilica, where the mystic marriage of the pope (as bridegroom) to the Catholic Church (as bride) was celebrated. Since the arches of Septimius Severus and Titus represented the endpoints of the original *via sacra*, the ancient monuments assumed a particular importance in the Christian context. Their integration into the processional route served a legitimation strategy for the popes. By visualising a symbolic continuity between the Roman Empire and the papacy, it suggested that the pope had acquired political power apart from his spiritual supremacy.

Venice, in turn, relied on symbolic aspects of the ceremonies of both *ingresso* and *possesso* in order to adopt imperial as well as sacred implications for its own political iconography. Allusion to the mystical marriage of the pope and the Catholic Church formally confirmed the Republic's divine mission as defender of Christianity and its role as *vicarius Dei*. Symbolic parallels to the marriage of the doge and the Virgin Mary enhanced the state's sacredness. In addition, the integration of a *via sacra* and the arch of Septimius Severus into the Venetian *via triumphalis* served not only as a reference to the Roman Empire but also to the empire of Charles V. Through the imperial iconography integrated in the arch at the Lido, Venice claimed the legitimacy of its rule over the land, just as the Sensa did over the sea. In this sense, it would be too modest to define Venice as an *altera Roma*, as it had traditionally been described by contemporary authors.[111] As in the case of Byzantium, Venetian state ideologists advanced an image of Venice which confirmed that the Republic had surpassed Rome in rank. In the hierarchy of rulers, it assumed the premier position, thereby ranking directly after God. This strategy of self-representation was further strengthened after the victory of Lepanto, when the Serenissima began to claim the defeat of the Ottomans exclusively for itself in literature and art.[112]

Close to the ephemeral arch, a loggia with ten Corinthian columns was erected (fig. 6.4).[113] Some festival reporters — including Marsilio Della Croce, Rocco Benedetti, Gregorio Manzini and Tommaso Porcacchi — describe it as a work designed by Palladio, while others do not name the architect.[114] Palladio's authorship has been challenged by scholars such as Wolfgang Wolters for stylistic reasons, but a recently reconstructed 3D model seems to prove it.[115] Though there is no known template for the loggia at the Lido, some drawings from Palladio might be possible models.[116] Symbolic parallels can be drawn to the Roman Forum concerning this loggia. South of the triumphal arch of Septimius Severus is the Rostra Augusti, the former speaker's platform, which was a locus for senators; north was the Curia Iulia, where the senators met. A similar sort of meeting place is implied by the Loggetta at the St Mark's Campanile, especially since it is located close to the Ducal Palace. At a formal level, the architectural style of the loggia, which connects the inside with the outside, alludes to its republican function. If this meaning of the Loggetta is extended to the ephemeral loggia, the latter gains high symbolic significance. Deborah Howard considers the Loggetta 'the most complete surviving visual representation of the "myth of Venice" – that is, the Venetian view of their own state as the perfect republic. […] The

Loggetta served not only to impress on foreign visitors the supremacy of the Venetian state, but also to remind Venetians themselves of the myth.'[117]

Howard's thesis is supported by Manfredo Tafuri, who defines the Loggetta as 'pure ideology' because it was a place of auto-glorification for the Venetian aristocracy, which appropriated the architectural structure of a triumphal arch for its own purposes.[118] Tafuri's perspective can be expanded upon, since an axis leads from the Loggetta through the Arco Foscari to the Scala dei Giganti. Thus, three elements of triumphal architecture were connected, not only forming a *via triumphalis* but also demonstrating how the Venetian aristocracy adapted imperial forms of representation to legitimise its rule. Though the Loggetta's originally existing democratic feature was hence reduced to the applauding audience outside, its role as an important component of the myth complex should not be neglected.[119]

The general function of the loggia as a place for religious ceremonies and, in the Venetian context, as a meeting point for the nobility is crucial. Both aspects were taken into consideration at the Lido. Four victories were painted on the ceiling of the loggia, which bore palm branches and crowns. With this decoration, Henry's coronation seemed to be staged when he entered the loggia. This allusion to a stage was intentional, since in the *Cerimoniali* the ephemeral loggia was called a 'theatre'.[120] On the back wall were ten statues of the virtues, an important element in the representational strategies of princely iconography. In the middle of the back wall was an altar with a painting of a crucifixion. Here the king knelt down and prayed.[121] Since others remained standing, this staging suggested a submission by Henry.

The loggia fulfilled a sacred function at several levels. Its derivation from the ancient temple, the central positioning of the altar, and the performance of liturgical acts already identified it as a consecrated place. The goddesses of Victory, which hovered above the altar and seemed to enact the virtual coronation of Henry III, could also be interpreted as a triumph of religion or faith. This aspect gains even more importance by the surrounding statues of the virtues as well as the direct iconographic reference to the triumphal arch, on which the king was depicted as *miles christianus* defending the true faith against the heretics.

Lionello Puppi interprets the structure of the festival architecture at the Lido as a series of intercommunicating scenarios reflecting a higher-level spectacle of power:

> If the arch corresponds to the opening of the *porta regalis*, the loggia distinguishes itself, even more than in the manner of the *sancta sanctorum* of the ceremony, as moving *columnatio*, both setting themselves as the front of a scene that the city generates, qualifying the representation as a spectacle and performance of power in which the counter-reformist vocation now meets the aristocratic hardening of the state.[122]

Though Puppi's assumption is essentially correct, the Signoria's attitude does not seem to be as rigid as originally supposed. Evidence of the government's adaptability to changing political requirements can be found in the political moves made after the separate peace with the Ottoman Empire was confirmed in 1573. Venice's disagreement with the resolutions issued by the Council of Trent had already provoked displeasure.[123] After the peace treaty, the image of the Serenissima as defender of the Catholic faith required urgent repair. Thus, in the midst of the Counter Reformation, the new French king was celebrated as a bearer of hope in the fight against the Huguenots on the triumphal arch at the Lido. The real strategic focus, however, was represented by the loggia, which depicted the elaboration of a new Christology featuring the motif of the Redeemer. Above the altar was a painting of Christ, because it is Christ, the bridegroom of *Venetia*, who refers to the divine foundation of the city as well as to the doge as *vicarius Dei*. The new iconographic programme designed for the Ducal Palace, the construction of the Redentore Church, and the festival architecture honouring Henry III were all linked by the special symbolism of Venetian topography. Since the conceptualization of this new ideology was still just beginning in 1574, it was realised in detail only in the subsequent perception of Henry's state visit by different media of visual culture.[124]

Conclusions

In the new iconography developed during the early modern era, the Republic of Venice was represented as a state created directly by God and thus as a paradise on earth. Since the figure of *Venetia* became interchangeable with the Virgin Mary, as well as with *Iustitia*, the Republic came to be seen as infallible in religious and public life. By means of the Sensa ceremony, Venice not only legitimised its claim of maritime supremacy, but assumed also a sacred status. The Serenissima created its own *via triumphalis* and *via sacra* on water, which started at San Nicolò and ended at St Mark but, in ideological terms, continued up to the doge's seat on the *tribunale* in the Hall of the Great Council. Festivals — like those celebrated on the occasion of the visit of Henry III — were state acts performed in the presence of sovereigns and foreign ambassadors in order to symbolically integrate the doge into the hierarchy of kings and emperors. In the case of the French king's reception in the ephemeral loggia in front of San Nicolò, it can even be understood as a competition between sacred figures. The *rex christianissimus* was staged as kneeling down to pray in front of an altar depicting Christ who, according to

Venetian iconography, was interchangeable with the doge, his *alter ego*. In this respect, the allusion to being crowned there by 'Venetian' victories strengthened the impression of the primacy of the Serenissima's sacredness.

An intercommunicating system of visual, acoustic, and topographical strategies of auto-celebration guaranteed a continuous process of self-affirmation for the state. After the victory of Lepanto, these performances began to assign a quasi-divine role to the doge as the Redeemer, identifying him with Christ as his *alter ego*. At the same time, in iconography and public ritual, the doge was staged as *princeps in republica* and *princeps in ecclesia*, a reference to the Byzantine emperor who embodied both religious and state supremacy. Of course, the doge's power and magnificence were not linked to his person but only to his office, in order to glorify state dignity.[125] According to the Venetian constitution, this 'paradoxical prince' had to act as *primus inter pares* while becoming godlike in the external projection of state policies.[126] It was precisely this dualism, embodied by each individual doge, that incited them to strive for more magnificence with the assistance of state ideologists. By strengthening their own 'sacredness', the doges enhanced the Republic's image as 'divine'.

In the course of the sixteenth century, architectural measures reinforced Venice's perception as an 'immortal Republic'. The programme of *renovatio urbis* transformed the two most important areas, St Mark's Square and Rialto, into urban spaces perfectly suited for the extended requirements of civic ritual and for supporting the 'myth of Venice'. The concept for reconstruction focused on combining sacred connotations with references to Roman imperial iconography. As a result, both areas show ideological and stylistic parallels. Their particular symbolic significance became clear since both locations were linked to the foundation 'myth' and were called 'piazza'. They even seemed to mirror each other in topographical terms. St Mark's Square was characterised by the Basilica facing San Geminiano and flanked by the Procuratie. Similarly, the '*insula*' was framed by San Giacomo di Rialto, San Giovanni Elemosinario and administration offices on opposite sides. Three of these churches were under the doge's *ius patronatus*, while San Geminiano had been rebuilt on ducal advice. All four churches were destinations of ducal processions ('*andare in trionfo*') either in the Holy Week or in the Easter Week. Therefore, a strong focus was set on the doge's image as 'Redeemer'. On a mystical level, a mutual exchange between the head of state and the topography took place. The doge was charged with sacredness by visiting sacred locations, whereas he himself transmitted sacredness to the spaces he visited. This autoreferential system guaranteed the city's sacralising capacity. The connection of the two 'sacred' areas of St Mark's Square and Rialto, generated by the Mercerie, created a sophisticated system of short and long *vie sacre* that adapted to the increased demands of civic ritual emerging in times of crisis. Thus, the 'sacred' role of topography became evident.

However, from the seventeenth century onwards hard political facts provoked a transformation of the Venetian myth complex. A loss of 'sacredness' and a resemantization of republican values characterised the performances of civic ritual. This development was accompanied by an economic decline due to long-lasting military conflicts and increasing piracy. The loss of political and economic power caused by defeats in the Mediterranean assigned Venice a new rank among European rulers, shifting the interests of the Venetian patriciate more and more towards the *Terraferma*. Against this international backdrop, the Serenissima's image as paradise on earth, a place guaranteeing peace and wealth for its subjects, seemed to lose its persuasive power. The deepening of social differences inside and outside the patriciate challenged the efforts to achieve social harmony and political stability through rituals. Consequently, the supposed strong emotional ties between the Republic and its subjects, acknowledged and feared by foreign ambassadors, vanished. Both the devotion to the state and the sense of collectiveness, which still in the sixteenth century created the basis for the admired harmony and stability supposedly making the Republic immortal, diminished. Nevertheless, or precisely for this reason, festival culture was expanded. The Serenissima became an European centre for amusement and part of the grand tour. Though sumptuous performances of civic ritual continued to be displayed, however, the Republic no longer felt divine.

1. See chapter 1 by Florio and Metlica. See also Muir, *Civic Ritual in Renaissance Venice*, pp. 13–63; Gaeta, 'Alcune considerazioni sul mito di Venezia'. On the myth and musical performances see Fenlon, *The Ceremonial City*; on the myth in the visual arts see Tagliaferro, 'Il "Mito" ripensato'; Rosand, 'Venezia figurata'; Wolters, *Der Bilderschmuck des Dogenpalastes*. On the actual genesis of Venice, see Ravegnani, *Venezia prima di Venezia. Mito e fondazione della città lagunare*; Ortalli, 'Nascere sull'acqua. La lunga genesi di Venezia'.
2. ASVE, COL, Cer., reg. 1 and 2; Renier Michiel, *Origine delle feste veneziane*; Ambrosini, 'Cerimonie, feste, lusso'; Muir, *Civic Ritual in Renaissance Venice*; Fortini Brown, 'Measured Friendship, Calculated Pomp'; Casini, *I gesti del principe*, pp. 149–84 and 277–357; Urban, *Processioni e feste dogali*; Korsch, '"Le ceremonie per occasion di venute de Prencipi"'; Cossalter, 'Dai porti alle isole'.
3. On the visit of Henry III, Korsch, *Bilder der Macht*; Nolhac and Solerti, *Il viaggio in Italia di Enrico III*; Della Croce, *L'Historia della publica et famosa entrata*; Porcacchi, *Le attioni d'Arrigo terzo*; Benedetti, *Le feste, et trionfi fatti*. On the coronation of Morosina Morosini, see Van Gelder, 'Ducal display and the contested use of space'; Wilson, '"il bel sesso, e l'austero Senato"'; Molmenti, *La dogaressa di Venezia*, pp. 285–305. Rota, *Lettera*; Tutio, *Ordine et modo tenuto nell'incoronatione*.
4. Distefano, *Atlante storico di Venezia*, pp. 450–67.
5. Bryant and Cecchinato, 'Venice, City of Music'.
6. On suppression of knowledge of public disorder, see Van Gelder and De Vivo, 'Papering over Protest'.
7. Da Mosto, *I dogi di Venezia*, pp. 312–16; Giomo, 'Le spese del nobil uomo Marino Grimani'.
8. Van Gelder, 'The People's Prince'.
9. Korsch, 'Die Stanzen von Celio Magno'. For the lyrics, see Magno, 'Stanze recitate nel convito'.
10. Magno, *Trionfo di Christo*.
11. For a detailed analyses of the 'Tragedia', see Korsch, *Bilder der Macht*, pp. 87–96. The scores by Claudio Merulo have not survived. For the lyrics, see Frangipane, *Tragedia*.
12. Korsch, *Bilder der Macht*, pp. 95–96; Solerti, 'Le rappresentazioni musicali di Venezia', pp. 506–07.
13. For this concept, see Korsch, 'Die Stanzen von Celio Magno', pp. 162–63; Korsch, *Bilder der Macht*, pp. 57–60.
14. Korsch, *Bilder der Macht*, p. 96.
15. This term was used for the first time by Paruta, *Discorsi politici*. On Venetian theories of the state, see Sinding-Larsen, *Christ in the Council Hall*, pp. 134–49.
16. For kings, see Kantorowicz, *The King's two Bodies*.
17. On the gift made by Henry III to doge Alvise Mocenigo, see Korsch, *Bilder der Macht*, pp. 106–10.
18. Bertelli, *The King's Body*, p. 70.
19. On the political significance of orations made on behalf of subject communities, see Florio, 'Celebrating the Prince from Afar', pp. 123–27. On communication between representatives of Venice and those of the dominions, see Florio, 'La formalizzazione di una funzione informale'.
20. On *Venetia* as the Virgin Mary in Venetian political iconography, see Tagliaferro, 'Le forme della Vergine'.
21. On Astraea in political iconography, see Yates, *Astraea*.
22. On the state in analogy to the sun, see Curtio, *Oratione*.
23. Trissino, *Oratione*: 'un principe giusto, e santo, e simile a Dio; che 'l Principe buono è proprio la imagine di Dio in terra'; Malmignatti, *Orazione*: 'questo celeberrimo Collegio, il quale rappresenta l'angelico choro del Paradiso'.
24. Masenetti, *Oratione*: 'Onde è stato necessario che ne sia stata concessa questa Republica Santa di Vinegia, nata per celeste consiglio, Imperatrice, libera, et christiana [...] quando uscì dalle onde salse ornata di mille corone la Città di Vinegia, uscì insieme con lei la Fede, la Giustitia, et le altre virtù'.
25. On secrecy as *instrumentum regni* and part of the myth, see De Vivo, *Information and Communication in Venice. Rethinking Early Modern Politics*, pp. 40–45.
26. Benzoni, 'Tra regno perduto e regno recuperato', p. 238: 'semplice mercadante' and 'marineri'; on Venice's image as an 'immortal republic', see Finlay, 'The Immortal Republic: The Myth of Venice during the Italian Wars (1494–1530)'.
27. De Vivo, 'Historical Justifications of Venetian Power in the Adriatic', pp. 159–176.
28. Benzoni, 'Tra regno perduto e regno recuperato: la sindrome della corona', p. 248.
29. Benzoni, 'Tra regno perduto e regno recuperato', pp. 284–85.
30. BMV, MSS It. VII 396 (7423), fol. 5: 'La sempre gloriosa veneta Republica trasse l'origine sua faustissima dal mare l'anno di nostra salute 421 il giorno dell'Annuntiatione di Maria Vergine destinato felice a tutta la Christianità. L'Eterno Padre considerando seco stesso perapunto nell'eternità di trovar sposa al di lui Unigenito Figliolo, rissolse, che si generassero nel ventre verginale in un istesso giorno Christo, e Venetia; ed ecco dello sposo, e della sposa li 25 marzo il pretiosissimo incalmo. Perché doveva esser asilio della cattolica fede, ecco che naque fra l'aque, e si rende immobile fra le turbolenze de flutti, e fra l'humane tempestose vicende. [...] è fortissima circondata da mobili mura diffesa dall'occhio, dall'unghie d'un leone di questa Ser.ma Dominante, rimarcabile impresa, com'anche dell'Evangelista San Marco glorioso, e faustissimo embloema; attufata nell'aque a guisa del sole più viva, più rinomata, e cospicua riluce, fatta spettacolo inimitabile, e da tutto il mondo ammirata'.
31. See Chapter 1 by Florio and Metlica.
32. 'Buon governo': Petrarca, *Letters of Old Age*, IV, 3; Commynes, *Mémoires sur les principaux*, fols. 135v-136v.
33. Altano, *Oratione*: 'O saggio, et santo pastore del piu bel gregge, che pasca in tutto l'ovile del Signore. O fedele, et innocente tutore della famosa virginità di questa donna, cui ne prima fù simil, ne seconda'.
34. The four paintings are Paolo Veronese, *Sebastiano Venier rende grazie al Redentore dopo la battaglia di Lepanto*, Jacopo Tintoretto, *Cristo morto adorato dai dogi Pietro Lando e Marcantonio Trevisan*, Jacopo Palma il Giovane, *Il Giudizio Universale*, Jacopo and Domenico Tintoretto, *Il Paradiso*.
35. Habert, 'Venezia e il *Paradiso*', p. 57: 'Cristo è un doge celeste, unico vero doge di Venezia, e il doge terreno è il suo vicario in terra'.
36. Tafuri, *Interpreting the Renaissance*, p. 221.
37. Bryant, 'Liturgia e musica liturgica nella fenomenologia del "Mito di Venezia"', p. 207: 'Il doge, *princeps in republica, princeps in ecclesia*, diviene una specie di moderno imperatore che sa unificare e rendere prospere nella reciproca posizione di un equilibrio, perduto nella stessa Bisanzio, la chiesa e lo stato'.
38. On the dictum in imperial contexts, Kantorowicz, *Laudes regiae*, pp. 1–12; Fasoli, 'Liturgia e cerimoniale ducale', I, pp. 282–84.
39. Metlica, 'Reshaping the Republican Ritual', p. 177.
40. Sansovino, *Venetia città nobilissima et singolare* (1663), p. 306.
41. Metlica, 'Reshaping the Republican Ritual', pp. 179–81.

42. On the building conditions of San Moisè, see Sansovino, *Venetia città nobilissima et singolare* (1663), p. 112.
43. Lorenzetti, *Venezia e il suo estuario*, p. 389.
44. On the Sensa ceremony, see Muir, *Civic Ritual in Renaissance Venice*, pp. 103–33; Urban, *Processioni e feste dogali*, pp. 89–96.
45. Lorenzetti, *Venezia e il suo estuario*, p. 389.
46. Nanetti, ed., *Il Codice Morosini*, II, §§ 100, 102 and 114; Schreiner and Korsch, 'Un imperatore bizantino tra le calli di Venezia'. Emperor Manuel II had appointed his son as co-ruler in 1421, and since 1423 John had taken over all the affairs of state. Therefore, John was addressed as 'emperor'.
47. Nanetti, ed., *Il Codice Morosini*, § 114.
48. Nanetti, ed., *Il Codice Morosini*, § 114: 'capissero la città e il porto'.
49. Nanetti, ed., *Il Codice Morosini*, § 114: 'montagne d'oro zecchino e perle e gioielli in grande moltitudine, con fili d'oro e perle e gioielli in grande varietà, e passarono accanto ai negozi e alle bancarelle di vendita per panni, stoffe dorate di ogni specie, e seta'.
50. Nanetti, ed., *Il Codice Morosini*, § 114: 'Così che lui [l'imperatore], vedendo, ammirando e ponderando lo splendore e la grande ricchezza della città di Venezia, e la sua magnificenza, lo riportasse ai suoi nobili e a tutti i greci: In tutto il mondo non c'è niente comparabile a questa città, se si è visto ciò che lui ha visto, e tali cose non avrebbe potuto mai prima né pensare né credere che esistano'.
51. Miller, 'The Emperor and the Ritual'; Carile, 'Le cerimonie musicali alla corte bizantina'.
52. On Veronese's painting, see Wolters, *Der Bilderschmuck des Dogenpalastes*, pp. 126–28. For presentations of *Venetia* in political iconography, see Tagliaferro, 'Le forme della Vergine'.
53. ASVE, COL, Cer., reg. 1, fol. 57v.
54. On the Sensa, see ASVE, COL, Cer., reg. 1, fol. 22v; PSM, *Procuratori "de supra"*, Chiesa, Reg., reg. 98, fols. 25r–v, 77r–v and 151v–152r. At the end of the sixteenth century the Marriage to the Sea took place at the port entrance and not anymore on the open sea. See Sansovino, *Venetia città nobilissima et singolare* (1663), pp. 501–02.
55. On this cross-system of marriages, see Korsch, 'Renaissance Venice and the Sacred-Political Connotations of Waterborne Pageants', pp. 88–89.
56. ASVE, COL, Cer., reg. 1, fols. 54v–55r; Benedetti, *Ragguaglio delle allegrezze, solennità, e feste*, without pagination.
57. Sansovino, *Venetia città nobilissima et singolare* (1663), pp. 292–94.
58. On the entry of Francesco Morosini, see Metlica, 'La "gioiosa entrata" di Francesco Morosini'. On Giovanni Pesaro, see Vincenti, *Gli apparati veneti*.
59. On the entry ceremony of Dogaressa Zilia Dandolo Priuli, see ASVE, COL, Cer., reg. 1, fols. 42r–44r; Molmenti, *La dogaressa di Venezia*, pp. 260–75. On the celebrations of the Victory of Lepanto, see Benedetti, *Ragguaglio delle allegrezze, solennità, e feste*.
60. ASVE, COL, Cer., reg. 1, fol. 42v: 'un Teatro […] dove eranvi due porte di mirabil prospettiva'. Sansovino, *Venetia città nobilissima et singolare* (1663), p. 410: 'un bello arco con un volto grande per testa'. Tondro, 'The First Temporary Triumphal Arch in Venice (1557)'. Unfortunately, I had no access to Tondro's doctoral dissertation: 'Memory and Tradition'.
61. Sansovino, *Venetia città nobilissima et singolare* (1663), pp. 410–11.
62. Tondro, 'The First Temporary Triumphal Arch in Venice', pp. 349–52.
63. *La venuta della Serenissima Bona Sforza*.
64. Tondro, 'The First Temporary Triumphal Arch in Venice (1557)', pp. 340–47; Tafuri, '"Sapienza di Stato" e "atti mancati": architettura e tecnica urbana nella Venezia del '500'.
65. On the discussion, to what extent Jacopo Sansovino's project for the Library affected the removal of the butchers' stalls, see Morresi, *Piazza San Marco. Istituzioni, poteri e architettura a Venezia nel primo Cinquecento*, pp. 96–104.
66. ASVE, PSM, *Procuratori "de supra"*, Chiesa, Reg., b. 32, processo 65, fasc. 2 (quoted from Tondro, 'The First Temporary Triumphal Arch in Venice', pp. 342 and 347): 'una cosa così brutta in mezo tante zogie com'è, la zecca, la libreria, il pallazzo della raggion situtata poi nel piu bel sitto della città'.
67. On the decorations of the arch and the 'macchina', see Wilson, '"il bel sesso, e l'austero Senato"'; Rota, *Lettera*; Sansovino, *Venetia città nobilissima et singolare* (1663), pp. 418–20; Urban, 'Apparati scenografici nelle feste veneziane', pp. 156–60 and 162–66.
68. For example, see Urban, *Processioni e feste dogali*, p. 130, and Gombrich, 'Celebrations in Venice', p. 64. On the festivities, see ASVE, COL, Cer., reg. 1, fols. 54v–55r; Benedetti, *Ragguaglio delle allegrezze, solennità, e feste*; Sansovino, *Venetia città nobilissima et singolare* (1663), pp. 415–16; Fenlon, *The Ceremonial City*, pp. 175–91.
69. ASVE, COL, Cer., reg. 1, fol. 55r. On Guzmán de Silva's mission in Venice, see Levin, 'Diego Guzmán de Silva and Sixteenth-century Venice'.
70. ASVE, COL, Cer., reg. 1, fol. 55r; Benedetti, *Ragguaglio delle allegrezze, solennità, e feste*, p. 8.
71. On the *ius patronatus*, see Cozzi, 'Il giuspatronato del doge su San Marco'.
72. Benedetti, *Ragguaglio delle allegrezze, solennità, e feste*, p. 8.
73. Benedetti, *Ragguaglio delle allegrezze, solennità, e feste*, p. 8: 'vi fu anco sua Serenità portandosi il Crocifisso innanzi, che commoveva grandemente ogn'uno nel considerare quanto grande, e immensa fusse la clemenza e possanza del Signore, che ci haveva campati di tante angustie, miserie, tribulationi, giatture e pericoli'.
74. Benedetti, *Ragguaglio delle allegrezze, solennità, e feste*, p. 6.
75. Groto, *Oratione fatta in Vinegia*, p. A ii: 'son peraventura le due più rare imprese, c'habbia mai fatta questa Rep.'; 'sacro Colleggio'.
76. Groto, *Oratione fatta in Vinegia*, p. A ii.
77. Benedetti, *Ragguaglio delle allegrezze, solennità, e feste*, p. 10.
78. Benedetti, *Ragguaglio delle allegrezze, solennità, e feste*, p. 11.
79. Sansovino, *Venetia città nobilissima et singolare* (1663), p. 362: 'la prima Piazza d'Europa'. On the 'insula', see Calabi and Morachiello, *Rialto*, pp. 5–15.
80. Sansovino, *Venetia città nobilissima et singolare* (1663), pp. 363–64; Schreiner and Korsch, 'Un imperatore bizantino tra le calli di Venezia', p. 228.
81. Sansovino, *Venetia città nobilissima et singolare* (1663), p. 198. Lorenzetti, *Venezia e il suo estuario*, p. 466, states that the church was actually built around 1100.

82 Sansovino, *Venetia città nobilissima et singolare* (1663), p. 197.
83 On the *renovatio urbis* project, see Tafuri, '"Renovatio urbis Venetiarum". Il problema storiografico'; Hirthe, *Il 'foro all'antica' di Venezia*. Regarding the applied *ius patronatus* on the church, see Moucheront, 'A Booklet of Documents Concerning the Reconstruction of the Church of San Giacomo di Rialto Around 1600'. It was completely rebuilt in 1600–01 respecting the typology of the medieval building and reusing some of the materials previously employed; Fenlon, *The Ceremonial City*, p. 182.
84 Benedetti, *Ragguaglio delle allegrezze, solennità, e feste*, pp. 11–12. I confirm about 150 steps.
85 Benedetti, *Ragguaglio delle allegrezze, solennità, e feste*, p. 14.
86 Polybios, *The Histories*, books 10, 16 and 23.
87 ASVE, COL, Cer., reg. 1, fol. 54r.
88 Benedetti, *Ragguaglio delle allegrezze, solennità, e feste*, p. 12.
89 On the Venetian art market, see Cecchini, *Quadri e commercio a Venezia durante il Seicento*, pp. 192–204.
90 Benedetti, *Ragguaglio delle allegrezze, solennità, e feste*, pp. 12–13; Sansovino, *Venetia città nobilissima et singolare* (1663), p. 415.
91 Benedetti, *Ragguaglio delle allegrezze, solennità, e feste*, p. 14: 'Veramente, che 'l portico tanto superbamente adornato con tanti lumi haveva del divino, et le tante harmonie faceano parere, che ivi si trovasse il choro delle Muse'.
92 Benedetti, *Ragguaglio delle allegrezze, solennità, e feste*, p. 13; Sansovino, *Venetia città nobilissima et singolare* (1663), p. 415.
93 Benedetti, *Ragguaglio delle allegrezze, solennità, e feste*, pp. 14–15; Sansovino, *Venetia città nobilissima et singolare* (1663), p. 416.
94 Sansovino, *Venetia città nobilissima et singolare* (1663), p. 416.
95 Sansovino, *Venetia città nobilissima et singolare* (1663), p. 416: 'una apparenza del tutto impossibile a dirsi'.
96 ASVE, SEN, Del., Misti, reg. 55, fol. 4v, 11.3.1424: 'la loza nostra da rialto laqual he reduto di nostri zentilhomeni'; fol. 8r, 23.3.1424: 'sera chosa perpetoa e piu bella e piu sana e piu honor de la signoria nostra'.
97 Sansovino, *Venetia città nobilissima et singolare* (1663), p. 307.
98 Tafuri, '"Renovatio urbis Venetiarum"'; Hirthe, *Il 'foro all'antica' di Venezia*.
99 Calabi and Morachiello, *Rialto*, pp. 142–59; Morresi, *Jacopo Sansovino*.
100 ASVE, SEN, Del., Terra, reg. 50, fols. 26v-27r.
101 Hochmann, 'La collection de Giacomo Contarini'.
102 Beltramini and Burns, 'Villa Barbaro a Maser', pp. 114–29.
103 Zorzi, *Le opere pubbliche e i palazzi privati di Andrea Palladio*, pp. 167–71.
104 Brilliant, *The Arch of Septimius Severus*.
105 Della Croce, *L'historia*, pp. 13–14. On Henry's coronation in Krakow, see *Le allegrezze et solennità fatte in Cracovia*; Buccio, *Le coronationi di Polonia*; McGowan, 'Festivals and the Arts'.
106 ASV, Miscellanea Armadi II, 130, fols. 128r-138v.
107 Cassius Dio, *Historia Romana*, LXXV, pp. 187–95.
108 Madonna, 'L'ingresso di Carlo V a Roma', I, pp. 50–65.
109 For details, see Tafuri, '"Renovatio urbis Venetiarum"'; Hirthe, *Il 'foro all'antica' di Venezia*.
110 Fagiolo, 'L'effimero di stato', II, pp. 8–25.
111 Marx, 'Venedig – "altera Roma" – Transformationen eines Mythos', pp. 325–73.
112 On the impact of Lepanto, see Gibellini, *L'immagine di Lepanto*, pp. 129–33.
113 Della Croce, *L'historia*, p. 14.
114 For example, Della Croce, *L'historia*, pp. 12–13.
115 Wolters, 'Le architetture erette al Lido per l'ingresso di Enrico III', pp. 281–82; Balletti, Guerra, Meneghello, and Romanato, 'The Digital Ephemer', pp. 33–40.
116 Puppi, *Palladio*.
117 Howard, *Jacopo Sansovino*, p. 34.
118 Tafuri, *Jacopo Sansovino e l'architettura del '500 a Venezia*, p. 70: 'ideologia pura'.
119 Muir, *Civic Ritual in Renaissance Venice*, pp. 185–250. On this topic, also see chapter 2 by Tagliaferro.
120 ASVE, COL, Cer., reg. 1, fol. 57v: 'theatro'.
121 Della Croce, *L'historia*, pp. 14–15.
122 Puppi, *Andrea Palladio*, II, p. 408: 'Se l'arco vale il vano della *porta regalis*, la loggia s'evidenzia, più ancora che nei modi di *sancta sanctorum* della cerimonia, quale mossa *columnatio*, ponendosi l'uno e l'altra come la *fronte* di una *scena* che la città accampa, qualificando la rappresentazione ch'è spettacolo e recita del *potere* in cui la vocazione controriformistica incontra ormai l'irrigidimento aristocratico dello stato'.
123 Kretschmayr, *Geschichte von Venedig*, III, pp. 39–40.
124 Korsch, *Bilder der Macht*, pp. 117–88.
125 Bardi, *Delle cose notabili della città di Venetia*, pp. 77–78.
126 Muir, *Civic Ritual in Renaissance Venice*, p. 251.

Umberto Cecchinato

7

BEYOND THE CEREMONIAL CITY

Music, Public Revelries, and Urban Spaces in Everyday Renaissance Venice

Since the publication of Jacob Burckhardt's classic *The Civilization of the Renaissance in Italy* (1860), Renaissance festivals have been studied as institutionalised occasions — mostly corresponding to sacred days on the religious calendar — that involved the entire community and helped to reinforce community bonds. Over the last six decades, Venice has proved fertile ground for research on this topic. Many studies have been devoted to festive rituals: civic and ecclesiastical celebrations, public games, and spectacles such as bullfights, *forze d'Ercole*, naval battles, etc. Among such works, Edward Muir's *Civic Rituals in Renaissance Venice* (1981) set a new methodological and theoretical standard that also influenced other research fields. His fruitful model inspired further studies of the political functions of ritual celebrations and the relationships between the latter and the urban fabric. During festivals, urban centres were transformed into ceremonial cities, in which architectural structures became stages for promoting the socio-political values of the community. This conceptual lens has informed many scholarly fields and continues to be relevant in general studies of Renaissance festivals. For example, historical musicologists hardly look beyond the main and more representative public settings, such as St Mark's Square and Basilica, the 'theatres of ceremony', as Iain Fenlon called them, where 'dramatic public rituals underpinned with musical and theatrical elements were performed.[1]

This approach looks at phenomena from above, taking the point of view of authorities and cultural elites. As a result, it limits festive experience and its social functions to specific frames of time and space — the 'special days' fixed on the liturgical calendar, according to Edward Muir[2] — underplaying the multiple ways in which individuals organised and constructed their own everyday lives. Urban historians' recent interest in street life invites us to look beyond these temporal and spatial borders.[3] Music, revelries, public games, and other festive activities were commonly performed throughout the city and often organised spontaneously, outside institutional frames. They had an important role in social life, taking place in multiple public settings and intertwining with other daily activities. This article will analyse a variety of indoor and outdoor urban settings — churches, palaces and dwellings, streets, and squares — to show how spontaneous revelries occupied them and shaped their social meaning.

Churches and sacred places

Churches of every size and importance dotted the Venetian urban space, like many other Italian Renaissance cities. According to Coryat, at the beginning of the seventeenth century, the city hosted 'two hundred churches in which are one hundred forty three paire of organs, fifty four monasteries, twenty six nunneries, fifty six tribunals or places of iudgement, seventeene hospitals, six companies or fraternities'.[4] In mentioning the organs, Coryat indexed the strong ties between sacred places and musical performances. Although musicologists have devoted considerable research to sacred music traditions and praxis, the continuous presence of sacred music performances on the entire urban fabric of the city and their deep connection to everyday social practice is still understudied. Churches are usually considered sacred spaces neatly separated from the rest of the urban context, especially during masses or other liturgical celebrations. From this perspective, church music helped separate ritual

7.1

Dirk Jansz van Santen,
View of the city of Venice (detail).
From *Atlas van der Hagen*,
Amsterdam, Pieter Mortier, c. 1690.
The Hague, Koninklijke Bibliotheek.

moments from ordinary life. Moreover, it is often opposed to street music, which is deemed more common and accessible. As Iain Fenlon put it, the music 'of *calle* and *campo* [...] was much more likely to be heard by the vast majority of Venetians than the polyphonic motets and masses that were performed in the elite environment of St Mark's Basilica and a handful of other churches in the city'.[5] The reality, however, was far more complex than this, and such a statement needs reconsideration.

Polyphonic music was by no means performed only in St Mark's Basilica and a handful of other churches: as Elena Quaranta has demonstrated, on holy days minor churches also hosted solemn celebrations in which music was seldom absent.[6] The data collected by Quaranta shows how these places of worship were distributed across the urban fabric (fig. 7.2). Polyphonic church music could be enjoyed in every part of the city. Guides such as the *Protogiornale* of Vincenzo Maria Coronelli advised visitors on where and when these activities would take place, and as Coronelli states, 'no day passes without the display of paraphernalia and festival in different locations'.[7]

Even the way people commonly enjoyed church music was not very different from how they consumed street songs and tunes. Today, we tend to imagine people attending mass and other church celebrations with pious and solemn behaviour. Yet this was not the case for many bystanders, who participated looking for social exchange with others. The celebration of a solemn mass attracted passers-by of all social conditions, genre and ages. Bachelors in particular saw masses as opportunities to declare or even make love and compete with rivals. Moralists often complained about the participation of such crowds and blamed the polyphonic and instrumental music, which was accused of moving people to sinful passions and distracting them from their religious duties. In 1528, Patriarch Geronimo Querini prohibited the use of instruments because, he argued, they attracted gangs of libidinous

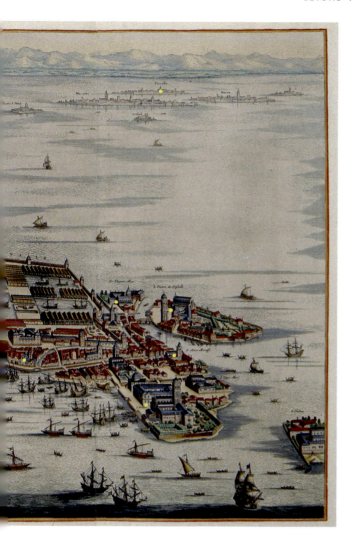

7.2
Map realised by the author, with yellow dots indicating musically active churches. Based on Dirk Jansz van Santen, *View of the city of Venice*. From *Atlas van der Hagen*, Amsterdam, Pieter Mortier, c. 1690. The Hague, Koninklijke Bibliotheek.

juveniles creating scandals and using violence one against the other. In his eyes, Venetian churches seemed to be 'meretricum scolae', guilds of sex workers, and were no different to the city's theatres and public dances.[8]

Churches were invaded by such crowds whenever liturgies were celebrated with music. The participation of large crowds was encouraged by organisers: the more people attended, the more the celebrations were honoured. Processions and musical masquerades paraded through the city a few days beforehand to announce that an event was taking place and attract as many people as possible.[9] Organisers also signalled the presence of a solemn feast by decorating the church itself. They covered façades and interior walls with wooden counter-walls, on which they hung silver masks, red, yellow, blue, or gold paper festoons, flowers, and symbolic plants, such as ivy. The windows were darkened with paper mounted to a wooden frame, which was sometimes also used to cover the doors.[10] The decorations created a special atmosphere and stimulated the senses of those who went inside, where lighting came from lamps and candles of various sizes: the visual impact was thus combined with olfactory stimuli, thanks to the use of incense, and auditory stimuli coming from the musical performances. The concerts themselves, filtering through the walls, also helped to attract crowds of passers-by during such celebrations.[11]

Many people in these crowds, as Querini noticed, were hardly there to attend mass. Bachelors' sexual needs were satisfied by *meretrices*, who were always present and looking for clients. They were usually seated in visible places, surrounded by suitors. For example, in 1618 a young woman was spotted sitting beside the musicians' stage and chatting with an old *ruffiana* during celebrations at Santa Marta's church.[12] In 1638, during the celebrations for the Annunciation, Marietta Bianchi was seated with her back to the altar of the Madonna, surrounded by several glamorous youngsters.[13] The most successful gained enough wealth to dress like noblewomen, attending the celebrations with many followers and occupying the most honoured pews.[14] This sometimes led to conflicts with noblewomen, who refused to be compared to the courtesans. In November 1611, the *famozisima meretrice* Novella entered Sant'Andrea's church followed by six maids, headed straight to the *coro* and asked permission to sit next to a noblewoman of Grioni's family. Grioni stiffly answered 'I know you as a dirty one' and refused. Novella responded by saying 'you call me dirty: you are the dirty one!' — starting a verbal dispute. Since the two women seemed peers in terms of their attire, some witnesses could not distinguish between the two and initially thought the fight was taking place between two noblewomen.[15]

From 1539 on, authorities tried to solve the 'disorders' created by sex workers throughout the city, while 'A lot of them stay on the public streets and in the main places of this city, exercising their art, giving a bad example to everyone, even at the time when the divine offices are being held'.[16] Sex workers had to be removed to preserve the prayers from debasement, 'so that they do not give an evil example with many acts, words and lascivious works to those who go in these churches' and to prevent violent clashes, because 'with their evil works they are most often the cause of many fights, scandals and failures'. 'Meretrices' and courtesans were therefore banned from 'any place in the nearby of churches and

7.3
Vittore Carpaccio, *Ambassadors' Return to the English Court* (detail). Featuring at the centre a member of the Compagnia della Calza while half kneeling. Venice, Gallerie dell'Accademia, 1495. Photo: Public Domain.

sacred spaces' and from going 'into any church on the day of the main feast and solemnity of that church' or faced a penalty of 200 lire.[17] The decree proved ineffective, since it had to be reiterated in 1571 and 1572, while on 20 December 1578 the court noted that, in order to circumvent the ban, sex workers entered churches 'dressed as wives and widows', and therefore forbade them to dress in this fashion.[18] Other sex workers used to parade in gondolas near the churches: in 1582, another law forbade them to 'row through the city, especially on feast days, solemnities and church pardons' and to go 'walking and stopping in the middle of the churches, making a lot of noise and doing dishonest things'. Many circumvented the prohibitions by going during the night, especially on Christmas, during the Holy Week, or on Holy Monday. Moreover, to attract passers-by and those gathered in the church, they presented themselves 'dressed in various lewd clothes and making many noises and using dishonest terms'.[19]

Prohibitions became stricter in the first half of the seventeenth century. In 1613, it was noted that the decrees had been regularly violated. Fines increased to 100 ducats and judges could add a ban, prison time, or corporal punishment at will.[20] Still, sex workers continued to disguise themselves to pass unnoticed and mingle with noblewomen. In 1615 they were consequently forbidden from going 'in any form of dress to the festivals or weddings of noble persons and of honourable life, or to the festivals, feasts, villa balls, in the churches and fairs and other public places'.[21] Penalties increased to five years of imprisonment and included public shaming practices, such as publicly cutting off their nose and ears in the space between the two columns of St Mark's Square, or pillorying and flagellation that proceeded from St Mark's to the Rialto. Even this punishment did not change the situation: in 1627, the authorities admitted that, despite the previous prohibitions, sex workers 'permit themselves to commit endless scandals, both by day and by night, particularly in churches' and once again reiterated the decrees from 1539 and 1582 with the increase in fines established in 1613. The same occurred the following year.[22]

Palaces and dwellings

The English diarist John Evelyn noted that during the Venetian carnival 'every place became accessible and everyone was free to enter'. Festive activities broke down the already blurred boundaries between the domestic and public sphere, making palaces and other dwellings open to all.[23] Attempts to reserve attendance for a selected few provoked general

disapproval. Sanudo records in his *Diarii* that in 1530, when the *Compagnia della Calza* (fig. 7.3) held a party in the Great Council hall, the fact that some people stood at the entrance limiting access to noblemen 'gave rise to much murmuring, since in such public festivities doors are usually kept open'.[24]

During the carnival, many dwellings hosted public meetings where people could freely enter and dance, paying the musicians at the end of the song. Such parties were held in 'the very houses of noblemen and gentlemen', noted Fynes Morison, which were 'open for any masked persons to enter'. A lantern decorated with garlands that hung on the residence's threshold invited passers-by.[25] Usually, these *feste da ballo* were organised by a *mazziere*: an entrepreneur who engaged the musicians and shared the profits with them. The *mazziere* was also responsible for maintaining order during the party. Since these events were open to anybody, violent clashes could arise. In December 1559, a *festin* organised by the dancer Lugrezia Barbiera in a house in Calle dei Fabbri, near St Mark's, gathered people of all kinds: notaries, craftsmen, nobles, and patricians. The house was so crowded that it was difficult to move, and participants perceived a feeling of suffocation: 'there were many people [...] pushing themselves. Some were pushing this way, some that way'. A quarrel between the servant of the Trevigiana count Claudio Collalto and a female dancer escalated into a bloody armed clash between the faction of Collalto and a gang of Venetian artisans.[26]

When no signs advised ongoing celebrations, passers-by could follow the music trickling into the street, as happened during church celebrations. In February 1556, some Rialto shopkeepers decided to dine 'in a secret place': the venue was in Murano in a palazzo of Geronimo Priuli, the godfather of one of the organisers. The banquet was accompanied by a dance: though it was only for a few close friends, the local *podestà* had forbidden music, so the young people tried to maintain secrecy; one of them stood at the entrance to prevent eventual passers-by attracted by the sound from entering. Over the course of the evening he chased away several other shopkeepers and a woman from Murano who came to borrow a pot. Nevertheless, his efforts did not prevent some local fishermen from entering the palazzo and playing 'four tunes improvising with the *lira*', nor the *podestà*'s henchman from discovering the illicit banquet.[27]

Sometimes these 'invasions' brought violence. Since the carnival of 1532, the Council of Ten had approved specific legislation aimed at limiting the attendance of unwanted guests at *feste* in private palaces. The carnival that year had witnessed bands of youths entering palaces during the revelries against owners' wishes, beating upon the doors, insulting and harassing the guests or provoking fights and quarrels. Authorities issued a fine of 100 ducats, six months of imprisonment, and exile for two years. The penalty for insulting the hosts or guests was five years of exile and a fine of 200 ducats. Using violence against a host, drawing arms, breaking glass, or attempting to enter by force drew a penalty of ten years of exile and a fine of 200 ducats.[28] These harsh measures may not have had the desired effect, since later sources show little change in the behaviour of youth, and notably of young nobles. In the early seventeenth century, for example, nobleman Leonardo Pesaro, who was later banned from the Republic for a series of hideous crimes, broke into a wedding party with his henchmen and started an attack against the palace dwellers, under the pretext of having previously been cast out for having addressed the bride in a rough manner. In 1670, Vincenzo Michiel, the son of a procurator of St Mark, was condemned for having entered 'by ruse, masked and with two pistols, the house of the nobleman Carlo Grimani, where a numerous company of ladies and patricians were engaged in a virtuous *accademia*'; the young nobleman 'improperly [addressed these] ladies of respectable condition' and, having attracted his hosts' attention, drew his pistols.[29]

Spontaneous celebrations frequently occupied taverns, places often indistinguishable from actual dwellings. Taverns were meeting places for different cultures, as well as social centres for the local community. Many people spent their leisure hours there, attending performances by musicians and singers of both sexes, playing cards and dice, and drinking. The community made tavern places for venting and resolving internal tensions, where rivals also had the opportunity to get even.[30] The authorities perceived the danger of meetings in taverns for political and moral reasons, since the practices that took place there diverted people from liturgical services.

In addition to the taverns, the *bastioni da vin* — where wine was sold at the retail price — also served as meeting places for festive gatherings. There it was possible to watch musical performances and buy cheap prints.[31] Authorities enacted laws to prevent people from crowding into such places. On 31 July 1571, an order by the Council of Ten made the existing penalties worse, punishing those who found themselves in these spaces to eat, drink, and gamble with eighteen months in the galley with irons on their feet; in the event of incapacity, they were banished for three years from the city with a fine of 100 lire. The wine sellers themselves were punished with a fine of 100 ducats. The same law forbade keeping these spaces open on official holidays and Sundays; only a small balcony could remain open. This *bando* was announced in Venice and Murano 'particularly where there are bastions, or wine and malmsey stores': we can draw up a list of these places for five of the six city districts and identify how they were distributed throughout the urban fabric.[32]

[*Cannaregio*] Sopra el canpo de San Bartolamio; a San Gresostemo; a San Cancian apreso el magazen dala malvasia; a Santo Apostolo apreso el magazen dal vin; a Santa Sofia apreso el magazen da malvasia; a San Felice; al ponte da Noal apreso el magazen da vin; a Santa Fosca; ala Madalena; in rio terà apreso el magazen dala malvasia; a San Marcuola apreso el magazen dal vin; ai Servi apreso el magazen dal vin; a Santo Avixe apreso el magazen da vin; a San Gieremia apreso el magazen da vin; a mezo canaregio apreso el magazin da vin

[*Castello*] in cale de le Rase, apreso li bastioni; in su la fondamenta di Sagavoni [Schiavoni], ala Pietà, arente el bastion da vin; sul campo de San Zuane bracola al bastion da la malvazia; a San Zuane Bracola, al bastion da vin; a Sant'Antolin, apreso el bastion dal vin; a cale de ruga Gagufa [Giuffa?] al bastion hover furata; sul ponte de Santa Maria Fermosa arente quel da la malvazia; a San Zuanne Nuovo arente quelo dala malvazia; a San Felippo, Iacomo arente quele furatole deli sagavoni [schiavoni]; a San Zuanne Pollo al bastion dal vin; in cale de Santo Antonio al ponte da ca' Balbi al bastion dala malvazia; sul campo de Santa Marina al bastion dala malvazia; in cale de la Madona, de le Fave, al bastion dale malvazie; sul campo de San Lio, al bastion dala malvazia; in cale de la Bisa, al bastion da la malvazia

[*Santa Croce*] a Santa Casa [?] sul canpo; a San Stai al magazen; a San Iaco dalorio; al magaze dei bari; a San Simio Picolo al bastio; a 3 ponti al bastio

[*San Marco*] San Samuel, Sant'Anzolo, a San Beneto, a San Fantin, a San Luca, in cale di Fuseri, a Santa Maria Zobenigo, a San Moisè

[*San Polo*] a Santo Aponal apreso el magazin da malvasia; a San Polo apreso el magazen dal vin; a San Toma; ai fra menori apreso el magazen da malvasia et da vin; a San Rocco apreso el magazen da malvasia

Nodes of public interactions: calli, campi, corti, fondamente

John Evelyn states 'that all the yeare long, al the markett places of great [Italian] Cittyes are full of montebankes or Ciarlatanes, who stand vpon tables like stages, and to sell their oyles, waters, and salues, drawe the people about them by musicke and pleasant discourse like Comedies, hauing a woman and a masked foole to acte these partes with them.' Venice was no exception. Although scholars attached much attention to St Mark's,[33] many other squares in the city — called *campi* – were usually crowded. During church celebrations, a varied crowd populated the adjacent *campi*. As in St Mark's Square, sellers, *cantimbanchi*, and entertainers offered passers-by all kinds of goods, from devotional tools like candles to miraculous potions and sweets (fig. 7.4). Authorities tried to regulate these spontaneous markets. In August 1578 the Cinque Savi alle mariegole — a court regulating the arts of Venice — forbade the selling of 'fruits, merchandise, biscuits, baskets, pots, weeds' or any other kind of goods, except for those regarding mariners, rope makers, and those who sold statues of saints. Four years later the prohibition to sell 'on church squares were the celebration is held' was extended to all art.[34] Those who wanted to sell their merchandise needed a special licence. This could be requested at a dedicated court. In October 1574, Antonio da Salò and his 'compagni dell'acqua vita' sought — and obtained — the Giustizia Vecchia to be allowed to sell their *acquavita*, because the product was deemed to have healing effects.[35] Among peddlers and sellers, visitors would also find music performances. Street concerts could be organised spontaneously, as Morison noted, by companies of wandering revellers who 'walke up and downe the markett places, and some leade musicke with them and table to place some instruments, where they play excelent musicke'.[36]

Nodes of public interaction such as *calli*, *corti* and *campi* regularly hosted a variety of leisure activities, similar to the streets and squares in other cities. Public competitions like fist fights, bull hunting, and ball games were organised outdoors despite being forbidden. All these festive gatherings were the object of repressive laws. In Venice, between 1558 and 1627 about 250 orders were issued by the court of *esecutori alla bestemmia* to eradicate spontaneous festive activities from the main squares, courtyards, and streets near sacred buildings and the palaces of the major patrician families, as well as from smaller squares, courtyards, *fondamente*, and ferry docks. The bans were proclaimed in various years in the same places. This demonstrates that repression was far from effective and that people identified specific urban areas as places for habitual festive meetings. Authorities were not able to delineate zones of order and decorum within the urban environment, contrary to what some scholarship suggests.[37]

By prohibiting games and revelries on both workdays and holidays, these laws also demonstrate the daily occurrence of urban festive gatherings. Precisely what happened during these events is difficult to tell. People could find a variety of leisure and entertainment activities: bull hunts, ball, dice, and card games, dancing, and music. Criminal proceedings and verdicts also make frequent reference to gambling, which allows us to shed some light on these ephemeral practices.

People of every age and condition gathered around playing tables to see how a game was going and try to participate. We know that crowds from different nations usually frequented St Mark's. In the part of the Piazza extending from the Clock Tower to the shore of the *bacino* gathered 'many Polonians, Slavonians, Persians, Grecians, Turks, Iewes, Christians of all the famousest regions of Christendome, and each nation distinguished from another by their proper and peculiar habits' (fig. 7.5).[38] A similar variety appears to have interacted in the other spots throughout the city dedicated to this entertainment. Card games had no nationality and were able to unite players coming from around the world. In 1582, the Armenian Abdenor and the Indian

7.4

Giacomo Franco, *Ducal Palace*. Engraving from Id., *Habiti d'huomeni et donne venetiane con la processione della Ser.ma Signoria ed altri particolari*, 1614. Detail of 3.4 featuring sellers and a singer with a dog..

Giandù were arrested while playing the 'gioco del trentuno' with cards. In July 1584, Giacomo Manfrini and Giacomo Strenghe, a Tuscan and a German, were also arrested. In March 1590, the sbirri seized Niccolò Sacca, a Greek, who was playing with a Jew, Marcho della Bella.[39] Cards also abolished differences in status or age. In 1582, Domenico *strazzaruol* — a cloth peddler — was arrested while playing with a fourteen-year-old nobleman, Giulio Marin. In November 1589, the *sbirri* raided a *ridotto* where eleven people were playing cards, among which were a Greek, two Venetian noblemen of the Barozzi and Bembo families, a goldsmith, a woman named Chiara de' Medici, and several representatives of the mechanical arts.[40]

Music was also involved. Though few of these orders openly referred to music or dances, many prohibited 'strepiti' — an aural category that also included the sound produced by a street performer.[41] Dances could arise spontaneously from the tunes of street musicians. Visitors noticed that people stood around to watch when somebody played an instrument, as during the 'dances of the young girls' recorded by Saint Didier. These dances took place wherever there was enough space to gather: large *calli* or *fondamente*, docks, and 'most commonly in the little squares of their quarters', i.e. courtyards. The sound of the tambourines and songs played by young women attracted many locals as well as foreigners. These dances allowed for freedom in the interactions between men and women, since soon the dancing girls were joined by someone from the public. The Venetians were not only spectators at these gatherings, because they offered 'easy

7.5

Giacomo Franco, *Procession in St Mark's Square during the recruitment of men for the fleet*. Engraving from Id., *Habiti d'huomeni et donne venetiane con la processione della Ser.ma Signoria ed altri particolari*, 1614. Detail of 1.4 featuring a crowd of foreigners.

opportunities of being familiar with these young lasses, and afterwards to choose from among 'em'.[42]

Outdoor dances could also be organised. At least since the first half of the seventeenth century, the organisation of dances was a prerogative of the *scuola de' sonadori*: unfortunately, there is little evidence of the guild's activities, since their archive was lost. However, according to a letter sent by the *provveditori di Comun* to the heads of the Council of Ten, the *sonadori* required the licence of the Council itself to build the ephemeral structures called 'casoni', or wooden lodges, under which they held public balls. The document, dated 2 February 1643, is interesting also because it records a problem that still affects public festivals today: damage to the common areas. The *provveditori* thus asked the Council of Ten to authorise a resolution that would oblige the organisers, using a *piezaria*, to take out a sort of insurance that would reimburse the sums incurred to repair the damage caused by the participants in these festivities 'by breaking the *sallizadi* and by damaging the wells with urine and other rubbish'.[43]

Conclusions

This paper shows how spontaneous revelry and merry-making were distributed throughout Venice, offering a glimpse into everyday festive life. Moving beyond the borders of overstudied ceremonial areas, such as St Mark's Square, it explored how people made use of different public settings to organise and participate in celebrations. Festivals were not only institutionalised occasions for urban elites to showcase their political and religious power. They were part of daily life and played an important role in the social interactions among individuals.

Many aspects of this festive universe are still unexplored. For instance, most of these practices mingled with other everyday activities, such as jobs and errands, or even with other institutional festive activities, such as the acts and behaviours that authorities tried to impose during church celebrations. How spontaneous merry-making and other practices were related is still unclear and requires further research. Since spontaneous festive behaviours usually collided violently with other activities, criminal archives and court acts offer an optimal starting point.

There was an economy of spontaneous festive practices. Street musicians, professional gamblers, and other entrepreneurs such as the *mazzier* all profited from an unofficial but rich market organised around the everyday needs of merry-makers. They had to catch any opportunity that street life would offer, adapting to a fluid demand that worked outside the cyclical seasons of the institutionalised festivals. How this hidden market functioned and what dimensions it reached is not clear yet, nor is how it interacted with other official festive markets. The presence of corporations like the *scuola de' sonadori* indicates the desire to control the income deriving from spontaneous activities through the promotion of organised and authorised events. Yet it is still unclear whether these efforts were successful and to what extent.

We tend to ignore the repertoire promoted by spontaneous merry-makers. Yet music was a strong political medium. Street musicians could disseminate state propaganda or become the vehicles of protest, as charlatans did.[44] Their repertoires should be found somewhere in the enormous mass of cheap prints still conserved in Italian libraries and archives. Moreover, some attention should be given to the identity of street performers: certainly, they did not completely improvise — but we do not yet know anything about their education or social conditions.

1. Muir, *Civic Ritual in Renaissance Venice*; Fenlon, *The Ceremonial City*; Fenlon, 'Urban Soundscapes'.
2. Muir, *Ritual in Early Modern Europe*, pp. 62–86.
3. Nevola, *Street Life in Renaissance Italy*; Fenlon, *Orality and Print*.
4. Coryat, *Coryat's Crudities*, II, p. 74.
5. Fenlon, *Orality and Print*, p. 82. For a critical survey on the studies on Venetian church music, see Bryant and Quaranta, *Produzione, circolazione e consumo*.
6. Quaranta, *Oltre San Marco*.
7. 'Non vi è giorno in tutto l'anno che con molto apparato non si esponga il Venerabile, e le feste in luoghi diversi'. Coronelli, *Guida de' forestieri*, p. 35. See also Bryant and Cecchinato, 'Venice, City of Music'.
8. Cit. in Quaranta, *Oltre San Marco*, p. 411.
9. The Scuola di Sant'Orsola, operating in the church of Santi Giovanni e Paolo, used to set up a ship with a stage where two people, usually young, represented St Ursula and an angel. On the eve of the celebrations in honour of the saint, this apparatus was carried through the Venetian call by about fifteen porters accompanied by a group of musicians, 'per denonziar la festa' (in order to publicize the feast). Quaranta, *Oltre San Marco*, p. 143.
10. The quality of the decorations varied according to the economic possibilities of the institution commissioning them. In Venice, in the year 1564 alone, payments to the *conzieri* who decorated churches on feast days were recorded in the account books of thirty one churches. Quaranta, *Oltre San Marco*, pp. 189–226.
11. On the diffusion and uses of sacred music at festivals organised by religious institutions and during processions, see Bryant and Pozzobon, *Musica devozione città*, Glixon, *Honoring God and the City*.
12. ASVE, PM, Atti, b. 256, 1618 July.
13. ASVE, PM, Atti, b. 268, 1638 *agosto*, fols. [1v-2r].
14. Church pews symbolised social hierarchies and were frequently objects of disputes. On this phenomenon specifically in Venice, see Carroll and Cecchinato, 'Violence and Sacred Space in Early Modern Venice'.
15. 'Te conosso per una sporca'; 'ti vuole che sia una sporca mi... ti è una sporca ti!'. This short dialogue is reported by a witness. ASVE, PM, Atti, b. 264, file 1611 November.
16. 'Ne sono infinite che stano sopra le strade publice et nelli principal luogi de questa città, exercitando tal loro arte, dando mal esempio ad ognuno, maxime a tempo che si celebrano li divini officii'. *Leggi e memorie venete sulla prostituzione*, pp. 101–02. On Venetian prostitution, see Scarabello, *Meretrices*.
17. 'Acciò non siano causa de mal exempio con molti acti, parole et opere lascive a quelli over a quelle che vano a bon fine in dicte chiesie,' 'con le loro male opere sono il più delle volte causa de molte risse, scandali et mancamenti'; 'habitar over stantiar in luoco alcuno che sia per mezo chiesie et luochi sacri'; 'in chiesia alcuna il zorno della festa et solennità principal di quella'. *Leggi e memorie venete sulla prostituzione*, pp. 101–02.
18. 'Vestite da maridate e da vedove, facendo atti disonesti'. *Leggi e memorie*, p. 122.
19. 'Vogar per la città, et massime nelli giorni delle feste, solennità et perdoni delle chiese'; 'passeggiando e fermandosi per mezzo esse chiese facendo molti chiassi e cose dishoneste'; 'vestite con diversi habiti lascivi et facendo molti chiassi et usando termini inhonesti'. *Leggi e memorie*, pp. 124–26.
20. *Leggi e memorie*, pp. 136–37.
21. 'In qualsivoglia abito alle feste o nozze di persone nobili et di honesta vita, overo alle sagre, feste, balli di villa, nelle chiese et alle fiere et altri luoghi pubblici'. *Leggi e memorie*, pp. 137–38.
22. 'Si fanno lecito così di giorno come di notte, particolarmente nelle chiese, commettere infiniti scandoli'. *Leggi e memorie*, pp. 148 e 151.
23. John Evelyn is cit. by Burke, *The Historical Anthropology of Early Modern Italy*, p. 186. See Bamji, 'The Control of Space'.
24. 'Dete molto mormorar, ché in simil feste publice si suol tenir le porte aperte', quoted in Pontremoli and La Rocca, *La danza a Venezia nel Rinascimento*, pp. 31–32.
25. Fynes, *An Itinerary*, pp. 457–58. On the door garlands, see Limojon de Saint-Didier, *The City and Republick of Venice*, III, pp. 68–69.
26. 'Ghe erano molte persone [...] che se spenzevano [...] chi spenzeva in qua et chi spenzeva in là'. ASVE, AC, 4297, fasc. 10, *Scattola Massimo, ferimento all'inguine al conte Claudio Collalto 1559*, fols. 28r-v.
27. 'In luogo che non si sapesse'; 'quattro versi soli alimprovisa con la lira'. ASVE, Pod. Mur., b. 61, file 2: '1555–1557 21 marzo Angelo Benedetto', subfile '1555 Denunce ecc.', deposition of Ludovico de Masi, 3 marzo 1556. See also Bryant and Cecchinato, 'Venice, City of Music'.
28. ASVE, CL, ser. I, b. 68, IV, fol. 267r-v.
29. 'Mascherato, munito di dui pistolle, stillo nella casa del nobil huomo ser Carlo Grimani, nella quale si faceva riddutione et accademia di virtù con concerto numeroso di donne nobili, et soggetti patritii'; 'donne di rispettabile conditione [...] con forme improprie'. MCV, Ms. P.D. 2107, n. 70.
30. See Ortalli, *Gioco e giustizia nell'Italia di comune*.
31. See Salzberg, *Ephemeral City*.
32. ASVE, CD, Proc. stampa, b. 1, 'Parte presa nell'eccelso Consiglio di Dieci 1571 à 31 luglio. In materia di quelli che vanno a mangiar nelli magazeni et giocano'.
33. Rospocher and Salzberg, 'Street Singers in Italian Renaissance Urban Culture and Communication'; Degl'Innocenti and Rospocher, 'Street Singers'.
34. 'Sopra i campi di quelle chiese dove è la festa'. ASVE, CL, S. I, b. 206, fols. 382r and 390r.
35. ASVE, CL, S. I, b. 206, fol. 376r.
36. Moryson, *Itinerary*, 457–58.
37. Derosas, 'Moralità e giustizia a Venezia nel '500-'600'.
38. Coryat, *Coryat's Crudities*, p. 220.
39. ASVE, EB, b. 57, reg. 'Notatorio di terminationi principia l'anno 1582', fols. 2r, 25v, and 177v.
40. ASVE, EB, b. 57, reg. 'Notatorio di terminationi principia l'anno 1582', fols. 19v and 148r-150r.
41. On noise as a sensorial category, see Pickering and Rice, 'Noise as "sound out of place"'.
42. Limojon de Saint-Didier, *The City and Republick of Venice*, pp. 82–84.
43. 'Col romper li sallizadi et col guastar li pozzi con l'immonditie dell'orinar et altro'. ASVE, CCD, Not., Fil., file 32, sub data. The document is cited by Vio, 'L'arte dei sonadori', p. 79.
44. Rospocher, '"In Vituperium Status Veneti"'.

Marco Bellabarba

8

POWER, FRIENDSHIP, AND PROTECTION

Venetian Rectors in Verona Between the Sixteenth and Seventeenth Centuries

A now lost cycle of frescoes, the Venetian *podestà* Agostino da Mula (fig. 8.1), and the Venetian mainland city of Verona form the backdrop for this chapter. The element binding the three together can be found in the biographical profile of Da Mula written many years ago by Gaetano Cozzi for the *Dizionario biografico degli Italiani*.[1] Elected *podestà* of Verona on 17 January 1613, Da Mula was no ordinary patrician. Indeed, he arrived in Verona following a brilliant political career. He had been *savio agli ordini* in 1587, *podestà* and captain of Belluno in 1593, and *savio di Terraferma* almost uninterruptedly for a decade between 1602 and 1612. He had furthermore been a part of Paolo Sarpi's circle during the Interdict, gaining a reputation as one of the Papacy's most intransigent adversaries among Venetian patricians. This was fitting, as Verona was no ordinary place either. Located 'in the heart' of the Venetian territorial state, at the starting point of the roads for Germany, and deemed the 'most beautiful and densely populated' ('più bella et populata') city on the Venetian mainland (Terraferma),[2] Verona was one of the most challenging towns in the dominion, since it was full of 'men of high intellect' ('cervelli alti'),[3] who were often uneasy about Venice's sovereignty, as captain Alvise Contarini put it in 1575.

Documentation from the period suggests that Da Mula encountered no significant obstacles during his rule (*reggimento*) in Verona. Except a disagreement with the local ecclesiastical inquisitor (when he held fast to his right to detain men and women on trial in the podesta's prisons)[4] and a few instances in which he had to intervene in matters pertaining to crimes carried out by members of the local nobility, the issues he addressed in his correspondence with the Senate and the heads (*capi*) of the Council of Ten fell within the bounds of ordinary administration.

Likewise, proceedings of the city council of Verona attest to no friction or tension between him and the city council as they executed their respective powers. Conversely, in the two years prior, between 1610 and 1612, the city council had been involved in a bitter jurisdictional dispute with the captain Girolamo Corner.[5] 'In spite of this, or perhaps precisely because of this', Da Mula had wanted to leave behind evidence of his time in the city, attesting to the 'peace and good harmony he'd been able to establish with the inhabitants of Verona'.[6] Thus, he commissioned Antonio da Gandino, Paolo Veronese's pupil, to produce a painting cycle to decorate the hall of the Palazzo Pretorio.

Antonio da Gandino followed the complex iconographic programme that Da Mula had solicited from Ottavio Rossi,[7] a man of letters from Brescia, who had already performed similar work for others in Da Mula's position. Graced with eighteen allegorical paintings, the programme involved elaborately decorated hall walls and a ceiling akin to the one in the Ducal Palace in Venice. The hall's walls were divided into panels bound by Corinthian columns that supported entablatures from which were suspended 114 shields showcasing the coats of arms of each *podestà* in service after 1517 (the year Verona was permanently conquered by Venice; some of the shields were left empty for subsequent office holders). Twelve niches between the columns housed the painted allegories, above which were depicted two large *Victories*. Atop each column were two golden coats of arms, commemorating Da Mula, in his capacity as *podestà*, and the captain in service alongside him, Silvestro Valier.[8]

Da Mula charged Francesco Pola, a noble man of letters from Verona,[9] with the task of explaining the painting cycle in a dialogue-form booklet, *Lo Stolone ovvero della sala pretoria veronese* (fig. 8.2). The book was published by a local printer in 1615, when the decoration of the hall was complete.[10] In the imagined dialogue, Pola described the many virtues, portrayed in the frescoes, required of a 'good rector', all of which Da Mula clearly possessed.

8.1
Bust of Agostino da Mula, Belluno, Museo Civico. Reproduced with permission.

8.2
Frontispiece of Francesco Pola, *Lo Stolone, ovvero della Sala pretoria veronese. Dialogo*, Verona, appresso Bortolamio Merlo, 1615. Photo: BnF, Gallica. Reproduced with permission.

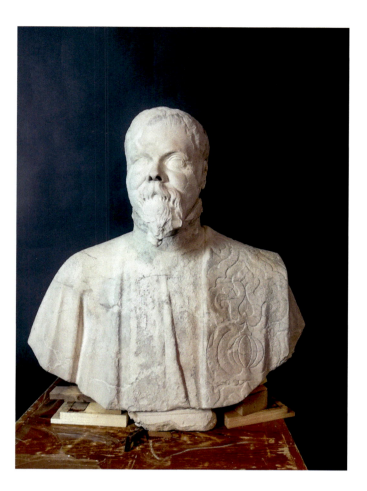

The painting cycle and Pola's booklet each attested, in Cozzi's words, to 'Da Mula's unbridled ambition, both as a man and as a Venetian patrician'. The cycle celebrated the power and wisdom of the Republic, but it was 'Da Mula, the depositary of that grandeur and wisdom, who stood in the foreground'. No one — as Stolone, the main character of the booklet's dialogue, declared — had ever exercised justice better, with more rigour, fairness, or patience, than Da Mula; and no Venetian rector could boast a nobility as grand as the one required to govern a city as important as Verona.[11]

Pola's dialogue was written in close proximity to an historical phase in which the Republic 'had had to exert effective and meaningful control over the state's many embodiments' in the dominion's largest cities, 'particularly those represented by forces that tended to be hostile'[12] towards Venice. By pushing their way into the Republic's most important magistracies (the Senate, the Collegio, the Council of Ten), the 'new' patrician families[13] had managed to implement a series of legislative measures extending the sphere of action of mainland rectors.[14]

The redundant extolling of Da Mula's virtues in *Stolone* seems to reflect these ongoing changes in the relationship between Venice and its subject cities during the early 1600s. It certainly attests to a shift when contrasted to the documents describing the duties of Venetian rectors published ever since Venice's early Renaissance territorial expansion. Well-known texts from the late 1400s (namely, *De bene instituta re publica* by Domenico Morosini[15] and *Rerum venetarum ab urbe condita libri XXXIII* by Marcantonio Sabellico[16]), as well as Giovanni Tazio's works published in the 1560s, list the essential virtues that a rector should possess. These included moderation and prudence, avoiding exceedingly close relations with subjects,[17] and being careful not to leave too strong a recollection of his rule in the local community, for instance in the form of paintings and sculptures, once his assignment was over.[18] Such precautions were also detailed in a substantial corpus of legislative measures. Starting in the early 1400s, laws had been in place to prohibit customs considered inappropriate. For instance, orations and ceremonial speeches ('sermones et arengas in laudem suam') were not to be delivered upon the rectors' arrival, armigeros were not to escort rectors during their entries, painted or sculpted decorations showcasing the rectors' coats of arms were not to be displayed on the walls of their residences, and, by 1545, rectors were not to be named godfathers or sponsors to the children of local families during baptism or confirmation ceremonies.

A Senate law promulgated on 22 June 1609, a few years before Da Mula arrived in Verona, summarised a detailed list of prohibitive measures passed over the course of the previous century by the sumptuary magistracy of the *provveditori alle pompe*. This once again clarified that rectors should not be accompanied by more than six Venetian patricians ('più dei sei nobili'), participate in parties or public banquets, or accept presents upon stepping down from their rule. Additional minute prescriptions — such as the instruction not to have more than twelve chairs in the house at any time (upholstered in velvet, 'without gold') or more than eight people in the combined staff of the stables and palace — explained the type of conduct rectors and their families were expected to observe during their daily lives.[19] Establishing exceedingly close relations with subjects, or becoming 'too tightly bound to one local pressure group or another, thus creating in them the illusion that they'd found, in the Venetian representative, a faithful and friendly intercessor with the Prince should the need arise',[20] were also censured behaviours, punishable by harsh penalties.

In fact, despite the many measures aiming to assign rectors to cities to which they lacked ties, the sixteen months of their office allowed for many encounters and the establishment of personal relations.[21] Rhetorical recommendations and legislative precepts were almost turned on their heads during rectors' entry rituals, which were so rife with political significance that local legislations were compelled to govern them in minute detail. The new Veronese statutes of 1450[22] opened with a paragraph titled 'De honorifico introitu Domini Potestatis': each new *podestà* arriving from Venice was to pass through Santo Spirito's gate, and go first to the Basilica of San Zeno; from there, the procession was to continue to Piazza delle Erbe (the *platea Communis*), where the *podestà* was to walk up the steps of the marble capital, receive the city sceptre (*sceptrum*), and listen to a speech delivered in his honour by a city council emissary.[23] The entry ceremonies for the *provveditore* and captain sent to the nearby fortress of Legnago were identical in form, albeit more sober.[24] The ritual likely took place in a similar fashion in other cities of the dominion (fig. 8.3). The passing of the procession through the city gates, the rector's meeting with the local notables either in the cathedral or beneath the loggia of the city hall (*Palazzo del Comune*), and his oath to abide by local laws were described with great care by the local statutes.[25] As for the instructions each rector was given before taking his office ('mandates' or 'commissions'), local statutes were fairly vague: they merely listed strict rules concerning the behaviours deemed unacceptable for those holding the office of captain or *podestà*, largely taken from decrees issued by Venetian magistracies.

Thus, no words other than those uttered in the administration of the office were to be exchanged between rectors and subjects, and no mingling was to occur apart from on public occasions. Yet this strict protocol, though reiterated repeatedly, nevertheless had a weak hold. In Verona, as we have seen, the veto on *sermones et arengas* delivered in honour of Venetian rectors was circumvented by local statutes. Indeed, in Verona and elsewhere, the literary genre of encomiastic orations sustained the publishing market, offering city printers an important revenue source. Other speeches praising rectors, often displaying an even more extravagant taste for the celebration of their virtues, were delivered at the end of their office. On the evening of 16 June 1560, a local jurist delivered an opening speech in exquisite Latin ('in bellissimo latino') before the rectors, Elders (*Anziani*, i.e. the city's heads), and city council of Bergamo extolling the achievements of the *podestà* Lorenzo Bragadin, who was about to leave his post in the hands of his successor Francesco Venier. In February, the Elders' council (*Consiglio degli Anziani*) had charged the painters Andrea Calepio and Marco Passi with affixing the insignia of Bragadin and the captain Pizzamano on the facades of the *Palazzo Pretorio*: the two men's heraldic figures, topped by the Serenissima's coat of arms, were completed at the beginning of June just in time for the scheduled handover.[26]

8.3

Pietro Damini, *The exchange of the baton and keys of the city of Padua between the city governors, the brothers Massimo and Silvestro Valier.* Padua, Musei Civici, 1621. Reproduced with permission.

At least in this case, Bergamo's *Anziani* had followed the law: as stated in a decree issued by the Council of Ten in 1540, frescos of rectors' coats of arms and names was allowed on public palaces so long as these renditions were 'simple' and not chiselled on the walls or made in stone. Conversely, they had completely disregarded the prohibition on reciting and printing orations extolling rectors. Repeatedly — in 1567, 1582, and 1616 — the Council of Twelve (the city assembly's executive body, comprising the uppermost echelons of the ruling class) had set forth regulations regarding how these speeches could be delivered in public; to avoid that the chance absence of certain councilmen might prevent the spectacle from taking place, it had been decided that the obligation to deliver the speech ('munus orationum') for the *podestà* and the captain would fall to the youngest jurist among the Twelve, or to another jurist purposefully elected by the Council itself.[27]

Celebration of the 'union and love' between the two rectors was an ever-present commonplace in the reports rectors read before the Venetian Collegio or Senate once returned to Venice. This practice was a way of recalling the bond between each 'patrician and the state-aristocratic body' they had kept alive during their months away from the lagoon.[28] Yet in the inscriptions commissioned in Bergamo — as in the cycle of frescoes painted in the Palace of Verona — reference to the harmony between the rectors described an emotional and social bond that had been built in the governed city. The traditional repertoire of patrician virtues (obedience, love for the Republic, humility, prudence) virtually shifted from the patriciate as a whole to individual interlocutors. The 'generous and grateful inhabitants of Verona' ('Veronesi, generosi e grati riconoscitori'), for instance, recognized captain Nicolò Corner's qualities as he was about to leave their city in August 1606, because he had ruled it with prudence. Corner had entered into 'reciprocal bonds of friendship' with the *podestà*, and above all — as highlighted by the oration's author, jurist Vincenzo Manueli — had been the 'most diligent executor of all laws, and mainly of those set forth in our own statutes and privileges'.[29]

Such comments point toward the existence of a dense network of relations, political and personal, which the urban aristocracies of the Venetian mainland entertained with rectors both during their *reggimenti* and after their return to Venice. Giovanni Florio has described this ongoing conversation as a relation 'at the intersection between kinship and clientelism' able to create a steady, two-way 'exchange of resources between the community-client and the rector-patron'.[30] Viewed within a rhetorical framework rife with stereotypes — in which the Republic figured as a 'mother', rectors as 'fathers' and 'patrons', and the subjects as 'children'[31] — these relations highlight an essential, constitutive feature of Venetian law, namely, the existence of a 'direct relationship between the subjects and the Republic's institutions',[32] which was to be unimpeded by obstacles or other forms of mediation apart from those the rectors themselves embodied.

A passage from *Stolone* — appearing significantly before

the lengthy description of the *podestà*'s virtues — clarifies the relationship envisioned between Da Mula and the subject community. When asked about the coat of arms hanging on the hall's left side, in front of the emblems belonging to the *podestà* and the captain, Stolone answers:

> That is the coat of arms of our city, which is placed under the holy protection of the Republic of Venice, of which the Lion is the glorious and famous symbol. And the *podestà* decided to place it amidst the other coats of arms in order to show the passionate and rightly-partial love that, throughout his ruling period, he showed towards [our city], her privileges, and her laws, of which he proved to be a devout custodian and guarantor.[33]

Da Mula offered the inhabitants of Verona his 'passionate love' and 'protection'. Similar terms often appeared in reference to Venetian authorities in the proceedings of the city council. In 1606, for example, they were used to explain the decision of sending orators to Venice to celebrate Leonardo Donà's ducal election. As representatives of Verona, the orators had 'to show the happiness of our city and our thankfulness to him for his patronage that will be remembered forever by future generations since he benignly helped us when the situation was most difficult'.[34] In 1614, upon the arrival of the *provveditore generale in Terraferma* ('mainland commander in chief') Antonio Lando, four orators were requested 'to provide humble assistance to the patron himself'.[35] In 1615, when another *provveditore*, Gerolamo Corner, the captain of Verona in 1610, was about to arrive, the Veronese councillors stated: 'we indeed are not just aware of the fact that he proved benign towards us more than once, but we are also familiar with his heroic virtues, and are ready to welcome the rich fruits of his paternal protection and his high authority'.[36] Thus, rectors and former rectors were constantly styled as protective figures (or patrons) for whom the exercise of authority implied 'paternal protection' (*paterna protezione*) towards their subjects. Proceedings from a council session held in 1616 in memory of the *podestà* Giacomo Contarini once again employ a formula ('he affectionately defended our hometown and our citizens')[37] that — precisely because it was so often repeated — must be understood within its proper lexical and institutional context.

In the earliest editions of the *Vocabolario della Crusca*, the word protection (*protezione*) and its variants encompassed several meanings: a political-institutional or personal introduction (*raccomandazione*, thus equivalent to the Latin words *defensio* and *tutela*), the gifting of something, or 'favours bestowed on others, protection, assistance, defence'.[38] Favours, graces, protection, and defence all describe the relationship subjects entertained with their rectors, who were the most immediate point of contact between their world and the Republic and, in many cases, the only tangible embodiment of Venetian sovereignty. Rectors were not ordinary officials, who — as in princely states — were mere conduits for orders from above but actual depositaries of a kind of republican sovereignty, thus preserving the irreducible difference in administrative structure between the *Dominante* and the *Terraferma*.[39] Given these premises, the concept of protection (and associated notions taken up by modern historiography, such as friendship, clientelism, mediation, and patronage brokerage) can only be understood within the institutional architecture of the time, in relation to the configuration of existing powers, hierarchical differences among patricians (based on wealth, career, family), and the relative weight of the cities where rectors carried out their posts.[40]

Verona's wealth and military position situated it among the 'first rate' *reggimenti*. This post was reserved for patricians from families close to the summit of republican power (as in the case of Da Mula in 1613) or endowed with financial resources adequate to allow them (and their retinue) to enjoy a lifestyle suitable to the prestige of the post. 'This lord must be a grand and rare senator',[41] the imaginary interlocutor in *Stolone* claims with conviction, drawing attention to the fact that only a member of the Venetian Senate — not one of the many, often poor patricians of the Great Council — would have what it takes to govern Verona. Further, it is thanks to his success in administering the city that Da Mula, 'God willing, will justly achieve the highest dignities of his grand Republic'.[42] As evoked in the *Stolone*, Da Mula's career seems to allow a contact between Verona and Venice, the provincial city and the capital. It is first and foremost Da Mula's personal qualities that make it possible for these two geographical poles to come into contact. Indeed, the political abilities listed in Pola's dialogue and painted in the fresco in the *Palazzo Pretorio* allow the *podestà* to take up his role as leading figure.

The logic of this argument appears reversed in the orations commissioned by the city council of Verona in those years to praise the leaving rectors. Homage was paid to the wisdom, moderation, and equity the rectors had shown during their rule (*reggimento*), as a matter of course, but the praise was framed differently. Indeed, texts foreground other virtues coming from the rectors' pasts and from events in their personal lives, which were interwoven with other virtues related to the patrician houses in which they had been raised. Looking at these speeches, a narrative built on elements that had been disregarded by *Stolone* is immediately apparent. For instance, in the *Oratione all'Illustrissimo Sig. Giovanni Cornaro, Capitano di Verona* written by Pola in 1596,[43] and in the text written shortly afterwards by Vincenzo Manueli for the captain Nicolò Corner, recollection of the rectors' governance of the city is conjoined with the praise of their descendance from one of the most powerful families in Venice. The Corners

8.4
Frontispiece of *Varie compositioni scritte in lode dell'illustrissimo sig. Giovanni Cornaro capitanio di Verona*, Verona, appresso Girolamo Discepolo, 1596. Photo: Roma, Biblioteca Universitaria Alessandrina, with permission from the Italian Ministry of Culture.

— an 'old', traditionally pro-papal, and extraordinarily rich patrician family — gain centre stage here.

As he praises the 'incomparable senator' ('Senatore incomparabile') now set to return to Venice, Pola compiles a celebratory catalogue of the ecclesiastical posts members of the Corner family have held throughout the years. He refers to the 'prelates, abbots, bishops, cardinals with which your house has always supplied the Christian Republic',[44] thus characterising the family's involvement in the church as a hereditary, almost undisputed legacy. Yet it is the family's immense wealth that Pola identifies as a distinguishing feature and dwells on most: 'che si potrebbe dire dell'immense vostre ricchezze? De' vostri monti d'oro? Chi non vede che le sustanze vostre eccedono lo stato senatorio? Che i tesori vostri s'agguagliano a Regii, a gli Imperatori?' ('What can one say of your immense richness? Of your piles of gold? Who does not see that your wealth exceeds that of a senator, and that your treasures are rather those of kings and emperors?'). This is not an occasional homage, for it is precisely the magnitude of the family's economic means, the 'heaps/piles of gold' owned by the Corners, that made possible for the rector 'la maniera di vivere più splendida et più magnifica' ('the most splendid and magnificent way of living') ever witnessed in Verona:

> Who has ever admired more virtuous, better-dressed, more numerous, and better-behaving servants than yours? Whenever have these walls, these rooms, this whole palace been more richly adorned with silk and gold, according to the different seasons of the year? [...] What governor has ever entertained with such courtesy, or offered more splendid banquets, or welcomed in his dwelling a higher number of distinguished guests and, not seldom, his first and wealthier citizens?[45]

'Magnanimous' and 'most magnificent', so generous he had sometimes paid out of his own pocket for the entertainment of the local citizenry, Giovanni Corner certainly benefited from the prestige and affluence of his house. While signs of the barefaced nepotism accompanying his later assignments, ending in his election as doge in 1624, were at the time still untraceable, his inclination to put familial logic ahead of his public role must have been easily detectable by the urban elite in Verona. Indeed, it was prominent enough to become the unifying element of the *Varie compositioni scritte in lode de l'Illustrissimo Sig. Giovanni Cornaro Capitano di Verona et de l'Illustrissima Sig. Chiara Delfina, sua consorte*, a collection of poetry in Latin, Italian vernacular, and the dialect of Verona printed in 1597 (fig. 8.4).

These poems all revolve around the 'exaltation of the virtues and nobility possessed by Giovanni and Chiara, their ancestors' political and military careers (from both the Cornaro and the Dolphin families), their erudition and their generosity'.[46] Though perhaps mitigated to avoid the most lavish praise of the personal qualities of the rector, this family-based model of oration was very influential, as attested by the text jurisconsult Manueli wrote for captain Nicolò Corner years later. Son-in-law of doge Marino Grimani and brother of Marco, the bishop of Padua, Corner was a 'most liberal lord' ('Signore liberalissimo') who enchanted the citizens of Verona with his incomparable standard of living:

> When has this palace ever been richer in all sorts of provisions? When has it been more richly adorned, according to the different seasons of the year? What representative of the Doge of Venice, as you are, had kinder manners, or a wealthier apparatus of gold and silverware, or has offered as many and as sumptuous state banquets, or had among his guests so many noble foreign and important citizens of this city, which is subject to your authority?[47]

Recollection of Corner's 'grandeur' takes over the pages of the oration. Inevitably, such grandeur produced a governing style marked more by clemency than justice, as Manueli himself highlighted in his speech: 'if justice lets laws be maintained in a city, clemency lets the subjects be kept in their homeland: this has happened (under your rule) more than once for your own glory and the satisfaction of the Veronese nobility'.[48]

Thus, what seemed decisive for a rector's destiny was neither his integrity nor his ability to govern but the rank of his lineage. Following this model, roughly all orations produced during this period positioned the *podestà* and captain within their family history,[49] suggesting that their permanence in Verona was not an isolated instance. It was always possible for authors to find documentary proof (authentic or not) of a *podesteria* held by the ancestors of the rector in office. This evidence was enough to speculate that a bond existed between the city and the rector's lineage, which had started in the past and would extend into the future.[50] After all, from the perspective of the Veronese nobility commissioning the work, the rector's wealth and fame demonstrated the importance of their own city. Praise for Giovanni Corner's lavish lifestyle — in the form of a tale in some cases resembling 'a parody' of the regulations in force — 'was perhaps intended to indicate that the inhabitants of Verona themselves maintained a knowing extraneousness from the attempts made by the Venetian state to regulate their socio-economic activities in the city, both publicly and privately'.[51] In Pola's and Manueli's texts, the public banquets, dozens of servants, and luxurious furnishings in the Palace of the *podestà* (*Palazzo podestarile*) reflected a type of sociability that was sensitive to public manifestations of status, something even the aristocratic families of Verona could not renounce. This was especially true in the late 1500s, when noblemen with a seat on the city council felt the need to commission dozens of family stories and grand fresco cycles evoking the former independence of Verona[52] as 'a veiled and prudent, but clear, political answer'[53] to Venetian sovereignty.

The strong comeback made by the local aristocratic identity involved a competition in prestige in which symbols were paramount (the ostentation of wealth and a certain lifestyle, the renovation of private and public residences). Venetian representatives themselves could not refrain from taking part in this game. Nonetheless, the chances that the nobility's self-awareness and promotion would lead to openly challenging the 'protection' ensured by rectors were, until the early 1600s, very slim. Far from rejecting the rectors' protection, the local nobility effectively viewed it as a reciprocal promise.

A very long oration delivered at the Accademia Olimpica in Vicenza in 1579 in honour of the *provveditore generale* in Terraferma Giacomo Soranzo addressed this issue, as it discussed the 'proper government' ('buon governo') of subjects. The oration's author spoke on the city's behalf, and his celebratory tone — for instance comparing the rectors to demigods ('Semidei') possessing heroic virtues ('eroiche virtù') — did not prevent him from reminding Soranzo of the promise he had made 'with sweet and courteous words' ('con sì cortesi et dolci parole') to offer Vicenza 'honoured protection' ('honorata protection'). The text explained at length what this promise entailed in practice: the privileges and exemptions acquired by the city were to be defended, and the pacts underwritten at the time of the city's first *deditio* were to be maintained. Soranzo's commitment to upholding his promise would result in the people's 'love and obedience' ('amore e ubbidiente') for 'their protector and benefactor forever, and in all places' ('sempre, et in ogni luogo nostro protetore et benefatore').[54]

With its multiplicity of variants and nuanced meanings, the vocabulary of protection cast light on the 'clearly strategic nature of rectors' position, placed at the intersection of an eminently political and mediatory role, as local terminals of the dominant power, and the heavy burden of the centuries-long communal tradition, which at least the *podestà* was to embody'.[55] Undoubtedly, government action frequently modelled on a fundamentally unchangeable power structure characterised each sixteen-month rule *reggimento*. However, compared to the first century of Venetian rule, the 'substantial isolation' in which Venetian rectors operated vis-à-vis the inhabitants of mainland cities had changed.[56] Though the dozens of aforementioned fifteenth-century laws aimed at preventing orations and other activities devised by rectors for purposes of self-glorification and at regulating entry rituals and the placement of coats of arms were accompanied by penalties — a hefty monetary fine and immediate removal from office — they were not enough to curb what, at first glance, appears to have been an uncontrollable 'privatisation' of the public space.

Yet the personal ambitions do not explain why such laws were completely ignored. More in-depth investigation of the events surrounding the renovation and rebuilding of podesta palaces as early as the period following the Battle of Agnadello (1509) suggests that subject communities were not forced to accept the imposition of an 'outside' architectonic style. Rather, they actively participated in this work, commissioning paintings and frescoes cycles in which episodes of the city's history were interwoven with those of the *Dominante*.[57] In 1595, for the birth of Giovanni Corner's and Chiara Dolfin's son, Verona's Council of Twelve hired artist Felice Brusasorzi to commemorate the event. His painting depicted a woman wearing a crown of stones, a symbol of Verona, as she passed the couple's son to the bishop so he could be baptised in the waters of the Adige. The iconography of this work was devoid of any reference to Venice. Conversely, attempts were made to connect the Corner dynasty to the independence of Verona[58] and exploit the rector's protection as a guarantor for the city vis-à-vis Venice. Similarly, the hundreds of painted or sculpted *armae* identifying the rectors — in open violation of an order by the Council of Ten from 1489 — which could be found not only on the palaces but also in many other public places throughout the subject cities (on squares, bridges, and gates) were mostly commissioned by the communities,[59] not the rectors themselves, who sometimes even objected to their production.

We can thus conclude that, once the submission phase[60] symbolised by the entry rituals and taking of office was over, the distance between rectors and subjects gave way to a myriad of private and public encounters, conversations held outside the palace, and occasions for friendly rapport (often in academies, as in Verona's case the Philharmonic Academy),[61] which regulations on conduct in Venetian law were in no way able to control.

This system of exchanged favours and network of different legal traditions and customs, identities and political ambitions,[62] surfaces in *Stolone* as well. The harmony Cozzi alludes to in relation to Da Mula's relationship with the city is marked by acts that were far from occasional. On 27 November 1614, 'optante Ill.mo D. Augustino Amulio optimo Praetore', the Council of Twelve resolved to allocate a sum of money to clean up the tombs of the Della Scala family in the cemetery of Santa Maria.[63] The Verona's nobility also seems to have played some part in the writing of *Stolone*, if the Council's resolution from March 1615 — the year the dialogue was published — to examine a 'librum eulogiorum' by Francesco Pola so it could be sent to press, is to be trusted.[64]

While it is uncertain whether the book referenced in the resolution is indeed *Stolone*, that Pola belonged to the urban milieu is beyond question. A man of letters well-informed about the politics of Verona, the author of encomiastic orations, and a jurist from the *studium* of Padua, Pola included the following affected declaration regarding the intimate bonds between the city and the rector at the end of his dialogue:

> So, be sure that the veneration of our city for this very man is immense, our city's love for him is extraordinary, his authority over us is uncontested, be also sure that the fame of all this spreads everywhere, the honour that he gained is triumphal, the glory that follows him is more than human, and the immortality of his name will last forever in our hearts.[65]

That the reciprocity between the 'veneration' ('Veneratione') the citizens of Verona felt for the *podestà* and the latter's 'incredible love' ('incredibile Amore') for the city were perceived as capable of potentially undermining the delicate balance of power on which the Venetian 'jurisdictional state' was founded is clear from the sudden acceleration of laws aimed at disciplining the rectors' sphere of action in the 1600s. The law promulgated in 1609, echoing similar measures from 1598 and 1600, was followed by a second law voted by the Senate on 11 March 1653.[66] Based on a long report by the *provveditori alle pompe*, the text made the catalogue of prohibited behaviours even more cogent and thorough, delving into the private, almost intimate sphere of the rectors' activity. Now the entire duration of a rector's assignment (not just the entry and exit rituals) was subject to a detailed protocol. Individual paragraphs addressed how the palace could be furnished, the style of clothing members of the *podestà*'s family could wear, and the type of carriages (indeed the number of horses) that were to be used in the city and in trips to the countryside. Even the daily lives of the rector's family members — the people they could frequent and the civil and religious ceremonies they could and could not attend — were regulated in detail.

Nearly fifty years apart, the two laws pursued the same end: they censored 'the overspending needlessly introduced' by rectors during their assignments ('le eccessive spese con molta superfluità') and called for a return to 'the moderation upon which the Republic has always modelled itself' ('quella moderatezza che è stata sempre di particolar instituto della Repubblica'). These problems were 'regrettably well known' ('purtroppo note'), the *provveditori alle pompe* added, and accounted for how difficult it was to find Venetian patricians willing to hold offices requiring such high expenditures. In those decades, political waters in Venice were troubled by conflicts originating from wealth imbalances within the patriciate that had been set off by Giovanni Corner's dogado.[67] The two laws regulating rectors' behaviours attempted to overcome those conflicts. However, the Senate did not confine itself to addressing its own representatives on the mainland: in the last few lines, after detailing the inquisitorial procedures awaiting those failing to fulfil their obligations, the Senate ordered that rectors immediately publish the laws in their cities of residence, though omitting the chapters regarding sumptuary excesses (furnishings in palaces, number of servants, ornaments for carriages, and so forth). The core of the prohibitions, about which everyone had to be informed, pertained to regulating the informal contacts and network of relationships linking rectors and their subject communities. This aim certainly was not lost on the senators, many of whom were former rectors and knew that the 'love' and 'protection' described in the orations commissioned by the subject cities referred to social bonds and forms of political obedience that could not be cancelled by a command from above. If the informality of these encounters could be accepted (on the grounds that the encounters ultimately benefited Venetian sovereignty), the fine line between Venice and its subject cities, between the former's patriciate and the latter's nobility, between relations of reciprocal 'friendship' and binding 'patron-client relations' nevertheless had to be walked very carefully.[68]

1. Cozzi, 'Da Mula, Agostino', 32.
2. The citations are from two reports by the inquisitorial syndics (*sindici inquisitori*) (1555 and 1591) published in Melchiorre, *Conoscere per governare*, p. 118 and pp. 185–86.
3. In Tagliaferri, ed., *Relazioni dei rettori veneti in terraferma*, IX, p. 97.
4. ASVE, SEN, Dis., Ret., Verona, f. 11, not numbered, 8 and 13 October 1614.
5. Some documents regarding the conflict with Corner can be found in *Statuti, ordini, e parti*, pp. 306ff. For a profile on Corner, see Derosas, 'Corner, Girolamo'.
6. Cozzi, 'Da Mula, Agostino', p. 379.
7. Marzullo, 'La raccolta di lettere di Ottavio Rossi', particularly pp. 347ff.
8. Guzzo, 'La decorazione della Sala pretoria', p. 48.
9. Information about Francesco Pola is rather scarce, except for a short biographical profile by Brugnoli, 'Una villa e una cappella di Francesco Pola a Negrar'. Born around 1568, Pola studied jurisprudence in Padua and practised law in Verona, holding prestigious positions in the city's political life despite his non-noble origins. A teacher at the *Studium* of Padua and member of the Philharmonic Academy of Verona, he probably died in 1616; Marzullo, 'La raccolta di lettere', pp. 348–49, footnote 85.
10. Pola, *Lo Stolone*.
11. Cozzi, 'Da Mula Agostino', p. 379.
12. Povolo, 'Un rapporto difficile e controverso', p. 406.
13. On the friction between 'old' and 'new' patrician families, see, first and foremost, Cozzi, *Venezia barocca*.
14. As observed by Povolo, *L'intrigo dell'onore*, p. 157, it is likely that many of the laws set forth by Venice, which were 'sometimes suspended, or corrected, and often adjusted a short time after being put into effect, also had the purpose of forcing ruling classes in subject cities to take concrete action for themselves, by allowing them to catch sight of other, heavier intrusions'.
15. Cozzi, 'Domenico Morosini e il *De bene instituta re publica*'.
16. Cozzi, *Ambiente veneziano, ambiente veneto*, pp. 13–86.
17. Thus, 'è cosa appartenente a colui che è in magistrato di esser molto cauto et circonspetto a fuggire la conversatione intrinsica de' sudditi, percioché, oltra che dalla molta famigliarità ne nasce un dispregio del magistrato'. Tazio, *L'ottimo reggimento del magistrato pretorio*, pp. 136–37.
18. Tazio, *La imagine del rettore*, pp. 115ff.
19. ASVE, SEN., Del., Terra, Fil., f. 191, not numbered, 22 June 1609.
20. Viggiano, *Governanti e governati*, p. 68.
21. For an eloquent example of these ties, see Chambers, 'Marin Sanudo, Camerlengo of Verona'.
22. On Venetian-era statutes, refer to the extensive description given by Varanini, 'Gli statuti della Terraferma veneta nel Quattrocento'; close relations between members of the local legal class, the renowned Bartolomeo Cipolla, and the podestà in office, Zaccaria Trevisan, who was referred to as the city's 'protector precipuus' (p. 282), are documented in Verona at the time the statutes were being written.
23. *Statutorum magnificae civitatis Veronae*, liber primus, pp. 1–2.
24. Vallerin, *Il Comune di Legnago nel XVI secolo*, pp. 106–14; Trecca, *Legnago fino al secolo XX*, pp. 146–51.
25. Papal legates entering subject cities following a protocol very similar to the one observed by Venetian rectors, according to the description provided by Fosi, '"Parcere subiectis, debellare superbos"', p. 111. As with all city rituals, entry rituals too 'were commentaries on the city, its internal dynamics, and its relationship with the outside world'. Muir, *Civic Ritual in Renaissance Venice*, p. 5.
26. Cappelluzzo, ed., *Lo 'Statuto del podestà' di Bergamo*, pp. 35–36.
27. On the 1567 law, see ASVR, AAC, Reg., reg. 87 (Atti del Consiglio, 1565–1569), fol. 147v, 9 November 1567; on the literary genre of orations praising the podestà, see the suggestive overview provided by Raines, *L'invention du mythe aristocratique*, I, pp. 208–25, where special attention is paid to the veritable surge in published orations in the early 1600s.
28. Del Negro, 'Forme e istituzioni del discorso politico veneziano', p. 431.
29. 'Scambievoli leggi d'amicitia'; 'esecutore diligentissimo di tutte le leggi, e di quelle principalmente che negli Statuti e privilegi nostri si contengono'. Manueli, *Orazione all'Illustrissimo Signor Nicolò Cornaro*, p. 37 and p. 39; citations are from the edition published in the 1800s *Per le faustissime e nobili nozze Bianchini-Dubois*, Venice 1863. On friendship in early modern period, see, to start: Dewald, *Aristocratic experience and the origins of modern culture*, pp. 104ff; Österberg, *Friendship and love, ethics and politics*; Descharmes, Heuser, Krüger, Loy, eds., 'Varieties of Friendship'.
30. Florio, 'Rappresentanti e rappresentazioni', p. 235 and p. 242.
31. Florio, 'Rappresentanti e rappresentazioni', p. 234.
32. Povolo, 'Un rapporto difficile e controverso', pp. 413–14.
33. 'Ella è l'arma publica de la città nostra, che sta sotto la protettione beata della Republica Vinitiana, di cui è non men gloriosa che notoria insegna il Leone. Et il Signor Podestà l'ha voluta qui in mezo collocare, per dar a divedere l'amore sviscerato et giustamente partiale, ch'egli in tutto il fortunato suo reggimento ha mostrato verso di lei, et de le ragioni et de le legi sue; de le quali egli è religiosissimo custode et conservatore'. Pola, *Lo Stolone*.
34. 'Ad declarandam patriae nostrae laetitiam, gratulationemque agenda per illudque in aeternum filiis, nepotibus, nostris memorandum patrocinium quod nobis benigne praestitit in rebus nostris magis arduis'. ASVR, AAC, Reg., reg. 100 (Atti del Consiglio, 1604–1607), fols. 77v–78r, 15 January 1606.
35. 'Ipsi patrono humillime assistant'. ASVR, AAC, Reg., reg. 102 (Atti del Consiglio, 1612–1616), fol. 101r, 25 November 1614: indeed, in the preceding lines Lando was referred to as 'eminentibus virtutibus ornatum et in primis propensum patriae nostrae cuius iura et Privilegia non semel benigne tutatus est'.
36. 'Nos enim non semel experti sumus benignam animi sui propensionem erga nos, novimusque Heroicas virtutes suas, uberrimosque percepimus fructus paternae protectionis et summae suae aucthoritatis'. ASVR, AAC, Reg., reg. 102 (Atti del Consiglio, 1612–1616), fol. 134v, 12 July 1615.
37. 'Patriam nostram, nosque singulos amanter protexit'. ASVR, AAC, Reg., reg. 102 (Atti del Consiglio, 1612–1616), fol. 168r, 12 April 1616.
38. 'Grazia, che si conferisce in altrui, protezione, aiuto, difesa'. *Vocabolario Crusca* (1612), *ad vocem* 'Favore'.
39. Povolo, 'Un sistema giuridico repubblicano'.
40. Povolo, *L'intrigo dell'onore*, p. 104.
41. 'Bisogna che questo Signore sia un grande e raro Senatore'. Pola, *Lo Stolone*.
42. 'Dio volente, conseguirà opportunamente le maggiori dignità della sua grande Repubblica'. Pola, *Lo Stolone*.
43. Pola, *Oratione all'Illustrissimo Sig. Giovanni Cornaro*, without page numbers. A profile of Giovanni Corner appears in Povolo, 'Corner, Giovanni'. Giovanni Corner was elected doge on 4 January 1625.
44. 'Prelati, gli Abbati, i Vescovi, i Cardinali, che la medesima vostra Casa ha sempre somministrato alla Repubblica Christiana'. Pola, *Oratione all'Illustrissimo Sig. Giovanni Cornaro*.

45 'Chi mirò mai la più nobile, la più attilata, la più numerosa, la più ben regolata servitù domestica di cotesta vostra? Qual vostro predecessore fece calcare le nostre strade da più generosi et leggiadri destrieri de' vostri? Quando mai queste pareti, questa sala, questo palagio tutto fu secondo le varie stagioni dell'anno più riccamente addobbato, con più sete et con più oro fregiato? […] Qual Preside mai con modi più cortesi, con conviti più lauti, ricevé nei suoi palagi più frequente numero di gran Signori Ospiti, et non rare volte i primarii cittadini et ottimati suoi soggetti?'. Pola, Oratione all'Illustrissimo Sig. Giovanni Cornaro.

46 The text, another work for which Pola was likely commissioned, is examined in Alison Smith's essay, p. 158, which contains much that is relevant and interesting to the issues addressed here.

47 'Quando mai questo palagio fu più abbondante di tutte le cose, quando fu secondo le varie stagioni dell'anno più riccamente addobbato? Qual Rappresentante di grandissimo Prencipe, come Voi, con modi più cortesi, con maggior apparato d'argento e d'oro, con più solenne pompa di tanti e suntuosi conviti hebbe nei suoi palagi più frequente concorso di gran Signori forestieri, et infinite volte de gli Ottimati di questa città al vostro Imperio soggetta?'. Manueli, Orazione all'Illustrissimo Signor Nicolò Cornaro, pp. 32–33.

48 'Se con la giustitia si conservano le leggi alla Città, con la clemenza si conservano i cittadini alla Patria: per la qual cosa con molta vostra gloria e soddisfatione della Nobiltà Veronese s'è veduto alcuna volta avvenire'. Manueli, Orazione all'Illustrissimo Signor Nicolò Cornaro, p. 38.

49 This genealogical glorification was shared by the rectors themselves (Pesaro, Badoer, Grimani, Morosini), as the texts dedicated to the cycles of frescoes inside the captain's tower make clear: Costantino, Napione, and Valdinoci, eds, La torre del capitanio.

50 The issue is addressed in depth by Povolo, 'Il protettore amorevole'.

51 Smith, 'Ersilia Spolverini', p. 156: 'forse voleva indicare che i veronesi stessi mantenevano una consapevole estraneità ai tentativi dello stato veneziano di regolare le loro attività socio-economiche in città sia pubblicamente sia privatamente'.

52 Varanini, 'L'uso pubblico della storia'.

53 'Una velata e prudente, ma chiara, risposta politica'. See Berengo, 'Patriziato e nobiltà: il caso veronese', pp. 194–95; see also Lanaro Sartori, Un'oligarchia urbana nel Cinquecento veneto.

54 Angiolello, Oratione de l'Angiolello Academico Olimpico. On Soranzo, one of the most influential Venetian patricians of the 1570s, refer to Caterina Caverzan's meticulously researched 'L'affaire Soranzo'.

55 Varanini, 'Gli ufficiali veneziani nella Terraferma veneta quattrocentesca', p. 162; also, by the same author, 'La Terraferma veneta nel Quattrocento'.

56 Varanini, Gli ufficiali veneziani, p. 164.

57 Matarrese, 'I Maganza per il Palazzo del Podestà di Vicenza'; more in general, Zucconi, 'Architettura e topografia delle istituzioni nei centri minori della Terraferma'.

58 As correctly noted by Smith, 'Ersilia Spolverini', p. 153.

59 ASVR, AAC, Reg., reg. 103 (Atti del Consiglio, 1617–1620), fol. 33r-v.

60 Fosi, '"Parcere subiectis, debellare superbos"', p. 111.

61 Rectors' participation in the gatherings of the Philharmonic Academy of Verona are well documented, as pointed out by the essays published in Magnabosco, ed., L'Accademia Filarmonica di Verona. For more on this topic, see Raines, L'invention du mythe aristocratique, pp. 221–23; Benzoni, 'Aspetti della cultura urbana nella società veneta del '5-'600'.

62 An important resource for anyone interested in this interpretation of the ceremonies is Benigno's Favoriti e ribelli, p. 125.

63 ASVR, AAC, Reg., reg. 102 (Atti del Consiglio, 1612–1616), c 102r, 27 November 1614, in Council of Twelve 'Pro purgando Mausoleis Scalligeris in cimiterio S. Mariae Antiquae optante Ill.mo D. Augustino Amulio optimo Praetore nostro ut mausolea praedicta purgentur, decretum fuit quod in opere ipso expendantur ducati decem currentes ex aere publico de quibus praesens consilium disponere potest'. Varanini, 'L'uso pubblico', p. 96, further observes that in the late 1500s, while the councilmen's attention was directed at the early communal period, they 'entirely disregarded the Della Scala cemetery and its sarcophagi […]. They left it in a complete state of abandonment, and showed the utmost indifference for the equestrian statue depicting Cangrande I, which, struck by lightning, lay on the ground for almost thirty years, damaged and mutilated'.

64 ASVR, AAC, Reg., reg. 102 (Atti del Consiglio, 1612–1616), fol. 121r 18 March 1615 'Pro Excell. D. Francisco Pola. Cum summo labore et virtute ipse Excell. Pola composuit librum elogiorum eumdemque dicaverit huic Magnifice Civitati manuscriptum, decretum fuit ut volumen ipsum videatur et recenseatur per Magn. cos DD. Provisores comunis et per Magn. um D. Petrum Paulum Malaspinam Marchionem et eo viso refferant huic consilio eorum opinionem circa impressionem'.

65 'Insomma, abbiate per constante che la Veneratione di questa Città verso questo Signore è immensa, incredibile l'Amore, l'autorità sua sopra di noi omnina et piena, che la fama che riporta, vola per tutto sonora, che l'Honore ch'egli s'ha acquistato è trionfale, che la Gloria che lo segue è più che humana, che l'immortalità del suo nome durerà eternamente ne' nostri cori'. Pola, Lo Stolone.

66 ASVE, SEN., Del., Terra, Fil., fol. 587: the Senate law is dated 11 March 1653; the attached report by the provveditori alle pompe is dated 3 March 1653.

67 Cozzi, Venezia barocca.

68 On this issue, see Eisenstadt 'Personal Relations, Trust and Ambivalence', p. 2: 'These relations are usually defined in terms of mutual intimacy, of moral and emotional obligations, stressing above all trust and empathy, and sometimes the sharing of common 'pure' pristine values, as well as some equality. In the relation of friendship, this mutual trust is consistently based on the relative equality of the participants in this relationship, while patron-client relations entail hierarchical differences between the patron and his protégé, his "client"'.

Erika Carminati

9

CELEBRATIONS OF VENETIAN *TERRAFERMA*'S *RETTORI*

From *the Good Fama* to its Subversion in *Bergamo's* Public Ritual Sphere

Twenty-five miles northeast of the Duchy of Milan's frontiers, since 1428 the city of Bergamo was the westernmost urban centre of the Venetian territorial state.[1] The heart of its public civic life was settled on the hills, in the upper city (*città alta*) bounded by the defensive walls that were built by the Republic of Venice in the second half of the sixteenth century.[2] The city centre entailed an architectural system of piazzas, churches (Santa Maria Maggiore's cathedral and Sant'Alessandro's cathedral), and governmental buildings that integrated the symbols of Bergamo's municipal identity with those of the Serenissima.[3] This concatenation of public spaces also served as a ceremonial civic stage: here the rectors periodically sent by Venice to rule the city (*podesta, capitani* and *provveditori*)[4] performed their ceremonial entries and interacted with city council's representatives (namely the *Deputati di mese*, or monthly Deputies) on several public occasions.[5]

This chapter will first present one of the most important ceremonial events characterising the ritual relation between the city and its Venetian governors: the celebration held at the end of each rector's assignment which aimed to enhance his reputation and to influence public memory. It will then consider some protest events that took place during these ceremonies to explore how the extra-institutional appropriation of ritual space contributed to shaping the civic political landscape and culture.

Ritual *celebrations* of Venetian *rettori* in Bergamo

The public image of a rector had to be shaped in accordance with his role as mediator of republican authority and representative of the aristocratic ruling class and its values. Since the very early stages of Venetian rule on the mainland, special sumptuary laws regulated not only the rectors' public behaviours and their social interactions with locals, but also their ceremonial and ritual functions.[6] Indeed, among this corpus of laws were various norms intended to manage their ceremonial entries into subject cities and to control the opulent celebrations typically planned for the end of their assignment. The ceremonial pattern that took place with the *podesta*'s first entry into the subject city reflected an intersection of Venetian law and local traditions and norms.[7] In the city of Bergamo, for instance, up to the eighteenth century this ceremony conserved a high degree of political symbolism entailing juridical effect: interactions between the *podestà* and municipal representatives ritually reproduced the terms of their political pact, in particular, through the rite of the solemn oath that was sworn by the rector on the city's statute.

At the end of their office, Venetian rectors were publicly celebrated by the subject city's council and aristocracy. In addition to older Venetian sumptuary law, local decrees and ceremonial protocols implemented by city councils regulated these ceremonies, which, because of their official character and opulent quality, often appeared in the pages of local chronicles.[8] In seventeenth and eighteenth-century Bergamo, these celebrations, formerly required by city council's decrees, included public recitation of a panegyric, presentation of a gift (often a commemorative plaque), and a final ceremonial cortege that accompanied the rector out of town.[9] Writers from the period recorded several of these festive events, highlighting the link among the ceremonial tribute, the unanimous acclaim of the local aristocracy, the warmhearted participation of the urban population, and the own merit of the celebrated one. In 1657, for example, Captain and Vice *podestà* Gradenigo left the city escorted by a retinue of four hundred men after being honoured with a public panegyric, a superb armour, a silver crown, and the placement of statues representing him, his relatives and their coat of arms on public buildings.[10] During the 1680s, individual members of the local aristocracy started to homage departing governors by commissioning their portraits.[11] Afterwards, the city council was asked to accept these portraits as gifts and permanently display them in public buildings to honour the former rectors' memories. During the seventeenth century, the custom of portraying *rettori* and decorating public offices with this genre of painting was widespread in the *Terraferma*. Though most of these paintings commissioned in the Bergamo area seem to have been lost, the series of ten portraits by Gian Giacomo Barbelli for the town hall of Crema's between 1640 and 1651 and Vicenza's stunning cycle of large-scale paintings accurately described by Marco Boschini in his *I gioielli pittoreschi* (fig. 9.2–9.7) are remarkable examples of this custom.[12]

In the second half of the century, Venice intensified its sumptuary laws regarding the placement of rector's permanent memories in subject cities, thus revealing the intention to avoid the cult of individual *rettori* or development of an exclusive relationship between them and the city in which they had served. In 1661, the Senate issued a decree aiming to stop the spread of statues and coats of arms of rectors across the dominion and to forbid public gifts such as armour, batons (fig. 9.1), flags, and other items which could refer to their rulership or suggest special affection toward them.[13] Thirty years later, facing a persistent violation of these sumptuary laws, the Senate took the extremely radical measure of ordering the removal of all statues in public spaces and the erasure of other permanent memories of past rectors, since the only 'monument' allowed was to be 'the good impression left in the subjects' heart by the representants' right justice'.[14] Nevertheless, rectors' celebration continued during the following century and right up to the fall of the Serenissima in 1797. In Bergamo, they were honoured with both orations and permanent memories commissioned by the city council or groups of local citizens. These included commemorative plaques, medals bearing their portraits, or even more impressive and extravagant presents: for example, in 1785, *podestà* Valmarana was honoured with a statue erected at the local fairground; Alvise Contarini (1778) and Nicolo' Corner (1795) received obelisks.[15]

In early modern Bergamo, celebration of *rettori* played a key role in the public political arena as a ritual mediating between governors and the governed city. If the ceremonial

9.1

Baton of the governor (rettore) of the city of Padua. Padua, Musei Civici, 1621. Reproduced with permission. Alessandrina, with permission from the Italian Ministry of Culture.

9.2
Francesco Maffei, *Glorification of the city governor (podestà) Gaspare Zane*. Vicenza, Museo Civico, 1645. Reproduced with permission.

9.3
Giulio Carpioni, *Glorification of the city governor (podestà) Vincenzo Dolfin*. Vicenza, Museo Civico, 1647. Reproduced with permission.

9.5
Francesco Maffei, *Glorification of the city governor (podestà) Girolamo Priuli*. Vicenza, Museo Civico, 1649. Reproduced with permission.

9.6
Francesco Maffei, *Glorification of the city governor (podestà) Alvise Foscarini*. Vicenza, Museo Civico, 1655. Reproduced with permission.

9.4
Giulio Carpioni, *Glorification of the city governor (podestà) Girolamo Bragadin*. Vicenza, Museo Civico, 1648. Reproduced with permission.

9.7
Francesco Maffei, *Glorification of the city governor (podestà) Tommaso Pisani*. Vicenza, Museo Civico, 1656. Reproduced with permission.

entries reproduced and renewed the constitutional pact at the base of the republican system, the ceremonies ending rectors' assignment corroborated it by publicly honouring their qualities, merits, and good administration. A comparative analysis of the panegyrics produced for these ceremonies clearly demonstrates that their content was based on fixed *topoi* sustaining this intent.[16] Indeed, the content of these panegyrics was based on a well defined set of arguments which crystallised in a rhetorical structure that can be summarised in three points: first, praise of the rector's bloodline and its ancient origins; second, a catalogue of the rector's virtues, which were transmitted by blood, shared by all the members of the patrician ruling class, and practised by the rector during his *reggimento*; third, declaration of the rector's loyalty to the Republic and exaltation of the special bond linking him and the subject city, which had resulted in his positive public reputation and ongoing praise. This last argument underpinned the whole celebrative system developed by the city of Bergamo to honour its rectors. Even the orations accompanying the presentation of rectors' portraits all follow this same logic. Indeed, in presenting the painting glorifying Captain Marcello, nobleman Francesco Tassi had claimed that since 'the prince and its representatives are fathers, to these the gratitude and love of subjects owe writings of their charms and offerings of devotion'.[17] Tassi then asked that the portrait be put in a worthy place at the Council's palace 'to the sight and veneration of the Citizens, so that the beneficial wishes of this Numen may never cease, who, like the great Planet, will be able even from afar to influence happiness and grace'.[18] In 1684 when *podestà* Cappello's portraits were presented, the city council decided to put them in their assembly room as proof of their regard for his merit and to perpetuate public praise of him.[19]

In the urban context of the Venetian subject cities, the rituals held at the end of the rectors' assignment and their perpetuation through written panegyrics, works of art or monuments became the very *lieux de memoires* of municipal political culture. From a Venetian perspective, the importance of rectors obtaining fame and a good place in public memory had been clear since the sixteenth century. According to the Capodistrian writer Giovanni Tazio, 'among the things he has to do and thanks to his virtuous and beneficent actions,' each Venetian rector 'is required to leave his distinguished memory to posterity'.[20] In another work discussing the qualities and good attitudes a rector must demonstrate towards his subjects — at his entrance as well as the end of his assignment — Tazio highlighted the importance of integrity and justice to 'earn a glorious name and leave in the chests and on the tongues of subjects a laudable memory and a distinguished shout'.[21] Gaspare Morari's later 1708 treatise for Venetian rectors too highlighted the fundamental and delicate role of *fama*:

> Fame is the big man's curse. Fame sees all, hears all and tells all. The light of the Prince makes his actions clear even if they are committed in the dark. [...] Thus, the rector has to live as the entire world is watching him. He not only has to moderate his public behaviour, but to be disciplined in the most secret cabinets too. He can be sure that each man, also those that belong to the viler populace, has eyes to observe his actions. He who presides over the government is subject to this unhappiness: he has to account to everybody for what he has done. It is true that conscience is the evidence of innocence, but only before God. To justify himself before the world, the approval of fame is required.[22]

The ceremony at the end of a rector office was a cyclical public ritual which not only validated the pact between the city and the Republic but also celebrated the individual Venetian officeholder and nourished his good *fama*.[23] These ceremonies and their memorial products can moreover be considered a sort of ritual exchange: the Venetian patrician class, as a depository of political virtues, promised good governance (*buongoverno*) of the mainland cities as well as respect for and protection of their interests, privileges, and identity; the cities reciprocated by glorifying the rectors in a manner that not only strengthened their symbolic capital but also improved the cumulative social capital of their families, and consequently of the entire patrician ruling class.[24]

Riot and protest in the ceremonial space

In the ceremonial framework delineated by repetition and protocols, two institutional agents — the Venetian rector and the representatives of the city council — were present on the ceremonial public stage, where their ritual interaction was constantly managed so that it would demonstrate the harmony of their political relationship.[25] Even if omitted by ceremonial protocols, crowds filled the street during these ceremonies, ensuring their success and attesting to collective appreciation of the celebrated one and his governance. However, circumstantial events could disturb or upset the established connotations of the ordinary pattern of the ceremony.

On 7 September 1756, after having attended the ritual entry of his successor, the former *provveditore* of Bergamo Pietro Priuli was ready to make his ceremonial exit from the city.[26] Traditionally, the carriages of local nobles paraded with the former rector along a ceremonial route which began just outside the his palace and followed the main street through the city, following the main sites of collective urban life (Piazza Nuova, Piazza Vecchia, Piazza Mercato delle Scarpe) to the city gates.[27] That evening, however, the ritual parade was disturbed by 'disdainful and offensive voices' from start to finish.[28] In fact, this kind of ceremony, and its parade in particular, constituted a breeding ground for disorder and protest. Throughout the Venetian domination of Bergamo, several such occurrences were recorded in local chronicles or in the proceedings of trials, as in the case of the revolts against Pietro Priuli and Ottavio Trento.[29] Moreover, sources show that that risk of revolt was perceived as most likely to occur in this specific ceremonial context. In his treatise addressing the first ceremonial entrance of the rectors, Gaspare Morari explained that the event could often be planned at night to avoid trouble.[30] In 1756, lieutenant Iseppo Gobetti declared that when he questioned a man in the crowd during the troubles of 7 September about what was happening, he was told that it was the habit: 'sometimes the people came to break carriage's glass when they didn't appreciate Representatives'.[31] Paolo Corner, Ottavio Trento's successor, maintained for days before the ceremony he had had a foreboding sense of the people's discontent towards Priuli. He thus ordered security chiefs 'to promptly investigate popular dispositions and to act in a careful way to prevent each possible attempt'.[32]

This kind of ephemeral manifestation of dissent shared characteristics with popular violence and politics in early modern Europe. Most witnesses of the revolt against Priuli, for instance, did not hesitate to identify its popular origins, openly despising the instigators and implicitly disqualifying from political relevance. Recent research on Venetian society has underscored popular involvement and protagonism in the public arena.[33] Moreover, historiography on early modern political violence has re-evaluated the dichotomy of popular and elite politics, shifting focus to spaces where they converged and interacted.[34] Also in the case of Bergamo, 'popular' protest practices were filled with political connotations and symbolic references, and the composition of revolting crowds seemed to be heterogeneous. In 1756, for example, Priuli's chaplain confessed that he could see at least two noble men and that he had reprimanded one of them, asking whether he felt ashamed.[35] During the trial following the events, suspicions concentrated on Count and Canon Ferrante Ambivere. In a letter addressed to the Venetian State Inquisitors (*Inquisitori di Stato*), Priuli's successor, Sebastiano Venier, reported that the first charges in the case had presented public complaints declaring that dislike of Priuli was nearly universal.[36]

During such events, it was the use of certain codes that defined them as violent and related to popular agency. Orality, for instance, such insults and aggressive shouting, is omnipresent. Shouting in the piazza and streets of Bergamo was quickly recognized as a threat: on the evening of 7 September, shouting at the rector's palace alerted the guards' captain Michelangelo Filiberti, who immediately suspected danger. His bad feeling then became a reality when the carriages arriving in the central piazza were met by the voices of innumerable people 'almost shewing an uprising'.[37] Then, as the ceremonial parade progressed, the vague shouting became more explicit, intelligible as mockery and insults constituting critique and challenge to the Venetian rector's reputation.[38] Crowds could also intervene in such events more physically, as lynching was a recurring element of these disorders. In 1676, when the carriages that escorted *podestà* Carlo Belegno reached the Sant'Agostino city gate, they found a group of women who began insulting the *rettore* and throwing soil and stones against the carriage.[39] Sometimes, such kind of protests operated more creatively: in 1629, the ceremonial parade of *podestà* Giulio Valier was disturbed by people who insulted and threw food rinds and other garbage at him.[40] In 1793 Ottavio Trento's carriage was attacked with beef manure and locusts, a biblical allusion to his supposed illicit fodder's administration.[41]

Another significant action frequently shaped contestation in the ceremonial context: the production of pasquinades often associated with manipulation of the *rettori*'s permanent memories, a practice that took place in Bergamo since the fifteenth century.[42] During the trial of 1756, for instance, the degradation of Priuli's commemorative plaque became the centre of the investigation. Indeed, some days after the rector's ceremonial exit, it was found smeared in mud with its decorative crown damaged. Count and Canon Ferrante Ambivere — who was seen by several witnesses throwing stones at it — swore that this was just the result of a game with his sisters of trying to hit the decorative crown.

Nevertheless, his past disagreements with Priuli increased the allegations against him as well as the new ephemeral inscription that covered and substituted the original one. Because of its sophisticated form, it was believed that 'some good brain made it':[43] 'Petro Priulo qui lapides non lapidem meruit/quique comuni civium et villicorum voto/abiit excessit erupit/ 7 septembri 1756' ('Pietro Priuli who hasn't deserved a commemorative stone, but stones/ with each citizen of the city's and of each countryman's vote/ has left, escaped and disappeared, 7 September 1756')[44]. The inscription, which recalls a passage of Cicero's Catiline orations, directly referred to the contestation that took place during Priuli's ceremonial exit. The iconoclastic action to the monument stressed its bond with the rector's public fame.

In the second half of the eighteenth century, another couplet widespread in Bergamo vividly attests to this habit in local collective culture: 'Urbs lapidosa quae semper dat saxa regenti: si male rexit dat lapides, si bene lapidem' ('Town of stones which always gives stones to rectors: if they misgovern, it gives them stones, if they govern well, it gives them commemorative stones')[45]. Such episodes reveal a common awareness in Bergamo of how to manipulate structural elements of Venetian rector celebrations to subvert their symbolic consequences. The repertoire of ephemeral practises — ordinarily associated with an irrational explosion of popular violence — could intervene in these ceremonies to modify not only their manifestations but also their institutional outcomes: when universal homage to the rector's merit is voluntarily substituted with public complaint, his reputation is degraded consequently.

Some days after the riot of 1756, a letter for Priuli's successor was found in the secret complaint box. Its anonymous writer started with an informal salutation, addressing the new rector by 'dear friend', and went on to argue that everybody knew the good disposition with which he was starting his *reggimento*, adding that Venier had an advantage in being 'the successor of a fool'[46] who had respected no law or reason. The writer continued with some benevolent words, affirming that he desired only 'that you can get your honour and that you can have as much praise as the blame that Priuli got'.[47] The new *rettore* of Bergamo was then warned about the people in the town who could take advantage of and betray him, and he was advised to follow the laws and to put his confidence in the professors of the public court and who occupied the leading offices of the city. The latter, he explained, gained no personal advantage from their assignments nor from the rector's position, since they acted just for honour. In the second part of the letter, the author drew up a list of ancient Venetian rectors of Bergamo who had been loved because they ruled for the common good: this was offered as the evidence that the people of Bergamo could recognize a rector's merit.[48] The anonymous writer finished by declaring he wanted 'to see in you the glories of these gentlemen duplicated'[49], maintaining that he would warn the new Venetian ruler if bad people approached him. The tone of this anonymous letter is notable. Oscillating between esteem and threat, it never questions the republican system itself, but shows how the subject city and its people took an active role in mediating Republican authority. The closing of the letter summarises this well: 'love me, because I love you'.[50]

Conclusions

After the riot of 7 September 1756 and the discovery of the degraded commemorative stone, Venice started investigations and opened a trial. The guilty parties were searched, but the efforts of Venetian authorities seemed more focused on discovering the extent and motivation for the collective disgust against Priuli. At the end of the investigations, Sebastiano Venier tried to mediate with the representatives of the city of Bergamo. They had denounced several aspects of Priuli's administration and asked for the respect of their privileges.[51] Venier assured them that he had succeeded in bringing the situation in Bergamo under control. As in the case of Ottavio Trento, the Venetian response to the event seemed aimed at decoupling the individual political acts of a single rector from the 'good government' of the Republic as a whole, which according to the 'myth' was supposed to fully respect subject cities' privileges and customs[52]: efforts were then concentrated on trying to restore the pre-existing harmony, as was normal in the ritual ceremonies at the end of each Venetian rector's assignment. Civic ceremonies constituted an essential dimension of the public sphere where the political relation between Venice and the municipality was not only represented but also legitimated, renewed, and maintained by the ritual's institutional power.[53] The political identity of Venice, as well as that of Bergamo, took shape in the celebrations at the end of a rector's assignment, during which the city could express the continuity of its loyalty to the Republic through glorification of its representatives and gratitude for their good actions.

Nevertheless, the repertoire of ceremonial codes, practices, and interconnected media, defined by ritual repetition at an official level, could be taken over through manipulation or subversion by extra-institutional agents expressing their political opinions. The institutional ceremonial dimension in this way became a public space of interaction where a plurality of voices could arise and divergent opinions could be expressed.[54] In their manifestation, these practices could transform the celebration of good government into a ritual of defamation and degradation of the rector's *fama*. Moreover, if rituals were for their nature ephemeral, their effects could have the most lasting impacts and reverberations. Since the celebration of *rettori* represented a constant and cyclical celebration of a well-balanced political relation, as well as an exaltation of the Venetian patriciate's superior moral qualities and virtues, its subversion could have more collective consequences: it could question and weaken the symbolic capital of the entire Venetian ruling class.

1. Belotti, *Storia di Bergamo*, III, pp. 130–36, 201–22.
2. Bonadei, ed., *Bergamo verso l'Unesco*.
3. Colmuto Zanella and Zanella, '"Città sopra monte excellentissime situada"'.
4. On the *rettori*, see Tagliaferri, ed., *Atti del convegno Venezia e la Terraferma*; Cozzi, *Ambiente veneziano, ambiente veneto*, pp. 291–352; Zamperetti, 'Magistrature centrali'.
5. BCBG, ASC, Ant. reg., Com. Bg, Canc., Cap., AB 94, fols. 10 r-11 v.
6. The *provveditori alle pompe* (which oversaw the regulation of expenditures and public displays of luxury) was constantly attentive to the public behaviour of *rettori*. The first directives regarding governors' ritual entries and celebrations were issued in the early stages of Venetian dominion of the Terraferma, during the fifteenth century. ASVE, PP, f. 7. Also see Bellabarba's contribution to this volume, chapter 8.
7. Carminati, 'La Repubblica in scena'.
8. For Bergamo, a very rich source of this kind is Calvi, *Effemeride sagro-profana*; Calvi, *Diario (1649–1678)*. For the nearby town of Brescia similar events are recorded in Guerrini, 'I Diari dei Bianchi'.
9. This is demonstrated by the uninterrupted emanation of decrees on the matter by the city council that are recorded in BCBG, ASC, Ant. reg., Com. Bg, Azioni. This is also confirmed by the eighteenth-century ceremonial protocols recorded in the city ceremonial book, BCBG, ASC, Ant. reg., Com. Bg, Canc., Cer., MMB 884.
10. Calvi, *Diario (1649–1678)*, p. 119.
11. BCBG, ASC, Ant. reg., Com. Bg, Azioni, regg. 73–75.
12. Boschini, *I gioielli pittoreschi*, pp. 195–212. On the Vicenza cycle, which was realised by Giulio Carpioni, Francesco Maffei, and the Fratelli Braganza, also see Avagnina, Binotto, and Villa, eds, *Pinacoteca civica di Vicenza*, pp. 154–60. On the series of portraits in Crema, see Colombo, Marubbi, and Miscioscia, eds, *Gian Giacomo Barbelli*, pp. 237–40. The habit of portraying the *rettori* was widespread in the local votive context too, showing the special bond established between Venetian patricians and local elites. See Boccato and Pasqualini Canato, *Il potere nel sacro*; Mancini, 'Sotto specie di laude'.
13. BCBG, ASC, Ant. reg., Com. Bg, Duc., Reg., Municipali, R 99 17, fol. 26r.
14. 'La buona impressione che lascia nel cuore de' sudditi la retta giustizia de' rappresentanti'. BCBG, ASC, Ant. reg., Com. Bg, Duc., Reg., Municipali, R 99 17, fol. 150r.
15. For the statue of Valmarana see Tassi, *Vite de' pittori, scultori e architetti Bergamaschi*, II, p. 137. For the obelisks: Rosa, 'Alvise II Contarini e l'obelisco di Santa Marta', pp. 9–14; Zanetti, 'L'obelisco di Nicolò Corner capitano veneto di Bergamo', pp. 6–8.
16. From the seventeenth century on there has been a general trend to increase the printing of this kind of panegyrics in the whole Venetian State. See Raines, *L'invention du mythe aristocratique*, I, pp. 213–14. I worked mainly on the printed panegyrics for the *rettori* of Bergamo of the seventeenth and the eighteenth century preserved in the Biblioteca Angelo Mai. It's significant to notice the recurrence of these topical subjects in the celebration of the procurators of St Mark too. See: Metlica, 'Magnificence and Atticism in Seventeenth-Century Venice'; Metlica, 'Reshaping the Republican Ritual'.
17. 'Il Principe et suoi Rappresentanti sono Padri, a questi la gratitudine e l'amore de sudditi devono le scritture de' carmi e l'holocausti della devotione'. BCBG, ASC, Ant. reg., Com. Bg, Azioni, reg. 73, fol. 280v.
18. 'Alla vista et alla veneratione de' Cittadini con che non habbino a cessarsi mai li auspicij benefici di questo Nume che a guisa del gran Pianeta saprà anche da lontano influire la felicità e gratie'. BCBG, ASC, Ant. reg., Com. Bg, Azioni, reg. 73, fol. 280v.
19. BCBG, ASC, Ant. reg., Com. Bg, Azioni, reg. 74, fols. 143r–144v.
20. 'Tra le altre cose che deve esequire, è tenuto con le sue virtuose operationi giovevoli alla città lasciar di sé illustre memoria alla posterità'. Tazio, *La imagine del Rettore*, pp. 131–32.
21. 'Acquistarsi un glorioso nome e di sé lasciarne nei petti e nelle lingue dei sudditi una memoria laudabile e un famoso grido'. Tazio, *L'ottimo Reggimento del Magistrato Pretorio*, p. 286.
22. 'Atroce flagello de Grandi è la Fama. Questa tutto vede, tutt'ode, e tutto dice. La luce del Prencipe fa, che sian chiare le di lui azioni, benché al buio commesse. […] Dovrà adunque il nostro Rettore Politico prefiggersi di vivere, come se tutt' il Mondo lo vedesse. Non solo doverà in publico pesare le proprie azioni; ma contenerle in disciplina anco ne' più secreti gabinetti; mentre può assicurarsi, che quasi ogn'uno anco della più vile feccia del volgo havera gl'occhi à prescutare le di lui operazioni, tutto che cautamente condotte. Chi presiede al Governo soggiace à tal forte d'infelicità, che delle proprie azioni deve rendere conto anco alla più minuta plebe. È vero, che la propria conscienza è buon testimonio dell'innocenza, con Dio però, ch'intende il linguaggio de cuori; ma per giustificarsi appresso il Mondo è necessaria l'approvazione della fama'. Morari, *Prattica de' reggimenti in Terraferma*, pp. 235–36.
23. Literature on the topic of *Fama* is vast. For a definition of this concept, see Gauvard, 'La Fama, une parole fondatrice'. Also see Fenster and Smail, eds, *Fama*, and Walker and Kerr, eds, *Fama and her Sisters*.
24. On the concept of symbolic capital and its relation to power, see Dubois, Durand and Winkin, 'Aspects du symbolique dans la sociologie de Pierre Bourdieu'. On the cumulative social capital of the Venetian patrician class, see Raines, *L'invention du mythe aristocratique*, pp. 187–236, 453–83.
25. On political harmony as performed in the ritual context, see Muir, *Ritual in Early Modern Europe*, pp. 252–55.
26. The events of 1756 are reported in ASVE, IS, Proc. crim., b. 1067.
27. It followed the same landmarks of the ceremonial entries into the city, in the reverse direction. This can be reconstructed by comparing the protocols recorded in the City Ceremonial Book, BCBG, ASC, Ant. reg., Com. Bg, Canc., Cer., MMB 884.
28. 'Sprezzanti e offensive voci'. ASVE, IS, Dis. Ret., b. 221, fol. 736r.
29. On the revolt against Ottavio Trento, see Povolo, 'Il processo a Ottavio Trento'. Other riots during Venetian governor ceremonial exits from Bergamo took place in 1560 (Lorenzo Bragadin), 1629 (Giulio Valier), and 1676 (Carlo Belegno).
30. Morari, *Prattica de' reggimenti in Terraferma*, pp. 39–40.
31. 'Alcune volte giungea il popolo sin a romper i vetri della carrozza quando i rappresentanti qui non incontravano'. ASVE, IS, Proc. crim., b. 1067, fol. 12v.

32 'Non solo di indagar destamente quali infatti si fossero le popolari disposizioni, ma anco di prestarsi in modo cauto per impedire possibilmente ogni attentato'. ASVE, IS, Proc. crim., b. 1185, fol. 1r.
33 De Vivo, Patrizi, informatori, barbieri; De Larivière, The Revolt of Snowballs; Van Gelder and Judde de Larivière, eds, Popular Politics in an Aristocratic Republic.
34 Wood, Riot, Rebellion and Popular Politics in Early Modern England; Cohen, 'Juger les juges'.
35 ASVE, IS, Proc. crim., b. 1067, fol. 20r.
36 ASVE, IS, Dis. Ret., b. 221, fol. 736r.
37 'Dimostravano quasi sollevazione'. ASVE, IS, Proc. crim., b. 1067, fol. 21v.
38 On the link between insults, popular politics, and political subversion see Haemers, 'Filthy and Indecent Words'.
39 Calvi, Diario (1649–1678), p. 253.
40 Benaglio, 'Relazione della carestia e della peste', p. 440.
41 Povolo, 'Il processo a Ottavio Trento', p. 251.
42 For example, in 1560, while *podestà* Bragadin was about to leave the city, the commemorative plaque which had been given to him by the city council was damaged and *scripturas infames* were affixed all over the town. See Cappelluzzo, ed., Lo 'Statuto del Podestà' di Bergamo, p. 36. In 1629, the evening of *podestà* Giulio Valier's celebration, a pasquinade alluding to his administration of fodder was seen on the door of his palace. Its text has been recorded in Calvi, Effemeride sagro-profana, p. 443. On this modality of expression in social-political conflicts in the nearby city of Brescia, see Valseriati, Tra Venezia e l'impero.
43 'Qualche buona testa chi la fece'. ASVE, IS, Proc. crim., b. 1067, fol. 11v.
44 ASVE, IS, Proc. crim., b. 1067, fol. 6v.
45 Vimercati Sozzi, Sulla moneta della città di Bergamo, p. 44.
46 'Il sucessore di un pezzo di matto'. The anonymous letter is contained in ASVE, IS, Proc. crim., b. 1067.
47 'Che ve fè onor, e che abiè altretanta lode, quanto xè 'l biasimo ch'à avudo el proveditor'. ASVE, IS, Proc. crim., b. 1067.
48 Niccolò Erizzo (in Bergamo in 1752), Paolo Querini (1737), Leonardo Dolfin (1740), Angelo Contarini da Mula (1729). The author arguably implicitly demonstrates that good actions are followed by a good and persistent memory.
49 'Veder in vu replicarse le glorie de sti galatomini'. ASVE, IS, Proc. crim., b. 1067.
50 'Voletemi ben, perché mi ve amo'. ASVE, IS, Proc. crim., b. 1067.
51 They in particular denounced Priuli's lack of legal formalities in judgement, frequent underserved incarcerations, violent hindrances of legal appeal, and ceremonial changes. As in the case of Ottavio Trento studied by Claudio Povolo, it seems that Priuli abused the employment of the *rito sommario*, overstepping municipal customs. See Povolo, 'Il processo a Ottavio Trento', p. 285.
52 For an overview of this vast and long-debated topic, see Martin and Romano, eds, Venice Reconsidered. For a specific focus on the Terraferma: Viggiano, 'Il Dominio da terrai'; Ortalli, 'Entrar nel Dominio'. On the iconography of the pacts of dedication and their link with the legitimation of the republican domination on the Terraferma, see Florio, 'Inchini e carte bollate'.
53 Bourdieu, 'Les rites d'institution', pp. 175–86.
54 Rospocher, ed., Beyond the Public Sphere.

Alfredo Viggiano

10

THE GOOD USE OF 'PEOPLE' IN FIFTEENTH-CENTURY VENICE

Reflections over a Controversial Term

Since the 1970s, anthropologists, legal historians, jurists, philosophers and historians of political doctrines, and, subsequently, linguists and 'general' historians, have challenged the paradigms by which the field of political action and its rationale were defined for over two centuries. Conflict versus peace, civil society versus the state, autonomy versus centralization, freedom versus constraint, discipline versus disorder: the discourse on human action in communities has long been constructed following binary oppositions, the either-or.

In this attempt at clarification, historiography has turned, often confusedly, to the social sciences in search of the basis of its lost legitimacy. Study of the political lexicon shaped by the communicative interactions among different social actors has represented a privileged subject of investigation. In order to decipher its function and use, scholars have employed tools drawn from various disciplines, such as social and structural anthropology, literary theory, the history of law and institutions. The reflections of anthropologists, linguists, and philosophers — from Claude Lévy-Strauss to Clifford Geertz, from Hans Robert Jauss to John Langshaw Austin, from Richard Posner to Hans Georg Gadamer, from Leo Spitzer to Vladimir Propp, from Ernesto de Martino to Antonio Gramsci — have been mobilised to explain lexical recurrences and stereotypes sedimented in the various types of documents consulted by historians. Within the general framework of this new 'cultural history', scholarship has examined the performative nature of political jargon, the social usage and manipulation of lexical ambiguity, as well as the ways in which norms impact society and are reshaped by it.[1] Such attention has not only allowed for a better understanding of the language of 'rulers' and power élites, it has strived to restore the voice of a plurality of subjects excluded or marginalised from the sphere of political decisions. In this way, the specific tonality of voices and experiences long thought to be 'marginal' or insignificant have been recovered.

Alongside research that has sought to understand the direction of 'popular *agency*' in specific contexts, other methods of research on the idioms and conceptions of politics have emerged. We will mention just two approaches that have influenced historical research in various ways. The first comes from German scholarship and features figures such as Werner Conze, Reinhart Koselleck, and Wolfgang Reinhard, the leading scholars of the extensive research project on the *Geschichtliche Grundbegriffe* ('Fundamental historical concepts').[2] The second approach, synthetically referred to as the 'Cambridge School', was pioneered by Quentin Skinner and John Grenville Agard Pocock. Skinner's and Pocock's early interests were indicative of a very precise choice of chronological scope: the early modern era, a period characterised by a profound reconfiguration of the political lexicon. Between the fifteenth and seventeenth centuries, terms such as *libertas*, *privilegium*, and *res publica* acquired new meanings through the influence of republican culture and classical rhetoric, from Cicero to Quintilian.[3]

The *Grundbegriffe* project was encyclopaedic in nature. The German edition spans eight extremely rich volumes, for a total of around nine thousand pages. These volumes are organised into one hundred and twenty-two preselected 'entries', decided by the curators and assigned to various authors. Lexemes reflecting analytical 'macro-categories' thus follow one another from volume to volume: *Heimat* and *Gesellschaft*, *Fortschritt* and *Demokratie*, *Faschismus* and *Imperialismus*. The philosophical foundation of this approach is evident: among the curators' referenced authors, the names of Heidegger and Gadamer stand out. On the 'trunk' of this hermeneutical framework were grafted contributions coming from historical sociology, such as those offered by Alfred and Max Weber, and from political and legal doctrines, especially the ideas of Carl Schmitt.[4] This genealogy left its mark on the project, which aimed to portray an all-encompassing history

(*Verfassungsgeschichte*), capable of capturing political action, legal frameworks, and socio-economic structures with the same overall view.

In some cases, individual lemmas were placed close to others thought to be similar. Among the clusters built by analogy, we can find, for instance, one that includes *Volk, Nation, Nationalismus, Masse*.[5] Just from the sequence of these four terms, one can grasp the strengths and limitations of the overall approach of the work. Despite the statements of the editors, who declared the intention of framing the terms under consideration within the 'intellectual' context, the reader still has the impression of being confronted with a work that is teleologically informed, regardless of its extraordinary importance. The ambiguity of the words, their multifunctionality, their flexibility, and their adaptability to various contexts do not fit with the hermeneutical perspective characterising the whole editorial enterprise. Additionally, one should consider that the sources cited by the different authors of individual entries belong mostly to high culture: texts by philosophers and jurists clearly predominate over other types of sources or writings drawing from other sensibilities less aware of their impact and relevance. Thus, the authors of the 'history of concepts' did not question one of the most traditional topics of intellectual history: the distinction, formalised over generations, between 'high' culture and 'low' culture.[6]

Similar considerations can be made about the research led by the main authors of the Cambridge School.[7] The intellectual reference points that most impacted Skinner and Pocock are well-known: on the one hand, the classics of Greek and Roman ethical-political literature read and interpreted during the modern age, with Aristotle and Cicero at the forefront; on the other hand, analytical philosophy and performative language theories, especially authors such as Ludwig Wittgenstein, John Langshaw Austin, Willard Van Orman Quine, and Donald Davidson.[8] While historians like Otto Brunner or Reinhart Koselleck focused on the impact and transformation of terms throughout Western history using a kind of Braudelian long-term (*longue durée*) approach, in the Anglo-Saxon tradition this chronological dimension, though not denied, appeared as a mere background allowing for clearer focus on the role of performative utterances and *speech acts* in shaping political cultures. According to the Cambridge School, the use of these *acts* within broad communicative spheres would have legitimised political cultures and made them recognizable.

During the 1980s, under the influence of Skinner's research and thanks to the reception of Michel Foucault's work,[9] the identity of *Intellectual History* (which has been further specified in recent years with adjectives like New, Global, etc.) was defined between the two shores of the Atlantic, largely between Cambridge, United Kingdom and Cambridge, Massachusetts.[10] The change in perspective is evident: historians like Robert Darnton or Martin Jay do not consider texts and topics belonging to the 'high' tradition of the European canon of political knowledge, let alone the republican paradigm, or to the reception of Roman political and legal literature within early modern political theories.[11] Their critical focus has shifted toward intensive analysis of less studied types of texts: letters, city chronicles, police records, travel accounts.[12] The social spectrum of the protagonists of political actions and claims has also become wider to include artisans, millers, fishermen, innkeepers. The aim of such historians has been to capture the culture of these unexpected political actors and the multidimensional, complex web of power relations in which their political actions were situated.[13]

Spaces and places between conflict and consensus

Within the very fragmented galaxy of 'urban history' of the late Medieval and early modern periods, recent research has devoted special attention to processes of constructing spaces as a result of the interplay among architectural projects, social (in)discipline, and institutional control.[14] Urban spaces are no longer understood as mere 'stages' where different actors enter and exit. The *piazza* has long been depicted as a neutral space, whose main feature is its disposition to be occupied by the protagonists, either active or passive, of political action. Representation of the relationship between active individuals and the static environments in which their behaviours are staged has been radically challenged by research that has emphasised the interactions among actors/social groups and the creation of spaces of jurisdiction.[15]

Starting from the 1980s and 1990s, studies on Venice too have experienced increasing interest in the social and anthropological construction of urban spaces. The works of Ed Miur and Matteo Casini shed light onto the importance of civic rituals (festivals, processions, triumphs) as a tool for political legitimisation.[16] Their analysis focuses on the ritual pacification of the different components of Venetian society rather than on the reasons underlying social conflicts. In the aforementioned research, the Venetian patriciate has played an important but not exclusive role: the attention given to its ability to reconcile differences has seemed to recreate a modern, functional version of the 'myth of Venice'. This approach has been challenged by a series of more recent studies. Authors such as Filippo de Vivo, Claire Judde de Larivière, Massimo Rospocher, Rosa Salzberg, and Maartje van Gelder[17] consider aspects of political agency that had been previously overlooked. The main contributions of this new historiographical approach can be summarised as follows: the diffusion of gossip as a means of political communication and acculturation; the definition of a new *spatial* turn in which the 'square' takes the form of a dynamic element. Rather than considering the square a passive object or sort of theatrical backdrop, indifferent to the actors playing their roles, this approach frames it as the protagonist in ongoing processes of interaction, interpretation, and sensemaking undertaken by individual or collective actors searching for legitimacy.[18] From the methodological point of view, the square is now recognised as the hub of a complex urban fabric where various spaces of power and jurisdiction blend and overlap. In this sense, it represents a space of confrontation between the different nuances of the notion of 'citizenship'[19] where processes of social inclusion and exclusion, approval and disapproval are defined together with the operational aspects of the 'emotions'.[20]

Given the nature of the sources produced and preserved there, and by the republican set-up of its constitution, early modern Venice certainly constitutes an excellent vantage-point for investigation of the 'invention of *popolo*' and analysis of the active 'popular' presence in public places of political decision-making and representation.[21] The circulation and manipulation of news, along with the role of gossip, represent new sets of historiographical concern. Scholarly interest in agency and ritual and ceremonial practices has aided in the identification of the various protagonists of the Venetian urban scene.[22] Family, religious, and guild conflicts not only moved within urban spaces but also shaped their outlook; the negotiation of interests and claims for justice 'from below' could not be articulated anywhere but in the urban space. What Laurie Nussdorfer claimed for early modern Rome indeed sheds light on the Venetian context as well: 'the city landscape itself became a substitute for participatory institutions'.[23]

The search for cultures 'other' than 'official' and 'learned' ones allows for innovative interpretation of historical documents: local chronicles, judicial verdicts, inquisitorial proceedings, theological and political treatises, correspondence. In many respects, the 'square' represents only the latest source considered by this branch of historiographical research investigating the plurality of politically active voices in the early modern period. However, it is important to highlight that the 'square' also carries a potential ambiguity. For a long period of European history, it was both the domain in which the values of *iustitia* and *bonum commune* were asserted and the arena where factional conflicts between different 'parties' got most fully expressed.[24] The square could welcome and amplify the radical voices of individuals who protested against the violation of fundamental rights, while also providing an extraordinary weapon for the sacralization of the power of an authority. The square was also the space where conflicts were neutralised: in this context, the peace-making role of preachers belonging to mendicant orders, especially the Dominicans, is relevant. Summoned by city councils, they would publicly condemn factional divisions before large crowds, accusing anyone who fuelled disagreements and conflicts.[25]

The tension between participation and repression, obedience and sedition, was thus expressed within the perimeter of the 'square' and defines its physiognomy and functions. It is certainly not coincidental that during the century spanning from the mid-1400s to the mid-1500s, political literature and legal treatises debated the nature of acts classified as *rebellio* and *tumultus*, and therefore their punishability.[26] For the most part, this new lexicon of order was elaborated by humanists hosted in the 'halls of power': this process of refining hermeneutic categories tended to draw an increasingly firmer line between savagery and civic behaviours, between *ignobilitas* and nobility.[27]

Throughout the fifteenth century, the Republic of Venice repeatedly reiterated an act framing any meetings or communications involving more than five individuals (*conventicula*) in public spaces as *seditio* ('sedition').[28] This measure might seem paradoxical, as it was conceived in a city that built part of its 'myth' on opening public spaces to community participation.[29] However, we must remember that such accessibility was subordinate to the control of political authority, which meticulously organised ritual and celebratory occasions.[30]

In the square, various ways of expanding the political sphere intersected, confronted one another, and blended. There, discourses on liberty and obedience also found the most fertile environment for their expression.[31]

Much has been written on the 'myth' of origins of Venice and its political structure: from technical literature — authored by personalities such as Lauro Quirini or Gasparo Contarini[32] — to chronicles that, even during the Middle Ages, attempted to establish the original features of the Venetian city-state.[33] Traits of this mythological construction can also be identified in the iconography decorating the halls of power.[34] The relative stability of these mythologies conceals and neutralises the social and constitutional tensions running through the Venetian polity over the centuries.

Military disasters — such as the one for which Antonio Grimani (1434–1523) was held responsible — often led to constitutional crises. As Niklas Luhmann highlighted, in such circumstances, the keywords, topics, and issues animating political discourse lost semantic weight and acquired new meanings, thus entering different interpretive circuits. According to Luhmann, such crises change the 'rules of attention'.[35] Indeed, faced with dramatic events, the republican system of values struggled to fully integrate elements of disorder and dissent. The climax of such crisis, stemming in this case from a humiliating defeat by the Turks, challenged various elements of the republican mythological system: the suspension of traditional 'institutionalised' forms of 'internal' political communication and difficulty in controlling the inevitable circulation of gossip in an 'open' city like Venice arose regardless of the apologetic discourse which, instead, would have tended to deny them.

The Grimani affair: infamy and honour

Close to the setting of the famous Battle of Lepanto, which took place in 1571, the waters of Cape Zonchio were the scene of the earlier battle intermittently fought from 12 to 25 August 1499 by the Venetian navy, led by Antonio Grimani, and the Ottoman fleet one, under the command of Kamal Reis.[36] This event belonged to the broader Turkish-Venetian conflict that unfolded between 1499 and 1503 and led to a weakening of Venice's presence in the Eastern Mediterranean, culminating in the definitive loss of the outposts of Modon and Coron. News of the defeat dismayed the members of the Great Council and caused a wave of indignation and agitation amongst the population, eventually leading to Grimani's impeachment. The Great Council gathered all adult male members of the patriciate, the closed aristocratic class that ruled the Republic by birthright. The so-called *Serrata* (Closing) of 1297 had restricted this privilege to the descendants of a limited number of lineages.[37] Nonetheless, in the subsequent centuries the Great Council could not avoid expanding into a plethoric assembly, which was far from functional to the speed and competence required to make decisions for a state now spanning from the Adda river to the Aegean Sea. During the Grimani trial, the participants in the judicial sessions of the Great Council were nearly 2000.

Amongst them was the notorious diarist Marin Sanudo[38], who gave a detailed account of the events following the battle of Cape Zonchio. In his *Diarii* he reported in detail the echoes of the defeat and its increasingly dramatic repercussions. As a firsthand observer of many of the events constituting the Grimani affair, Sanudo carefully gathered testimonies and gossip circulating within the patrician magistratures. Antonio Grimani, the negative protagonist and scapegoat of the naval defeat, was a member of one of the wealthiest families in the Venetian patriciate.[39] Born in 1434 to Marino and Agnesina Montaner from Coron, Antonio lost his parents at four years old and was raised by an uncle. He distinguished himself in the spice trade from a young age, particularly in the trade of pepper, quickly accumulating significant wealth and proving to have leadership charisma in the mercantile environment. Grimani's political career was therefore successful: starting from the 1480s, he was elected to the most prestigious offices of the Republic (*avogadore di Comun*, *savio del consiglio*, ambassador to Milan). In 1494, he was appointed as naval commander-in-chief (*capitano generale da mar*), the premier role in the maritime fleet. At the beginning of spring 1499, he offered the Serenissima 40,000 ducats to support the costs of the war against the Turks. It is difficult to speculate whether his appointment as supreme commander of the navy was favoured by a similar dedication to the Republic's cause or whether the significant monetary contribution had the purpose, clearly unsuccessful, of avoiding needing to be elected to this military office, which was considered particularly risky and burdensome.

The defeat at Zonchio stirred up criticism from part of the Venetian patriciate, revealing the presence of internal divisions within the ruling class that had hitherto remain latent. As documented by coeval chroniclers such as Marin Sanudo and Domenico Malipiero, the difference in fortunes amongst patrician families had fuelled a climate of resentment. While the wealthy lineages were engaged in trades and investments on the mainland and managed the politics of ecclesiastical benefices, the lower patriciate was excluded from access to such significant resources.[40]

At the beginning of the sixteenth century, the proclaimed aristocratic equality of all members of the Great Council was perceived by many patricians as merely rhetorical and celebratory. Resentment on the part of the lower patricians spread, especially within the milieu of the navy. For the lower patriciate holding military posts on the galleys, the conquest of military-commercial outposts and the construction of an empire spanning from the Adriatic coast to Turkey represented an opportunity for redemption, via both legal and illicit means. The defeat deprived both individuals and lineages of material and immaterial resources (i.e. spoils of war, administrative and military positions, prestige, and honour to be invested in the political arena), leaving them to an uncertain fate. The defeat at Zonchio also opened deep wounds in the political body of the Republic. However, the republican political tradition had devised a remedy to mend such wounds: the person responsible for the defeat had to undergo a political trial to adjudicate their responsibility.

This cure, though, was not painless: giving voice to the mounting resentment harboured by the patriciate hit by the crisis would have posed a risk to the stability of the system. Part of the patriciate was indeed starting to consider the power of Antonio Grimani and his clan as clear evidence of the corruption of the values of equity, mediation, and moderation on which the republican model was founded. The marriage of Grimani's father to a non-noble 'commoner' played a role in this process of constructing an internal enemy.

Grimani was not the first and certainly would not have been the last to experience the humiliating ritual of undergoing a criminal trial. In 1350, Marco Ruzzini was accused of facilitating the sacking of the port of Negroponte by the Genoese fleet with his cowardice. In 1379, similar charges hit Vettor Pisani, the protagonist of a shameful naval debacle during the long conflict between Venice and Genoa over control of the Mediterranean.[41] Francesco Morosini faced a similar fate in 1670 when he was accused of causing the defeat that led Venice to give Crete up to the Ottoman empire after a 24-year-long war.[42]

News of the Zonchio defeat preceded the arrival of its responsible party. In his *Diarii*, Sanudo noted an increasing display of discouragement, anger, and fear in the city. The proclaimed harmony of the patriciate was torn apart by bitter conflicts: latent clan rivalries became more evident, incidents of violence between members of the 'Case Vecchie' and 'Nuove' were more frequent, as were the insults that young, unemployed patricians addressed to the wise and elderly '*patres patriae*' leading the Republic. Challenged by such displays of resentment, the equality of opportunity and prestige between wealthy and less fortunate nobles, a fundamental premise of the republican constitution, looked like empty rhetoric. The military setback of 1499 triggered a process of claim-making with deep roots. The tumultuous journey of the 'war news' travelling from Corfu to the Venetian lagoon caused an amplification and dramatisation of the event. Letters, dispatches, and oral accounts laid the groundwork for a sensational trial that operated on two levels from its inception: the official level, determined by the procedures and rites of the magistratures, and the more fluid and generic level marked by the voices and pressures exerted by the inhabitants of Venice. '*Terra*' (Land) is the term Sanudo adopted to define this latter actor, which presented itself as the driving force behind the indictment of the naval commander-in-chief. Sanudo's *Diarii* represent the most extensive collection of vernacular words of common use circulating in Venice during the early modern era. They can therefore be used as a primary source to access the political lexicon of the period.

Sanudo's usage of the term '*Terra*' reveals the existence of at least three semantic fields that appear tightly intertwined with each other. The first encompasses a dimension that could be defined as spatial-territorial: it expresses the nature of the *civitas Veneciarum* in its monumental and architectural dimension, representing the whole set of its stones and buildings. Thus usage constitutes a verbal translation of what, just a year later, Jacopo de' Barbari would visually represent in his remarkable bird's-eye view map of Venice.[43]

The second meaning of the term conveys the constitutional and political authority of the patriciate: in this usage, '*Terra*' entails the whole entangled set of patrician magistratures composing the Republic, and therefore the 'myth' of the 'law in action'. At times, Sanudo employs the term '*Terra*' in a narrower sense, as a synonym for the normative/legislative activity of the Great Council. Here a metonymic process — substituting the part for the whole — is obviously at play. 'Terra' defines the function of the institution that served as the basis of legitimisation for all the city's other magistratures. The republican 'myth' developed between the fifteenth and the first half of the sixteenth century replicated this pattern. The Republic was composed of members who were essentially equal, as they were equally included in the Great Council; in an apparent paradox, their individual identity was given by their participation in collective institutions politically acting towards the 'common good'.

The third meaning of 'Terra' encompasses the entirety of the city's inhabitants, who were simultaneously actors and spectators in an uninterrupted performance. In this case, 'Terra' is an equivalent of 'popolo' in its broadest and most indefinite sense. Here the people are perceived as an indistinct collective which was nonetheless ever-present during the most decisive moments of the city's history. The 'popolo' could promote and legitimise, comply with or challenge the decisions made by political institutions. In Sanudo's narrative, the 'popolo' played a twofold role: at times, it actively manifested its presence, while at other times, it seemed to be stuck in a kind of aphasia, appearing subordinate to logics of political action and power above it. The duplicity of this position is evident: the people both provided support in terms of discipline/obedience for the construction of republican harmony and emerged as an autonomous subject potentially capable of representing a threat.

Representation of the 'people'

It is important to remember that in the Venetian political lexicon — and thus in the Republic's conscious self-representation — the term 'popolo' acquired a constitutional significance that we have not yet considered, and which took on a specific connotation during the Grimani trial. The word 'popolo' identified the social class of the privileged *cives*, i.e. the individuals who occupied the upper ranks of the bureaucratic apparatus.

These individuals actually granted the perfect equilibrium of the republican polity 'from below': they were the lower layer of a tripartite structure at the centre of which stood the aristocratic element represented by the ensemble of patrician magistratures and whose apex was occupied by the *doge*, the monarchic element of the Venetian 'mixed constitution'. The conceptual framework through which Sanudo saw the Republic's military and political crisis had little to do with this idealised representation, which hailed back to various Venetian translations/adaptations of the Aristotelian and Polybian political models. Only apparently *évenementielle*, the narrative proposed by Sanudo ascribed the *populus* a function which was more dynamic and multifaceted than that proposed by coeval theories of the *De bene instituta re publica*. Similarly, in the *Diarii*, the relationship between what we can call the *internal legitimisation* of the republican constitution (built on the rhetoric of solidarity and equality among all nobles in the Great Council) and an *external legitimisation* appeared much more entangled. The latter seemed to be determined by the contribution made to the city's peace by non-patrician elements of Venetian society. This social segment (which actually represented the majority of the Venetian urban milieu) has recently aroused great historiographical interest: yet recent research tends to ascribe all subjects who did not belong to the inner circle of the patriciate (who are indifferently identified, at times, with the constellation of artisans gravitating around the *Scuole piccole*, and, at other times, with the city residents as a whole) a substantially indistinct character. In such historiographical representations, the 'popolo' exists and exerts pressure on institutional power structures. While this perspective has expanded the scope of the analysis of political action to a series of previously overlooked actors, it must be underscored that it risks ascribing to the pre-modern category of the 'popolo' an antagonistic acceptation and an almost metaphysical cohesion that are totally absent in the available historical sources.

The crisis experienced by the Venetian Republic at the beginning of the sixteenth century uncovered several layers of tension — between nobles and non-nobles, between the rich and the poor, between subjects of the mainland and those of the maritime state, between rulers and ruled — and ideological projection. The unfolding of events recounted 'in real time' by Sanudo did not significantly differ, in essential features, from other contemporary testimonies of the case, such as fragments of chronicles and trial sentences that summarise its key phases. However, the details of the events that Sanudo captured on paper allow us to question the role of the 'popolo' in this incident, since the diarist placed it at the crucial turning point of the Grimani *affair*.

Indeed, Sanudo noted that 'Sier Antonio Grimani's rule of the fleet raised great discontent in the city. The fallen soldiers and sunken ships at Lepanto: not for many years had news reached Venice of a defeat on such a scale'. External to institutional judicial procedure but equally significant in ritualistic meanings, the rising of this rumours was the most striking manifestation of the gap that was emerging between the 'Terra' and those who had been elected to represent it in the Mediterranean war. As Sanudo recalled, in the days preceding the debate on Grimani's trial, groups of 'puti' (young boys) roamed Venetian streets and squares (the 'Terra') singing a mocking refrain: 'Antonio Grimani, ruin of the Christians, rebel against the Venetians, may you and your children be eaten by dogs and puppies'.[44]

Sources of this kind can certainly prompt questions. Might it be possible to relate these defamations to the spread of patriotic feelings amongst undefined sectors of Venetian urban society? In this case, the community's disapproval of the commander, turning him into a scapegoat, could be read as a response to feelings of fear and shame which were unsettling the city. It is equally valid to wonder if such derisive acts and words could be attributed to members of a patrician faction that may have wanted to seize the opportunity presented by the political and military crisis to strengthen its identity in the republican arena. In this case, the origin of the 'popular' protest against the commander would be found in the sphere of the Venetian patriciate composed of individuals and families with limited economic and political wealth, who opposed powerful plutocratic clans like the Grimanis. As chroniclers such as Sanudo and Priuli described, a plethora of micro-conflicts — regarding elections to administrative posts and the allocation of ecclesiastical benefices, civic rituals, and testamentary lawsuits — revealed the multiple roots of this deep-seated resentment.[45] In this case, the trial of Antonio Grimani would need to be placed in the context of an intraclass conflict between privileged and marginalised patricians, or, according to the lemmas in use at the time, between 'grandi' and 'mezzani'.

As chroniclers and diarists reported, the ritual of humiliation performed by the people awaiting Grimani's arrival, which was initiated by the dissemination of defamatory pamphlets and the rhymes recited by 'infanti' (young boys), was characterised by immediacy and spontaneity. According to these sources, there is no evidence to suggest that the collective stigmatisation of the naval commander-in-chief came from outside the 'people'. However, it is possible to discern interesting relationships between the 'institutionalised' justice that took place within the courtroom through formalised judicial procedures and this primary justice carried out by the people demanding exemplary punishment as a form of compensation for the humiliation suffered by the Republic. The construction of the figure of the 'infante', as Ottavia Niccoli has productively explained, reflected a powerful ambiguity from the time of its origins in the late antique period. The duplicity of this figure was mirrored in the image of the 'popolo'. Reflecting an original innocence beyond good and evil, the 'infante' emerged as a 'disturbing' figure.[46] Without the right to hold public office — indeed, 'deprived of the ability to articulate speech', the etymology of 'infans' — individuals classified with this label were entrusted with the task of carrying out forms of primary justice we could define as 'zero-degree' justice. Through acts of ritualised violence, they rebuilt the shattered fabric of the community. The category of 'infante' often preceded that of the 'young' in the order of life stages. The transition between the two was not precisely outlined by the theologians, preachers, and jurists who engaged, for different reasons, with these concepts during the late medieval and early modern period. Nevertheless, we can still observe that this second transitional stage toward 'maturity' was situated, like the first, in a kind of boundary zone.

Those who inhabited the liminal space between the largely undefined area of personality development and the full acquisition of positive rights (such as, in our case, acquiring civilitas, citizenship, and the possibility of accessing political resources) were entrusted with the task of restoring the community order previously shattered by subversive elements. In other words, the state of emergency could only be mended by those who had preserved their otherness with respect to the established powers, and, consequently, their 'purity', as opposed to the 'contamination' suffered by the body politic. Sanudo's representation of the Grimani affair made use of the image of the 'people in action' in a manner akin to the biological and anthropological categories just discussed. His attention to the 'people' as the restorer of social and political order enables Sanudo to record some exceptional events shortly preceding the Zonchio defeat in which Grimani seems like a magnet for negative events: the crisis of the republican political and constitutional order was accompanied by disruptions in climatic, meteorological, and biological regularities. During December 1499, which 'felt like spring', Venice had been plagued by 'storms', 'fogs', 'thunders', and an unprecedented amount of 'snow'. The fact that Domenico Capello's wife gave birth 'not knowing she was pregnant, as there was no sign of her state' had caused great 'wonder'. Even the traditional norms that regulated the first cell of social harmony, the family, changed: children rebelled against their fathers, and there were countless 'fights between brothers'; the atavistic custom of feuds and vendettas spread in the city of peace[47]. Against the backdrop of this increasing anomie, the Grimani trial appeared as a ritual of atonement aimed at restoring order by turning back the hands of time, synchronising them with the mythical moment of origin.

The values of the republican constitution predated history as a succession of events: the 'myth of Venice' was a puzzle made up of many pieces that come apart just when we think we have found their order. Different narrative fragments overlap, and no hierarchy can be discerned among them. We can name, for example, the letter from Cassiodorus that sketched out the socio-cultural image of the ancestors of the Venetians, the inhabitants — or populi — of the marshes between Grado and Ravenna, who were extremely skilled at building and sailing ships; or the extraordinary feats of Buono di Malamocco and Rustico di Torcello, protagonists of the theft and transportation of the body of Mark the evangelist to Venice between 827 and 829; or the acclaim of the legendary Paulino Anafesto, named first doge by an early council and later by the tribunes; or still other crucial dates marked by military feats (the conquest of Constantinople in 1204) and miraculous events.[48] If we shift our attention from the account offered by medieval chronicles and 'public historiography' (i.e. the official repository of Venetian political and institutional memory)[49] to the cycles of paintings in the Ducal Palace, the list of extraordinary moments marking the history of the Republic could be extended. Rather than 'myth', we should refer to a 'mythological machine' or patchwork woven from many images and discourses. The 'myth of Venice' was a language of stories and legends in which social actors (men of government, merchants, judges, members of guild associations, etc.) could intervene, adapting it to their interests or ideas of justice.[50] The role of the people must for this reason always be historically situated, if we are to understand the specific network of relationships in which it was actually enwrapped.

The Grimani affair highlights an interesting mode of ritual and rhetorical building of politics. The 'piazza', as we have observed, turned into a theatre and tribunal: the 'popolo' played a double role, as both actor and judge. The collective and unanimous condemnation of Antonio Grimani linked the action of the people to the reaction of the virtuous part of the Venetian patriciate. Drawing from Hasso Hoffman's pivotal analysis of the polysemic notion of representation — a fundamental lemma in the European political lexicon — we can say that the modes of representation as Stellvertretung (i.e. the mobilisation of power relations by various actors) reflected the idea of representation as repraesentatio identitatis (the formalisation of an order of reality expressed in theological and political terms).[51] There was a natural coherence between acts that impact reality and metaphors that placed them within an ordered system. The vernacular songs sung by the 'people' to stigmatise the betrayal of the naval commander-in-chief, and the indignant voices that stirred the city, were intended to overcome and publicly denounce the Grimani clan's attempt to suppress the news of Antonio's arrival in Venice. Yet these chants and voices were also exploited by the magistrature in charge of the prosecution — the avogadori di Comun — which struggled to bring the defendant before the Great Council. This plan was countered by an influential part of the patriciate itself and by the wishes of the Grimani lineage, which insisted on bringing the trial to the Council of Ten. Even the presidents of this tribunal claimed the superiority of their jurisdiction in this case. The tensions undermining the republican constitution in the years between the fifteenth and the sixteenth centuries thus became evident. The Avogaria and the Council of Ten represented two opposed conceptions of power: the former identified it with law, the latter with authority.[52]

The avogadori di Comun held different political and judicial prerogatives. All political treatises about the Venetian magistratures written between the fourteenth and sixteenth centuries summarised them with one incisive definition: they were the 'observadori de la leze' (observers or guardians of the law). This concise gloss conceals an array of jurisdictions. As was the case in Antonio Grimani's trial, they acted as public prosecutors in the criminal trials taking place in Venice — this is why they received the naval commander at his arrival. The avogadori also judged on appeal the criminal sentences issued by the magistrates of both the Dominante and its subject provinces; it was within their power to invalidate the decisions taken by the sovereign councils — except those of the Council of Ten — which contradicted Venetian statutes or disregarded the principle of equity (*equitas*), the most important virtue of the Venetian political system.[53] The *avogador* operated on juridical and political levels that seemed to contradict each other. As recipients of appeals from the dominions, they were obliged to safeguard local privileges granted by the *pacta deditionis*,[54] but as guardians of the republican spirit and holders of discretionary powers, they had a power of interference incomparable to that granted to any other magistrature. Both as public prosecutors and as promoters of appeals, the *avogador* could represent themselves, at their discretion, to the magistrature (Senate and Great Council, Serenissima Signoria, or *Quarantine*) that seemed most suitable to resolving their specific case.

The jurisdiction appointed to the *avogadori* was thus ambivalent: they could appear as uncompromising guardians of a higher order, but in other circumstances as meticulous examiners of matters of minimal relevance. The *avogador* were in this sense the 'chameleons' of the Venetian constitution. They were often called upon to mediate between local legal systems and Venetian law or to negotiate between the use of informal customary procedures and the literal application of written norms, as well as to reconcile the resilience of archaic conventions with the need for flexible adaptation to current events, or to oscillate between the moods and political emotions of the '*piazza*' and those of the many magistratures hosted in the '*palazzo*'. The uniqueness of their position in the interplay of the Republic's institutions was both their strength and their weakness: the fragmentation of their responsibilities risked blurring the institutional profile of the magistrature and advancing the protagonistic desires of the nobles elected to the Avogaria.

The indefiniteness of the Avogaria's profile seems to explain the attempt to legitimise its position undertaken, between the mid-fifteenth and mid-sixteenth centuries, by numerous Venetian and non-Venetian political writers, including an anonymous French author from the late fifteenth century and the Florentine Donato Giannotti, who was exiled after the restoration of Alessandro de Medici in 1530.[55] These authors attempted to draw comparisons between the plebeian tribunes in Republican Rome and the Venetian Avogaria.[56] The moderate and limited view of the popular tribunate that took shape in Venice was far from Machiavelli's radical reading of Tito Livio's pages. In comparison with the *tribune plebis*, the task of protecting the polity in charge of the Avogaria was restrained by the application of the law. However, the analogies between the two magistratures, which deserve more thorough analysis, come to an end when faced a decisive difference: the Roman tribune possessed the authority to propose laws responding only to the 'concilium plebis', the representative institution of the plebeian council; the *avogador* acknowledged the existence of a legal system in which they could not interfere except through their capacity to interpret the law. The veil of aristocratic privilege thus enveloped and limited the *avogador*'s sphere of action: the equality they had to uphold was that of the aristocratic class before the laws of the Great Council.

During the investigation of Grimani, the rhetoric of severity and mediation, *raison d'état* and paternalism, publicity and secrecy manifest decisively. While we will not delve into these details here, as it is not within the scope of this article to trace the existential, familial, and political events shaping the fate of Grimani, who was condemned by the Great Council to the island of Cherso (Cres). The need for a public execution, expressed from the outset of the affair, had thus been satisfied. However, the verdict allowed for both material and metaphorical escape routes. The network of relationships of the Grimani clan extended well beyond the borders of the Republic. In the late fifteenth century, the clan distinguished itself for its ability to acquire substantial ecclesiastical benefices. Grimani's exile would make the interactions between his relatives and the Roman curia even more frequent.[57] This indeed played a role in Grimani's reintegration into the Venetian political system, to the point of allowing his election, in 1521, to the *dogado*, the highest magistracy of the republic.

Conclusions

The semantics of the '*popolo*' and its long-term transformation from the Middle Ages to the contemporary age are now at the centre of many research projects.[58] It seems that a rupture between the 'before' and the 'after' in the meaning of this term occurred in the period between the second half of the eighteenth century and the first half of the nineteenth: the period that Reinhard Koselleck called 'Sattelzeit' ('saddle' or transitional period).[59]

Between the Seven Years' War and the Revolutions of 1848, new forms of political action were defined, and new legal and constitutional perspectives were articulated. Literature, philosophy, and visual arts increasingly invoked public opinion. According to Koselleck, this transitional age was characterised by complex forms of coexistence and conflict between ancient and novel structures. Within this transformation of society's underlying structures, narratives concerning the 'people' too underwent a radical rewriting. A similar unstable coexistence existed between the fifteenth and sixteenth centuries, an era in which the meanings in force during the Middle Ages coexisted with other meanings that became increasingly prominent during the sixteenth and seventeenth centuries.[60]

The ensemble of discourses that sprang up during the Grimani affair highlight the overlapping of several discursive and rhetorical levels. For a long period, the *'populus'* occupied a position of prominence in medieval theological thought and canon law. The term *'popolo'* denoted all those belonging to the basic church constituency: the parish. This administrative identity, centred around the care of souls, was presented as the basic element of a sacralising conception of the people, understood as an expression of the universal church (*ecclesia*).

Between the thirteenth and fifteenth centuries, representations of the *'popolo'* also multiplied in the fields of political and legal thought. Here the vitality of a reinterpreted tradition that went back to Aristotle's and Cicero's thought is evident. In his work *De re publica*, Cicero stated that 'not every agglomeration of men assembled in any way is a people, but rather a gathering of associated people whose foundation is the observance of justice and the commonality of interests' (De re publica, I, 25). This idea can be found in a multitude of texts criticising the political role of city factions and asserting the civic values of peace and harmony: from Brunetto Latini to the Sienese frescoes of *Buongoverno*, from Dante's *De Monarchia* to Petrarca's humanistic rhetoric, from Marsilio da Padova's political theology to Bartolo da Sassoferrato's legal foundation for opposition to tyranny.[61]

In the fourteenth century, the multifaceted silhouette of the *'popolo'* offered by Roman-imperial law proposed two opposing paradigms that were both bound to be revisited and modified during the modern era. As highlighted by Walter Ullmann, the *'popolo'* acted as a point of orientation in the processes of legitimising civil authority. The theory of 'ascending of power' positions the 'people' as the subject holding inalienable rights and main contracting party in the constitutive pact the *'popolo'* itself makes with the sovereign/emperor in acknowledging their authority. This representation is opposed to the theory of 'descending power'.[62] In this case, the sovereign is placed at the top of the social and political hierarchy, as the point from which all other political, institutional, and representative authorities derive their power. Throughout the early modern era, fragments of these two paradigms were, on the one hand, integrated into the genesis of absolutist theories of power, and, on the other hand, provided the basis for the concept of 'ius resistendi' — the right to resist a tyrannical sovereign.

A new model emerged out of the complex stratification of these theories, where legal and theological theories intermingled with common idioms and political claims of legitimacy. This model accompanied the processes of aristocratization that spread throughout Italian and European society from the beginning of the sixteenth century. Consequently, the ambiguity inherent in the concept of *popolo* became greatly simplified. The most significant interpreter of this critical moment is Francesco Guicciardini; from his *Ricordi*, so rich in references to the period of Florentine history between Savonarola and the Medici restoration, it is worth quoting some rather illustrative passages:

> 140. He who said a people truly said a mad animal, full of a thousand errors, of a thousand confusions, without taste, without delight, without stability.
> 141. Often between the palace and the square is so thick a fog, or so thick a wall, that the eye of men cannot penetrate into it, so much knows the people of what those who govern do, or of the reason why they do it, as of the things they do in India; and therefore the world is easily filled with erroneous and vain opinions.[63]

1. Scattola, 'Storia dei concetti e storia delle discipline politiche'; Richter, 'Lessico dei concetti politici e giuridici europei', pp. 16–24.
2. Brunner, Conze, and Koselleck, *Geschichtliche Grundbegriffe*, Bd. 1–8,2; Schiera, 'Considerazioni sulla Begriffsgeschichte'. Dipper, 'I Geschichtliche Grundbegriffe'.
3. See Schiera, 'Considerazioni sulla Begriffsgeschichte'; Scattola, 'Storia dei concetti e storia delle discipline politiche'; Scattola, *Dalla virtù alla scienza*.
4. Consolati, *Dominare tempi inquieti*.
5. See Koselleck, Gschnitzer, Werner, and Schönemann, 'Volk, Nation, Nationalismus, Masse'.
6. See Ginzburg, 'L'alto e il basso', pp. 107–32.
7. Skinner, *Visions of Politics*, I; Skinner, *Liberty Before Liberalism* and Skinner, *Reason and Rhetoric in the Philosophy of Hobbes*; Pocock, *The Machiavellian Moment*.
8. See Brett and Tully, eds, *Rethinking the Foundations of Modern Political Thought*; Anderson and Burgess, eds, *The Political Imagination in History*; Palonen, *Quentin Skinner*.
9. See Foucault, 'Sui modi di scrivere la storia'; also see Levi, 'I tempi della storia', in which the author underlines the shift in the study of 'classical' thinkers – such as Marx, Weber, Durkheim, Bourdieu, Braudel, Lefebvre – to study of the works of figures such as Freud, Benjamin, Warburg, Foucault.
10. Armitage, Battini, and Ruhel, 'Una discussione intorno alla "Modern Intellectual History"'.
11. LaCapra, *Rethinking Intellectual History*.
12. See Darnton, 'Intellectual and Cultural History', p. 337: Darnton thought considered intellectual history to include the history of ideas (he referred mostly to 'the study of informal thought, climates of opinion and literary movements'), the social history of ideas, and cultural history.
13. Arcangeli, *Cultural History*.
14. Folin, 'Introduzione'.
15. See Torre, *Luoghi*. This interpretation avoids falling into the naivete found in much contemporary English-language historiography. From a microhistorical perspective, it identifies the authors and networks of authorship of documents (judicial, cartographic, normative, etc.), and therefore grasps actual power dynamics and forms of legitimation in their concreteness. The idea that historical testimonies, even when produced by holders of power, would express the genuine needs of a metaphysical 'society' – somehow independent and autonomous from power – corresponds to an understanding of historiography that has predominantly focused on the study of governing institutions.
16. Muir, *Civic Ritual in Renaissance Venice*; Muir, *Ritual in Early Modern Europe*; Casini, *I gesti del Principe*; Metlica, *Lessico della propaganda barocca*.
17. De Vivo, *Patrizi informatori barbieri*; Judde de Larivière, *The Revolt of Snowballs*; Rospocher and Salzberg, *Il mercato dell'informazione*; Van Gelder and Judde de Larivière, eds, *Popular Politics in an Aristocratic Republic*.
18. On the relationship between revindication of rights and creation of spaces of legitimation, see Torre, *Luoghi*.
19. Two different analytical perspectives are Berengo, *L'Europa della città*, and Prak, *Citizens without Nations*.
20. The history of emotions can be subdivided according to different perspectives. For a critical analysis, see Ferente, 'Storici ed emozioni'; Rosenwein, 'Worrying about Emotions in History'.
21. Judde de Larivière and Salzberg, 'The People Are the City'.
22. Salzberg, *Ephemeral City*.
23. Nussdorfer, 'The Political Space in Early Modern Rome', p. 162.
24. A fundamental synthesis of these themes is offered by Mineo, 'La repubblica come categoria storica', pp. 126–7 and Mineo, *Popolo e bene comune*.
25. Bruni, *La città divisa*.
26. De Benedictis, *Neither disobedients nor rebels*.
27. See, Todeschini, *Visibilmente crudeli*.
28. Viggiano, *Governanti e governati*, pp. 145–46.
29. See Arcangeli, 'I rituali urbani fra storia e antropologia. Un bilancio'. Some interesting points are also made in Casini, 'Rituali del potere', Fenlon, *The Ceremonial City*; Fenlon, *Piazza San Marco*.
30. Arcangeli, 'Introduzione'.
31. Trexler, 'Ritual Behaviour in Renaissance Florence'.
32. See, Gaeta, 'Storiografia, coscienza nazionale e politica culturale'; Gaeta, 'Alcune considerazioni sul mito di Venezia'; Gilmore, 'Myth and Reality in Venetian Political Theory'; Finlay, 'The Immortal Republic'; Crouzet-Pavan, *Venezia trionfante*. See also Cozzi, *Ambiente veneziano, ambiente veneto* and Ventura, *Scritti di storia veneziana*.
33. For an overview on the sources, see Ortalli, *Venezia inventata*.
34. See, Wolters, *Il palazzo ducale di Venezia*, Tagliaferro, 'Martiri eroi, principi e beati'; Tagliaferro, 'Le forme della Vergine'.
35. Luhmann, *Stato di diritto e sistema sociale*, pp. 100–01.
36. See Cogo, 'La guerra di Venezia contro i Turchi', pp. 20–76; Zille, 'Il processo Grimani'; Viggiano, 'Il processo al Capitano generale da Mar Antonio Grimani'. From here, I take all citations referred to the case Grimani.
37. Maranini, *La Costituzione di Venezia*, pp. 44–45.
38. Melchiorre, 'Sanudo, Marin il Giovane'.
39. Zago, 'Grimani, Antonio'.
40. Cozzi, *Repubblica di Venezia e stati italiani*, pp. 152–60.
41. Lane, *Venice, a Maritime Republic*, pp. 177–79.
42. Gullino, 'Morosini, Francesco'. Also see chapter 1 by Florio and Metlica.
43. Schulz, 'Printed Plans and Panoramic Views of Venice', pp. 17–22; Schulz, 'Jacopo de' Barbari's View of Venice'.
44. 'Tanto è stà despiazevole a tutta la cità nostra el governo de sier Antonio Grimani, considerando la quantità de homeni peridi; el grandissimo numero di l'armada nostra, za molti e molti anni non audito sì grande e più mazor legni; e il perder di Lepanto, che i puti andavano criando per la terra: Antonio Grimani/Ruina de' cristiani/ rebello de' venetiani/ Puostu esser manzà da' canni/ da' canni e da cagnolli/ ti e to fiulli. E su molte botege, su muri, vidi jo scritto: Antonio Grimani / Rebello de' venetiani!'. Sanudo, *I diarii*, III, col. 5.

45 Finlay, Politics in Renaissance Venice.
46 Niccoli, Il seme della violenza.
47 'A di 20 dezembrio. In questo zorno fo cosse fuora di modo, zoè fo caligo, niolo, tempesta, neve, toni, ch'è cossa miranda da questi temi che pareva primavera [...]. Non voglio restar da scriver, come la moier di sier Domenego Capello, *quondam* sier Nicolò, fia di sier Francesco Bernardo, non si sapendo fusse graveda, né parendo alcun signal, in questi giorni parturì uno fiol, cossa fè a tuti gran maraveglia [...]. Molte lite tra fradelli sussitoe in questa terra'. Sanudo, I diarii, III, col. 71.
48 Ortalli, Venezia inventata.
49 Cozzi, 'Cultura politica e religione'.
50 In this regard, it could be useful to consult Jesi, Materiali mitologici and for a Jesian reading of the 'myth of Venice' Metlica, 'La macchina mitologica della venezianità'. The more or less official sources that contributed to build the 'myth of Venice' can be analysed starting from the questions formulated by Veyne, Les grecs ont-ils cru à leurs mythes?.
51 See Hoffmann, Rappresentanza-rappresentazione; Duso, La rappresentanza politica; Accarino, Rappresentanza.
52 Cozzi, 'The Authority and the Law'.
53 On the development of these duties in the fifteenth century, see Viggiano, Governanti e governati. Setti, 'L'Avogaria di Comun come magistratura media d'appello'.
54 Cozzi, Repubblica di Venezia e Stati italiani, pp. 118–42.
55 See Braunstein and Mueller, eds, Descripcion; Gilbert, 'The Venetian Constitution in Florentine Political Thought'.
56 On the genealogy and diffusion of this paradigm during the early modern period, see Galtarossa, L'idea del Tribunato nella storia della Repubblica di Venezia'. De Benedictis, 'Da Confalonieri del popolo a tribuni della plebe'; Savelli, 'Sul concetto di popolo'.
57 Paschini, Il cardinale Marino Grimani.
58 Although the turning point mentioned in the text is not in the following book, it is still of great interest: Ruocco and Scuccimarra, eds, Il governo del popolo.
59 Kosselleck, Future Past.
60 See Mineo, Popolo e Bene Comune, and Savelli, 'Sul concetto di popolo'.
61 Quaglioni, '"Quando supervenit iustus dominus"'.
62 See Ulmann, The Individual and Society in the Middle Ages.
63 '140. Chi disse uno popolo disse veramente uno animale pazzo, pieno di mille errori, di mille confusione, sanza gusto, sanza diletto, sanza stabilità. 141. Spesso tra el palazzo e la piazza è una nebbia sí folta, o uno muro sí grosso, che non vi penetrando l'occhio degli uomini, tanto sa el popolo di quello che fa chi governa, o della ragione perché lo fa, quanto delle cose che fanno in India; e però si empie facilmente el mondo di opinione erronee e vane'. Guicciardini, Ricordi.

Matteo Casini

VENICE BEYOND VENICE

The Foreign Approach to Venetian Rituals, 1400–1600s*

For a long time, foresti ('foreigners') used Venetian rites, images, and objects in public rituals inside the city and abroad. The foreign ceremonial gaze at Venice materialised in multiple and complex forms, depending on the individual's time of residence and involvement in the Venetian urban life or the knowledge or perception of Venice that people had in other places such as Lyon, Florence, Parma, London and others. In this chapter I will consider two kinds of events that occurred largely between the early sixteenth and late seventeenth centuries: first, events organised by people living in Venice for long or short periods, such as resident foreign communities, foreign dignitaries, or other temporary visitors; second, festivals abroad that incorporated Venetian themes and objects, for which there are interesting — if sometimes scarce — bibliographical sources. Inquiring into how foreign rituals conceived Venice will help us first see how, and then how accurately, non-Venetians perceived Venice and her mythology. It also foregrounds how these myths and discourses impacted ceremonial play abroad, in particular in societies with non-republican political systems and audiences possessing little or no knowledge of Venetian history and propaganda.

We can start with the foresti who lived permanently in Venice and were promoters of initiatives sometime in concert and at other times in conflict with the Venetian government. The Florentines, for instance, had a long history of celebrations in Venice, at least since 1441, when they attended the huge wedding of Jacopo Foscari. Moreover, during the carnival of 1498 the community organised a sort of theatre-joust that moved from the Ducal Palace to the rest of the city. The area of San Polo was a favourite location: here the election of the Medici pope Leo X was celebrated in March 1513; then, in October 1532 Lorenzo Strozzi held a great patrician banquet at the nearby ca' Bernardo, on the Grand Canal, with 'beautiful women and dancers'. The Florentines also attended the San Polo baptisms of Jews performed by Venetian religious authorities.[1]

The German community is interesting as well. They started participating in Venetian festivals during the Middle Ages when, in 1285, the officials of the Fondaco dei Todeschi (the German market) were asked to participate in the 'solemn feasts of the Major Council'.[2] Later, in the early 1500s, the Fondaco organised popular spectacles and games modelled on Venetian customs, such as mock-jousts, bull and bear hunts, mummies, triumphal chariots, balls, masks, and other activities. Famous local characters were engaged, such as the 'buffon' Zuan Polo.[3] Later in the century, in May 1597, the German pistori ('bakers') held a lavish 'military' cortege at the Ducal Palace to feast the wife of the doge, Morosina Morosini Grimani. They carried many silver objects 'as [was] their custom' and celebrated Ceres, the Roman goddess of agriculture and grain, symbol of abundance.[4] Moreover, from the first half of the 1600s on, the Germans of the Fondaco were involved in the ceremonial introductions of newly elected procurators of St Mark. In that period the starting point of the cortege accompanying the procurators moved from San Moisè to San Salvador, not far from the Fondaco.[5] Finally, the Germans were also active participants in the huge celebrations for the end of Vienna's siege in September 1683, which included 'solemn feasts, burning statues and distributing bread, wine and money'.[6]

The Dutch and Greek communities were involved in Venetian celebrations as well, and here we can consider a couple of examples. The Dutch were involved in the aforementioned celebrations for Morosina Morosini Grimani in May 1597, organizing a sort of water joust in front of St Mark's Basilica (familiar thanks to a famous print by Giacomo Franco: fig. 11.2). The game resurrected the tradition of Venetian naumachie — the

11.1
Valois tapestry, Water Festival at Bayonne. Detail of 11.6.

most famous example of this entertainment taking place in October 1530 to welcome Francesco Sforza — while the doge Marino Grimani collaborated with the Dutch by offering white and red liveries to the players.[7] On 24 June 1649 the Greek community arranged and were notably present in the day's huge celebrations of the Venetian victory at Foça in the War of Candia. A great Greek procession left their church of San Giorgio for St Mark's Basilica with 'chariots', 'pyramids of silver', banners, and musical instruments. At the Basilica they prayed before images of the Virgin Mary and relics of saints.[8]

As these examples suggest, further research in this area is needed. As a general point, however, it seems clear (and natural) that foreign communities designed their festivities to conform to Venetian ones. One motivation for *foresti* was the desire to emulate Venetian customs and integrate into Venetian society. Through such festivities, foreigners residing in the city sought social recognition and engagement, aiming to become an honourable and respected part of the society.

Apart from this communal participation, individual foreigners also engaged in Venetian ritual life. These figures included resident ambassadors or preeminent visitors such as dignitaries, princes, captains, or aristocratic families. Interestingly, they usually came from monarchies or princely states, and thus from polities very different from the Venetian aristocratic republic.

Though little evidence of individually initiated festivities is available for the 1500s, Sanudo's chronicles recount a few episodes, mostly regarding ambassadors' private parties. For instance, the Count of Chariati, a Spanish envoy, hosted a solemn dinner in June 1512, with important foreign and local guests. The ambassador of Mantua tried to hold a feast with twenty-five women in January 1523, together with the ambassadors of Rome and England; but the sumptuary exemptions requested of the government were not approved. More successful was the papal Legate who, in June 1526, sponsored a feast and banquet at the house of the Marquis of Este, in front of the Grand Canal, to honour the League of Cognac. Trumpets, flutes, and buffoons were invited while great luminaries enlightened the palace, and many ships filled the Canal in front of it. The representatives of France, England, and Milan also hosted luminaries at similar celebrations.[9]

A different scenario arose in the 1600s, when the birth of the opera and addition of the theatrical season attracted greater international interest in and attendance at carnival.[10]

11.2
Giacomo Franco, *The dogaressa gets on the Bucintoro*. Engraving from Id., *Habiti d'huomeni et donne venetiane con la processione della Ser.ma Signoria ed altri particolari*, 1610. New York, Metropolitan Museum of Art. Photo: Public Domain.

New private parties were held by ambassadors, for instance, with growing involvement by the Venetian authorities and population. This was the true of gatherings hosted by French representatives, in particular the ambassador Claude Mallier du Houssay. In January 1633 he arranged a lavish baptism for his son at the church of San Geremia. The Venetian government was invited as godfather and sent in the *savio del consiglio* Angelo Contarini in their name. The mass was officiated by Patriarch Federico Corner, a protagonist of Venetian life in those years. At the end of the ceremony, the newborn was given the golden chain with St Mark, a sign of the knighthood of the Republic.[11]

Five years later the same ambassador Mallier decided to host notable festivals to celebrate the birth of the Dauphin. Religious accoutrements were set up on the island of San Giorgio and many other events took place in Eastern Cannaregio, near the French palace. Among them were lavish dinners at the palace, the offer of bread and wine to monasteries and the poor (a wine fountain was built on a canal, too), performances of a bull and bear hunt by members of the Venetian populace, the *Forze d'Ercole* (acrobatic games), and a dance of swords called *moresca*.[12] Then an ephemeral architectural structure called 'Theater of the World' comprising a square stage with four columns and a spherical roof was mounted on the canal in front of the palace. The square hosted a ball, fireworks, and a play involving fighters with large swords made of firecrackers who represented Hercules and the Hydra. The idea was to acknowledge Louis XIII as a Gallic Hercules, 'tamer of all monsters of rebellion and division of France'. Also, a *naumachia* portraying a castle assaulted by galleons and galleys was arranged to present Louis as a triumphant leader of the Mediterranean. During the last night of celebrations 'silver bowls full of Genoa pastries, candied fruits, marzipans, pistachios and other sorts of sweets were left to be ransacked by the people, following an international custom present in Venice since the 1470s.[13]

The events of 1638 demonstrate that the French ambassador made extensive use of Venetian and international festive modes — both theatrical and playful — in the rather marginal area of Eastern Cannaregio (which would remain a central site for future French celebrations, especially because of the nearby church of Madonna dell'Orto).[14] In this way, both the royal character of French power and the participation of the French embassy in Venetian local life were dignified. This highlights the potential of ritual as a mixture of different languages and as a tool to reach multiple audiences.

Similar themes emerge in the rich, festive life of two princely seventeenth-century non-republican families which interacted extensively with Venetian society. The first is the German family of the Dukes of Braunschweig-Lüneburg, which arrived in Venice during the mid-1500s[15], a period of growing German interest in Venetian amusements, particularly carnival, which princes of the German area had already replicated.[16] The Braunschweig-Lüneburg's participation in local Venetian festivals grew stronger in the following century, mainly from the 1660s on, when they supported the Republic in the dramatic conflicts of Candia and Morea (and thus received generous gifts in return for their loyalty).[17] The family's involvement in the local Baroque festive life started after the 1660s: a theatrical piece was dedicated to George William in 1662, while Johann Frederick paid for a 'most beautiful regatta' in September 1664.[18]

The real protagonist, though, was Duke Ernest Augustus, particularly in the 1680s. At carnival 1682, he held a ball and 'most superb' banquet for 80 dames and cavaliers, which included abundant wildfowl and sweets. In May 1685 he set up artificial 'bushes' at the Lido (a strategic area on the border with the sea) where rooms for guests were prepared and a military exhibition and a nocturnal grand ball were organised. In June, the Duke built a 'machine' in front of his palace where two comedies were presented; in August, he was the main guest at one of the most famous feasts held at the villa of procurator Marco Contarini in Piazzola sul Brenta[19]. Furthermore, on the 25 of June 1686, Ernest Augustus was the patron of the majestic regatta honouring the recent conquest of Navarino in the Peloponnesus and the Venetian holiday of the 'apparition of St Mark'. The boat parade featured bizarre and well-adorned *peote* ('ceremonial vessels') seating many nobles, including cavaliers, ambassadors, and other important foreign guests such as the prince of Parma, Alessandro Farnese, and Juan Tomás Enríquez de Cabrera, the count of Melgar and former governor of Milan. On the same occasion, an enormous ephemeral structure called a 'machine' was assembled in the figure of a whale carrying other sea creatures and ridden by the god Neptune (fig. 11.3). The structure celebrated the sea power of the Republic and her victories in the Levant (and the contributions of Duke's soldiers to that conflict); it was carried to the regatta's arrival at Ca' Foscari on the Grand Canal, where the prizes were distributed.[20]

Indeed, foreigners such as Duke Augustus loved the Venetian regatta, which combined the sophisticated arts of *peote* and

11.3

Alessandro Dalla Via, *'Machina' of Neptune on the Grand Canal*. Engraving from Giovanni Maria Alberti, *Giuochi festivi e militari, danze, serenate, macchine, boschereccia artificiosa, regata solenne et altri sontuosi apprestamenti di allegrezza*, Venezia, Poletti, 1686. Photo: Bibliotheca Hertziana. Reproduced with permission.

macchine with popular competition.[21] The high degree of Ernest Augustus's immersion in Venetian festive life is demonstrated also by his participation in some of its 'darker' aspects: in February 1685, just after his arrival, the Duke organised a private party with two hundred sex workers superbly dressed and gave out as refreshment the luxurious food he had just received as gift from the Republic.[22]

The second princely family of *foresti* under consideration is that of the Farnese of Parma who, according to my research, had a very interesting relationship with Venice in the 1680s. In December 1682 Alessandro Farnese, the brother of Duke Ranuccio II, was nominated General of the Venetian forces in the Levant; in the following years, Alessandro and his brother sojourned in the lagoon and participated in its local amusements. For instance, in March 1683 Alessandro was a protagonist in a local *cavallerizza* ('horse game') and staged a Florentine drama at his palace. In April and May, he was in Dolo, in the 'villeggiatura' ('vacation in a villa') on the river Brenta. In July he organised a 'most beautiful serenade on the Grand Canal' in front of his palace; and in September he contributed to the amusements planned for the end of the siege in Vienna, 'sparkling' his palace with gunshots and offering a ball[23]. Then, in February 1685, he attended the carnival, and in June 1686 the regatta sponsored by Ernest Augustus.[24] In October and November 1688, Alessandro's brother Ranuccio, the Duke of Parma, came to Venice and lodged in the French palace. He was notably generous, giving hundreds of coins called *scudi*, diamonds, silver, and other expensive things to various people and places in town. He also went to Padua to make a vow to St Anthony, leaving large gifts there as well.[25]

It seems that the Farnese family carried their knowledge of and fascination with Venetian culture and spectacle home. Consider what happened in Parma in spring 1690 during the spectacular nuptials between Ranuccio's son Odoardo and Dorothea Sophie von der Pfalz, the princess of Neuburg. The celebrations were announced by Venetian sources, which

11.4
Domenico and Gasparo Mauro, *Floating chariots of Neptune and Thetis*. Engraving from *La gloria d'amore spettacolo festivo fatto rappresentare dal serenissimo sig. Duca di Parma*, Parma, nella Stampa Ducale, 1690. Photo: Biblioteca Universitaria di Bologna, A.V.Tab.I.N.I.171/2, 10. With the permission from Alma Mater Studiorum Università di Bologna — Biblioteca Universitaria di Bologna.

wrote of 'feasts, jousts, and other amusements' to be held in Parma with more than 3000 people.[26] Venetian culture dominated these celebrations indeed. On the 24 of May, the fishpond of the Ducal Gardens hosted the spectacular theatrical piece 'Glory of Love', created by a number of Venetians: Aurelio Aureli, working at the Farnese court during the period, who wrote the text; Orazio Franchi, who made the costumes; the musician Bernardo Sabadini, at court as the Master of Chapel, who composed the music;[27] and the Venetian family of the Mauro, who were among the most important scenographers and architects of Baroque Europe and crafted huge ephemeral theatres and boats provoking general astonishment (fig. 11.4).[28] Moreover, the chronicler of the nuptials, Giuseppe Notari, noticed that the artificial bridges on the fishpond built for the spectacle were 'not really different [...] from the bigger ones to be seen on the canals of the famous Venice'.[29]

In addition, according to contemporaneous news previously unconsidered by historians, the Farnese wedding in Parma incorporated both the elites of Venice and its non-patrician population. Venetian sources report that in April, just before the wedding, a 'quantity of workers' moved from the lagoon to Parma, 'particularly an incredible number of *Nicoloti* and *Castelani*'. These were the two factions into which the lower classes of Venice were divided, who confronted each other in various sports. The workers' trip to Parma occurred because of the 'will [of] the Most Serene Duke [of Parma] to make a sumptuous war of *pugni* ('fists') in his garden'. We have confirmation of this fight by Emmanuele Cicogna who, according to a (now lost) pamphlet published in Venice in 1690 devoted to Parmesan festivals, affirmed that the 'war' actually took place during the aforementioned piece 'Glory of Love'.[30] Additional sources from Parma tell us that on the 22 of May the Nicolotti and Castellani performed another of their specialties: the acrobatic demonstration called *Forze d'Ercole* (also performed in the French festival in Venice). A special stage was set up in the central Piazza del Castello for 24 Venetians who, dressed in liveries, enacted 'marvellous forces'— or rather, gymnastic feats — to the great satisfaction of spectators. It is clear that in May 1690 the population of Parma had the extraordinary opportunity to witness authentic Venetian popular games.[31]

The Duke's export of Venetian games abroad was not unprecedented. The *pugni* had already performed in Bologna in 1670 in observance of the famous local feast of St Bartholomew. A fight had been organised between 'bandits' exiled from Venice belonging to the Nicolotti and Castellani — with even the involvement of local soldiers. Nevertheless, the performance in Parma in 1690 was unique because the *pugni* and the *forze* were played by members of the Venetian lower classes who had travelled abroad.[32]

In fact, the Farnese sponsorship of popular Venetian culture is unsurprising given that the *pugni* — and other games or

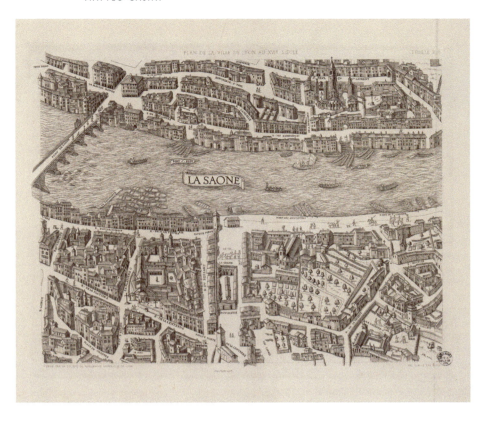

11.5a-b
Theatrical plan of the city of Lyon, 21 (detail), c. 1550. Ville de Lyon, Archives municipales, cote: 2SAT6. Photo: Public Domain.

sports, including regattas and bull and bear hunts — were notorious among visitors of Venice as symbols of the strength and courage of the Venetian lower classes; indeed, the government itself regularly organised these games for the most prestigious guests. News of them spread far abroad, as demonstrated by the fact that in September 1668 the Russian ambassador declared he had heard about the game. Moreover, the ambassadors of Malta and Spain had fighters among their servants, including the famously tough 'Black Moor' at the service of the Marquis of Fuentes. Apparently a real rivalry arose between Spain and France, as they supported different sporting factions.[33]

The Braunschweig-Lüneburg's and Farnese's feasts and games demonstrate that European princely families were particularly attracted by the capacity of Venetian spectacle to combine theatre and intricately well-crafted structures with the muscles and courage of the Venetian populace. This mix of cultural quality and common skills could be exported to non-'republican' environments, thereby bypassing the particular nature of the Venetian government and society, which were dominated by a fairly large aristocracy.

This fascination with Venetian boats and games among foreign princes encourages study of celebrations abroad that incorporated similar themes or protagonists. The most interesting traces are found in a non-republican context, sixteenth-century France, and particularly in the triumphal royal welcome stages in the city of Lyon. Lyon hosted three important visits of the king in 1548, 1564, and 1595.[34] In September 1548, for instance, when Henry II and Caterina de Medici entered Lyon they found, according to reports of the event, 'Gondolas expressly made for the service & commodity of the Majesty'. Another source, an Italian ambassador, mentions two 'Venetian style gondolas', one from Marseille and the other made by artisans from Lyon. Even Venetian light boats appeared, including a *peotina*, a *fisolera*, and even a *gran schelmo* (possibly the Venetian *paraschelmo*). According to a French source, some of these boats were sent directly from Venice. The official script of the event also discusses a 'barque longue' in which 14 *mattelotz* (mariners), dressed in white and green livery, rowed 'à la Venitiane'.[35] I wonder if Lyon had a rowing tradition similar to that of Venice, judging from a couple of interesting prints of the famous 'Plan scénographique' of the city (fig. 11.5).

On the same occasion, a huge French ship or '*bucentaure*' also appeared, designed by the cardinal Ippolito d'Este — the master of ceremonies and connoisseur of Venetian triumphal entries, which he had experienced in 1530, 1534, and 1541.[36] It was 'one of the grandest ships of the river' and was characterised by the Ferrarese ambassador as 'such a beauty, possibly more beautiful than the Venetian one'. Occupying the centre of the ship was a wide hall closed by two doors in the 'antique' fashion, surrounded by glass windows. Within the room a gallery extended along the water. Above the hall was 'a viewing

gallery with a balustrade around which guests could walk, while the king had a viewing platform of his own'.[37] A special mechanism was created to reveal a table with fine liqueurs and precious sweets for the king's pleasure, which impressed observers. The bucintoro was used multiple times to carry the king and his court and was accompanied by 'Brigantines, Fustes, & Gondolas & other vessels full of Princes, Dames & Seigneurs'. At a certain point, the boats were so numerous that the 'fishes were entirely covered'. A witness compared this cortege to Jason leaving to conquer the Golden Fleece with his ship Argo and fleet, and the sight might well have recalled the majestic Venetian parades surrounding the doge's Bucintoro in the St Mark basin or Grand Canal.[38]

The 1548 French bucintoro in Lyon set a precedent. In June 1564, for instance, two huge ships were crafted for the arrival of Charles IX and for Catherine of Medici, with balustrades in the form of galleries and a large hall.[39] In September 1574, the new king Henry III was met at his arrival on the river Saone by 'a bucintoro in [the] form of a Castle in [the] Venetian style'. The ship had a 'castle with four small towers on the four corners, & magnificent galleries around', and a beautiful and spacious hall with glass windows. Indeed, Catherine de Medici and the citizens of Lyon wanted to celebrate the new king most sumptuously after the great welcome Henry had received in Venice just two months before.[40]

Finally, in September 1595 another large boat was built in Lyon for Henry IV, 'a beautiful & rich structure, with twelve roars' and luxury textile adornments. The stern carried 'a lyon in golden bronze', the bow 'the coats of arms of France & Navarre'.[41] In fact, compared to the previous Lyon examples, the 1595 royal ship looked much more like the Venetian Bucintoro; for example, the golden lion positioned on the stern recalled the statue of Justice on the bow of the Venetian ducal vessel. The same might be said of the ceremonial boat built in Bayonne in June 1565. It is pictured on the famous Valois tapestry of the 'Whale' representing the water games arranged by Catherine de Medici for the christening of the son of her second daughter Claude and Duke Charles III of Lorraine (fig. 11.6). The boat, intended to carry important guests, appears to be a small bucintoro which seems almost Venetian. Frances Yates does not describe the boat but states that the artisans, Lucas de Heere and his friends, were 'careful to make the "Whale" tapestry correspond as closely as possible to what actually took place at Bayonne'.[42]

To conclude, it seems that most of the French bucintoros — particularly those of Lyon — were not so much ships in the Venetian style as they were water theatres or floating dining halls. In Italy these would have been called 'theatres of the world', and they were found in Renaissance Venice as well.[43] Furthermore, the term 'bucintoro' was already in use in fifteenth-century Italy to define the vessels used by Italian princes for river navigation.[44] Nevertheless, in sixteenth-century France the display

11.6
Valois tapestry, Water Festival at Bayonne.
Florence, Gallerie degli Uffizi, 1565.

II.7
Chariot of Neptune.
Engraving from Raffaello Gualterotti, *Feste nelle nozze del serenissimo don Francesco Medici gran duca di Toscana; et della sereniss. sua consorte la sig. Bianca Cappello*, Firenze, stamperia de' Giunti, 1579. Photo: Yale University Library.

of ephemeral water architectures called 'bucentaure', as well as the use of Venetian-style ships and the Venetian rowing style, could be considered a way of celebrating both the monarchy and the city of Lyon as a sort of 'other Venice'.

Not all ceremonial mentions of Venice were positive in sixteenth-century France. We cannot forget the famous *Description de la superbe et imaginaire entree faicte à la Royne Gijllette passant à Venise* (1582), which belongs to the literature defaming Henry III and his court. The *Description* is a chaotic narrative involving a long series of stereotypes about Venice, and one of its targets is to make a mockery of the famous triumphal entry of Henry into Venice in 1574.[45] Here Venice appears full of amazing things and events, including huge bucintoros in the shape of great monsters, 'gondoliers from Rialto' offering gifts in glass, extravagant and wealthy Venetian noblewomen giving lace to the Queen, a banquet sea monsters and animals crafted in sugar, a sort of St Mark's tower also made of sugar, and big exotic fights in the main square. Finally, a water battle between Venetian 'crabs' and Protestant 'casserons' (small squids) that recalled the siege of La Rochelle in spring 1573.[46]

The *Description* should be studied not just as a literary attack on Henry III but also in relation to the long history of the French 'anti-myth' of Venice, which lasted from the Wars of Italy in the early 1500s to Amelot de la Houssaie in the late 1600s.[47] In any case, the use of Venetian-oriented objects in French festivals continued under Henry IV, as we have seen.

Recalling the city of Venice in monarchic France was integral to memorialisation of the triumph on water of the king and the city, and in this process Venetian forms were adapted to new designs and symbols more fitting to local taste and festive culture.

Beyond France, additional research is necessary to determine whether Venetian culture infused festival ritual in other European nations. For instance, in 1662–1663 the first member of the Mauro family, Francesco, created a decorated bucintoro with Francesco Zanti (another Venetian) on Starnberg Lake in Bavaria[48]. In early 1600s Piedmont, the Savoys had various gala boats based on Venetian examples. Among them, bucintoros for navigating the Po River were 'fabricated in [the] shape of palaces with most beautiful ornaments in and out' (so they possibly looked similar to the French royal examples).[49] In Florence, Venice was obviously a protagonist in the wedding of Francis I Medici and his Venetian bride Bianca Cappello in October 1579. The most famous spectacle during the nuptials was a 'Sbarra' displaying various chariots — the first with a dolphin representing the sea of Venice, the Adriatic, which, for love of Bianca, 'contracted perpetual friendship and kinship' with the Tyrrhenian sea of Tuscany.[50] A second chariot carried Venus and two knights from Venice she had chosen to participate in the 'Sbarra' (the figure of Venus-Venice would reappear later in Parma, as a central character in the aquatic cortege of the 1690 'Glory of Love')[51]. A third chariot was led by

Neptune (fig. 11.7), a popular protagonist in Venetian-oriented events (already seen in Venice and Parma). This chariot celebrated the Christian triumph of Lepanto with the 'Venetian cavalier' Count Germanico Savorgnan in charge of defending the beauty of Venetian women.[52]

Looking more broadly around Europe, we know that regattas were held in water festivals at the Buen Retiro in Madrid in the first half of the 1600s (though we do not know whether they were in the Venetian form).[53] Moreover, the notable aquatic pageantry on the Thames in London in honour of the new Lord Mayor evoked Venice. In 1610, for instance, the prince of Anhalt Christianus said of London that 'none state or city in the world accompanies the election of its magistrates with such splendour, apart [from] the city of Venice, to which the city of London is almost equal'.[54] Fifteen years later the dramatist John Webster mentioned Venice while discussing the celebrations on the Thames in his *Monuments of London*. Describing an imaginary apparition of the god Thetis, Webster wrote that the god would call London a 'bride' and liken her to Venice, as on St Mark's Day 'the Duke and Senats their course hold / To wed our Empire with a Ring of Gold' — a reference to the Venetian ritual of the 'Wedding of the Sea'. Webster also drafted an imaginary account of a Thames ceremony for the new mayor in which Venice was personified, sitting together with other mythical cities.[55]

The writer Thomas Dekker also mentioned the famous 'Wedding of the Sea' — but considered it 'a poore Lantscip' in comparison to the 'full Bravereis of Thamesis'. Sometimes patriotism assumed a religious flavour, as when the playwright and author Thomas Heywood invoked the conflict between Puritans and Catholics in comparing a 'strong' Protestant barge with the 'wanton' gondola.[56] Still, the government of Venice understood the importance of the London water festivals and sent two gondolas to the King in 1661: the following year they were used to welcome Catherine of Braganza, the spouse of King Charles II.[57]

Though we could continue with further examples of the appropriation of Venetian festival rituals by other European courts, for instance international performances of the *commedia dell'arte* (a famous case being the performance at the wedding of Wilhelm of Bavaria in Munich in 1568), it is time for a conclusion.[58] What we can say for now is that study of the comments and events promoted by foreigners, both in Venice and abroad, help clarify how the celebratory system built by the politics and culture of Venice was received, absorbed, and re-purposed by actors partly or entirely familiar with its politics and culture. As we have seen, at any given time the 'foreign' utilisation of Venetians themes, rites, and games reproduced their original aspects or refashioned them emphasising their transgressive features. In general, the 'ritual Venice' displayed by foreigners was inspired by a mixture of various elements: the necessity of integrating into the larger Venetian community and its everyday life and politics through the wise use of city spaces; emotional reconstruction of ephemeral water theatres, boats, and water corteges according to the simple and impressionistic idea of the city as 'queen of the sea'; admiration for Venetian popular games and their ability to display prowess and loyalty.

In foreign ceremonies Venice became a *civitas* of water, craft, and muscles — a peculiar blending of elite and popular culture that could be exported and appreciated by diverse, even non-'republican' audiences. In this representation, however, the main absents were the Venetian ruling class and the aristocratic civic pride it most loved, as the ritual vision of *foresti* did not grant much attention to the incessant codification of myths and obsessive legislative action by Venetian intellectuals and authorities. More than glorifying the immortal 'republicanism' of Venice, what mattered instead was her unique society: the princely allure of the doge — manifest in the Bucintoro — or the magnificence and strength obtained through water and popular play. Beyond Venice, in local but especially foreign contexts, the city's 'myth' had to be ritually adapted and transformed in new and alternative ways to be digested and constantly reproduced according to local tastes and wills. In this way the 'Republic' of Venice could finally mutate into a 'monarchy'.

* I am deeply thankful to Pat Reeve for his revision and comments. All translations are my own.

1. Casini, 'Feste a San Polo nel lungo Rinascimento', p. 148.
2. Thomas, ed., *Capitolare dei Visdomini del Fontico dei Tedeschi*, p. 22.
3. Sanudo, *I diarii*, VII, col. 756, 18 February 1509; XXIII, col. 583, 12 February 1517; col. 604, 25 February 1517; XXVIII, col. 270, 20 February 1520. See also Braunstein, *Les Allemands à Venise*, pp. 178–79.
4. Tutio, *Ordine et modo tenuto nell'incoronatione*.
5. Sansovino, *Venetia città nobilissima et singolare* (1663), p. 306. Examples of the German celebrations for the procurators of St Mark are in Vincenti, *Gli apparati veneti*, pp. 39–41; Mariani, *L'ingresso trionfale*, pp. 2–3; Ivanovich, *Minerva al tavolino*, p. 123.
6. BMV, Ms. IT, VI, 460 (12104), fol. 210r.
7. Rota, *Lettera*, Hv-H2v; Van Gelder, *Trading Places*, pp. 63–66, and Casini, *I gesti del principe*, p. 305.
8. Dalla Spada, *Giubili e acclamationi*.
9. Sanudo, *I diarii*, IV, p. 323, 13 June 1512; XXXIII, p. 599, 31 January 1523; XLII, pp. 79–80, 8 June 1526.
10. Johnson, *Venice Incognito*; Bertrand, *Histoire du carnaval de Venise*.
11. ASVE, COL, Cer., Reg., reg. III, fol. 100r-v. On Corner, see Barcham, *Grand in design*.
12. On the *moresca* and acrobatic games in sixteenth century Italy, see Katritzky, 'A Court Festival set in the Garden of an Italian Villa'. On the Venetian *Forze d'Ercole*, see Zanotto, 'Le Forze d'Ercole dei veneziani'; Urban, *Le Forze d'Ercole*.
13. Fausto, *Venetia festiva*. On the Venetian 'theaters of the world', see Urban, 'Teatri e 'Teatri del Mondo''. On Venetian sugar sculptures in the Renaissance, see Casini, 'Gifts of Sugar and Aristocratic Magnanimity'.
14. Selfridge-Field, *Pallade veneta*, pp. 152–3.
15. See, for instance, ASVE, CD, Del., Comuni, Reg., reg. 21, fol. 145r, dated 1.12.1554; SEN., Del., Terra, Reg. reg. 53, 88r, 27 September 1580.
16. Katritzky, 'German Patrons of Venetian Carnival Art'.
17. For what follows, see Luckhardt, *Malerei und Divertissement*; Lanza, 'Karneval und kulturelle Vernetzung'; Lanza, ''I principi di Brunsvich capitarono qui…''; Watanabe-O'Kelly, 'Sailing towards a Kingdom'. For an example of a member of the family, Maximilian Wilhelm, serving the Republic in the Levant, see ASVE, COL, Cer., Reg., reg. III, 201v-202r, 28 April 1685; fols. 202r-v, 2 April 1686.
18. Aureli, *Le fatiche d'Ercole per Deianira*; MCV, Ms. *Codice Cicogna* 2597, Fasc. 241, 14 September 1664.
19. On the feasts in Piazzola, see Visentini, 'Feste, musica e spettacoli'.
20. *La sontuosa regatta grande*, pp. 6–7; Casini, 'Cerimoniali', pp. 140–41. Also see Garbero Zorzi, '"Giostre di legni in mare"'.
21. Casini, 'Cerimoniali', pp. 138–41; Perocco, 'Introduzione'.
22. ASVE, IS, b. 663, 14 February 1685.
23. BMV, Cod. IT, VI, 460 (12104), 22r, fols. 148r-v, 186v, 210v.
24. BMV, Cod. IT, VI, 462 (12106), 125v; Mariani, *Il trionfo di Nettuno*, pp. 49–50.
25. BMV, Cod. IT, 465 (12109), fols. 191v-192r, 194r.
26. BMV, Cod. IT, 467 (12111), 15 November 1690.
27. Mutini, 'Aureli, Aurelio'; Bianconi and Brown, 'Bernardo Sabadini'. The spectacle's costumist, Orazio Franchi, had also worked in Venetian theatres, while Venetian painter Sebastiano Ricci was employed later during the nuptials (Bracca, *L'occhio e L'orecchio*, pp. 211, 213).
28. Mamczarz, '"La gloria d'amore"'; Cirillo and Godi, *Il trionfo del barocco a Parma*. On the Mauros see Povoledo, *Mauro*, pp. 310–11, and Bracca, *L'occhio e L'orecchio*, 202, who considers the Mauros the leaders in spreading Venetian 'orchestration of nautical spectacles'.
29. Notari, *Descrittione delle feste*, p. 46.
30. BMV, Cod. IT, 467 (12111), 15 November 1690; MCV, Cod. Cicogna 3276, fasc. 13, 'Pugni', 5.
31. Notari, *Descrittione delle feste*, p. 44. On the 1690 wedding in Parma see now Casini, *Gloria d'Amore 1690-2021*.
32. MCV, Cod. Cicogna 3161, fasc. 22, fols. 27–9. Apparently, the 'Forze' took place in Bologna again in 1759 and 1765 (Urban, *Le Forze d'Ercole*, p. 18). One example of human pyramids in sixteenth Rome is described in Katritzky, 'A Court Festival set in the Garden of an Italian Villa'.
33. MCV, Cod. Cicogna 3161, fasc. 19, fol. 5; fasc. 15, fol. 2; Davis, *The War of the Fists*, pp. 135, 139–40.
34. A general presentation of the events can be found in Diefendorf, 'Lyon se présente à son roi'.
35. Scève, *The entry of Henri II*, pp. 22–4, IV-I2v.
36. Pacifici, *Ippolito II d'Este*, pp. 12, 20, 77–78.
37. McGowan, 'Lyon', pp. 39, 41–42
38. Scève, *The entry of Henri II into Lyon*, pp. 23–4, 122, 124, IV-I2v, K2r-v, K4v, L3, p. 323. On later (1574) French perceptions of Venetian water parades, see Poirier, 'Le retour de Pologne d'Henri III', pp. 45–46.
39. *Discours de l'entrée de tresillustre*, pp. 43–44.
40. *Les feux de joye*, p. 24; *L'ordre tenu à l'arrivée du treschrestien Roy de France*, pp. 5, 9–10. On the knowledge in France of Henry's entry in Venice, see Poirier, 'Le retour de Pologne d'Henri III', pp. 45–46.
41. Matthieu, *L'entrée de tresgrand, tres-chrestien, tres-magnanime, et victorieux prince*, p. 6; Godefroy, *Le Cérémonial françois*, I, p. 933.
42. Yates, *The Valois Tapestries*, pp. 57–8; Francastel, 'Figuration et spectacle'.
43. On Venetian 'theatres of the world', see note 13.
44. Luzio and Renier, *Delle relazioni di Isabella d'Este*, p. 15; Cappelli, 'Guiniforte Barzizza, maestro di Galeazzo Sforza', p. 407; Gallo, 'L'autobiografia artistica di Giovanni Ambrosio', pp. 198–99.
45. Poirier, 'La description de la superbe'; Poirier, *Henri III de France en mascarades imaginaires*, pp. 111–13.
46. *La description de la superbe*.
47. Sherman, 'Political Propaganda and Renaissance Culture'; Del Negro, 'Forme e istituzioni del discorso politico veneziano', pp. 420–21.
48. Lipowsky, *Baierisches Kuenstler-Lexikon*, II, p. 67; Bracca, *L'occhio e L'orecchio*, p. 203.
49. Arnaldi de Balme, 'Le feste di Corte a Torino tra spazi reali e itinerari simbolici', p. 36.
50. Gaci, *Poetica descritione d'intorno all'inventioni della sbarra*, p. 12;
51. Bracca, *L'occhio e L'orecchio*, pp. 212–13.
52. Gualterotti, *Feste nelle nozze del serenissimo don Francesco Medici*, pp. 51–52; Schrade, 'Les fêtes du mariage'; Else, *The Politics of Water*, pp. 133–34.
53. Sanchez Cano, '"Naumachiae" at the Buen Retiro in Madrid', p. 320.
54. Robertson, 'Rapports du poète et de l'artiste', p. 270.
55. Briest, *Married to the City*, pp. 141, 162; Bergeron, 'Venetian State Papers and English Civic Pageantry', p. 38.
56. Hill, *Pageantry and Power*, pp. 155, 321.
57. Palmer, *Ceremonial barges on the river Thames*, pp. 10, 177. The Venetian gondola was object of great fascination for the travellers of the Grand Tour (Gordon Brown, 'Water, Windows and Women', pp. 13–15).
58. Katritzky, 'The Diaries of Prince Ferdinand of Bavaria'.

LIST OF ABBREVIATIONS

ABW = Albertina Bibliothek Wien

ASBS = Archivio di Stato di Brescia
    Bib. = Biblioteca
        OL = Opuscoli e libretti

ASPD = Archivio di Stato di Padova
    ACA = Archivio Civico Antico
        Ducali = Ducali
        Nunzi = Nunzi e ambasciatori

ASV = Archivio Segreto Vaticano

ASVE = Archivio di Stato di Venezia
    AC = Avogaria di Comun
    CCD = Capi del Consiglio dei dieci
        Not. = Notatorio
    CD = Consiglio dei dieci
        Del. = Deliberazioni
            Com. = Comuni
            Crim. = Criminali
            Miste = Miste
        Proc. stampa = Proclami a stampa
    CL = Compilazione delle leggi
        s. I = Prima serie
        s. II = Seconda serie
    COL = Collegio
        Cer. = Cerimoniali
    Correr = Archivio privato Correr
    EB = Esecutori contro la bestemmia
    IS = Inquisitori di Stato
        Dis. Ret. = Dispacci dei rettori ed altre cariche
        Proc. crim. = Processi criminali
    MC = Maggior Consiglio
        Del. = Deliberazioni
    SE = Savi all'eresia
    SEN = Senato
        Dis. = Dispacci
            Ret. = Dispacci dei rettori
                Verona = Verona e Veronese
        Del. = Deliberazioni
            Misti = Misti
            Terra = Terra
    PM = Provveditori sopra monasteri
    Pod Mur. = Podestà di Murano
    PP = Provveditori, Soprapprovveditori e Collegio alle pompe
    PS = Provveditori al sal
        Misc. = Miscellanea

PSM = Procuratori di San Marco
Reg: registri
Fil: filze

ASVR = Archivio di Stato di Verona
    AAC = Archivio antico del Comune
        Reg. = Registri

BCBG = Biblioteca Civica Angelo Mai di Bergamo
    ASC = Archivio storico comunale
        Ant. reg. = Sezione di Antico regime
            Com. Bg = Comune di Bergamo (1428–1810)
                Azioni = Azioni dei consigli
                Canc. = Atti dei cancellieri comunali
                Cap. = Capitolari degli uffici
                Cer. = Cerimoniali
                Duc. = Lettere ducali (1428–1796)
                Municipali = Registri di ducali municipali

BAV = Biblioteca Apostolica Vaticana

BCBVI = Biblioteca Civica Bertoliana di Vicenza
    AT = Archivio Torre

BMV = Biblioteca Nazionale Marciana, Venezia

MCV = Biblioteca del Museo Correr, Venezia

SGSM = Staatliche Graphische Sammlung, Munich

BIBLIOGRAPHY

Accarino, B., *Rappresentanza* (Bologna: Il Mulino, 1999).

Algazi, G., Groebner V., and Jussen, B., eds, *Negotiating the Gift. Pre-Modern Figurations of Exchange* (Göttingen: Vandenhoeck & Ruprecht, 2003).

Altano, A. da Servarolo, *Oratione nella creatione del serenissimo principe M. Girolamo Priolo* (Venice: Andrea Arrivabene, 1560).

Alvarez-Ossorio Alvariño, A., '"Pervenire alle orecchie della Maestà": el agente lombardo en la corte madrileña', in *Annali di storia moderna e contemporanea*, 3 (1997), pp. 173–223.

Alvarez-Ossorio Alvariño, A., 'Corte, reinos y ciudades en la monarquía de Carlos II: las legaciones provinciales', in *Pedralbes: Revista d'Història Moderna*, 18 (1998), 2, pp. 221–50.

Alvarez-Ossorio Alvariño, A., 'Del reino al palacio real: la negociación del embajador de la ciudad de Nápoles en la Corte de Carlos II', in *Estudis: Revista de Historia Moderna*, 42 (2016), pp. 9–34.

Ambrosini, F., 'Cerimonie, feste, lusso', in *Storia di Venezia. Dalle origini alla caduta della Serenissima, V, Il Rinascimento. Società ed economia*, ed. by A. Tenenti and U. Tucci (Roma: Istituto della Enciclopedia Italiana, 1996), pp. 441–520.

Ammerman, A. J., 'Venice before the Grand Canal', *Memoirs of the American Academy in Rome*, 48 (2003), pp. 141–58.

Anderson, B., *Imagined communities. Reflections on the Origin and Spread of Nationalism* (London: Verso, 1983).

Anderson, P., and Burgess, G., eds, *The Political Imagination in History: Essays Concerning J. G. A. Pocock* (Baltimore: Owlworks, 2006).

Angiolello, Antonio Maria, *Oratione de l'Angiolello Academico Olimpico all'Illustrissimo et Eccellentissimo Signore, il Signor Giacomo Soranzo, Nella quale sommariamente si discorre quale d'i Prudenti et giusti Signori verso i loro sudditi debba essere il buon governo* (Vicenza: Georgio Angeleri, 1579).

Angulo Morales, A., 'Representación y negociación. Agencias y embajadores provinciales de los parlamentos vascos en el Madrid del Seiscientos', in *Los embajadores. Representantes de la soberanía, garantes del equilibrio, 1659-1748*, ed. by C. Bravo Lozano and A. Álvarez-Ossorio Alvariño (Madrid: Marcial Pons, 2021), pp. 295–316.

Arbel, B., 'Venice's Maritime Empire in the Early Modern Period', in *A Companion to Venetian History, 1400–1797*, ed. by E. Dursteler (Leiden-Boston: Brill, 2013), pp. 125–253.

Arcangeli, A., *Cultural History. A Concise Introduction* (London: Routledge, 2012).

Arcangeli, A., 'Introduzione', in *Rituali civici e continuità istituzionali nelle città italiane della prima età moderna*, ed. by di G.M. Varanini (Roma: Viella, 2023), pp. VII–XXI. Arcangeli, A., 'I rituali urbani fra storia e antropologia. Un bilancio', in *Rituali civici e continuità istituzionali nelle città italiane della prima età moderna*, ed. by di G.M. Varanini (Roma: Viella, 2023), pp. 15–28.

Armitage, D., Battini, M., and Ruhel, M., 'Una discussione intorno alla "Modern Intellectual History"', in *Ricerche di Storia Politica*, 3 (2018), pp. 323–34.

Arnaldi di Balme, C., 'Le feste di Corte a Torino tra spazi reali e itinerari simbolici', in *Feste barocche. Cerimonie e spettacoli alla corte dei Savoia tra Cinque e Settecento*, ed. by C. Arnaldi Di Balme and F. Varallo (Milano: Silvana, 2009), pp. 27–40.

Arslan, E., *I Bassano*, 2 vols (Milano: Ceschina, 1960).

Assonica, P., 'Fragmentum chronicæ ab anno circiter 1509 ad 1512', in *Miscellanea di Storia italiana*, 5 (1868), pp. 279–355.

Atkinson, N., 'The Italian Piazza. From Gothic Footnote to Baroque Theater', in *A Companion to Renaissance and Baroque Art*, ed. by B. Bohn and J. M. Saslow (Hoboken, NJ: Wiley 2013), pp. 561–81.

Aureli A., *Le fatiche d'Ercole per Deianira* (Venezia: per Francesco Nicolini, 1662).

Avagnina, M. E., Binotto, M., and Villa, G. C. F., eds, *Pinacoteca civica di Vicenza. Dipinti del XVII e XVIII secolo* (Milano: Silvana Editoriale, 2004).

Backouche, I., Cosandey, F., Duhamelle, C., Ducreux, M. E., Haddad, E., Joly, L., and Marraud, M., 'Borders, Thresholds, Boundaries: A Social History of Categorizations', in *L'Atelier Bis* (2021). URL: https://journals.openedition.org/acrh/12040?lang=en#text [2023/11/03].

Baiocchi, A., 'Paolo Paruta: ideologia e politica nel Cinquecento veneziano', in *Studi veneziani*, 17–18 (1975–1976), pp. 157–233.

Baldin, G., 'Filosofie della sovranità: Sarpi e Hobbes eredi di Bodin', in *Giornale Critico della Filosofia Italiana*, 98 (2019), pp. 55–74.

Balletti, C., Guerra, F., Meneghello, C., and Romanato, G., 'The Digital Ephemer: Henry III of France in Venice (1574)', in *ISPRS Annals of the Photogrammetry, Remote Sensing and Spatial Information Sciences*, VIII-M-1 (2021), pp. 33–40.

Bamji, A., 'The Control of Space. Dealing with Diversity in Early Modern Venice', in *Italian Studies*, 62/2 (2007), pp. 175–88.

Barcham, W. L., *Grand in design: the life and career of Federico Cornaro, prince of the Church, patriarch of Venice and patron of the arts* (Venezia: Istituto veneto di Scienze, Lettere ed Arti, 2001).

Bardi, G., *Vittoria navale ottenuta dalla Repubblica di Venezia contra Ottone figliuolo di Federigo I Imperatore per la restituzione di Alessandro III Pontefice Massimo venuto a Venezia* (Venezia: Francesco Ziletti, 1584).

Bardi, G., *Dichiaratione di tutte le Istorie che si contengono ne i quadri posti nuovamente nelle Sale dello Scrutinio, et del Gran Consiglio, del Palagio Ducale della Serenissima Republica di Vinegia […]* (Venezia: Felice Valgrisio, 1587).

Bardi, G., *Delle cose notabili della città di Venetia* (Venezia: Altobello Salicato, 1601).

Bazzoni, A., 'Le annotazioni degli Inquisitori di Stato di Venezia', in *Archivio Storico Italiano*, s. III, 11 (1870), pp. 3–72.

Bellabarba, M., 'Controlling Officials: Judicial and Administrative Practices in Early Modern Italian States', in *The Officer and the People: Accountability and Authority in Pre-Modern Europe*, ed. by M. Ángeles, M. Romera, and H. Ziegler (Oxford: Oxford University Press, 2021), pp. 201–23.

Bellabarba, M., 'Rettori veneti e città di Terraferma nel primo Seicento: immagini e parole', in *Rituali civici e continuità istituzionale nelle città italiane in età moderna*, ed. by G.M. Varanini (Roma: Viella, 2023), pp. 31–47.

Bellavitis, A., 'Family and Society', in *A Companion to Venetian History* (Leiden: Brill, 2013), pp. 319–51.

Bellina, A. L., 'Brevità, frequenza e varietà: Cristoforo Ivanovich librettista e storico dell'opera veneziana', in 'Musica e storia', VIII (2000), pp. 367–90.

Belotti, B., Storia di Bergamo e dei bergamaschi, 9 vols (Bergamo: Bolis Edizioni, 1989).

Beltramini, G., and Burns, H., 'Villa Barbaro a Maser', in Palladio, ed. by G. Beltramini and H. Burns (Venezia: Marsilio, 2008), pp. 114–29.

Benaglio, M., 'Relazione della carestia e della peste di Bergamo e suo territorio negli anni 1629 e 1630', in Miscellanea di storia italiana, ed. by G. Finazzi, 6 (Torino: Stamperia reale, 1895), pp. 409–86.

Benedetti, R., Ragguaglio delle allegrezze, solennità, e feste, fatte in Venetia per la felice Vittoria (Venezia: Gratioso Perchaccino, 1571).

Benedetti, R., Le feste, et trionfi fatti dalla Sereniss. Signoria di Venetia nella felice venuta di Henrico III. Christianiss. Re di Francia, et IIII. di Polonia, et in questa seconda edition sono aggiunti molti, diversi, et degni particolari (Venezia: alla libreria della Stella, 1574).

Benigno, F., Favoriti e ribelli. Stili della politica barocca (Roma: Bulzoni, 2011).

Benzoni, G., 'Aspetti della cultura urbana nella società veneta del '5-'600', in Archivio veneto, 108 (1977), pp. 87–159.

Benzoni, G., 'Tra regno perduto e regno recuperato: la sindrome della corona', in L'inestinguibile sogno del dominio: Francesco Morosini, ed. by G. Ortalli, G. Gullino, and E. Ivetic (Venezia: IVSLA, 2021), pp. 233–55.

Berengo, M., La società veneta alla fine del Settecento: ricerche storiche (Firenze: Sansoni, 1956).

Berengo, M., 'Patriziato e nobiltà: il caso veronese', in Potere e società negli stati regionali italiani del '500 e '600, ed. by E. Fasano Guarini (Bologna: il Mulino, 1978), pp. 194–95.

Berengo, M., L'Europa della città. Il volto della società urbana europea fra Medioevo ed età moderna (Torino: Einaudi, 1999).

Bergeron, D. M., 'Venetian State Papers and English Civic Pageantry, 1558–1642', Renaissance Quarterly, 23, no. 1 (1970), pp. 37–47.

Bergamini, G., and Puppi, L., eds, La galleria d'arte antica dei Civici Musei di Udine, I, Dipinti dal XIV alla metà del XVII secolo (Vicenza: Terra Ferma edizioni, 2002).

Bertelli, S., The King's Body: Sacred Rituals of Power in Medieval and Early Modern Europe, trans. by R. Burr Litchfield (Philadelphia: Pennsylvania University Press, 2003).

Bertrand, G., Histoire du carnaval de Venise: XIe-XXIe siècle (Paris: Pygmalion, 2013).

Bianconi, L., and Williams Brown, J., 'Bernardo Sabadini', in The New Grove Dictionary of Music and Musicians, 22 (London: Macmillan, 2001), pp. 60–1.

Bistort, G., Il Magistrato alle Pompe nella Repubblica di Venezia. Studio storico (Venice: Deputazione Veneta di Storia Patria, 1912).

Boccato, C., and Pasqualini Canato, M. T., Il potere nel sacro: i rettori veneziani nella Rotonda di Rovigo (1621–1682) (Rovigo: Minelliana, 2001–2004)

Bolduc, B., La Fête imprimée: spectacles et cérémonies politiques (1549–1662) (Paris: Classiques Garnier, 2016).

Bonadei, R., ed., Bergamo verso l'Unesco: Terra di San Marco, da frontiera di pietra a paesaggi vivi di pace, (Bergamo: Grafica & arte, 2016).

Boschini, M., I gioielli pittoreschi: virtuoso ornamento della Città di Vicenza: cioè l'endice di tutte le pitture publiche della stessa città: Venetia MDCLXVI, ed. by W. De Boer (Firenze: Centro Di, 2008).

Bourdieu, P., 'Les rites comme actes d'institution', in Actes de la recherche en sciences sociales, 43 (1982), pp. 58–63.

Bourdieu, P., 'Les rites d'institution', in Langage et pouvoir symbolique (Paris: Édition du Seuil, 2001), pp. 175–86.

Bouwsma, W. J., Venice and the Defense of Republican Liberty; Renaissance values in the age of the Counter Reformation (Berkeley: University of California Press, 1968).

Bouwsma, W. J., 'Venice and the Political Education of Europe', in Renaissance Venice, ed. by J. R. Hale (London: Faber and Faber, 1973), pp. 445–66.

Bowd, S., 'The Republic of Ideas: Venice, Florence and the Defence of Liberty, 1525–1530', in History, 85 (2000), pp. 404–27.

Bowd, S., '"The Tune Is Marred": Citizens and People in Gasparo Contarini's Venice', in European Review of History: Revue Européenne d'histoire, 7.1 (2000), pp. 83–97.

Bracca, S., L'occhio e L'orecchio. Immagini per il dramma per musica nella Venezia del '600 (Ponzano Veneto: ZeL edizioni, 2014).

Braunstein, P., and Mueller, R., eds, Descripcion ou Traicté du gouvernement et regime de la cité et Seigneurie de Venise. Venezia vista dalla Francia ai primi del Cinquecento (Venezia: Istituto Veneto di Scienze Lettere ed Arti, 2015).

Braunstein, P., Les Allemands à Venise (1380–1520) (Roma: École française de Rome, 2016).

Brown, I. G., 'Water, Windows and Women: the Significance of Venice for Scots in the Age of the Grand Tour', in Eighteenth Century Life, XXX, 3 (2006), pp. 1–50.

Breen, M.P., 'Addressing La Ville des Dieux: Entry Ceremonies and Urban Audiences in Seventeenth-Century Dijon', in Journal of Social History, 38 (2004), 2, pp. 341–64.

Brett, A., and Tully, J., eds, Rethinking the Foundations of Modern Political Thought (Cambridge: Cambridge University Press, 2006).

Briest, S., Married to the City: The Early Modern Lord Mayor's Show, Between Emblematics and Ritual (Heidelberg: Winter, 2019).

Briggs, A., and Burke, P., A Social History of the Media: From Gutenberg to the Internet (Cambridge: Polity Press, 2009).

Brilliant, R., The Arch of Septimius Severus in the Roman Forum (Roma: University of Michigan Press for the American Academy in Rome, 1967).

Brugnoli, P., 'Una villa e una cappella di Francesco Pola a Negrar', in Studi per Gianpaolo Marchi, ed. by R. Bertazzoli, F. Forner, P. Pellegrini, and C. Viola (Edizioni ETS: Pisa, 2011), pp. 207–21.

Bruni, F., La città divisa. Le parti e il bene comune da Dante a Guicciardini (Bologna: il Mulino, 2003).

Brunner, O., Conze W., and Koselleck, R., eds, Geschichtliche Grundbegriffe. Historisches Lexikon zur politisch-sozialen Sprache in Deutschland (Stuttgart: KlettCotta, 1972–1997).

Bryant, D., 'Liturgia e musica liturgica nella fenomenologia del "Mito di Venezia"', in Mitologie. Convivenze di musica e mitologia. Testi e studi, ed. by G. Morelli (Venezia: La Biennale, 1979), pp. 205–14.

Bryant, D., and Pozzobon, Michele, Musica devozione città. La Scuola di Santa Maria dei Battuti (e un suo manoscritto musicale) nella Treviso del Rinascimento (Treviso: Canova, 1995).

Bryant, D. D., and Quaranta, E., Produzione, circolazione e consumo. Consuetudine e quotidianità della polifonia sacra nelle chiese monastiche e parrocchiali dal tardo Medioevo alla fine degli antichi regimi (Bologna: il Mulino, 2006).

Bryant, D. D., and Cecchinato, U., 'Venice, City of Music. Festivities and Entertainment in Early Modern Age', in Musik und Vergnügen am Hohen Ufer. Fest- und Kulturtransfer zwischen Hannover und Venedig in der Frühen Neuzeit, ed. by S. Meine and others (Regensburg: Schnell und Steiner, 2016), pp. 27–48.

Buccio, P., Le coronationi di Polonia, et di Francia del Christianiss. Re Henrico III. con le attioni, et successi de' suoi viaggi (Padova, 1576)

Burson, J. D., 'Entangled History and the Scholarly Concept of Enlightenment', in *Contributions to the History of Concepts*, 8.2 (2013), pp. 1–24.

Burke, P., *Venice and Amsterdam: A Study of Seventeenth Century Élites* (London: Temple Smith, 1974).

Burke, P., *The Historical Anthropology of Early Modern Italy. Essay on Perception and Communication* (Cambridge: Cambridge University Press, 1987).

Bury, M., *The Print in Italy: 1550–1620* (London: British Museum Press, 2001).

Bussels, S., and Van Oostveldt, Bram, '"Restored Behaviour" and the Performance of the City Maiden in Joyous Entries into Antwerp', in *Netherlandish Culture of the Sixteenth Century: Urban Perspectives*, ed. by E. M. Kavaler and A. L. Van Bruaene, 41 (Turnhout: Brepols, 2017), pp. 147–66.

Butazzi, G., 'Intorno al "Cavaliere in nero": note sulla moda maschile tra Cinquecento e Seicento', in *Giovanni Battista Moroni: il cavaliere in nero: l'immagine del gentiluomo nel Cinquecento*, ed. by A. Zanni and A. Di Lorenzo (Milano: Skira, 2005), pp. 47–55.

Calabi, D., and Morachiello, P., *Rialto: le fabbriche e il Ponte 1514–1591* (Torino: Einaudi, 1987).

Calabi, D., *La città del primo Rinascimento* (Roma: Laterza 2001).

Calvi, D., *Effemeride sagro-profana di quanto di memorabile sia successo in Bergamo, sua diocese, et territorio da suoi principii fin'al corrente anno*, 3 vols (Bergamo: Francesco Vigone, 1676–1677).

Calvi, D., *Diario (1649–1678)*, ed. by M. Bernuzzi (Bergamo: Officina dell'Ateneo-Sestante, 2016).

Candiani, G., 'Conflitti d'intenti e di ragioni politiche, di ambizioni e di interessi nel patriziato veneto durante la guerra di Candia', in *Studi Veneziani*, 36 (1998), pp. 145–275.

Cappelli, A., 'Guiniforte Barzizza, maestro di Galeazzo Sforza,' in *Archivio Storico Lombardo*, s. III (1894), 21, pp. 399–442.

Cappelluzzo, G., ed., *Lo 'Statuto del podestà' di Bergamo. Commissione dogale per Lorenzo Bragadin*, (Bergamo: Comune di Bergamo, 1992).

Carile, A., 'Le cerimonie musicali alla corte bizantina', in *Da Bisanzio a San Marco. Musica e liturgia*, ed. by G. Cattin (Bologna: Il Mulino, 1997), pp. 43–60.

Carminati, E., 'La Repubblica in scena. Cerimonie rituali politici nei domini veneziani', in *Ludica. Annali di Storia e di civiltà del gioco*, 25 (2019), pp. 105–17.

Carroll, S. M., and Cecchinato, U., 'Violence and Sacred Space in Early Modern Venice', in *Acta Histriae*, 27/4 (2019), pp. 561–80.

Casella, L., ed., *Rappresentanze e territori. Parlamento friulano e istituzioni rappresentative territoriali nell'Europa moderna. Atti del Convegno internazionale di studi, Udine, 22–23 novembre 2001* (Udine: Forum, 2003).

Casella, L., *Il Parlamento friulano in età moderna. Verbali delle sedute (1471–1805)* (Udine: Forum, 2018).

Casini, M., 'Realtà e simboli del Cancellier Grande veneziano in età moderna (sec. XVI–XVII)', in *Studi veneziani*, n.s. 22 (1991), pp. 195–251.

Casini, M., *I gesti del principe. La festa politica a Firenze e Venezia in età rinascimentale* (Venezia: Marsilio, 1996).

Casini, M., 'Cerimoniali', in *Storia di Venezia. Dalle origini alla caduta della Serenissima*, VII, *La Venezia Barocca*, ed. by G. Benzoni and G. Cozzi (Rome: Istituto della Enciclopedia italiana, 1997), pp. 107–60.

Casini, M., 'Rituali del potere nella città capitale e nella Terraferma', in *Terra d'Este*, 9 (1999), fasc. 17 (gennaio-giugno), pp. 125–28.

Casini, M., 'Immagini dei capitani generali "da Mar" a Venezia in età barocca', in *Il 'Perfetto Capitano'. Immagini e significati del 'capitano' fra Cinque e Seicento*, ed. by M. Fantoni (Roma: Bulzoni, 2001), pp. 219–70.

Casini, M., 'Some Thoughts on the Social and Political Culture of Baroque Venice', in *Braudel Revisited: The Mediterranean World 1600–1800* (Toronto: University of Toronto Press, 2010), pp. 177–206.

Casini, M., 'Rituali e violenza pubblica a Venezia fra medio evo ed età moderna', in G. M. Cantarella, A. De Benedictis, and P. Dogliani, *Concezioni e pratiche del potere e della violenza dall'antichità all'età contemporanea* (Roma: Edizioni di Storia e Letteratura, 2012), pp. 27–47.

Casini, M., 'Gifts of Sugar and Aristocratic Magnanimity in the Renaissance', in *'Ebbi fame e mi deste da mangiare'. Luoghi, principi e funzioni della charitas veneziana, 1260–1806*, ed. by G. Matino and N. Gietz (Modena: Panini, 2018), pp. 105–20.

Casini, M., 'Feste a San Polo nel lungo Rinascimento', in *La chiesa e la parrocchia di San Polo. Spazio religioso e spazio pubblico*, ed. by G. Matino and D. Raines (Roma: Viella, 2021).

Casini, M., *Gloria d'Amore 1690–2021: Parma-Venezia, Venezia-Parma*, in *Gloria d'Amore 2021: Catalogo della mostra nella Peschiera del Parco Ducale di Parma* (Venezia: Artlife for the World, 2022), pp. 5–8.

Cassius Dio, L., *Historia Romana*, ed. by E. Cary (London/Cambridge: Harvard University Press, repr. 1982).

Cavalcanti, G., *Istorie Fiorentine*, ed. by Guido di Pino (Milano: Martello, 1944).

Cavazzana Romanelli, F., 'Contarini, Andrea', *Dizionario biografico degli italiani*, 28 (Roma: Istituto dell'Enciclopedia Italiana, 1983).

Caverzan, C., 'L'affaire Soranzo. Una vicenda giudiziaria nella Venezia di fine Cinquecento' (unpublished master thesis, University of Venice, 2016–2017).

Cecchetti, B., *Il Doge di Venezia* (Venezia: tip. di P. Naratovich, 1864).

Cecchi, A., Conigliello, L., and Faietti, M., eds, *Jacopo Ligozzi, 'pittore universalissimo'*, (Livorno: Sillabe; Firenze: Firenze musei, 2014).

Cecchini, I., *Quadri e commercio a Venezia durante il Seicento. Uno studio sul mercato dell'arte* (Venezia: Marsilio, 2000).

Chambers, D. S., 'Marin Sanudo, Camerlengo of Verona (1501–1502)', in *Archivio Veneto*, 109 (1977), pp. 37–66.

Chambers, D. S., '"Merit and Money: The Procurators of St Mark and Their Commissions, 1443–1605", in *Journal of the Warburg and Courtauld Institutes*, 60 (1997), pp. 23–88.

Checa Cremades F., and Fernández-González, L., eds, *Festival Culture in the World of the Spanish Habsburgs* (Farnham: Ashgate, 2015).

Chojnacki, S., 'Political adulthood in fifteenth century Venice', in *American Historical Review*, 91 (1986), pp. 798–801.

Chojnacki, S., 'Social Identity in Renaissance Venice: The Second Serrata', in *Renaissance Studies*, 8, no. 4 (1994), pp. 341–58.

Chojnacki, S., 'La formazione della nobiltà dopo la Serrata', in *Storia di Venezia*, III, *La formazione dello Stato patrizio*, ed. by G. Arnaldi, G. Cracco and A. Tenenti (Roma: Istituto della Enciclopedia Italiana, 1997), pp. 641–725.

Chojnacki, S., 'Identity and Ideology in Renaissance Venice: The Third Serrata', in *Venice Reconsidered. The History and Civilization of an Italian City-State*, ed. by J. J. Martin and D. Romano (1297–1797) (Baltimore: The Johns Hopkins University Press, 2000), pp. 263–94.

Christ, G., and Morche, F. J., eds, *Cultures of Empire: Rethinking Venetian Rule, 1400–1700. Essays in Honour of Benjamin Arbel* (Leiden-Boston: Brill, 2020).

Cirillo, G., and Godi, G., *Il trionfo del barocco a Parma nelle feste farnesiane del 1690* (Parma: Banca Emiliana, 1989), pp. 97–138.

Cocke, R., *Veronese's Drawings: A Catalogue Raisonne* (London: Sotheby Publications, 1984).

Cogo, G., 'La guerra di Venezia contro i Turchi (1499–1501)', in *Nuovo Archivio Veneto*, 18 (1899), pp. 5–76, 348–421; 19 (1900), pp. 97–138.

Cohn, S. K. Jr, *Popular Protest and Ideals of Democracy in Late Renaissance Italy* (Oxford: Oxford University Press, 2021).

Cohen, D., 'Juger les juges: ouverture d'un espace critique socialement mixte? L'exemple de l'affaire des Cévennes, 1782–1785', in *Justice et espaces publics en Occident, du Moyen-Âge à nos jours. Pouvoirs, Publicité et citoyenneté*, ed. by P. B., D. Fyson, J. P. Garneau, and T. Nootens (Québec: Presses de l'Université du Québec, 2014), pp. 287–98.

Colmuto Zanella, G., and Zanella, V., '"Città sopra monte excellentissime situada". Evoluzione urbana di Bergamo in età veneziana', in *Storia economica e sociale di Bergamo. Il tempo della Serenissima. L'immagine della bergamasca*, ed. by A. De Maddalena, M. Cattini, and M. A. Romani (Bergamo: Fondazione per la storia economica e sociale di Bergamo, 1995), pp. 59–151.

Colombo, G., Marubbi, M., and Miscioscia, A., eds, *Gian Giacomo Barbelli: l'opera completa*, (Azzano San Paolo: Bolis Edizioni, 2011).

Colombo, S., 'Portraits of Sovereignty: Jacopo Palma Giovane and the Doges' Commemorative Cycle in the Doge's Palace', in *Artibus et Historiae*, 75 (2017), pp. 127–48.

Commynes, P. de, *Mémoires sur les principaux faicts, et gestes de Louis onzième et de Charles huictième, son fils, Roys de France* (Paris: Galiot du Pré, 1552).

Consolati, I., *Dominare tempi inquieti. Storia costituzionale, politica e tradizione europea in Otto Brunner* (Bologna: Il Mulino, 2019).

Contarini, G., *De magistratibus et republica Venetorum libri quinque*, (Paris: ex officina Michaëlis Vascosani, 1543)

Contarini, G., *La Republica e i magistrati di Vinegia di M. Gasparo Contarini nuovamente fatti volgari* (Venezia: Girolamo Scotto, 1544).

Contarini, G., *Gasparis Contareni cardinalis opera* (Paris: Apud Sebastianum Nivellium, 1571).

Contarini, G., and others, *Della republica et magistrati di Venetia libri V di m. Gasparo Contarini che fu poi cardinale con un ragionamento intorno alla medesima di m. Donato Giannotti fiorentino et i discorsi di M. Sebastiano Erizzo et di M. Bartolomeo Cavalcanti* (Venezia: presso Aldo [Manuzio], 1591).

Contarini, G., and others, *The Commonwealth and Government of Venice* (London: Imprinted by Iohn Windet for Edmund Mattes, 1599).

Contarini, G., *Casparis Contareni patricii Veneti, de Republica Venetorum libri quinque* (Leiden: Elzevier, 1628).

Contarini, G., *The Republic of Venice: De Magistratibus et Republica Venetorum*, ed. by F. Sabetti, trans. by G. Pezzini and A. Murphy (Toronto: University of Toronto Press, 2020).

Conti, V., *Consociatio civitatum: le repubbliche nei testi elzeviriani: 1625–1649* (Firenze: Centro editoriale toscano, 1997).

Conti, V., 'The Mechanization of Virtue: Republican rituals in Italian political thought in the sixteenth and seventeenth centuries', in *Republicanism*, II, *The Values of Republicanism in Early Modern Europe*, ed. by M. van Gelderen and Q. Skinner (Cambridge, UK: Cambridge University Press, 2002), pp. 73–83.

Cooper, T., 'Prolegomenon to a Quarrel of Images', in *Coming About...: A Festschrift for John Shearman*, ed. by L. R. Jones and L. C. Matthew (Cambridge, MA: Harvard University Art Museums, 2001), pp. 141–48.

Coronelli, V., *Guida de' forestieri sacro-profana per osservare il più ragguardevole nella Città di Venezia* (Venezia: Per Gio. Battista Tramontin, 1706).

Coryat, T., *Coryat's Crudities*, 2 Vols. (Glasgow: J. MacLehose and Sons, 1905) [First edition: Coryat, T., *Coryat's Crudities* (London: William Stansby, 1611)].

Cossalter, S., 'Dai porti alle isole. Cerimoniali di accoglienza nella Serenissima', in *Spazi veneziani. Topografie culturali di una città*, ed. by S. Meine (Roma: Viella, 2014), pp. 125–48.

Costantino, A., Napione, E., and Valdinoci M., eds, *La torre del capitanio. Restauri, scoperte e ricerche*, (Verona: Antiga edizioni, 2009).

Cozzi, G., 'La società veneziana del Rinascimento in un'opera di Paolo Paruta: "Della perfettione della vita politica"', in *Atti della Deputazione di Storia Patria per le Venezie*, 3 (1961), pp. 13–47.

Cozzi, G., 'Cultura politica e religione nella "publica storiografia" veneziana del '500', in *Bollettino dell'Istituto di Storia e Società dello Stato Veneziano*, 5–6 (1963), pp. 215–94.

Cozzi, G., 'Domenico Morosini e il *De bene instituta re publica*', in *Studi veneziani*, 12 (1970), pp. 405–58.

Cozzi, G., 'The Authority and the Law', in *Renaissance Venice*, ed. by J. R. Hale (London: Faber, 1973), pp. 293–345.

Cozzi, G., 'La venuta di Alessandro III a Venezia nel dibattito religioso e politico tra il '500 e il '600', in *Ateneo veneto*, 15 (1977), pp. 119–32.

Cozzi, G., *Repubblica di Venezia e Stati italiani. Politica e giustizia, secoli XVI-XVIII* (Torino: Einaudi, 1982).

Cozzi, G., 'La Repubblica di Venezia in Morea: un diritto per il nuovo Regno (1687–1715)', in *L'età dei lumi. Studi storici sul Settecento europeo in onore di Franco Venturi*, 2 vols (Napoli: Jovene, 1985), pp. 739–89.

Cozzi, G., 'Da Mula, Agostino', *Dizionario Biografico degli Italiani*, 32 (Roma: Istituto della Enciclopedia Treccani, 1986).

Cozzi, G., *Venezia barocca. Conflitti di uomini e idee nella crisi del Seicento veneziano* (Venezia: Il Cardo, 1995).

Cozzi, G., *Ambiente veneziano, ambiente veneto: saggi su politica, società, cultura nella Repubblica di Venezia in età moderna* (Venezia: Marsilio, 1997), pp. 155–83.

Cozzi, G., 'Dalla riscoperta della pace all'inestinguibile sogno di dominio', in *Storia di Venezia*, VIII, *La Venezia barocca*, ed. by in G. Benzoni and G. Cozzi (Roma: Istituto della Enciclopedia Italiana, 1997), pp. 3–104.

Cozzi, G., 'Venezia regina', in *Ambiente veneziano, ambiente veneto. Saggi su politica, società, cultura nella Repubblica di Venezia in età moderna*, ed. by G. Cozzi (Venezia: Marsilio, 1997), pp. 3–11.

Cozzi, G., 'Il giuspatronato del doge su San Marco: diritto originario o concessione pontifica', in *La società veneta e il suo diritto. Saggi su questioni matrimoniali, giustizia penale, politica del diritto, sopravvivenza del diritto veneto nell'Ottocento*, G. Cozzi (Venezia: Marsilio, 2000), pp. 231–47.

Cozzi, G., 'Venezia, una Repubblica di principi?', in *La società veneta e il suo diritto. Saggi su questioni matrimoniali, giustizia penale, politica del diritto, sopravvivenza del diritto veneto nell'Ottocento*, G. Cozzi (Venezia: Marsilio, 2000), pp. 249–65.

Craik, K. A., 'Reading "Coryats Crudities" (1611)', in *Studies in English Literature, 1500–1900*, 44.1 (2004), pp. 77–96.

Craik, K. A., 'Eating His Words: Thomas Coryat and the Art of Indigestion', in *Reading Sensations in Early Modern England*, ed. by K. A. Craik (London: Palgrave Macmillan UK, 2007), pp. 93–114.

Crouzet-Pavan, E., 'Potere politico e spazio sociale: il controllo della notte a Venezia nei secoli XIII–XV', in *La notte. Ordine, sicurezza e disciplinamento in età moderna*, ed. by M. Sbriccoli (Firenze: Ponte alle Grazie, 1991), pp. 46–66.

Crouzet-Pavan, E., '*Sopra le Acque Salse*': espaces, pouvoir et société à Venise à la fin du Moyen Âge, 2 vols (Roma: École Française de Rome, 1992).

Crouzet-Pavan, E., 'Les mots de Venise: Sur le contrôle du langage dans une Cité-État italienne', in *La circulation des nouvelles au moyen age* (Roma: École Française de Rome, 1994), pp. 205–18.

Crouzet-Pavan, E., *Venezia trionfante. Gli orizzonti di un mito* (Einaudi: Torino, 2001).

Curtio, L., *Oratione al Serenissimo Principe Luigi Mocenigo, nella sua essaltatione al Principato, in nome della città di Belluno* (Ceneda: Marco Claseri, 1601).

Da Porto, L., *Lettere storiche di Luigi da Porto vicentino dall'anno 1509 al 1528*, ed. by Bartolomeo Bressan (Firenze: Le Monnier, 1857).

Da Deppo, M., ed., *Venezia in Cadore 1420–2020* (Treviso: Antiga edizioni, 2020).

Da Mosto, A., *I dogi di Venezia* (Firenze: Giunti, 2003).

Dalla Corte, G., *L'istoria di Verona del sig. Girolamo Dalla Corte gentil'huomo Veronese, diuisa in due parti, et in 22 libri*, 2 vols (Verona: nella stamparia di Girolamo Discepolo, 1596).

Dalla Spada, V., *Giubili, e acclamationi della città di Venetia per la vittoria contro l'armata turchesca, ottenuta l'anno 1649 a' 12 Maggio dall'Armi della Serenissima Republica in Asia nel Porto di Focchie* (Venezia: Pinelli, 1649).

Damerini, G., *Morosini* (Milano: Edizioni Alpes, 1929).

Darnton, R., 'Intellectual and Cultural History', in *The Past Before Us: Contemporary Historical Writing in the United States*, ed. by M. Kammen (Ithaca: Cornell University Press, 1980), pp. 327–54.

Davanzo Poli, D., *Abiti antichi e moderni dei Veneziani* (Vicenza: Neri Pozza, 2001).

Davis, R. C., *The War of the Fists. Popular Culture and Public Violence in Late Renaissance Venice* (New York-Oxford: Oxford University Press, 1994).

Davis, R. C. and Marvin, G. *Venice, the Tourist Maze: A Cultural Critique of the World's Most Touristed City* (Berkeley: University of California Press, 2004).

De Benedictis, A., 'Da Confalonieri del popolo a tribuni della plebe: onore, insegne e visibilità di una magistratura popolare (Bologna XIV–XVI secolo)', in *Essere popolo. Prerogative e rituali d'appartenenza nella città italiane d'antico regime*, ed. by G. Delille and A. Savelli, *Ricerche storiche*, 32 (2002), pp. 221–46.

De Benedictis, A., *Neither disobedients nor rebels. Lawful resistance in Early Modern Italy*, (Rome: Viella 2018).

De Certeau, M., *The Practice of Everyday Life* (Berkeley: University of California Press, 1984).

De Franceschi, S. H., 'Entre antiromanisme catholique et républicanisme absolutiste: Paolo Sarpi (1552–1623) et la défense du bien public au temps de la crise de l'Interdit vénitien (1606–1607)', in *Les clercs et les princes. Doctrines et pratiques de l'autorité ecclésiastique à l'époque moderne*, ed. by P. Arabeyre and B. Basdevant-Gaudemet (Paris: Publications de l'École nationale des chartes, 2013), pp. 357–71.

De Luca, M. E., and Faietti, M., eds, *Jacopo Ligozzi, 'altro Apelle'* (Milano: Giunti, 2014).

De Nores, G., *Breve institutione dell'ottima republica* (Venezia: Paolo Megietti, 1578).

De Vivo, F., 'Historical Justifications of Venetian Power in the Adriatic', in *Journal of the History of Ideas*, 64 (2003), 2, pp. 159–76.

De Vivo, F., *Information and Communication in Venice: Rethinking Early Modern Politics* (Oxford: Oxford University Press, 2007).

De Vivo, F., 'Pharmacies as Centres of Communication in Early Modern Venice', in *Renaissance Studies*, 21 (2007), pp. 505–21.

De Vivo, F., 'I luoghi della cultura a Venezia nel primo Cinquecento', in *Atlante della letteratura italiana*, 1, *Dalle Origini al Rinascimento*, ed. by A. De Vincentiis (Torino: Einaudi, 2010), pp. 708–18.

De Vivo, F., *Patrizi, informatori, barbieri. Politica e comunicazione a Venezia nella prima età moderna* (Milano: Feltrinelli, 2012).

De Vivo, F., 'Walking in Sixteenth-Century Venice: Mobilizing the Early Modern City', in *I Tatti Studies in the Italian Renaissance*, 19 (2016), 1, pp. 115–41.

Degl'Innocenti, L., and Rospocher, M., 'Street Singers: An Interdisciplinary Perspective', in *Italian Studies*, 71/2 (2016), pp. 149–53.

Del Negro, P., 'Forme e istituzioni del discorso politico veneziano', in *Storia della cultura veneta*, 4 vols, II, *Il Seicento* (Vicenza: Neri Pozza editore, 1984), pp. 407–36.

Del Torre, G., *Venezia e la Terraferma dopo la guerra di Cambrai. Fiscalità e amministrazione (1515–1530)* (Milano: FrancoAngeli, 1986).

Del Torre, G., and Viggiano, A., eds, *1509–2009: l'ombra di Agnadello: Venezia e la terraferma: atti del Convegno internazionale di studi, Venezia 14–15-16 maggio 2009* (Venezia: Ateneo veneto, 2011).

Della Croce, M., *L'historia della publica et famosa entrata in Vinegia del Serenissimo Henrico III. Re di Francia, et Polonia* (Venice: no publisher, 1574).

Della Misericordia, M., '"Como se tuta questa universitade parlasse". La rappresentanza politica delle comunità nello Stato di Milano (XV secolo)', in *Ad Fontes* (2010). URL: http://www.adfontes.it/biblioteca/scaffale/mdm-mixv/principi.pdf [2023/11/03].

Delorenzi, P., *La galleria di Minerva. Il ritratto di rappresentanza nella Venezia del Settecento* (Verona: Cierre, 2009).

Delorenzi, P., 'Pallade in caccia di notizie. L'arte a Venezia nelle fonti periodiche di fine Seicento', in *Saggi e Memorie di storia dell'arte*, 42 (2018), pp. 153–63.

Derosas, R., 'Moralità e giustizia a Venezia nel '500-'600: gli Esecutori contro la Bestemmia', in *Stato società e giustizia nella Repubblica veneta (sec. XV–XVIII)*, ed. by G. Cozzi (Roma: Jouvence, 1980).

Derosas, R., 'Corner Girolamo', *Dizionario Biografico degli Italiani*, 39 (Roma: Istituto della Enciclopedia Treccani, 1983).

Descendre, R., *Lo Stato del mondo. Giovanni Botero tra ragion di Stato e geopolitica* (Roma: Viella, 2022).

Descharmes, B., Heuser, E. A., Krüger C., and Loy T., eds, *Varietes of Friendship. Interdisciplinary Perspectives on social relationships* (Göttingen: V&R unipress, 2011).

Dewald, J., *Aristocratic experience and the origins of modern culture. France, 1570–1715* (Berkeley: University of California Press, 1993).

Diefendorf, B. B., 'Lyon se présente à son roi: les joyeuses entrées de 1548, 1564 et 1595', in *Cités humanistes, cités politiques (1400–1600)* (Paris: PUPS, 2014), pp. 71–86.

Dipper, C., 'I Geschichtliche Grundbegriffe dalla storia dei concetti alla teoria delle epoche storiche', in *Società e storia*, 19 (1996), pp. 385–402.

Discours de l'entrée de tresillustre, Trespuissant, Treschrestien & Tresvictorieux Prince Charles de Valois neuvième de ce nom Roy de France en sa tresrenommée & fameuse ville de Lyon (Lyon: Auguste Brun, 1884).

Distefano, G., *Atlante storico di Venezia* (Venezia: Supernova, 2008).

Doglio, M. L., 'La letteratura ufficiale e l'oratoria celebrativa', in *Storia della cultura veneta*, 4 vols, I, *Il Seicento*, ed. by G. Arnaldi and M. Pastore Stocchi (Vicenza: Neri Pozza, 1983), pp. 163–87.

Doglioni, G. N., *La città di Venezia con l'origine et governo di quella eti dogi che vi sono stati et tutte le cose notabili chedi tempo in tempo vi sono avvenute dal principio della sua edificatione sino a questi tempi* (Venezia: Bertelli, 1594).

Dubois, J., Durand, P., and Winkin, Y., 'Aspects du symbolique dans la sociologie de Pierre Bourdieu. Formation et transformations d'un concept générateur', in CONTEXTES: *Revue de Sociologie de la Littérature* (2013).

URL: https://journals.openedition.org/contextes/5661 [2023/03/23].

Dumolyn, J., and Haemers, J., '"A Bad Chicken was Brooding": Subversive Speech in Late Medieval Flanders', in *Past and Present*, 214 (2012), pp. 45–86.

Dumolyn, J., Haemers, J., Oliva Herrer, H. R., and Challet V., eds, *The Voices of the People in Late Medieval Europe. Communication and Popular Politics*, special issue of *Urban History*, 33 (2014).

Duso, G., *La rappresentanza politica. Genesi e crisi del concetto* (Milano: Giuffrè, 2003).

Eglin, J., *Venice Transfigured: The Myth of Venice in British Culture, 1660–1797* (New York: Palgrave, 2001).

Eisenstadt, S. N., 'Personal Relations, Trust and Ambivalence in Relation to the Institutional Order', in *Patrons, clients and friends. Interpersonal relations and the structure of trust in society*, ed. by S. N. Eisenstadt and L. Roniger (Cambridge, New York and Melbourne: Cambridge University Press, 1987), pp. 1–18.

Elet, Y., 'Seats of Power: The Outdoor Benches of Early Modern Florence', in *Journal of the Society of Architectural Historians*, 61 (2002), pp. 444–69.

Else, F. M., *The Politics of Water in the Art and Festivals of Medici Florence. From Neptune Fountain to Naumachia* (London: Routledge, 2018).

Faggion L., and Verdon, L., eds, *Le don et le contre-don: usages et ambiguïtés d'un paradigme anthropologique aux époques médiévale et moderne* (Aix-en-Provenc: Université de Provence, 2010).

Fagiolo, M., 'L'effimero di stato. Dal conclave al possesso', in *La festa a Roma dal Rinascimento al 1870*, ed. by M. Fagiolo, 2 vols (Torino: Allemandi, 1997), 2, pp. 8–25.

Faietti, M., Nova, A., and Wolf, G., eds, *Jacopo Ligozzi 2015* (Firenze: Kunsthistorisches Institut, 2015).

Fausto, C., *Venetia festiva per gli pomposi spettacoli fatti rappresentare dall'Illustriss. & Eccellentiss. Sig. d'Hussè Ambasciatore di S. M. Cristianissima, per la nascita del Real Delfino di Francia* (Venezia: Andrea Baba, 1638).

Favilla, M., and Rugolo, R., 'Venezia, 1772: le "molto ben architettate apparenze" per l'entrata del cancellier grande Giovanni Girolamo Zuccato', in *Studi Veneziani*, n.s. LXI (2010), pp. 193–211.

Favilla, M., and Rugolo, R., 'Frammenti dalla Venezia barocca', in *Atti dell'Istituto Veneto di Scienze, Lettere ed Arti. Classe di scienze morali, lettere ed arti*, 163 (2004–2005), pp. 47–138.

Fasoli, G., 'Nascita di un mito (Il mito di Venezia nella storiografia)', in *Studi storici in onore di Gioacchino Volpe*, 1 (Firenze: Sansoni, 1958), pp. 445–79.

Fasoli, G., 'Liturgia e cerimoniale ducale', in *Venezia e il Levante fino al secolo XV*, ed. by A. Pertusi, 1 (Firenze: Olschki, 1973), pp. 261–93.

Fenlon, I., *The Ceremonial City: History, Memory and Myth in Renaissance Venice* (New Haven, CT: Yale University Press, 2007).

Fenlon, I., 'Sung Histories: The Battle of Lepanto between Orality and Print', in *Antropologia della musica nelle culture mediterranee: interpretazione, performance, identità: alla memoria di Tullia Magrini*, ed. by P. V. Bohlman and M. Sorce Keller (Bologna: Il Mulino, 2009), pp. 71–80.

Fenlon, I., *Piazza San Marco* (London: Profile Books, 2010).

Fenlon, I., *Orality and Print: Singing in the Street in Early Modern Venice*, in *Interactions between Orality and Writing in Early Modern Italian Culture*, ed. by L. Degl'Innocenti, B. Richardson, and C. Sbordoni (London and New York: Routlegde, 2016).

Fenlon, I., 'Urban Soundscapes', in *The Cambridge History of Sixteenth-Century Music*, ed. by I. Fenlon and R. Wistreich (Cambridge: Cambridge University Press, 2019), pp. 210–11.

Fenster, T., and Smail, D. L., eds, *Fama: The Politics of Talk and Reputation in Medieval Europe* (Ithaca: Cornell University Press, 2003).

Ferente, S., 'Storici ed emozioni', in *Storica*, 15, no. 43–45 (2009), pp. 371–92.

Fink, Z. S., *The Classical Republicans: An Essay in the Recovery of a Pattern of Thought in Seventeenth-Century England* (Evanston: Northwestern University Press, 1962).

Finlay, R., *Politics in Renaissance Venice* (New Brunswick, NJ: Rutgers University Press, 1980).

Finlay, R., 'The Immortal Republic: The Myth of Venice during the Italian Wars (1494–1530)', in *The Sixteenth Century Journal*, 30 (1999), fasc. 4, pp. 931–44.

Fioravanti, L., *Dello specchio di scientia universale* (Venezia: Heredi di Marchio Sessa, 1572).

Florio, G., 'L'inventio della consuetudine. Congratulazioni al doge di Venezia tra norma e prassi', in Florio, G., and Viggiano, A., eds, *La Repubblica degli esperti. Misurare, mediare, raccontare nella Repubblica di Venezia (secc. XV–XVIII)*, (Palermo: Mediterranea, forthcoming).

Florio, G., 'Rappresentanti e rappresentazioni delle comunità di Terraferma nella Venezia dell'Interdetto (1606–1607)' (unpublished doctoral thesis, University of Venice, 2014).

Florio, G., 'Venezia e le Comunità di Terraferma di fronte all'Interdetto (1606–1607). Protagonisti e forme di un dialogo asimmetrico sul tema della sovranità', in *Ateneo Veneto*, s. III, no. 201, 13 (2014), II, pp. 119–44.

Florio, G., 'La formalizzazione di una funzione informale. La rappresentanza politica dei corpi sudditi nella Venezia della prima età moderna', in *Imperial. Il ruolo della rappresentanza politica informale nella costruzione e nello sviluppo delle entità statuali (XV–XXI secolo)*, ed. by G. Ambrosino and L. De Nardi (Verona: QuiEdit, 2017), pp. 19–38.

Florio, G., 'S'incliner devant au Prince républicain. Images de la souveraineté et de l'assujettissement dans les ambassades d'obéissance aux doges de Venise', in *L'humiliation. Droit, récits et représentations (XIIe–XXIe siècles)*, ed. by L. Faggion, C. Regina, and A. Roger (Paris: Classiques Garnier, 2019), pp. 221–39.

Florio, G., '"Ai piedi di Sua Serenità". Media e elezioni ducali nella Venezia di fine Seicento', in *I media nei processi elettorali. Modelli ed esperienze tra età moderna e contemporanea*, ed. by C. Cornelissen and M. Cau (Bologna: Il Mulino 2020), pp. 137–62.

Florio, G., 'Inchini e carte bollate: iconografia delle dedizioni alla Repubblica di Venezia (secoli XVI–XVII)', in *Annali dell'Istituto storico italo-germanico in Trento*, 2 (2021), pp. 69–92.

Florio, G., '"Acciocché i popoli tutti maggiormente si sdegnino e si sollevino contro il Prencipe". Una prospettiva sull'Interdetto veneziano del 1606–1607', in *Séditions et révoltes dans la réflexion politique de l'Europe moderne*, ed. by A. Merle and M. Mestre Zaragozá (Paris: Classiques Garnier, 2022), pp. 149–71.

Florio, G., 'Celebrating the Prince from Afar. Echoes from the Jubilant Dominions in the Orations to the Newly Elected Doges (XVI–XVII Century)', in *Geographies of Sound. Sounding and Listening to the Urban Space of Early Modern Italy with a Contemporary Perspective*, ed. by L. Collarile and M. R. De Luca (Tournhout: Brepols, 2023), pp. 107–44.

Florio, G., *Micropolitica della rappresentanza* (Roma: Carocci, 2023).

Florio, M. S., '"So Flourishing a Commonwealth": some aspects of Lewkenor's translation (1599) of Contarini's la republica e i magistrati di Vinegia (1544)' (unpublished doctoral thesis, Università Ca' Foscari, 2010).

Folin, M., 'Introduzione', in Città italiana e città europea. Ricerche storiche, ed. by M. Berengo (Reggio Emilia: Diabasis, 2010).

Fontana, A., and Fournel, J.-Louis, 'Piazza, Corte, Salotto, Caffè', in Letteratura italiana, 5, Le questioni, ed. by A. Asor Rosa (Torino: Einaudi, 1986), pp. 634–86.

Fontana, A., 'La piazza del Cinquecento come "topos" rappresentativo', in Discours littéraires et pratiques politiques: travaux du Centre de Recherche sur l'Italie à l'époque de la Réforme et de la Contre-Réforme, ed. by A. C. Fiorato (Paris: Publications de la Sorbonne, 1987), pp. 163–82.

Fortini Brown, P., 'Painting and History in Renaissance Venice', in Art History, 7 (1984), 3, pp. 263–94.

Fortini Brown, P., Venetian Narrative Painting in the Age of Carpaccio (New Haven: Yale University Press, 1988).

Fortini Brown, P., 'Measured friendship, calculated pomp: the ceremonial welcomes of the Venetian Republic', in 'All the world's a stage…': Art and Pageantry in the Renaissance and Baroque, ed. by B. Wisch and S. Munshower, 2 vols (Pennsylvania: University Park, 1990), pp. 136–86.

Foscari, A., and Tafuri, M., L'armonia e i conflitti: la chiesa di San Francesco della Vigna nella Venezia del '500 (Torino: Einaudi, 1983).

Foscari Malacrea, M., 'Il doge nelle cerimonie pubbliche', in Il serenissimo Doge, ed. by U. Franzoi (Treviso: Canova, 1986), pp. 105–91.

Fosi, I., '"Parcere subiectis, debellare superbos". L'immagine della giustizia nelle cerimonie di possesso a Roma e nelle legazioni dello Stato pontificio nel Cinquecento', Cérémonial et rituel à Rome (XVIe-XIXe siècle) (Roma: École Française de Rome, 1997), pp. 89–115.

Fosi, I., Signorotto, G., and Visceglia, M. A., 'Court and City in the Ceremony of the Possesso in the Sixteenth Century', in Court and Politics in Papal Rome, 1492–1700, ed. by G. Signorotto and M. A. Visceglia (Cambridge: Cambridge University press, 2002).

Foucault, M., 'Sui modi di scrivere la storia', in Follia, scrittura, discorso, M. Foucault, 1, Archivio Foucault. Interventi, colloqui, interviste, 1961–1970 (Milano: Feltrinelli 1974), pp. 48–57.

Fragnito, G., 'Contarini, Gaspar', Dizionario Biografico Degli Italiani, 28 (Roma: Istituto della Enciclopedia Treccani, 1983).

Francastel, P., 'Figuration et spectacle dans les tapisseries des Valois', Les fêtes de la Renaissance, Études réunies et présentées par J. Jacquot, 1 (Paris: Éditions du Centre Nationale de la Recherche Scientifique, 1956), pp. 101–05.

Francesco Morosini 1619–1694. L'uomo, il doge, il condottiero (Roma: Istituto poligrafico e Zecca dello Stato italiano – Libreria dello Stato, 2019).

Franco, G., Habiti d'huomeni et donne venetiane con la processione della ser.ma Signoria et altri particolari cioe trionfi, feste et cerimonie publiche della nobilissima città di Venetia (Venezia: Giacomo Franco forma in Frezzaria all'insegna del sole, 1610).

Frangipane, C., Tragedia, al Christianissimo et invittissimo Henrico III. Re di Francia, e di Polonia, recitata nella Sala del Gran Consiglio di Venetia (Venezia, 1574).

Franzoi, U., Storia e leggenda del Palazzo Ducale di Venezia (Venezia: Storti, 1982).

Franzoi, U., and Leonardi, E., Il Palazzo Ducale di Venezia nella rappresentazione grafica dal XV al XIX secolo (Treviso: Canova, 1989).

Frecavalli, M., 'Oratione dell'eccellentissimo signor Mario Frecavalli, ambasciator di Crema', in Le glorie immortali del Serenissimo Prencipe di Vinegia Marino Grimani, ed. by A. Michele (Venezia: Francesco Bariletti, 1596), pp. 46–58.

Friedensburg, W., ed., Nuntiaturberichte aus Deutschland nebst ergänzenden Aktenstücken. IV. Legation Alexanders 1538–1539 (Gotha: Friedrich Andreas Perthes, 1893).

Frontain, R. J., 'Thomas Coryate and the Epistemology of Travel', in CEA Critic, 64.1 (2001), pp. 59–69.

Gaci, C., Poetica descritione d'intorno all'inventioni della sbarra combattuta in Fiorenza nel cortile del palagio de' Pitti in honore della sereniss. signora Bianca Cappello gran duchessa di Toscana (Firenze: stamperia de' Giunti, 1579).

Gaeta, F., 'Alcune considerazioni sul mito di Venezia', in Bibliothèque d'Humanisme et Renaissance, 23, (1961), pp. 58–75.

Gaeta, F., 'Storiografia, coscienza nazionale e politica culturale nella Venezia del Rinascimento', in Dal primo Quattrocento al concilio di Trento, Storia della cultura Veneta, ed. ed. by G. Arnaldi M. Pastore Stocchi, 3 (Vicenza: Neri Pozza, 1980), pp. 1–91.

Gaeta, F., 'L'idea di Venezia', in Storia della cultura veneta, III, Dal primo Quattrocento al Concilio di Trento (1981), pp. 565–641.

Gaeta, F., 'Venezia da "Stato misto" ad "aristocrazia esemplare"', in Storia della cultura veneta, ed. by G. Arnaldi and M. Pastore Stocchi, 10 vols (Vicenza: Neri Pozza, 1976–1986), IV, Il Seicento, 2 (1984), pp. 437–94.

Gaier, M., Facciate sacre a scopo profano. Venezia e la politica dei monumenti fra Quattro e Settecento (Venezia: Istituto veneto di lettere ed arti, 2002).

Gaier, M., Architettura 'Venetiana': i proti veneziani e la politica edilizia nel Cinquecento (Sommacampagna: Cierre, 2019).

Gaille-Nikodimov, M., ed., Le gouvernement mixte: de l'idéal politique au monstre constitutionnel en Europe (XIIIe–XVIIe siècle), (Saint-Étienne: Publications de l'Université de Saint-Étienne, 2005).

Gallo, A. F., 'L'autobiografia artistica di Giovanni Ambrosio (Guglielmo Ebreo) da Pesaro', in Studi Musicali, 12 vols, 2 (1983), pp. 189–202.

Galtarossa, M., 'L'idea del Tribunato nella storia della Repubblica di Venezia', in Diritto @ Storia. Rivista internazionale di Scienze giuridiche e Tradizione Romana, 7 (2008). URL: http://www.dirittoestoria.it/7/Memorie/Galtarossa-Idea-Tribunato-Repubblica-Venezia.htm [2023/11/03].

Garbero Zorzi, E., '"Giostre di legni in mare". Le 'regate grandi' a Venezia dal tardo Seicento alla fine del Barocco', in Le capitali della festa 2007, pp. 299–304.

Garzoni, T., La Piazza Universale di tutte le professioni del mondo, 2 vols (Torino: Einaudi, 1996).

Gauvard, C., 'La Fama, une parole fondatrice', in Médiévales, 24 (1993), pp. 5–13.

Geertz, C., 'Religion as a Cultural System', in Anthropological Approaches to the Study of Religion, ed. by M. Banton (1966), pp. 1–46.

Geertz, C., 'Centers, Kings, and Charisma: Reflections on the Symbolics of Power', in Culture and Its Creators: Essays in Honor of Edward Shils, ed. by J. Ben-David and T. N. Clark (Chicago: University of Chicago Press, 1977), pp. 150–71.

Geertz, C., Local Knowledge: Further Essays in Interpretative Anthropology (New York: Basic Books, 2000).

Giani, M., 'Paolo Paruta: Il lessico della politica' (unpublished doctoral dissertation, Università Ca' Foscari, Venezia, 2010–2011).

Giannotti, D., Dialogi de Repub. Venetorum (Leiden: Elzevier, 1631).

Giannotti, D., Opere Politiche, ed. by F. Diaz (Milano: Marzorati, 1974).

Gibellini, C., L'immagine di Lepanto. La celebrazione della vittoria nella letteratura e nell'arte veneziana (Venezia: Marsilio, 2008).

Gilbert, F., 'The date of the composition of Contarini's and Giannotti's books on Venice', in *Studies in the Renaissance*, 14 (1967), pp. 172–84.

Gilbert, F., 'The Venetian Constitution in Florentine Political Thought', in *Florentine Studies*, ed. by N. Rubenstein (London: Faber and Faber, 1968), pp. 463–500.

Gilbert, F., 'Religion and Politics in the Thought of Gasparo Contarini', in *Action and Conviction in Early Modern Europe: Essays in Memory of E.H. Harbison*, ed. by Theodore K. Rabb and Jerrold E. Seigel (Princeton: Princeton University Press, 1969), pp. 90–116.

Gilmore, M. P., 'Myth and Reality in Venetian Political Theory', in *Renaissance Venice*, ed. by J. Rigby Hale (London: Faber and Faber, 1973), pp. 431–44.

Ginnasi, L. 'Celsi, Lorenzo', *Dizionario biografico degli italiani*, 23 (Roma: Istituto della Enciclopedia Treccani, 1979).

Ginzburg, C., 'L'alto e il basso: il tema della conoscenza proibita nel Cinquecento e Seicento', in C. Ginzburg, *Miti, emblemi e spie. Morfologia e storia* (Torino: Einaudi, 1986), pp. 107–32.

Giomo, G., 'Le spese del nobil uomo Marino Grimani nella sua elezione a doge di Venezia', in *Archivio Veneto*, 33 (1887), pp. 443–54.

Girgensohn, D., ed., *Francesco Foscari: promissione ducale 1423* (Venezia: La Malcontenta, 2004).

Gleason, E. 'Reading Between the Lines of Gasparo Contarini's Treatise on the Venetian State', in *Historical Reflections / Réflexions Historiques*, 15 (1988), 1, pp. 251–70.

Gleason, E. *Gasparo Contarini: Venice, Rome, and Reform* (Berkeley: University of California Press, 1993).

Glixon, J., *Honoring God and the City. Music at the Venetian Confraternities 1260–1807* (Oxford: Oxford University Press, 2003).

Godefroy, T., *Le Cérémonial françois*, ed. by D. Godefroy, I (Paris: Sébastien Cramoisy, 1649).

Gombrich, E. H., 'Celebrations in Venice of the Holy League and of the Victory of Lepanto', in *Studies in Renaissance and Baroque Art presented to Anthony Blunt on his 60th Birthday*, ed. by A. Blunt (London: Phaidon, 1967), pp. 62–68

Gordon, S., *Controlling the State: Constitutionalism from Ancient Athens to Today* (Cambridge, MA: Harvard University Press, 1999).

Goy, R. J., *Building Renaissance Venice: Patrons, Architects and Builders, C. 1430–1500* (New Haven: Yale University Press, 2006).

Grendler, P. F., 'The Leaders of the Venetian State, 1540–1609: A Prosopographical Analysis', in *Studi Veneziani*, 19 (1990), pp. 35–85.

Grevembroch, G., *Gli abiti de veneziani di quasi ogni età con diligenza raccolti e dipinti nel secolo XVIII*, 4 vols (Venezia: Filippi, 1981).

Groto, L., *Oratione fatta in Vinegia, per l'allegrezza della vittoria ottenuta contra Turchi dalla santissima Lega* (Venezia: appresso Sigismondo Bordogna e Francesco Patriani, 1571).

Groto, L., *Le orationi volgari* (Venezia: Fabio & Agostino Zoppini, 1586).

Grubb, J., 'When Myths Lose Power: Four Decades of Venetian Historiography', in *Journal of Modern History*, 58 (1986), pp. 43–94.

Gualterotti, R., *Feste nelle nozze del serenissimo don Francesco Medici gran duca di Toscana; et della sereniss. sua consorte la sig. Bianca Cappello* (Firenze: stamperia de' Giunti, 1579).

Guerrini, P., 'I Diari dei Bianchi', in *Fonti per la storia bresciana*, 4 (Brescia: Edizioni del Moretto, 1930).

Guicciardini, F., *Ricordi*, ed. by M. Fubini (Milano: Rizzoli, 1977).

Guicciardini, F., *The History of Italy*, ed. by S. Anglo (Princeton NJ: Princeton University Press, 1984).

Guicciardini, F., *Ricordi*, introduction and commentary by C. Varotti (Rome: Carocci, 2013).

Gullino, G., 'Erizzo, Francesco', *Dizionario biografico degli Italiani*, 43 (Roma: Istituto della Enciclopedia Italiana, 1993).

Gullino, G., 'L'evoluzione costituzionale', in *Storia di Venezia*, IV, *Il Rinascimento*, ed. by A. Tenenti and U. Tucci (Roma: Istituto della Enciclopedia Italiana, 1996), pp. 345–78.

Gullino, G., 'Mocenigo, Tommaso', *Dizionario biografico degli Italiani*, 75 (Roma: Istituto della Enciclopedia Italiana, 2011).

Gullino, G., 'Morosini, Francesco', *Dizionario biografico degli Italiani*, 77 (Roma: Istituto della Enciclopedia Italiana, 2012).

Gullino, G., 'Zen, Ranieri', *Dizionario biografico degli Italiani*, 100 (Roma: Istituto della Enciclopedia Italiana, 2020).

Guzzo, E. M., 'La decorazione della Sala pretoria: un'impresa per il bresciano Antonio Gandino e due lettere di Ottavio Rossi', in *Civiltà veronese*, 4 (1991), pp. 43–51.

Habert, J., 'Venezia e il Paradiso. Un concorso a Palazzo Ducale', in *Il Paradiso di Tintoretto. Un concorso per Palazzo Ducale*, ed. by J. Habert (Paris / Milano: 5 Continents, 2006), pp. 17–59.

Hadfield, A., *Literature, Travel and Colonial Writing in the English Renaissance* (Oxford: Clarendon Press, 1998).

Haemers, J., 'Filthy and Indecent Words. Insults, Defamation, and Urban Politics in the Southern Low Countries, 1300–1550', in *The Voices of the People in Late Medieval Europe: Communication and Popular Politics*, ed. by J. Dumolyn, J. Haemers, H. R. Oliva Herrer, and Vincent Challet (Turnhout: Brepols, 2014), pp. 247–67.

Haitsma Mulier, E. O. G., *The Myth of Venice and Dutch Republican Thought in the Seventeenth Century* (Assen, Netherlands: Van Gorcum, 1980).

Hankins, J., *Virtue Politics: Soulcraft and Statecraft in Renaissance Italy* (Cambridge, MA: Harvard University Press, 2019).

Harrington, J., *The Commonwealth of Oceana, A System of Politics*, ed. by J. G. A. Pocock (Cambridge: Cambridge University Press, 1992).

Haskell, F., *History and Its Images: Art and the Interpretation of the Past* (New Haven and London: Yale University Press, 1993).

Haskell, F., *Mecenati e pittori. L'arte e la società italiana nell'epoca barocca*, ed. by T. Montanari (Turin: Einaudi, 2019).

Hill, T., *Pageantry and Power: A Cultural History of the Early Modern Lord Mayor's Show, 1585–1639* (Manchester and New York: Manchester University Press, 2010).

Hirschkop, K., *Mikhail Bakhtin: An Aesthetic for Democracy* (Oxford: Oxford University Press, 2002).

Hirthe, T., *Il 'foro all'antica' di Venezia. La trasformazione di Piazza San Marco nel Cinquecento* (Venezia: Centro Tedesco di Studi Veneziani, 1986).

Hochmann, M., 'La collection de Giacomo Contarini', in *Mélanges de l'École française de Rome. Moyen Age – Temps Modernes*, 99 (1987), 1, pp. 447–89.

Hochmann, M., *Peintres et commanditaires à Venise, 1540–1628* (Roma: École française de Rome, 1992).

Hochmann, M., 'Giuseppe Porta e la decorazione di palazzo Contarini dalle Figure', in *Arte Veneta*, 59 (2002), pp. 238–46.

Hochmann, M., 'Giacomo Contarini', in *Il collezionismo d'arte a Venezia: dalle origini al Cinquecento*, ed. by M. Hochmann, R. Lauber, and S. Mason (Venezia: Fondazione di Venezia – Marsilio, 2008), p. 260.

Hoffmann, H., *Rappresentanza-rappresentazione. Parola e concetto dall'Antichità all'Ottocento* (Milano: Giuffrè, 2007).

Holden Evers, S., 'The Art of Paolo Veronese: Artistic Identity in Harmony with Patrician Ideology' (unpublished doctoral dissertation, University of California at Berkeley, 1994).

Horodowich, E., *Language and Statecraft in Early Modern Venice* (Cambridge: Cambridge University Press, 2008).

Horodowich, E., 'Speech and Oral Culture in Early Modern Europe and Beyond', in *The Journal of Early Modern History*, ed. by E. Horodowich, 16 (2012), pp. 301–13.

Howard, D., *Jacopo Sansovino: Architecture and Patronage in Renaissance Venice* (New Haven: Yale university press, 1975).

Howard, D., 'Venice as a Dolphin: Further Investigations into Jacopo de' Barbari's View', in *Artibus et Historiae*, 18.35 (1997), pp. 101–11.

Hunecke, V., *Il patriziato veneziano alla fine della Repubblica: 1646–1797. Demografia, famiglia, ménage* (Roma: Jouvence, 1997).

Hunecke, V., 'Il corpo aristocratico', in *Storia di Venezia. Dalle origini alla caduta della Serenissima*, VI, *L'ultima fase della Serenissima*, ed. by Piero Del Negro and P. Preto (Roma: Istituto della Enciclopedia Italiana, 1998), pp. 359–429.

Hunecke, V., 'I Savi Grandi: gli oligarchi di Venezia?', in *Acta Histriae*, 7 (1999), pp. 141–52.

Infelise, M., 'Professione reportista. Copisti e gazzettieri nella Venezia del Seicento', in *Venezia. Itinerari per la storia della città*, ed. by S. Gasparri, G. Levi, and P. Moro (Bologna: Il Mulino, 1997), pp. 183–209.

Infelise M., and A. Stouraiti, eds, *Venezia e la guerra di Morea: guerra, politica e cultura alla fine del '600* (Milano: FrancoAngeli, 2005).

Infelise, M., *Gazzetta. Storia di una parola* (Venezia: Marsilio, 2017).

Irace, E., 'Una voce poco fa. Note sulle difficili pratiche della comunicazione tra il centro e le periferie dello Stato ecclesiastico (Perugia, metà XVI-metà XVII secolo)', in *Offices, écrits et papauté (XIIIe-XVIIe siècle)*, ed. by A. Jamme and O. Poncet (Roma: École française de Rome, 2007), pp. 273–99.

Ivanovich, C., *Minerva al tavolino. Parte seconda* (Venezia: Appresso Nicolò Pezzana, 1688).

Jesi, F., *Materiali mitologici. Mito e antropologia nella cultura mitteleuropea* (Torino: Einaudi, 1979).

Johnson, J. H., *Venice Incognito: Masks in the Serene Republic* (Berkeley: University of California Press, 2011).

Jones, A. R., 'Italians and Others: Venice and the Irish in "Coryat's Crudities" and "The White Devil"', in *Renaissance Drama*, 18 (1987), pp. 101–19.

Judde de Larivière, C., 'Du Broglio à Rialto: cris et chuchotements dans l'espace public à Venise, au XVIe siècle', in *L'espace public au moyen age*, ed. by P. Boucheron and N. Offenstadt (Paris: Presses universitaires de France, 2011), pp. 119–30.

Judde de Larivière, C., and Salzberg, R., 'The People Are the City. The Idea of the *Popolo* and the Condition of the *Popolani* in Renaissance Venice', in *Annales. Histoire, Sciences Sociales* (2013/4), pp. 1113–40.

Judde de Larivière, C., *The Revolt of Snowballs: Murano Confronts Venice, 1511* (London-New York: Routledge 2018).

Judde de Larivière, C., 'De quel peuple parle-t-on? Le popolo dans les écrits historico-politiques vénitiens de la fin du Moyen Âge', in *Revenue Historique*, 1 (2022), pp. 35–67.

Kantorowicz, E. H., *Laudes regiae. A Study in Liturgical Acclamations and Mediaeval Ruler Worship* (Berkeley: University of California Press, 1946; repr. 1958).

Kantorowicz, E. H., *The King's Two Bodies: A Study in Medieval Political Theology* (Princeton: Princeton University Press, 2016).

Katritzky, M. A., 'The Diaries of Prince Ferdinand of Bavaria: commedia dell'arte at the Wedding Festivals of Florence (1565) and Munich (1568)', in *Italian Renaissance Festivals and Their European Influence*, ed. by J. R. Mulryne and M. Shewring (Lewiston: Edwin Mellen Press, 1992), pp. 143–72.

Katritzky, M. A., 'A Court Festival set in the Garden of an Italian Villa', in *Theatre Research International*, 23 (1998).

Katritzky, M. A., 'German Patrons of Venetian Carnival Art: Archduke Ferdinand II of Tyrol's Am bras Collections and the 1579 Travel Journal of Prince Ferdinand of Bavaria', in *Von kurzer Dauer? Fallbeispiele zu temporären Kunstzentren der Vormoderne*, ed. by B. U. Münch, A. Tacke, M. Herzog, and S. Heudecke (Petersberg: Michael Imhof, 2016), pp. 126–42.

Kettering, S., 'Gift-Giving and Patronage in Early Modern France', in *French History*, 2, 2 (1988), pp. 131–51.

King, M. L., *Venetian Humanism in an Age of Patrician Dominance* (Princeton: Princeton University Press, 1986).

Kingston, R., 'Mind Over Matter? History and the Spatial Turn', in *Cultural and Social History*, 7, 1 (2010), pp. 111–21.

Knapton, M., 'The Terraferma State', in *A Companion to Venetian History, 1400–1797*, ed. by Eric R. Dursteler (Leiden-Boston: Brill, 2013), pp. 85–124.

Kocka, J., 'Comparison and Beyond', *History & Theory*, 42, no. 1 (2003), pp. 39–44.

Koenigsberger, H. G., 'The Italian parliaments from the origins to the end of the eighteenth century', in *The Journal of Italian History*, 1 (1978), pp. 18–49.

Korsch, E., *Bilder der Macht. Venezianische Repräsentationsstrategien beim Staatsbesuch Heinrichs III. (1574)* (Berlin: Akademie Verlag, 2013).

Korsch, E., 'Renaissance Venice and the Sacred-Political Connotations of Waterborne Pageants', in *Waterborne Pageants and Festivities in the Renaissance. Essays in Honour of J. R. Mulryne*, ed. by M. Shewring (Aldershot: Ashgate, 2013), pp. 79–97.

Korsch, E., 'Die Stanzen von Celio Magno zur Dogenkrönung Alvise Mocenigos (1570) im Kontext venezianischer Repräsentationsstrategien', in *Musik und Vergnügen am Hohen Ufer*, ed. by S. Meine, N. K. Strohmann, and T. C. Weißmann (Regensburg: Schnell & Steiner, 2015), pp. 155–64.

Korsch, E., '"Le ceremonie per occasion di venute de Prencipi". Das Empfangszeremoniell der Serenissima im Kontext der Zeremonialbücher (1450–1600)', in *Prinzen auf Reisen. Die Italienreise von Kurprinz Karl Albrecht 1715/16 im politisch-kulturellen Kontext*, ed. by A. Zedler and J. Zedler (Köln: Böhlau, 2017), pp. 139–60.

Koselleck, R., Gschnitzer, F., Werner, K. F., and Schönemann, K., 'Volk, Nation, Nationalismus, Masse', in *Geschichtliche Grundbegriffe. Historisches Lexikon zur politisch-sozialen Sprache in Deutschland*, ed. by R. Koselleck, W. Conze, and O. Brunner, 6 (Stuttgart: Klett-Cotta, 1992), pp. 141–431.

Koselleck, R., *Future Past. On the Semantics of Historical Time*, trans. and with an introduction by K. Tribe (New York: Columbia University Press, 2004).

Köster, G., '24 luglio 1177: la Pace di Venezia e la guerra delle interpretazioni', in *Venezia: i giorni della storia*, ed. by U. Israel (Roma: Viella, 2011), pp. 47–90.

Kretschmayr, H., *Geschichte von Venedig*, 3 vols (Stuttgart, 1934; repr. Aalen: Scientia, 1964).

Kruft, H.W., 'L'idea della Piazza rinascimentale secondo i trattati e le fonti visive', *Annali di Architettura*, 4–5 (1992/1993), pp. 215–29.

Kümin, B., ed., *Political Space in Pre-industrial Europe* (Farnham: Ashgate, 2009).

Kurtzman, J. G., 'Civic Identity and Civic Glue: Venetian Processions and Ceremonies of the Sixteenth and Seventeenth Centuries', in *Yale Journal of Music & Religion*, 2, No. 2 (2016), pp. 49–76.

L'ordre tenu a l'arrivée du treschrestien Roy de France et de Pologne, Henry de Valois troisiéme de ce nom faicte à Lyon (Lyon: B. Rigaud, 1574).

La description de la superbe et imaginaire entree faicte à la Royne Gijllette passant à Venise, en faveur du Roy de la Malachie son futur espoux, le premier jour de Septembre 1582 (Paris: à l'Olivier rue S. Jacques, 1582).

La sontuosa regatta grande fatta nella Regina del Mare Veretia li 25 giugno 1686 (Venezia: Batti, 1686).

La venuta della Serenissima Bona Sforza et d'Aragona Reina di Polonia et Duchessa di Bari nella Magnifica Città di Padova a ventisette di marzo, con l'entrata nella inclita città di Vinegia il dì 26 aprile 1556 et la sua partita per Bari (Venezia, 1556).

Le allegrezze et solennità fatte in Cracovia città principale del regno de Polonia, nella Coronatione del Serenissimo Re Enrico di Valois fratello di Carlo IX. Christianissimo Re di Francia (s. l., 1574).

LaCapra, D., *Rethinking Intellectual History. Texts, Contexts, Language* (Ithaca: Cornell University Press, 1983).

Lamberti, A. M., *Memorie degli ultimi cinquant'anni della Repubblica di Venezia*, ed. by M. Pastore Stocchi and M. Zorzi (Venezia: Istituto Veneto di Scienze, Lettere ed Arti, 2019).

Lanaro Sartori, P., *Un'oligarchia urbana nel Cinquecento veneto. Istituzioni, economia, società* (Torino: G. Giappichelli editore, 1992).

Lane, F. C., *Venice, a Maritime Republic* (Baltimore: The Johns Hopkins University Press, 1973).

Lanza, E., 'Karneval und kulturelle Vernetzung. Die Reisen Herzog Anton Ulrichs nach Venedig', *"...einer der Grossten Monarchen Europas..."?! Neue Forschungen zu Herzog Anton Ulrich*, herausgegeben von Jochen Luckhardt (Petersberg: Michael Imhof, 2014), pp. 118–49.

Lanza, E., '"I principi di Brunsvich capitarono qui…". The Venetian journeys of the Guelph family in the 17th century', in *Musik und Vergnügen am Hohen Ufer. Fest- und Kulturtransfer zwischen Hannover und Venedig in der Frühen Neuzeit*, ed. by Herausgegeben von Sabine Meine, N. K. Strohmann and T. C. Weißmann (Regensburg: Schnell und Steiner, 2016), pp. 165–72.

Laus Venetorum a miraculo per dialogum [Venezia: 1509].

Lavarda, S., *Vicenza nel Seicento. Uomini, poteri, istituzioni* (Verona: Cierre, 2019).

Leggi e memorie venete sulla prostituzione fino alla caduta della Repubblica (Venezia: Marco Visentini, 1870–1872).

Les feux de joye faicts a Paris pour l'arrivee du Roy en France, avec l'Ordre tenu à son entree et reception en la ville de Lyon (Paris: Denis du Pré, 1574).

Leti, G., 'Dialogo quarto. Nel quale si discorre s'è bene che i prencipi e republiche permettino ad ogni uno la libertà di parlare di cose di politica e di materie di stato', in *Dialoghi politici o vero la Politica che usano in questi tempi, i prencipi e Republiche italiane per conservare i loro Stati e Signorie*, 1 (Roma: Moneta [but Pietro Chouet, Geneva] 1666), pp. 241–66.

Lettera scritta ad un cavalliere in Milano da un suo confidente nella quale li dà ragguaglio del pomposo ingresso dell'illustriss. et eccellentiss. sign. Francesco Morosini cavallier procurator, e già due volte capitan general da Mar (Venezia: s.e., 1670).

Levi, G., 'I tempi della storia', in *The Historical Review/La revue historique*, 7 (2009), pp. 42–51.

Levin, M. J., 'Diego Guzmán de Silva and Sixteenth-century Venice: A Case Study in Structural Intelligence Failure', in *The Dangerous Trade: Spies, Spymasters and the Making of Europe*, ed. by D. Szechi (Edinburgh: Edinburgh University Press, 2010), pp. 22–44.

Limojon de Saint-Didier, A.T., *The City and Republick of Venice* (London: Printed for Henry Brome, at the Gun at the West End of St Paul's Church-Yard, 1699).

Lipowsky, F. J., *Baierisches Kuenstler-Lexikon*, 2 (München: Fleischmann, 1810).

Logan, O., *Culture and Society in Venice 1470–1790: The Renaissance and Its Heritage* (London: Batsford, 1972).

Lorenzetti, G. and others, *Venezia e il suo estuario: guida storico artistica* (Padova: Erredici, 2002).

Lorenzi, G., *Monumenti per servire alla storia del Palazzo Ducale di Venezia. Parte I dal 1523 al 1600* (Venezia: Tipografia del Commercio di Marco Visentini, 1868).

Luckhardt, J., *Malerei und Divertissement: Reisen Herzog Anton Ulrichs und seiner Familie nach Venedig* (Braunschweig: Herzog Anton Ulrich-Museum 2002).

Luhmann, N., *Stato di diritto e sistema sociale* (Napoli: Guida Editori, 1990).

Luzio, A., and Renier, R., *Delle relazioni di Isabella d'Este Gonzaga con Ludovico e Beatrice Sforza* (Milano: Tipografia Bortolotto di Giuseppe Prato, 1890).

Machiavelli, N., *Discorsi sopra la prima deca di Tito Livio (seguiti dalle «Considerazioni intorno ai Discorsi del Machiavelli di Francesco Guicciardini»)*, ed. by C. Vivanti (Torino: Einaudi, 1983).

Madonna, M., 'L'ingresso di Carlo V a Roma', in *La festa a Roma dal Rinascimento al 1870*, ed. by M. Fagiolo, 2 vols (Torino: Allemandi, 1997), 1, pp. 50–65.

Magnabosco, M., ed., *L'Accademia Filarmonica di Verona dalla fondazione al Teatro. Tre saggi* (Verona: Accademia Filarmonica di Verona, 2015).

Magno, C., *Trionfo di Christo per la vittoria contra Turchi rappresentato al Sereniss. Prencipe di Venetia il dì di San Stefano* (Venezia: appresso Domenico, & Gio. Battista Guerra, fratelli, 1571).

Magno, C., 'Stanze recitate nel convito fatto dopo la creatione del Sereniss. Luigi Mozanigo Principe di Vinegia', in *Primo volume della scielta di stanze di diversi autori toscani, et di nuovo con ogni diligenza ricorrette*, ed by A. Ferentelli (Venezia: [Heredi di Marchiò Sessa], 1579), pp. 545–49.

Malipiero, D. and Dolfin, P., 'Annali veneti dall'anno 1457 al 1500', in *Archivio Storico Italiano*, 7 (1843), pp. 5–720.

Malmignatti, B., *Orazione per la Creazione del Doge Veniero* (Venezia: Griffio, 1554).

Mamczarz, I., '"La gloria d'amore" d'Aurelio Aureli et les naumachies aux XVIe et XVIIe siècles', in *Problèmes, interférences des genres du théâtre et des fêtes en Europe*, ed. by I. Mamczarz (Paris: Presses Universitaires de France, 1985), pp. 191–201.

Mancini, V., 'Sotto specie di laude: immagini celebrative di magistrati in Terraferma', in *Il buono e il cattivo governo: rappresentazioni nelle arti dal Medioevo al Novecento*, ed. by G. Pavanello (Venezia: Marsilio, 2004).

Mancini, V., Guerriero, S., and Casini, M., eds, *La 'splendida' Venezia di Francesco Morosini (1619–1694): cerimoniali, arti, cultura* (Venezia: Marsilio, 2022).

Mandelli, V., ed., *La copella politica: esame istorico-politico di cento soggetti della Repubblica di Venezia (1675)* (Roma: Viella, 2012).

Mannori, L., *Il sovrano tutore: pluralismo istituzionale e accentramento amministrativo nel principato dei Medici (secc. XVI–XVIII)* (Milano: Giuffrè 1994).

Manueli, V., *Orazione all'Illustrissimo Signor Nicolò Cornaro, Capitano di Verona nella sua partenza per nome della medesima città tenuta il 20 agosto 1605, in Per le faustissime e nobili nozze Bianchini-Dubois,* (Venezia: Naratovich, 1863).

Manuzio, A., *Il perfetto gentil'huomo* (Venezia: s.n.t., 1584).

Maranini, G., *La Costituzione di Venezia dopo la Serrata del Maggior Consiglio* (Firenze: La Nuova Italia, 1931).

Marconi, S., 'Giannotti, Donato', *Dizionario Biografico degli Italiani*, 54 (Roma: Istituto della Enciclopedia Treccani, 2000).

Marcus, L. S., Mueller, J., and Rose, M. B., eds, *Elizabeth I: Collected Works* (Chicago and London: The University of Chicago Press, 2000).

Mariani, M., *Il trionfo di Nettuno* (Venezia, 1686).

Mariani, M., *L'ingresso trionfale dell'illustr. et eccell. signor Leonardo Donato procurator meritissimo di S. Marco* (Venezia: Per Pietro d'Orlandi, 1686).

Martin, J., and Romano D., eds, *Venice Reconsidered: The History and Civilization of an Italian City-State, 1297–1797* (Baltimore and London: The John Hopkins University Press, 2000).

Martínez Aznal, R., 'El agente navarro en la Corte. Nuevas perspectivas sobre el estudio de la "diplomatie vom type ancien" en la Monarquía Hispánica', in *Nuevas perspectivas de investigación en Historia Moderna: economía, sociedad, política y cultura en el mundo hispánico*, ed. by María Ángeles Pérez Samper and José Luis Betrán Moya (Madrid: Fundación Española de Historia Moderna, 2018), pp. 886–97.

Marx, B., 'Venedig – "altera Roma" – Transformationen eines Mythos', in *Quellen und Forschungen aus italienischen Archiven und Bibliotheken*, 60 (1980), pp. 325–73.

Marzullo, G., 'La raccolta di lettere di Ottavio Rossi', in *'Testimoni dell'ingegno'. Reti epistolari e libri di lettere nel Cinquecento e nel Seicento*, ed. by Clizia Carminati (Sarnico: Edizioni di Archilet, 2019), pp. 325–56.

Masenetti, G. M., *Oratione fatta nella creatione al principato del serenissimo Francesco Veniero principe di Vineggia* (Padova: Gratioso Perchacino, 1554).

Matarrese, O., 'I Maganza per il Palazzo del Podestà di Vicenza e un'ipotesi per il Palazzo Pretorio di Verona', in *Verona Illustrata. Rivista del Museo di Castelvecchio* (1998), pp. 21–29.

Matthieu, P., *L'entrée de tresgrand, tres-chrestien, tres-magnanime, et victorieux prince. Henry IIII. roy de France & de Navarre, en sa bonne ville de Lyon, le IIII. septembre l'an M. D. XCV* (Lyon: de l'imprimerie de Pierre Michel, 1595).

Mauro, I., Flores, M. L., 'Una ceremonia coral: las entradas virreinales en Nápoles', in *Pedralbes: revista d'història moderna*, 34 (2014), pp. 101–31.

Mauro, I., 'La rete diplomatica delle capitali senza re. Il sistema di "delegazioni interne" della monarchia spagnola', in *Capitali senza re nella monarchia spagnola. Realtà, relazioni, immagini (sec. XVI–XVIII)*, ed. by R. Cancila (Palermo: Mediterranea, 2020), pp. 471–94.

Mazzarotto, T., *Le feste veneziane: i giochi popolari, le cerimonie religiose e di governo* (Firenze: Sansoni, 1980).

McGowan, M. M., 'Lyon: a centre for Water celebrations', in *Waterborne Pageants and Festivities in the Renaissance: Essays in in Honour of J.R. Mulryne*, ed. by M. Shewring (Farnham: Ashgate Pub., 2013), pp. 37–49.

McGowan, M. M., 'Festivals and the Arts in Henri III's Journey from Poland to France (1574)', in *Europa Triumphans*, ed by J. R. Mulryne, H. Watanabe-O'Kelly, and M. Shewring (London: MHRA; Aldershot: Ashgate, 2004), pp. 122–29.

McLuhan, M., Fiore, Q., *The Medium is the Massage: An Inventory of Effects* (New York: Bantam Books, 1967).

Melchiorre, M., 'Sanudo, Marin il Giovane', *Dizionario Biografico degli Italiani*, 90 (Roma: Istituto della Enciclopedia Treccani, 2017).

Melchiorre, M., *I patti con Padova (1405–1406). Dalla guerra alla Bolla d'oro* (Roma: Viella, 2012).

Melchiorre, M., *Conoscere per governare. Le relazioni dei Sindici inquisitori e il dominio veneziano in Terraferma (1543–1626)* (Udine: Forum, 2013).

Memmo, G. M., *Dialogo […] nel quale dopo alcune filosofiche dispute, si forma un perfetto Prencipe, et una perfetta Republica, e parimente un Senatore, un Cittadino, un Soldato, et un Mercatante* (Venezia: Gabriele Giolito de' Ferrari, 1564).

Messedaglia, L., *La dedizione di Verona a Venezia e una bolla d'oro di Michele Steno* (Venezia: off. graf. Carlo Ferrari, 1936).

Metlica, A., *Le seduzioni della pace. Giovan Battista Marino, le feste di corte e la Francia barocca* (Bologna: il Mulino, 2020).

Metlica, A., 'La macchina mitologica della venezianità. Retorica barocca e imperialismo fascista', in *SigMa. Rivista Di Letterature Comparate, Teatro E Arti Dello Spettacolo*, 5 (2021), pp. 343–70.

Metlica, A., 'La "gioiosa entrata" di Francesco Morosini. La festa veneziana in tipografia', in *La 'splendida' Venezia di Francesco Morosini (1619–1694): cerimoniali, arti, cultura*, ed. by M. Casini, S. Guerriero, and V. Mancini (Venezia: Fondazione Cini, 2022), pp. 159–67.

Metlica, A., *Lessico della propaganda barocca* (Venezia: Marsilio, 2022).

Metlica, A., 'Magnificence and Atticism in Seventeenth-Century Venice', in *Magnificence in the Seventeenth Century. Performing Splendour in Catholic and Protestant Contexts*, ed. by G. Versteegen, S. Bussels, and W. Melion (Leiden: Brill, 2022), pp. 261–75.

Metlica, A., 'Reshaping the Republican Ritual: The Entry of the Procurators of St Mark in Early Modern Venice', in *Discourses of Decline: Essays on Republicanism in Honor of Wyger R.E. Velema*, ed. by J. Oddens, M. Rutjes, and A. Weststeijn (Leiden: Brill, 2022d), pp. 168–81.

Michiel, A., *Delle orationi di Agostino Michele* (Venezia: Giovanni Battista Bonfadini, 1590).

Milanesi, M., *Vincenzo Coronelli Cosmographer (1650–1718)* (Turnhout: Brepols, 2016).

Miller, D. A., 'The Emperor and the Ritual. Magic and Harmony', in *Byzantine Studies Études Byzantines*, 6 (1979), pp. 117–28.

Milner, S., 'Citing the Ringhiera: The Politics of Place and Public Address in Trecento Florence', in *Italian Studies*, 55 (2000), pp. 53–82.

Milner, S., 'The Florentine Piazza della Signoria as Practiced Place', in *Renaissance Florence. A Social History*, ed. by Roger J. Crum and J. T. Paoletti (Cambridge: Cambridge University Press, 2006), pp. 83–103.

Mineo, I. E., 'La repubblica come categoria storica', in *Storica*, 43–45 (2009), pp. 125–66.

Mineo, I. E., *Popolo e bene comune in Italia fra XII e XIV secolo* (Roma: Viella 2018).

Minuzzi, S., *Il Secolo di carta. Antonio Bosio artigiano di testi e immagini nella Venezia del Seicento* (Milano: Franco Angeli, 2009).

Molho A., and Sznura, F., eds, *Alle bocche della piazza. Diario di anonimo fiorentino (1382–1401)*, (Firenze: Olschki, 1986).

Molmenti, P., *La dogaressa di Venezia* (Torino; Napoli: L. Roux, 1887).

Molmenti, P., 'Venezia alla metà del secolo XVII. Relazione inedita di monsignor Francesco Pannocchieschi', in *Rendiconti della Reale Accademia dei Lincei. Classe di Scienze morali, storiche e filologiche*, 25 (1916), pp. 187–242.

Morari, G., *Prattica de' reggimenti in Terraferma* (Padova: Giuseppe Corona, 1708).

Morosini, P., 'De rebus ac forma reipublicae venetae', in *Bibliotheca manuscripta ad S. Marci Venetiarum, codices Mss Latini*, ed. by G. Valentinelli, 3 (Venezia: Ex Typographia Commercii, 1870), pp. 231–64.

Morresi, M., *Piazza San Marco. Istituzioni, poteri e architettura a Venezia nel primo Cinquecento* (Milano: Electa, 1999).

Morresi, M., *Jacopo Sansovino* (Milano: Electa, 2000).

Moryson, F., *An Itinerary written by Fynes Moryson, gent. First in the Latine Tongue, and then Translated by Him into English. At London. Printed by John Beale, dwelling in Aldersgate Street 1617* (London: John Beale, 1617).

Moucheront, N., 'A Booklet of Documents Concerning the Reconstruction of the Church of San Giacomo di Rialto Around 1600', in G. Guidarelli, M. Pilutti Namer, and M. Agazzi, *Layers of Venice. Architecture, Arts and Antiquities at Rialto* (Venezia: Università Ca' Foscari, 2023), pp. 111–28.

Mueller, R. C., 'The Procurators of San Marco in the 13th and 14th Centuries: A Study of the Office as a Financial and Trust Institution', in *Studi Veneziani*, 13 (1971) pp. 105–220.

Muhle, M., 'Reenactments du pouvoir. Remarques sur une historiographie médiale', in *Rue Descartes*, 77 (2013), pp. 82–93.

Muir, E., 'The Doge as Primus inter pares: Interregnum Rites in Early Sixteenth-Century Venice', in *Essays Presented to Myron P. Gilmore*, ed. by S. Bertelli and G. Ramakus, 2 vols (Firenze: La Nuova Italia, 1978), I, pp. 145–60.

Muir, E., 'Images of Power: Art and Pageantry in Renaissance Venice', in *The American Historical Review*, 84 (1979), pp. 16–52.

Muir, E., *Civic Ritual in Renaissance Venice* (Princeton, NJ: Princeton University Press, 1981).

Muir, E., *Ritual in Early Modern Europe* (Cambridge: Cambridge University Press, 2005).

Mulryne, J. R., Aliverti, M. I., and Testaverde, A. M., eds, *Ceremonial Entries in Early Modern Europe. The Iconography of Power*, (Burlington: Ashgate, 2015).

Mulryne, J. R., 'Ceremony and the Iconography of Power', in *Ceremonial Entries in Early Modern Europe: The Iconography of Power*, ed. by J. R. Mulryne, M. Ines Aliverti, and A.-M. Testaverde (Farnham: Ashgate, 2015), pp. 1–13.

Mulryne, J. R., De Jonge, K., Morris, R. L. M., and P. Martens, eds, *Occasions of State. Early Modern European Festivals and the Negotiation of Power* (London-New York: Routledge, 2019).

Murphy, N. *Ceremonial Entries, Municipal Liberties and the Negotiation of Power in Valois France, 1328–1589* (Leiden-Boston: Brill, 2016).

Musatti, E., *Storia della promissione ducale* (Padova: tip. del seminario, 1888).

Mutini, C., 'Aureli, Aurelio', *Dizionario Biografico degli Italiani*, 4 (Roma: Istituto della Enciclopedia Treccani, 1962).

Nanetti, A., ed., *Il Codice Morosini. Il mondo visto da Venezia (1094–1433)* (Spoleto: Fondazione Cisam, 2010).

Nefedova, O., *A Journey into the World of the Ottomans: The Art of Jean-Baptiste Vanmour (1671–1737)* (Milano: Skira, 2009).

Nevola, F., *Street Life in Renaissance Italy* (New Haven: Yale University Press, 2020).

Newton, S. M., *The Dress of the Venetians, 1495–1525* (Aldershot: Scolar Press, 1988).

Niccoli, O., *Il seme della violenza. Putti, fanciulli e mammoli nell'Italia tra Cinque e Seicento* (Roma-Bari: Laterza, 1995).

Nicolicchia, M. A., 'Lettera di ragguaglio sopra [...] la solenne entrata di procuratore di S. Marco fatta li 18 gennajo del 1707 dall'illustriss. ed eccellentiss. signor cavallier Carlo Ruzzini', in *La Galleria di Minerva*, 5 (1707), pp. 237–38.

Nolhac, P. de, and Solerti, A., *Il viaggio in Italia di Enrico III re di Francia e le feste a Venezia, Ferrara, Mantova e Torino* (Torino: L. Roux, 1890).

Notari, G., *Descrittione delle feste eseguite con reale magnificenza nella città di Parma, il mese di maggio 1690* (Parma: Galeazzo Rosati, 1690).

Nussdorfer, L., 'The Political Space in Early Modern Rome', in *Memoirs of American Academy in Rome*, 42 (1997), pp. 161–82.

Nuti, L., 'Alle origini del Grand Tour: Immagini e cultura della città italiana negli atlanti e cosmografie del secolo XVI', in *Storia Urbana*, 27 (1984), pp. 3–54.

O'Connell, M., *Men of Empire. Power and Negotiation in Venice's Maritime State* (Baltimore: The Johns Hopkins University Press, 2009).

O'Connell, M., *The Multiple Meanings of Ritual: Orations and the Tensions of Venetian Empire*, in *Rituals of Politics and Culture in Early Modern Europe. Essays in Honour of Edward Muir*, ed. by M. Jurdjevic and R. Strøm-Olsen (Toronto: Centre for Reformation and Renaissance Studies, 2016), pp. 91–110.

O'Connell, M., 'Voluntary Submission and the Ideology of Venetian Empire', in *I Tatti Studies in the Italian Renaissance*, 20 (2017), pp. 9–39.

O'Connell, M., 'Venetian Empire in Oratory and Print in the Later Fifteenth Century', in *Cultures of Empire: Rethinking Venetian Rule 1400–1700. Essays in Honour of Benjamin Arbel*, ed. by G. Christ and F. J. Morche (Brill: Leiden-Boston, 2020), pp. 41–62.

Olivato, L., 'Politica e retorica figurativa nella Venezia del Settecento. Alla riscoperta di un pittore singolare: Felice Boscarati', in *Arte Veneta*, 31 (1977), pp. 145–56.

Ord, M., 'Textual Experience in Thomas Coryat's Crudities (1611)', in *Travel and Experience in Early Modern English Literature* (Palgrave Macmillan US, 2008), pp. 123–54.

Ortalli, G., *Gioco e giustizia nell'Italia di comune* (Treviso-Roma: FBSR-Viella, 1993).

Ortalli, G., 'Entrar nel Dominio: le dedizioni delle città alla Repubblica Serenissima', in *Società, economia, istituzioni. Elementi per la conoscenza della Repubblica Veneta, I, Istituzioni ed economia* (Caselle di Sommacampagna: Cierre, 2002), pp. 49–62.

Ortalli, G., 'Nascere sull'acqua. La lunga genesi di Venezia', in *L'acqua nei secoli altomedievali* (CISEM, Spoleto, 2008), pp. 141-82.

Ortalli, G., Schmitt, O. J., and Orlando, E., eds, *Il Commonwealth veneziano tra 1204 e la fine della Repubblica. Identità e peculiarità* (Venezia: Istituto veneto di Scienze, Lettere ed Arti, 2015).

Ortalli, G., Gullino, G., and Ivetic, E., eds, *L'inestinguibile sogno del dominio. Francesco Morosini* (Venezia: Istituto veneto di scienze, lettere ed arti, 2021).

Ortalli, G., *Venezia inventata. Realtà e leggenda della Serenissima* (Bologna: Il Mulino 2021).

Österberg, E., *Friendship and Love, Ethics and politics. Studies in Medieval and Early Modern history* (Budapest - New York: Central European University Press, 2010).

Pacifici, V., *Ippolito II d'Este cardinale di Ferrara: da documenti originali inediti* (Tivoli: Tip. Ripoli, 1984).

Palmer, K. N., *Ceremonial barges on the river Thames: a history of the barges of the City of London livery companies and of the crown* (London: Unicorn Press, 1997).

Palmer, P. S., '"The Progress of Thy Glorious Book": Material Reading and the Play of Paratext in "Coryats Crudities" (1611)', in *Renaissance Studies*, 28 (2014), 3, pp. 336–55.

Palonen, K., *Quentin Skinner: History, Politics, Rhetoric* (Cambridge: Polity Press, 1999).

Panciera, W., *La Repubblica di Venezia nel Settecento* (Roma: Viella, 2014).

Pannocchieschi D'Elci, F., 'Relazione sulle cose di Venezia', in *Curiosità di storia veneziana*, ed. by Pompeo Molmenti (Bologna: Zanichelli, 1919), pp. 310–358.

Parr, A., 'Thomas Coryat and the Discovery of Europe', *Huntington Library Quarterly*, 55 (1992), 4, pp. 579–602.

Paruta, P., *Della perfettione della vita politica* (Venezia: Domenico Nicolini da Sabbio, 1579).

Paruta, P., *Discorsi politici ne i quali si considerano diversi fatti illustri, e memorabili di principi, e di republiche antiche, e moderne* (Venezia: Domenico Nicolini, 1599).

Paruta, P., *Opere politiche*, ed. by Cirillo Monzani, 2 vols (Firenze: Felice Le Monnier, 1852).

Paschini, P., *Il cardinale Marino Grimani e la sua famiglia* (Roma: Facultas Theologica Pontificiae Universitatis Lateranensis, 1960).

Pasero, C., 'Giacomo Franco, Editore, Incisore e Calcografo Nei Secoli XVI e XVII', in *La Bibliofilía*, 37, no. 8/10 (1935), pp. 332–56.

Patrizi, F., *Della historia diece dialoghi di M. Francesco Patritio. Ne' quali si ragiona di tutte le cose appartenenti all'historia, et allo scriverla, et all'osservarla* (Venezia: Andrea Arrivabene, 1560).

Paul, B., ed., *Celebrazione e autocritica. La Serenissima e la ricerca dell'identità veneziana nel tardo Cinquecento* (Roma: Viella, 2014).

Pecchioli, R., *Dal 'mito' di Venezia all'"ideologia americana": itinerari e modelli della storiografia sul repubblicanesimo dell'età moderna* (Venezia: Marsilio, 1983).

Peretti, G., Artoni, P., Marini, P., and Napione, E., eds, *Museo di Castelvecchio. Catalogo generale dei dipinti e delle miniature delle collezioni civiche veronesi*, 3 vols (Cinisello Balsamo: Silvana, 2018).

Perocco, D., 'Introduzione', in *Poesie per le regate: testi veneti dal XVI al XIX secolo*, ed. by D. Perocco (Venezia: Marsilio 2006), pp. 7–31.

Petrarca, F., *Letters of Old Age: Books I–IX* (Baltimore and London: John Hopkins University Press, 1992).

Pezzolo, L., 'Fra potere politico e controllo dell'ordine: il capitan grande del Consiglio dei Dieci', in *Le polizie informali*, ed. by L. Antonielli (Soveria Mannelli: Rubbettino, 2010), pp. 91–100.

Pickering, H., and Rice, T., 'Noise as "sound out of place": investigating the links between Mary Douglas' work on dirt and sound studies research', in *Journal of Sonic Studies*, 14 (2017). URL: https://www.researchcatalogue.net/view/374514/374526/0/0 [2022/03/16].

Pin, C., 'Progetti e abbozzi sarpiani sul governo dello Stato "in questi tempi assai turbolenti"', in P. Sarpi, *Della potestà de' prencipi*, ed. by N. Cannizzaro (Venezia: Marsilio, 2006), pp. 89–120.

Pocock, J. G. A., *The Machiavellian Moment: Florentine Political Thought and the Atlantic Republican Tradition* (Princeton, NJ: Princeton University Press, 1975).

Poirier, G., 'Le retour de Pologne d'Henri III: images alexandrines du roi au Bucentaure', in *Renaissance and Reformation / Renaissance et Réforme*, New Series / Nouvelle Série, XXI, no. 4 (1997), pp. 42–55.

Poirier, G., *Henri III de France en mascarades imaginaires: mœurs, humeurs et comportements d'un roi de la Renaissance* (Paris: Presses de l'Université Laval, 2011).

Poirier, G., 'La description de la superbe et imaginaire entrée faicte à la Reyne Gijllette passant à Venise', in *Les Arts du spectacle dans la ville (1404–1721)*, ed. by M.F. Wagner and C. Le Brun-Gouanvic (Paris: H. Champion, 2001), pp. 159–83.

Pola, F., *Oratione all'Illustrissimo Sig. Giovanni Cornaro, Capitano di Verona* (Verona: Girolamo Discepolo, 1596).

Pola, F., *Elogium Augustini Delbenii et alia de eodem scripta* (Verona: typis Tamianis, 1614).

Pola, F. *Lo Stolone ovvero fella sala pretoria veronese dall'Illustrissimo Sig. Agostino Amulio Podestà restaurata* (Verona: Bortolamio Merlo, 1615).

Poliziano, A., *Opera* (Venezia: Aldo I Manuzio, 1498).

Polybios, *The Histories*, ed. by H. J. Edwards (Harvard: Harvard University Press, 1922–27).

Pontremoli, A., and La Rocca, P., *La danza a Venezia nel Rinascimento* (Vicenza: Neri Pozza, 1993).

Porcacchi, T., *Le attioni d'Arrigo terzo Re di Francia, et quarto di Polonia* (Venezia: appresso Giorgio Angeleri, 1574).

Povoledo, E., Mauro, in *Enciclopedia dello Spettacolo*, 7 (Roma: Casa Editrice Le Maschere, 1960), pp. 310–11.

Povolo, C., 'Corner, Giovanni', *Dizionario Biografico degli Italiani*, 29 (Roma: Istituto della Enciclopedia Treccani, 1983).

Povolo, C., 'Crasso, Nicolò', *Dizionario Biografico Degli Italiani*, 30 (Roma: Istituto della Enciclopedia Treccani, 1984).

Povolo, C., 'Centro e periferia nella Repubblica di Venezia. Un profilo', in *Origini dello Stato. Processi di formazione statale in Italia fra Medioevo ed età moderna*, ed. by G. Chittolini, P. Schiera, and A. Molho (Bologna: Il Mulino, 1994), pp. 207–21.

Povolo, C., *L'intrigo dell'onore. Poteri e istituzioni nella Repubblica di Venezia tra Cinque e Seicento* (Verona: Cierre edizioni, 1997).

Povolo, C., 'Il processo a Ottavio Trento, cartina di tornasole dei conflitti sociali (Lo stato delle cose)', in *Storia economica e sociale di Bergamo. Il tempo della Serenissima. Settecento, età del cambiamento*, ed. by A. De Maddalena, M. Cattini, and M. A. Romani (Bergamo: Fondazione per la storia economica e sociale di Bergamo, 2006), pp. 249–95.

Povolo, C., 'Un rapporto difficile e controverso: Paolo Sarpi e il diritto veneto', in *Ripensando Paolo Sarpi*, ed. by C. Pin (Veneziae: Ateneo Veneto, 2006), pp. 395–416.

Povolo, C., 'Un sistema giuridico repubblicano: Venezia e il suo stato territoriale (secoli XV–XVIII)', in *Il diritto patrio tra diritto comune e codificazione (secoli XVI–XIX)*, ed. by I. Birocchi and A. Mattone (Roma: Viella, 2006c), pp. 297–353.

Povolo, C., 'Uno sguardo rivolto alla religiosità popolare: l'inchiesta promossa dal Senato veneziano sulle festività religiose (1772–1773)', in *Il culto dei santi e le feste popolari nella Terraferma Veneta: l'inchiesta del Senato veneziano, 1772–1773*, ed. by S. Marin (Costabissara: A. Colla, 2007).

Povolo, C., 'Ambigue descrizioni: feste devozionali e feste di precetto nell'inchiesta veneziana di fine Settecento', in VJESNIK ISTARSKOG ARHIVA, 20 (2013), pp. 157–207.

Povolo, C., 'Il protettore amorevole. Magnifica Patria della Riviera del Garda 1570–1630', in *Sul lago di Garda tra passato e futuro. Lingua, storia, letteratura*, ed. by Ateneo di Salò, 2 (Brescia: Liberedizioni, 2020), pp. 87–124.

Pozza, M., 'Zeno, Ranieri', *Dizionario Biografico degli Italiani*, 100 (Roma: Istituto della Enciclopedia Treccani, 2020)

Prak, M. R., *Citizens without Nations. Urban Citizenship in Europe and in the World* (Cambridge: Cambridge University Press 2018).

Preto, P., *Persona per hora secreta. Accusa e delazione nella Repubblica di Venezia* (Milano: Il Saggiatore, 2003).

Priuli, G., *I Diarii [AA. 1499–1512]*, ed. by Roberto Cessi, 3 vols (Bologna: Zanichelli, 1940).

Promissio serenissimi Venetiarum ducis, serenissimo Silvestro Valerio duce edita [Venezia: Pinelli], 1694.

Prosperi, A., *Tra evangelismo e Controriforma. G.M. Giberti (1495–1543)* (Roma: Edizioni di storia e letteratura, 1969).

Puppi, L., *Andrea Palladio*, 2 vols (Milano: Electa, 1973).

Puppi, L., *Palladio. Corpus dei disegni al Museo Civico di Vicenza* (Milano: Skira, 1989).

Quaglioni, D., '"Quando supervenit iustus dominus". Cambi di regime e nascita del linguaggio della politica (tra Bartolo e Machiavelli)', in *Dal Leone all'Aquila. Comunità, territori e cambi di regime nell'età di Massimiliano I, Atti dei Convegno Rovereto 14–15, maggio 2010*, ed. by S. Bonazza and S. Seidel Menchi (2010), pp. 11–26.

Quaranta, E., *Oltre San Marco. Organizzazione e prassi della musica nelle chiese di Venezia nel Rinascimento* (Firenze: Olschki, 1998).

Quondam, A., *Tutti i colori del nero: moda e cultura del gentiluomo nel Rinascimento* (Costabissara: Angelo Colla Editore, 2007).

Raines, D., *L'invention du mythe aristocratique. L'image de soi du patriciat vénitien au temps de la Sérénissime*, 1 (Venezia: Istituto Veneto di Scienze Lettere ed Arti, 2006).

Rau, S., *History, Space, and Place* (London: Routledge, 2019).

Ravegnani, G., *Il doge di Venezia* (Bologna: Il Mulino, 2013).

Ravegnani, G., *Venezia prima di Venezia. Mito e fondazione della città lagunare* (Roma: Salerno Editrice, 2020).

Redford, B., *Venice & the Grand Tour* (New Haven: Yale University Press, 1996).

Renier Michiel, G., *Origine delle feste veneziane*, 6 vols (Venezia: Tipografia Alvisopoli di Gaetano Longo, 1852).

Reolon, G., 'La "Dedizione del Cadore a Venezia" di Cesare Vecellio. Per una lettura iconografica e contestuale', in *Venezia in Cadore 1420–2020*, ed. by M. Da Deppo (Vicenza: Antiga Edizioni, 2020), pp. 59–73.

Revest, C., 'Ciceronianismo e ideale repubblicano nell'età dell'espansione veneziana in Terraferma', in *Storica*, 82 (2022), pp. 17–64.

Richter, M. 'Lessico dei concetti politici e giuridici europei: opzioni e ostacoli', in *Sui concetti giuridici e politici della costituzione dell'Europa*, ed. by G. Duso and S. Chignola (Milano: Franco Angeli, 2005), pp. 15–38.

Rizzi, A., (2015), 'Dominante e dominati: strumenti giuridici nell'esperienza "statuale" veneziana', in *Il Commonwealth veneziano tra 1204 e la fine della Repubblica. Identità e peculiarità*, ed. by G. Ortalli, E. Orlando, and O. J. Schmitt (Venezia: Istituto Veneto di Scienze Lettere ed Arti, 2015), pp. 235–71.

Robertson, J., 'Rapports du poète et de l'artiste dans la preparation des cortèges du Lord Maire (Londres 1553–1640)', in *Les fêtes de la Renaissance*, ed. by J. Jaquot, 2 vols, 1 (1956), pp. 265–78.

Robey, D. and Law, J. E., 'The Venetian Myth and the *De Republica Venetia* of Pier Paolo Vergerio', in *Rinascimento*, 15 (1975), pp. 3–59.

Rosa, C., 'Alvise II Contarini e l'obelisco di Santa Marta', in *La Rivista di Bergamo*, 6 (1927), pp. 9–14.

Rosand, D., 'Venezia figurata. The Iconography of a Myth', in *Interpretazioni veneziane. Studi di storia dell'arte in onore di Michelangelo Muraro*, ed. by D. Rosand (Venezia: Arsenale editrice, 1984), pp. 177–96.

Rosand, D., *Myths of Venice: the Figuration of a State* (Chapel Hill: University of North Carolina, 2005).

Rosand, E., *Opera in Seventeenth Century Venice* (Berkeley: University of California Press, 1991).

Rose, P. L., 'Two Venetian Patrons of the Renaissance of Mathematics. Francesco Barozzi and Giacomo Contarini', in *Studi Veneziani*, 13 (1971), pp. 119–78.

Rose, P. L., 'Jacomo Contarini (1536–1595), a Venetian Patron and Collector of Mathematical Instruments and Books', in *Physis*, 18 (1976), 11, pp. 117–30.

Rose, P. L., 'A Venetian Patron and Mathematician of the Sixteenth Century: Francesco Barozzi (1537–1604)', in *Studi Veneziani*, n. s. 1 (1977), pp. 119–78.

Rosenthal, M. F., 'Clothing, Fashion, Dress, and Costume in Venice (c.1450–1650)', in *A Companion to Venetian History, 1400–1797*, ed. by E. R. Dursteler (Leiden: Brill, 2013), pp. 889–928.

Rosenwein, B., 'Worrying about Emotions in History', in *American Historical Review*, 107 (2002), pp. 828–45.

Rospocher, M., and Salzberg, R., '"El vulgo zanza": spazi, pubblici, voci a Venezia durante le guerre d'Italia', in *Storica*, 48 (2010), pp. 83–120.

Rospocher, M., and Salzberg, R., 'An Evanescent Public Sphere. Voices, Spaces, and Publics in Venice during the Italian Wars', in *Beyond the Public Sphere*, (2012), pp. 93–114.

Rospocher, M., and Salzberg, R., 'Street Singers in Italian Renaissance Urban Culture and Communication', in *Cultural and social history*, 9 (2012), pp. 9–27.

Rospocher, M., 'Beyond the Public Sphere: A Historiographical Transition', in *Beyond the Public Sphere: Opinions, Publics, Spaces in Early Modern Europe (XVI–XVIII)*, ed. by M. Rospocher (Bologna: Il Mulino; Berlin: Duncker & Humblot, 2012), pp. 9–28.

Rospocher, M., ed., *Beyond the Public Sphere: Opinions, Publics, Spaces in Early Modern Europe*, (Bologna: Il Mulino; Berlin: Duncker & Humblot, 2012).

Rospocher, M., '"In Vituperium Status Veneti": The Case of Niccolò Zoppino', *The Italianist*, 34 (2014) 3, pp. 349–61.

Rospocher, M., 'Battle for the Piazza. Creative Antagonism Between Itinerant Preachers and Street Singers in Late Medieval and Early Modern Italy', in *Voices and Texts in Early Modern Italian Society*, ed. by S. Dall'Aglio, B. Richardson, and M. Rospocher (London: Routledge, 2017), pp. 212–28.

Rospocher, M., and Salzberg, R., *Il mercato dell'informazione. Notizie vere, false e sensazionali nella Venezia del Cinquecento* (Venezia: Marsilio, 2022).

Rospocher, M. and Valseriati, E., 'Politics in the street: the materiality of urban public spaces in Renaissance Italy', in *Urban History* 50/4.

Rösch, G., 'The Serrata of the Great Council and Venetian Society, 1286–1323', in *Venice Reconsidered. The History and Civilization of an Italian City-State (1297–1797)*, ed. by J. J. Martin and D. Romano (Baltimore: The Johns Hopkins University Press, 2000), pp. 67–88.

Rota, G., *Lettera nella quale si descrive l'ingresso nel Palazzo Ducale della Serenissima Morosina Morosini Grimani Principessa di Venetia* (Venezia: Gio. Antonio Rampazetto, 1597).

Rubenstein, N., 'Italian reactions to terraferma expansion in the fifteenth century', in *Renaissance Venice*, ed. by J. R. Hale (London: Faber and Faber, 1973), pp. 197–217.

Ruocco, G., Scuccimarra, L., eds, *Il governo del popolo*, 1, *Dall'Antico Regime alla Rivoluzione* (Roma: Viella, 2021).

Russell, N., and Visentin, H., eds, *French ceremonial entries in the Sixteenth century: event, image, text* (Toronto: Centre for reformation and Renaissance studies, 2007).

Salzberg, R., *Ephemeral City. Cheap Print and Urban Culture in Renaissance Venice* (Manchester: Manchester University Press, 2014).

Salzberg, R., 'Spaces of unrest? Policing hospitality sites in early modern Venice', in *Popular Politics in an Aristocratic Republic*, ed. by M. Van Gelder and C. Judde de Larivière (London: Routledge, 2020), pp. 105–28.

Sanchez Cano, D., '"Naumachiae" at the Buen Retiro in Madrid', in *Waterborn Pageants* (London: Routledge, 2017), pp. 313–28.

Sansovino, F., *Tutte le cose notabili e belle che sono in Venetia* (Venezia: s.e., 1556).

Sansovino, F., *Delle Orationi recitate a Principi di Venetia da gli ambasciadori di diverse città* (Venezia: Apud Franciscum Sansovinum, 1562).

Sansovino, F., *Delle orationi volgarmente scritte da molti huomini illustri de tempi nostri* (Venezia: Francesco Rampazetto, 1562).

Sansovino, F., *Dialogo di tutte le cose notabili che sono in Venetia* (Venezia: s. e., 1564).

Sansovino, F., *Venetia città nobilissima et singolare* (Venezia: Iacomo Sansovino, 1581).

Sansovino, F., *Delle cose notabili della città di Venetia*, (Venezia: Valgrisio, 1587).

Sansovino, F., *Le cose meravigliose dell'inclita città di Venetia, riformate, accomodate, e grandemente ampliate da Leonico Goldioni* (Venezia: Domenico Imberti, 1603).

Sansovino, F., *Venetia città nobilissima et singolare*, ed. by G. Stringa (Venezia: presso Altobello Salicato, 1604).

Sansovino, F., *Venetia città nobilissima et singolare*, ed. by G. Martinioni, (Venezia: Appresso Steffano Curti, 1663).

Sansovino, F., *Sansovino's Venice: A Translation of Francesco Tatti Da Sansovino's Guidebook to Venice of 1561*, ed. and trans. by V. Hart and P. Hicks (New Haven: Yale University Press, 2017).

Sanudo, M., *Cronachetta*, ed. by R. Fulin (Venezia: Visentini, 1880).

Sanudo, M., *I diarii*, ed. by R. Fulin and others, 58 vols (Venezia: Visentini, 1879–1903; repr. Bologna: Forni, 1969–70).

Sarpi, P., *Consulti*, ed. by C. Pin, 2 tomi (Pisa: Istituti editoriali e poligrafici internazionali, 2001).

Sarpi, P., *Della potestà de' prencipi*, ed. by Nina Cannizzaro (Venezia: Marsilio, 2006).

Savelli, A., 'Sul concetto di popolo: percorsi semantici e note storiografiche', in *Laboratoire Italien. Politique e societé*, 1, *Le peuple. Formation d'un sujet politique* (2001), pp. 9–24.

Savini Branca, S., *Il collezionismo veneziano nel '600* (Padova: CEDAM, 1964).

Scarabello, G., and Morachiello, P., *Guida alla civiltà di Venezia* (Milano: Mondadori, 1987).

Scarabello, G., *Meretrices. Storia della prostituzione a Venezia tra il xiii e il xviii secolo* (Venezia: Supernova, 2006).

Scattola, M., *Dalla virtù alla scienza. La fondazione e la trasformazione della disciplina politica nella prima età moderna* (Milano: Franco Angeli 2003).

Scattola, M., 'Storia dei concetti e storia delle discipline politiche', in *Storia della storiografia*, 49 (2006), pp. 95–124.

Scève, M., *The Entry of Henri II into Lyon: September 1548*, a facsimile with an introduction by R. Cooper (Temple: Medieval and Renaissance texts and studies, 1997).

Schiera, P., 'Considerazioni sulla Begriffsgeschichte, a partire dai Geschichtlichen Grundbegriffe di Brunner, Conze e Koselleck', in *Società e storia*, 19 (1996), 72, pp. 403–11.

Schrade, L., 'Les fêtes du mariage de Francesco dei Medici et de Bianca Cappello', *Les fêtes de la Renaissance*, ed. by J. Jacquot, 1 (1956), pp. 107–31.

Schreiner, P., and Korsch, E., 'Un imperatore bizantino tra le calli di Venezia. La visita di Giovanni VIII (1423–24) nella cronaca di Antonio Morosini e l'autocelebrazione della Serenissima', 2 parts, in *Atti dell'Istituto Veneto di Scienze, Lettere ed Arti*, 178 (2019–20), pp. 207–40.

Schulz, J., 'Printed Plans and Panoramic Views of Venice', in *Saggi e Memorie di Storia dell'Arte*, 7 (1970), pp. 17–22.

Schulz, J., 'Jacopo de' Barbari's View of Venice: Map Making, City Views, and Moralized Geography before the Year 1500', in *The Art Bulletin*, 60 (1978) 3, pp. 425–74.

Scott, J. C., 'Preface', in *Political Space in Pre-industrial Europe*, ed. by B. Kümin (Farnham: Ashgate, 2009).

Selfridge-Field, E., *Pallade veneta. Writings on Music in Venetian Society 1650–1750* (Venezia: Fondazione Levi, 1985).

Setti, C., 'L'Avogaria di Comun come magistratura media d'appello', in *Il diritto della Regione*, 1 (2009), pp. 143–71.

Setti, C., *Una Repubblica per ogni porto. Venezia e lo Stato da Mar negli itinerari dei Sindici inquisitori in Levante (secoli XVI–XVII)* (Milano: Unicopli, 2021).

Sherman, M., 'Political Propaganda and Renaissance Culture: French Reactions to the League of Cambrai, 1509–1510', in *Sixteenth Century Journal*, 8 (1977) 2, pp. 96–128.

Sigonio, C., *Historiarum de regno Italiae Libri Quindecim* (Venezia: Giordano Ziletti, 1574).

Silvano, G., *La 'Republica de' Viniziani': ricerche sul repubblicanesimo veneziano in età moderna* (Firenze: L.S. Olschki, 1993).

Sinding-Larsen, S., *Christ in the Council Hall. Studies in the Religious Iconography of the Venetian Republic* (Roma: L'Erma di Bretschneider, 1974).

Skinner, Q., *Visions of Politics*, I, *Regarding Method* (Cambridge: Cambridge University Press, 2002).

Skinner, Q., *Reason and Rhetoric in the Philosophy of Hobbes* (Cambridge: Cambridge University Press, 2010).

Skinner, Q., *Liberty Before Liberalism* (Cambridge: Cambridge University, 2012).

Smith, A., 'Ersilia Spolverini e la moglie del capitano veneziano: le donne nell'ambiente culturale e politico alla fine del Cinquecento', in *Donne a Verona. Una storia della città dal medioevo a oggi*, ed. by P. L. Sartori and A. Smith (Verona: Cierre, 2011), pp. 147–62.

Soldini, H., 'Les républiques de Donato Giannotti: une biographie d'un républicain florentin du XVIe siècle' (unpublished doctoral thesis, European University Institute, 2014).

Solerti, A., 'Le rappresentazioni musicali di Venezia dal 1571 al 1605 per la prima volta descritte', in *Rivista Musicale Italiana*, 9 (1902), pp. 503–58.

Špoljarić, L., 'Power and Subversion in the Ducal Palace: Dalmatian Patrician Humanists and Congratulatory Orations to Newly Elected Doges', in *Neo-Latin Contexts in Croatia and Tyrol: Challenges, Prospects, Case Studies*, ed. by N. Jovanović, J. Luggin, L. Špoljarić, and L. Šubarić (Wien: Böhlau, 2018), pp. 81–104.

Statuti, ordini, e parti, con altre publiche scritture, e terminationi concernenti 'l beneficio, e buon governo del territorio veronese (Verona: Bartolomio Merlo, 1613).

Statutorum magnificae civitatis Veronae libri quinque (Venezia: apud Leonardum Tivanum, 1747).

Stefani, C., 'Franco, Giacomo', *Dizionario Biografico Degli Italiani*, 50 (Roma: Istituto della Enciclopedia Treccani, 1998).

Stouraiti, A., *War, Communication, and the Politics of Culture in Early Modern Venice* (Cambridge: Cambridge University Press, 2023).

Stringa, G., *Venetia città nobilissima et singolare, descritta già in XIIII libri da m. Francesco Sansovino et hora con molta diligenza corretta, emendata, e più d'vn terzo di cose nuoue ampliata* (Venezia: Presso Altobello Salicato, 1604).

Svalduz, E., '"Atorno questa nostra città": dai marginamenti cinquecenteschi alle Fondamenta Nuove', in *I limiti di Venezia*, ed. by G. Zucconi, 17 (2003), pp. 23–32.

Tafuri, M., *Jacopo Sansovino e l'architettura del '500 a Venezia* (Padova: Marsilio, 1969; repr. 1972).

Tafuri, M., '"Sapienza di Stato" e "atti mancati": architettura e tecnica urbana nella Venezia del '500', in *Architettura e Utopia nella Venezia del Cinquecento*, ed. by L. Puppi (Milano: Electa, 1980), pp. 16–39.

Tafuri, M., '*Renovatio urbis*'. *Venezia nell'età di Andrea Gritti*, ed. by M. Tafuri (1523–1538) (Roma: Officina, 1984).

Tafuri, M., '"Renovatio urbis Venetiarum". Il problema storiografico', in '*Renovatio urbis*'. *Venezia nell'età di Andrea Gritti*, ed. by M. Tafuri (1523–1538) (Roma: Officina, 1984), pp. 9–55.

Tafuri, M., *Venezia e il Rinascimento: religione, scienza, architettura* (Torino: Einaudi, 1985).

Tafuri, M., *Interpreting the Renaissance: Princes, Cities, Architects* (New Haven/London: Yale University Press, 2006).

Tagliaferri, A., ed., *Relazioni dei rettori veneti in terraferma*, IX, *Podestaria e Capitanato di Verona* (Milano: Giuffrè editore, 1977).

Tagliaferri, A., ed., *Atti del convegno Venezia e la Terraferma attraverso le relazioni dei Rettori: Trieste, 23–24 ottobre*, (Milano: Giuffré, 1981).

Tagliaferro, G., 'Quattro Jacopo per Montemezzano', in *Venezia Cinquecento*, 11 (2001), 21, pp. 141–54.

Tagliaferro, G., 'Le forme della Vergine: la personificazione di Venezia nel processo creativo di Paolo Veronese', in *Venezia Cinquecento*, 15, no. 30 (2005), pp. 5–158.

Tagliaferro, G., 'Martiri eroi, principi e beati: i patrizi veneziani e la pittura celebrativa nell'età di Lepanto', in *Guerre di religione sulle scene del Cinque-Seicento*, ed. by F. Doglio e M. Chiabò (Roma: Torre d'Orfeo, 2006), pp. 337–74.

Tagliaferro, G., 'Il "Mito" ripensato: trasformazioni della pittura veneziana tra Lepanto e l'Interdetto', in *Celebrazione e autocritica. La Serenissima e la ricerca dell'identità veneziana nel tardo Cinquecento*, ed. by B. Paul (Roma: Viella, 2014), pp. 193–231.

Tamassia Mazzarotto, B., *Le feste veneziane: i giochi popolari, le cerimonie religiose e di governo* (Firenze: Sansoni, 1961).

Tassi, F. M., *Vite de' pittori, scultori e architetti Bergamaschi*, 2 vols (Bergamo: Stamperia Locatelli, 1793).

Tassini, G., *Curiosità Veneziane, ovvero origini delle denominazioni stradali di Venezia* (Venezia: Grimaldo, 1872).

Tazio, G., *L'ottimo reggimento del magistrato pretorio* (Venezia: Francesco de' Franceschi, 1564).

Tazio, G., *La imagine del Rettore della ben ordinata Città* (Venezia: Gabriel Giolito, 1573).

Tenenti, A., 'L'uso scenografico degli spazi pubblici 1490–1580', in *Tiziano e Venezia* (Vicenza: Neri Pozza, 1980), pp. 21–26.

Terribile, C., *Del piacere della virtù: Paolo Veronese, Alessandro Magno e il patriziato veneziano* (Venezia: Marsilio, 2009).

Terry-Fritsch, A., 'Networks of Urban Secrecy: Tamburi, Anonymous Denunciations and the Production of the Gaze in Early Modern Florence', in *The Visual Culture of Secrecy in Early Modern Italy*, ed. by G. Fiorenza, T. D. McCall, and S. Roberts (Kirksville: Truman State University Press, 2013), pp. 162–81.

Thomas, G. M., ed., *Capitolare dei Visdomini del Fontico dei Tedeschi / Capitular des Deutschen Hauses in Venedig* (Berlin: Verlag Von A. Asher & Co, 1874).

Tipton, S., 'Diplomatie und Zeremoniell in Botschafterbildern von Carlevarijs und Canaletto', in *RIHA Journal*, 8 (2010).

URL: http://www.riha-journal.org/articles/2010/tipton-diplomatie-und-zeremoniell/ [2021/6/15].

Todeschini, G., *Visibilmente crudeli. Malviventi, persone crudeli e gente qualunque fra Medioevo ed Età Moderna* (Bologna: il Mulino, 2007).

Toffolo, S., *Describing the City, Describing the State: Representations of Venice and the Venetian Terraferma in the Renaissance* (Leiden: Brill, 2020).

Tondro, M. L. S., 'Memory and Tradition: the Ephemeral Architecture for the Triumphal Entries of the Dogaresse of Venice in 1557 and 1597' (unpublished doctoral thesis, University of Cambridge, 2002).

Tondro, M. L. S., 'The First Temporary Triumphal Arch in Venice (1557)', in *Court Festivals of the European Renaissance. Art, Politics and Performance*, ed. by J.R. Mulryne and E. Goldring (Aldershot: Ashgate, 2002), pp. 335–62.

Torre, A., *Luoghi. La produzione di località in età moderna e contemporanea* (Venezia: Marsilio 2011).

Traister, D., *The Elsevier Republics. Guide to the Microfiche Edition* (Bethesda, MD: CIS Academic Editions, 1988).

Trebbi, G., 'Priuli, Antonio', *Dizionario biografico degli italiani*, 85 (Roma: Istituto della Enciclopedia Treccani, 2016).

Trecca, G., *Legnago fino al secolo XX* (Verona: Tipografia Antonio Gurisatti, 1900).

Trexler, R., 'Ritual Behaviour in Renaissance Florence: the Setting', in *Medievalia et Humanistica*, 4 (1973), pp. 125–44.

Trissino, G., *Oratione al Serenissimo Principe di Venetia Andrea Gritti* (Roma: Lodovico de gli Arrighi, 1524).

Tully, J., ed., *Meaning and Context: Quentin Skinner and his Critics*, (Princeton: Princeton University Press, 1988).

Tutio, D., *Ordine et modo tenuto nell'incoronatione della Serenissima Moresina Grimani Dogaressa di Venetia* (Venezia: per Nicolò Peri libraro all'insegna di Fiorenza à S. Giuliano, 1597).

Ulmann, W., *The Individual and Society in the Middle Ages* (Baltimore: Johns Hopkins University Press, 1966).

Urban, L., 'Teatri e 'Teatri del Mondo' nella Venezia del Cinquecento', in *Arte Veneta*, 20 (1966), pp. 137–46.

Urban, L., 'Apparati scenografici nelle feste veneziane cinquecentesche', in *Arte Veneta*, 23 (1969), 145–55.

Urban, L., 'Feste veneziane cinquecentesche', in *Italian Renaissance Festivals and Their European Influence*, ed. by J. R. Mulryne and M. Shewring (Lewiston, Queenston, and Lampeter: Edwin Mellen Press, 1992), pp. 95–104.

Urban, L., 'L'"andata" dogale a San Vio: rituali, un quadro, una "beata", una chiesa', in *Studi veneziani*, 28 (1994), pp. 191–202.

Urban, L., *Le Forze d'Ercole* (Centro Internazionale della Grafica: Venezia, 1988).

Urban, L., *Processioni e feste dogali: 'Venetia est mundus'* (Vicenza: Neri Pozza, 1998).

Vallerin, P. U., *Il Comune di Legnago nel XVI secolo: il diritto-le istituzioni* (Verona: Editrice Anabasi, 1993).

Valseriati, E., 'Ingressi e uscite dei rettori veneziani a Brescia tra cerimoniale e infamia pubblica (sec. XVI)', in *Rituali civici e continuità istituzionale nelle città italiane in età moderna* (2023), pp. 49–66.

Van Cootwijck, J., *Itinerarium Hierosolymitanum et Syriacum: accessit synopsis reipublicae Venetae* (Antwerp: Verdussium, 1619).

Van der Sman, G. J., 'Print Publishing in Venice in the Second Half of the Sixteenth Century', *Print Quarterly*, 17 (2000) 3, pp. 235–47.

Van Gelder, M., *Trading Places: The Netherlandish Merchants in Early Modern Venice* (Boston-Leiden: Brill, 2009).

Van Gelder, M., 'Ducal Display and the Contested Use of Space in Late Sixteenth-Century Venetian Coronation Festivals', in *Occasions of State: Early Modern European Festivals and the Negotiation of Power*, ed. by J. R. Mulryne, K. De Jonge, R. L. M. Morris, and P. Martens (London: Routledge, 2018), pp. 167–95.

Van Gelder, M., 'The People's Prince: Popular Politics in Early Modern Venice', in *Journal of Moodern History*, 90 (2018), 2, pp. 249–91.

Van Gelder, M., and Judde de Larivière, C., eds, *Popular Politics in an Aristocratic Republic: Political Conflict and Social Contestation in Late Medieval and Early Modern Venice* (London-New York: Routledge, 2020).

Van Gelder, M., 'Protest in the Piazza. Contested space in early modern Venice', in *Popular Politics in an Aristocratic Republic*, ed. by M. Van Gelder and C. J. de Larivière (London: Routledge, 2020), pp. 129–56.

Van Gelder, M., and De Vivo, F., 'Papering over Protest: Contentious Politics and Archival Suppression in Early Modern Venice', in *Past and Present*, 258, 1 (2023), pp. 44–78.

Van Kessel, E., 'Artists and Knowledge in Sixteenth-Century Venice', in *The Artist as Reader: On Education and Non-Education of Early Modern Artists*, ed. by H. Damm, M. Thimann, and C. Zittel (Leiden and Boston: Brill, 2013), pp. 221–40.

Van Kessel, E., 'Venetian Thinking on the Lives of Paintings in the Early Modern Doge's Palace', in *The Secret Lives of Artworks: Exploring the Boundaries between Art and Life*, ed. by C. van Eck, J. van Gastel, and E. van Kessel (Leiden: Leiden University Press, 2014), pp. 95–115.

Varanini, G. M., 'Gli statuti della Terraferma veneta nel Quattrocento', in *Statuti e territori in Italia e Germania tra medioevo ed età moderna*, ed. by G. Chittolini and D. Willoweit (Bologna: Il Mulino, 1991), pp. 247–317.

Varanini, G. M., 'Gli ufficiali veneziani nella Terraferma veneta quattrocentesca', in *Annali della Scuola Normale Superiore di Pisa*, 4 (1997) 1, pp. 155–80.

Varanini, G. M., 'La Terraferma veneta nel Quattrocento e le recenti tendenze della storiografia', in *Ateneo Veneto*, 197 (2010), pp. 13–63.

Varanini, G. M., 'L'uso pubblico della storia. Il Medioevo nelle tele dipinte per la sala del consiglio civico di Verona (fine Cinquecento - inizi Seicento)', in *Iconologia del potere. Rappresentazioni della sovranità nel Rinascimento*, ed. by Da. Carpi and S. Fiorato (Verona: Ombre corte, 2011), pp. 86–105.

Varanini, G. M., 'Gli angusti orizzonti. Lessico delle dedizioni e «costituzione materiale» negli Stati territoriali italiani: l'esempio della Terraferma veneziana (secolo XV e ss.)', in *Des chartes aux constitutions: autour de l'idée constitutionnelle en Europe (XIIe-XVIIe siècle)*, ed. by F. Foronda and J.P. Genet (Paris: Éditions de la Sorbonne, 2019), pp. 417–40.

Varanini, G. M., ed., *Rituali civici e continuità istituzionale nelle città italiane in età moderna*, (Roma: Viella, 2023).

Vecellio, C., *De gli habiti antichi, et moderni di diverse parti del mondo libri due* (Venezia: Damian Zenaro, 1590).

Ventura, A., *Nobiltà e popolo nella società veneta del '400 e '500* (Bari: Laterza, 1964).

Ventura, A., *Scritti di storia veneziana*, ed. by P. Del Negro and M. Knapton (Venezia: Istituto veneto di Scienze Lettere ed Arti, 2006).

Venturelli, P., 'Mito di Venezia e governo misto in *Della perfettione della vita politica* di P. Paruta', in *Sifp. Rivista elettronica della Società Italiana di Filosofia Politica* (1961), pp. 1–19.
URL: https://sifp.it/wp-content/uploads/2021/10/Mito-di-Venezia.pdf [2022/05/13].

Venturelli, P., 'La costituzione mista e il "mito" di Venezia nel Rinascimento. Alcune considerazioni sugli scritti etico-politici di Donato Giannotti e di Gasparo Contarini', in *Studi di storia della cultura. Sibi suis amicisque*, ed. by Domenico Felice (Bologna: CLUEB, 2012), pp. 135–82.

Versteegen, G., Bussels, S., and Melion, W. S., eds, *Magnificence in the Seventeenth Century* (Leiden-Boston: Brill, 2021).

Veyne, P., *Les grecs ont-ils cru à leurs mythes? Essai sur l'imagination constituante* (Paris: Edition du Seuil, 1983).

Viggiano, A., *Governanti e governati: legittimità del potere ed esercizio dell'autorità sovrana nello Stato veneto della prima età moderna* (Treviso: Canova, 1993).

Viggiano, A., 'Il Dominio da terra: politica e istituzioni', in *Storia di Venezia. dalle origini alla caduta*, ed. by A. Tenenti and U. Tucci, 4 (Roma: Istituto della Enciclopedia italiana, 1996), pp. 529–75.

Viggiano, A., 'La disciplina dei rettori nello stato veneto del '400', in *Annali della Scuola normale superiore di Pisa*, 4 (1997) 1, pp. 181–90.

Viggiano, A., 'Il processo al Capitano generale da Mar Antonio Grimani "ruina de' Christiani", "rebello de' Venetiani", 1499–1500', in *Le procés politique (XIVe-XVIIe siècle)*, ed. by Y. M. Bercé (Roma: Collection de l'École française de Rome, 2007), pp. 251–27.

Vimercati Sozzi, P., *Sulla moneta della città di Bergamo nel secolo decimoterzo* (Bergamo: Stamperia Mazzoleni, 1842).

Vincenti, D., *Gli apparati veneti, overo le feste fatte nell'elezione in procuratore dell'illustrissimo et eccellentissimo signor Giovanni da Pesaro cavalier* (Venezia: Presso Pietro Miloco, 1641).

Vio, G., 'L'arte di sonadori e l'insegnamento della musica a Venezia', in *Recercare*, 18 (2006) pp. 69–111.

Visentini, M. A., 'Festivals of State: The Scenography of Power in Late Renaissance and Baroque Venice', in *Festival Architecture*, ed. by Sarah Bonnemaison and Christine Macy (London: Routledge, 2008).

Visentini, O., 'Feste, musica e spettacoli in Villa Contarini', in *Le capitali della festa. Italia Settentrionale, Atlante tematico del Barocco*, ed. by M. Fagiolo, 1 (Roma: De Luca, 2007), pp. 341–47.

Vocabolario degli Accademici della Crusca, con tre indici delle voci, locuzioni e proverbi latini e greci posti per entro l'opera (Venezia: appresso Giovanni Alberti, 1612).

Walker, C., and Kerr, H., eds, *Fama and her Sisters. Gossip and Rumour in Early Modern Europe* (Turnhout: Brepols, 2015).

Warf, B., and Arias, S., eds, *The Spatial Turn: Interdisciplinary Perspectives* (London-New York: Routledge, 2009).

Watanabe-O'Kelly, H., 'Sailing towards a Kingdom: Ernst August von Braunschweig-Lüneburg (1629–1698) in Venice in 1685 and 1686', in *Waterborne Pageants and Festivities in the Renaissance*, ed. by M. Shewring (London: Routledge, 2017), pp. 391–403.

Welch, E., 'Space and Spectacle in the Renaissance Pharmacy', in *Medicina & Storia*, 15 (2008), pp. 127–58.

Weststeijn, A., *Commercial Republicanism in the Dutch Golden Age: The Political Thought of Johan & Pieter de La Court* (Leiden: Brill, 2011).

Weststeijn, A., 'Imperial Republics: Roman Imagery in Italian and Dutch Town Halls, c. 1300–1700', in *Renovatio, Inventio, Absentia Imperii. From the Roman Empire to Contemporary Imperialism*, ed. by W. Bracke, J. Nelis, and J. De Maeyer (Turnhout: Brepols, 2018), pp. 93–116.

Williamson, F., ed., *Locating Agency: Space, Power and Popular Politics*, (Newcastle: Cambridge Scholars Publishing, 2011).

Wilson, B., '"Il bel sesso, e l'austero Senato": The Coronation of Dogaressa Morosina Morosini Grimani', in *Renaissance Quarterly*, 52 (1999), pp. 73–139.

Wolters, W., 'Le architetture erette al Lido per l'ingresso di Enrico III a Venezia nel 1574', in *Bollettino del Centro Internazionale di Studi di Architettura Andrea Palladio*, 21 (1979), pp. 273–89.

Wolters, W., 'Der Programmentwurf zur Dekoration des Dogenpalastes nach dem Brand vom 20 Dezember 1577', in *Mitteilungen des Kunsthistorischen Institutes in Florenz*, 12 (1966), pp. 271–318.

Wolters, W., *Der Bilderschmuck des Dogenpalastes* (Stuttgart: Franz Steiner Verlag, 1983).

Wolters, W., *Storia e politica nei dipinti di Palazzo Ducale: aspetti dell'autocelebrazione della Repubblica di Venezia nel Cinquecento* (Venezia: Arsenale, 1987).

Wolters, W., 'L'autocelebrazione della Repubblica nelle arti figurative', in *Storia di Venezia, VI, Dal Rinascimento al Barocco*, ed. by G. Cozzi and P. Prodi (Roma: Istituto della Enciclopedia Italiana, 1994), pp. 469–513.

Wolters, W., *Il Palazzo Ducale di Venezia: un percorso storico-artistico* (Caselle di Sommacampagna: Cierre, 2010).

Wood, A., *Riot, Rebellion and Popular Politics in Early Modern England* (New York: Palgrave, 2001).

Woodward, D., 'Paolo Forlani: Compiler, Engraver, Printer, or Publisher?', in *Imago Mundi*, 44 (1992), pp. 45–64.

Yates, F. A., *Astraea. The Imperial Theme in the Sixteenth Century* (London and Boston: Routledge and Kegan Paul, 1975).

Yates, F. A., *The Valois Tapestries* (London: Routledge and Kegan Paul, 1975).

Zago, R., 'Grimani, Antonio', *Dizionario biografico degli Italiani*, 59 (Roma: Istituto dell'Enciclopedia Italiana, 2002).

Zamperetti, S., 'Magistrature centrali, Rettori e ceti locali nello Stato regionale veneto in età moderna', in *Comunità e poteri centrali negli antichi Stati italiani. Alle origini dei controlli amministrativi*, ed. by L. Mannori (Napoli: Cuen, 1997), pp. 103–15.

Zamperini, A., *Palazzo Ducale: il Mito e il Potere* (Schio: Sassi, 2014).

Zanetti, U., 'L'obelisco di Nicolò Corner capitano veneto di Bergamo', in *La rivista di Bergamo*, 1 (1990), pp. 6–8.

Zanotto, F., 'Le Forze d'Ercole dei veneziani', in *Emporio artistico-letterario, ossia Raccolta di amene letture, novità, aneddoti e cognizioni utili in generale*, 3 (1850), pp. 238–40.

Zeller, T., 'The Spatial Turn in History', in *German Historical Institute Bulletin*, no. 35 (2004), pp. 123–24.

Zemon Davis, N., *The Gift in Sixteenth-Century France* (Madison: The University of Wisconsin Press, 2000).

Zenobi, L., 'Venice's Terraferma Expansion and the Negotiation of Territories in Late Medieval Italy', in *Ateneo Veneto*, 18 (2019) 2, pp. 187–214.

Zerner, H., 'Looking for the Unknowable: The Visual Experience of Renaissance Festivals', in *Europa Triumphans. Court and Civic Festivals in Early Modern Europe*, ed. by J. R. Mulryne and others, 2 vols (Aldershot: Ashgate, 2004) 1, pp. 75–98.

Zille, E., 'Il processo Grimani', in *Archivio Veneto*, s. V, 36 (1945), pp. 137–94.

Zorzi, G., *Le opere pubbliche e i palazzi privati di Andrea Palladio* (Venezia: Neri Pozza, 1965).

Zucconi, G., 'Architettura e topografia delle istituzioni nei centri minori della Terraferma (XV e XVI secolo)', in *Studi Veneziani*, 17 (1989), pp. 27–50.

NOTES ON CONTRIBUTORS

MARCO BELLABARBA is Professor of Early Modern History at the University of Trento

ERIKA CARMINATI is Independent Researcher

MATTEO CASINI is Lecturer of Renaissance and Mediterranean History at the University of Massachusetts

UMBERTO CECCHINATO is Researcher at the University of Trento

ISEABAIL CAMERON ROWE is Independent Researcher

GIOVANNI FLORIO is Postdoctoral Research Fellow in History of Political Institutions at the University of Padua

EVELYN KORSCH is Independent Researcher

ALESSANDRO METLICA is Associate Professor of Comparative Literature at the University of Padua

MONIQUE O'CONNELL is Professor of History at Wake Forest University.

MASSIMO ROSPOCHER is Director of the Italian-German Historical Institute of Trento

GIORGIO TAGLIAFERRO is Associate Professor in the History of Art Department, University of Warwick

ALFREDO VIGGIANO is Professor of History of Political Institutions at the University of Padua